Building Systems from Commercial Components

Kurt C. Wallnau
Scott A. Hissam
Robert C. Seacord

 **Addison-Wesley**

Boston • San Francisco • New York • Toronto
London • Munich • Paris • Madrid
Capetown • Sidney • Tokyo • Singapore • Mexico City

Carnegie Mellon
Software Engineering Institute

The SEI Series in Software Engineering

The publisher offers discounts on this book when ordered in quantity for special sales. For more information, please contact:

Pearson Education Corporate Sales Division
One Lake Street
Upper Saddle River, NJ 07458
(800) 382-3419
corpsales@pearsontechgroup.com

Visit AW on the Web: www.awl.com/cseng/

Library of Congress Cataloging-in-Publication Data
Wallnau, Kurt C.
    Building systems from commercial components / Kurt C. Wallnau, Scott A. Hissam,
  Robert C. Seacord.
        p. cm.
    Includes bibliographical references and index.
    ISBN 0-201-70064-6
    1. System design. 2. Component software. I. Hissam, Scott. II. Seacord, Robert C. III.
  Title.

QA76.9.S88 W345 2002
005.1'2dc21
                                                                        2001022846

0-201-70064-6
Text printed on recycled paper
1 2 3 4 5 6 7 8 9 10—EB—0504030201
First printing, July 2001

To my wife, Jeannemarie, and to my children, Zachary, Victoria, Gemma, and Bryn. You were all beginning to suspect that I would never finish the book. So was I. Without your love and support, I never would have.

—KW

I deeply want to thank my wife Jackie for her patience and support in the authoring of this book, she had to endure some of the early chapters and now knows more about PKI than she ever wanted to. I also want to thank my sons, Derek and Zachery, for showing me how to build systems from Legos! Love and thanks to them as they give reason to everything I do.

—SH

I would like to acknowledge my family for supporting my efforts in writing this book. My wife Rhonda, whose encouragement and support was essential, and my daughter Chelsea and my son Jordan without whom everything would be meaningless.

—rCs

Contents

Preface

There is a real *and growing* gap between the theory and practice of component-based software design.

There are, of course, books on component-based design. However, these books assume that the design task is to develop specifications for software components when most component-based design relies on *preexisting* components. There is room for both perspectives. However, preexisting components introduce new and novel design challenges, and their use is becoming increasingly prominent. Pre existing components mean preexisting component specifications, and these are constraints on—not artifacts of—a design.

Current component-based design methods are focused on the *less interesting* and *less encountered* design problem. The more common and more interesting aspects of the design process are those that are no longer under the control of *the designer.*

- Use of preexisting components involves a completely different class of design problem than arises from component specification. Preexisting components involve the designer in *selection decisions*, while the freedom to define component interfaces involves the designer in *optimization decisions*. The difference between these classes of design problem are only gradually becoming evident to software engineers, and design methods have not yet caught up with this growing awareness.

- Use of preexisting components involves a significant loss of control over fundamental design decisions: how a system is partitioned into components, what functionality is provided by components, and how components coordinate their activities. In software engineering theory, these are architectural (that is, design) decisions. This leads to the mistaken conclusion that aggressive use of preexisting components is antithetical to, or at least incompatible or disjunctive with, software design.

We have described briefly the state of component-based design methods today, but have not yet supported the assertion that there is a growing gap between the theory and practice of component-based development. In fact, the gap does exist and is self-evident, once you know where to look for it.

The trend toward component-based development has been well under way for more than fifteen years, and has its roots in the commercial software marketplace. Software products, such as relational database management systems, transaction monitors, message brokers, event managers, encryption services, Web browsers and servers, geographic information systems, product data management systems, *ad infinitum*, all satisfy the essential criteria of software component, at least as this term is coming to be understood by industry. That is, they all are implementations of functionality, are in binary form, are independently deployed, are described by a programmatic interface, and support third-party integration.

The commercial marketplace is the primary source of software components. This is true today, and will remain so for the indefinite future. Indeed, we believe that components and the software component marketplace are inextricably linked. Szyperski, in his influential book, shares this belief by observing that a component must be defined to fill a market niche [Szyperski 98]. However, Szyperski's notion of market was largely (although not completely) metaphorical. In contrast, our use of the term *component market* refers to something that demonstrably exists today, complete with component suppliers, component infrastructure providers, third-party component integrators, and, ultimately, consumers.

Ignoring the effects of the marketplace on software engineering would be analogous to ignoring the effects of friction on mechanical engineering. In particular, there are three qualities of commercial software components that together account for a significant share of the challenges posed by software components.

1. Commercial software components are *complex*. This complexity is needed to justify and sustain a component market. Many components are sufficiently complex that even experts in their use do not know all their features. There are invariably unknowns about component features and behavior.

2. Commercial software components are *idiosyncratic*. Standards are useful, but innovative features attract consumers. This means component knowledge is vendor-specific, and integration difficulties arise due to mismatches among innovative (that is, nonstandard) features.

3. Commercial software components are *unstable*. New features must be introduced to motivate upgrade, and are needed where competitors have copied successful features. Component knowledge has a short half-life, and design assumptions based on component features are fragile.

These qualities of software components, as they are found in the practice of building real systems, confound the assumptions of an orderly process that underlie traditional software design methods. However, these new complexities require a methodological response, since all component-based roads lead to the commercial component marketplace.

Methodological Response

A central proposition of our approach is that a principal source of risk in component-based design is a lack of knowledge about how components should be integrated, and how they behave when integrated. To mitigate this risk, component-based design inherently involves exploration and discovery. Acquiring and sustaining technology (component) competence is a principal motivation for this exploration.

This proposition may appear to some to be a heretical departure from the canons of software process improvement, which emphasize management skills over technical skills, and collective behavior over individual contributions. Indeed, phrases such as "that's just plumbing" in reference to component integration details, and "we need to get beyond individual heroics" in reference to reliance on software engineers with extraordinarily deep technology competence, are indicative of a mismatch between *perceptions* of what is important in software process, and the *reality* of what is needed in component-based development. In fact, the feasibility of a design is often dependent on "plumbing." Moreover, the overall design conception often depends on these low-level details. And there is no escaping the fact that deep technology competence is essential if these details are to be mastered.

The following are core elements of our methodological response:

1. We introduce component *ensemble* as a fundamental design abstraction. Ensembles expose component dependencies, and shift the emphasis from selecting individual components to selecting sets of components that work together (that is, ensembles).

2. We introduce *blackboards* as a fundamental design notation. Blackboards depict what is currently known about an ensemble and, just as important, what remains to be discovered. Blackboards serve to document a design and known areas of design risk.

3. We introduce a risk-driven discovery process, called R^3, for exposing design risk, and for defining ensemble feasibility criteria. We also introduce a prototyping process, called *model problems*, for generating situated component expertise, and for establishing ensemble feasibility.

4. We introduce the *design space*, defined in terms of ensemble relations and predicates. The design space captures dependencies among ensembles that arise in response to anticipated market events such as new component releases, and design hedges where ensemble feasibility is in doubt.

The methodological challenge is to meet the challenge posed by the commercial component market without allowing a) the design process to degenerate into an exercise in hacking, and b) innovative but unstable technology features to dominate a design and result in excessive and unnecessary design risk. The approach we prescribe, we believe, meets this challenge.

About This Book

GOALS OF THIS BOOK

Our goals are straightforward. Our first goal is to show that software components pose new methodological challenges for software engineering. In making this argument, we hope to clarify the nature of these challenges, with particular emphasis on those challenges rooted in the dynamics of the component market. Our second goal is to describe, in detail, processes and techniques that respond to these challenges. We believe these processes and techniques are a necessary foundation for any methodological response to software components. Our final goal is to illustrate, in a realistic case study drawn from our own experience in developing a large enterprise system, the complexity of component-based design, and the efficacy of our proposed processes and techniques.

INTENDED AUDIENCE

This book is intended for individuals participating in a component-based development effort, and for students of software engineering. Although the whole of the book provides useful information for all of these roles, emphasis may vary.

System Architect.   The lead designer will find ensembles, and the techniques for reasoning about ensemble repair and feasibility, welcome additions to his or her repertoire. The design space provides the system architect the conceptual language for managing the many layers of contingency and repair that characterize complex component-based systems.

Chief Engineer.   While the system architect is responsible for the conceptual integrity of a design, the chief engineer is responsible for demonstrating its feasibility in practice. The chief engineer will find the R^3 and model problem processes essential to exposing latent design risks that are otherwise masked by the complexity of components and their interactions.

Project Manager.   Project management is concerned first and foremost with identifying and mitigating project risk. The aggressive search for technical risk that drives R^3 (one of the Rs is **R**isk Identification) meets these concerns. The design space provides a concise snapshot of the status of a design, and provides a structure for allocating and tracking engineering effort versus project objectives.

Chief Technology Officer (CTO).   Modern enterprise systems are universally composed from commercial components. Such large-scale and long-lived systems never leave the design phase and, in fact, inhabit all phases of the development life cycle at all times. The CTO will find all of the concepts and techniques we describe useful for managing technology refresh.

Software Engineers and Programmers.   The frontline developer is the true unsung hero of component-based development. Project success depends upon developers to remain current with technology trends. This book provides ammunition for developers who wish to convince their management to invest in technology training in addition to the usual process training.

HOW TO READ THIS BOOK

This book has three parts, as follows:

- Part I explores the engineering challenges posed by commercial components. We describe engineering techniques that meet these challenges, and describe, wherever possible, workflows for incorporating these techniques into an enclosing development process.

- Part II presents an extended case study of a project that we were involved with starting in 1998. Each chapter illustrates the challenges posed by commercial components and the techniques used to meet these challenges.

- Part III provides advice on how to get started using the techniques described in this book. We also dust off our crystal ball and make predictions about the future of component-based development.

Chapter 1 introduces the problems inherent in component-based development. Chapters 2 through 4 explain why it is necessary to abandon as unworkable some of the more staid precepts of software process. Chapter 5 describes component ensembles and blackboards, both essential concepts in their own right and for the material presented in this book. Chapter 6 defines process models for exploratory design and design risk reduction. Chapters 7 and 8 describe how design documentation developed by these processes can be managed and reused, respectively. The remaining chapters in Part I describe specific techniques (really, families of techniques) for developing component-based systems. These can be read in any order; you can also skip these and head straight for the case study and return to the techniques as needed.

The case study describes a chain of events and so these chapters are linked by a running narrative. However, the chapters are designed to be relatively standalone, although the motivation for the work described in each chapter may be less than clear if you read them out of order. Chapter 14, which provides a mini-tutorial on public key infrastructure (PKI) and security, is one exception. If you already understand PKI, skip this chapter. Otherwise, you will need to read it to understand the details of the case study.

ACKNOWLEDGMENTS

First, the authors wish to express their gratitude to Daniel Plakosh, David Carney, and Fred Long for their contribution of chapters in this book. We also owe a debt of gratitude to our manager, John Foreman, for his strong support for this book, without which we would not have succeeded.

We are also grateful to the reviewers of this book whose insightful comments are reflected throughout our work: Santiago Comella-Dorda, Judith Stafford, Paul Clements, Tom Shields, Hans Polzer, Will Tracz, Alan Brown, and John Dean. We also happily acknowledge the intellectual contributions of members of the SEI COTS-Based Systems project not already mentioned: Howard Slomer, Wilfred Hansen, Patricia Oberndorf, Cecilia Albert, Lisa Brownsword, Edwin Morris, John Robert, and Patrick Place.

Special thanks go to our in-house editor, Len Estrin, for his excellent editing under a tight deadline. Also, Peter Gordon from Addison-Wesley deserves our thanks for agreeing to publish this work, and for his timely interventions to keep things on track.

Last, the authors are indebted to the Software Engineering Institute (SEI) for providing an unparalleled environment for conducting research in software engineering practice. In particular, we want to acknowledge our tireless librarians Karola Yourison, Shiela Rosenthal, and Terry Ireland. We offer special thanks to Steve Cross, the Director of the SEI, for his enthusiastic endorsement of the ideas expressed in this book.

PART ONE

FUNDAMENTALS

In Completing one Discovery we never fail to get an imperfect knowledge of others of which we could have no idea before, so that we cannot solve one doubt without creating several new ones.
—Joseph Priestly

1

Components
Everywhere

Water, Water, every where, Nor any Drop to Drink.
—Samuel Taylor Coleridge
The Rime of the Ancient Mariner

The belief that using commercial components will simplify the design and implementation of systems is widely held, but is, unfortunately, belief in a compelling myth. Imagine you are the architect or chief engineer for a project that is developing a large, mission-critical information system. For whatever reason, it has been decided that the only practical—though a very promising—means to this end is to build the system from commercially available components. Before the project makes substantial progress, though, it is confronted by the obstacles that follow:

- Many crucial design decisions revolve around component interfaces that are deficient in several respects, but are not subject to negotiation. Yet these same interfaces are often unexpectedly modified by their vendor, simultaneously invalidating previous design workarounds and introducing new integration difficulties.

- The components have been designed to be easy to integrate with some vendors' components but difficult to integrate with others. Unfortunately, the best components reside in different vendor camps. You discover that the question of which components to use is more complex than anticipated, with each selection decision contingent on some set of other selection decisions.

- The components that have been selected are sufficiently complex that no one on the project knows exactly how they work. When integrated, the component assembly exhibits baffling and incorrect emergent behavior. The vendors have never seen this behavior before, but they are *certain* the fault lies with another vendor's component.

Does this sound familiar? How did this state of affairs come about, and what can practicing designers and software engineers do about it? Can predictable and repeatable software engineering methods be established in the face of these challenges? We believe the answer is yes.

1.1   The Software Component Revolution

Software components are everywhere—or perhaps we should say this about magazine articles, scholarly papers, market forecasts, and (yes) books about software components. Judging by all that has been written, and continues to be written, the software industry is quickly moving toward component-based development. Add to this the avalanche of commercial software methods and tools that support component-based development and the conclusion seems inevitable.

A closer look at the evidence, however, presents a picture that is far less clear. We do not argue against this trend. Instead, we propose that this trend, far from being unified and coherent, is a splintering of many trends, some competing, some reinforcing, and some wholly independent. Organizations interested in adopting component-based development for competitive or other reasons are immediately confronted by a nearly impenetrable and fast-growing thicket of technological, methodological, and organizational options.

To state the conclusion first, software components are real and are already profoundly altering the practice of software engineering. Despite signs of progress, the challenges posed by systems that are constructed predominantly from *commercial off-the-shelf components* have yet to be addressed adequately. Indeed, the more general challenges posed by large-scale reuse of existing components, regardless of their origin, have yet to be addressed. Further stipulating the commercial origin of components merely adds further complexity to these already unaddressed challenges.

To be sure, there are several accepted and well-defined component-based development methods, notably Cheesman and Daniels' UML Components [Cheesman+ 00], D'Souza and Wills' Catalysis [D'Souza+ 99], and Herzum and Sims' Business Component Factory [Herzum+ 00], each recently published and each a truly excellent contribution in its own right. However, these methods assume that the design task is, predominantly, one of component specification for later implementation rather than one of component selection for later assembly. Only Herzum and Sims recognize this apparent contradiction between the premise of currently published component-based development methods and the *consequence* of adopting a component-based paradigm; namely, that applications would be assembled from existing components rather than from custom-developed components. Herzum and Sims address this by describing a reuse process (the business component factory) that shifts, ever so gradually, the emphasis from custom development to reuse of existing components.

But surely this misses two key points. First, design methods that assume the freedom to define component interfaces are fundamentally different from methods that lack this freedom.[1] Defining a method for the former condition in the hopes of transitioning this same method to the latter condition is doomed to failure. Second, there are many systems being built today whose fundamental design challenge stems from an aggressive use of commercial software components. By commercial components we mean things such as Web browsers, HTTP servers, object request brokers, relational database management systems, message-oriented middleware, public key infrastructure, transaction monitors, and geographic information systems. Software engineers need design methods to deal with this class of component-based system *now*, not in some indefinite future.

Our book addresses this gap in software engineering methodology. In particular, we define concepts, techniques, and processes to address the design challenges uniquely posed by the use of commercial software components. These include, but are not limited to, the challenges that follow.

- Critical design decisions must be made in the face of incomplete and often mistaken understanding of the features and behavior of commercial software components. Knowledge gaps are inevitable and are a major source of design risk.

- Whatever knowledge is obtained about one commercial software component does not translate easily to components from different vendors, and all component knowledge tends to degrade quickly as components evolve through new releases.

- Competitive pressures in the software marketplace force vendors to innovate and differentiate component features rather than stabilize and standardize them. This results in mismatches that inhibit component integration and inject significant levels of wholly artificial design complexity.

- Use of commercial components imposes a predisposition on consumers to accept new releases despite disruptions introduced by changing component features. These disruptions take on a random quality across all phases of development as the number of components used grows.

These challenges all derive from the same root cause: a loss of design control to market forces. Perhaps the reason why no methods have yet been developed to address these challenges is that we have been trained to think of market forces as beyond the scope of software engineering methods. But it is a poor engineering method that fails to accommodate practical reality. These market

---

[1] Design *with* interface freedom reduces to a form of continuous optimization tradeoff wherein each component interface represents a variable that can be arbitrarily modified to produce more or less optimal results. Design *without* interface freedom reduces to a form of selection tradeoff wherein each component interface represents one choice among a discrete set of choices. These two modes require fundamentally different approaches to design.

forces play as much a part in software engineering as friction plays in mechanical engineering.

Before delving into details we must first set some context. We describe the class of design problem addressed by this book, especially with respect to different conceptions of *software component* and *component-based development*. Then, we outline our assumptions about the software engineering methods and processes that we expect to be in place already. Lastly, we deal with terminology.

1.2   Component Space

Although the term "component-based development" does not refer to the development of just one type of system, or to the use of just one type of component, most conceptions of component-based development share a few fundamental concepts. Foremost of these is that components are software implementations that have interfaces and that are units of independent substitution. But beyond this, there are numerous variations, both large and small. We have found three dimensions of variation to be particularly apt for describing the big picture.

The first dimension concerns the source of software components. As we noted earlier, published component-based software methods share a premise: that the principal task of the design effort is to produce component specifications. This premise is clearly invalid in situations in which most or all of the components already exist. The distinction we make, then, is between development efforts that specify their own custom components and efforts that are constrained to use only preexisting components. Today, the most important source of preexisting components is the software component marketplace. It is the marketplace that leads to economies of scale and that truly differentiates component-based development from other software engineering paradigms.

The second dimension concerns the environments into which components are deployed and in which they execute. Again, there are two major distinctions. Some components are deployed directly onto a native operating system. This class of component need only comply with the interfaces and conventions imposed by that operating system. Other components are deployed into a higher-level environment that is variably referred to as a component framework [Bachmann+ 00] [Szyperski 98], business component virtual machine [Herzum+ 00], or component standard [Cheesman+ 00]. Whatever it is called, the distinction between framework-based and operating system-based components is an important one, since a component framework constrains component developers and simplifies component integration.

The third dimension concerns the use of components to implement *application* versus *infrastructure*. Obviously this distinction is subjective: the best definition of infrastructure that we know of is "whatever it is that I need to do my job."[2]

---

[2] We are indebted to Len Bass for this definition.

Consequently, one engineer's infrastructure may well be another engineer's application. Nevertheless, the idea of infrastructure does have substantive meaning for one very large class of system—the enterprise information system. Enterprise information systems tend to be, among other things, large, heterogeneous, distributed, multi-user, persistent, transactional, and secure. By infrastructure, we mean the software that implements this functionality. In contrast, enterprise information systems use the infrastructure to implement and deliver business services to users.

Some people refer to infrastructure dismissively as "plumbing" as a way of suggesting that this functionality *should* be assumed to exist within a component framework, that the problems of infrastructure are, by and large, solved, and that the *real* software engineering problems reside elsewhere. We agree that one of the benefits of component frameworks is that they bundle infrastructure services [Seacord+ 99]. In principle, we agree with Herzum and Sims (and many others) that component technology will evolve in the direction of more complete and robust frameworks. However, we do not expect one standard framework to emerge, but rather a variety of component frameworks, each tailored to its own requirements. Such frameworks will themselves need to be integrated, and new releases of frameworks must be installed and integrated. There is no escaping infrastructure, and building and sustaining an enterprise infrastructure is an excruciatingly complex undertaking. Software engineering methods are needed here, too.

Figure 1-1 depicts these as three orthogonal dimensions in a Cartesian coordinate system. We, of course, understand that the world of components is far more complex than can be accommodated by these three dimensions. But the resulting picture of "component method space" adequately situates the subject matter of this book with respect to different classes of component-based system and their related development methods.

As mentioned earlier, Cheesman and Daniels' UML Components targets the design of applications built using frameworks (upper right rear of figure). Although their method includes a step to search for existing components, doing so *after* defining component interfaces practically guarantees that no components will be found. Herzum and Sims are even more aggressive in postulating component frameworks than Cheesman and Daniels. They assume frameworks exist at each conceptual layer (user, workstation, enterprise, and resource) in their canonical system design. Both of these methods focus on application rather than infrastructure. That is, they assume the existence of an infrastructure rather than describe a method to construct one. Likewise, both methods assume the design task is predominantly one of specifying components rather than assembling systems from existing components. D'Souza and Wills' Catalysis, however, differs from UML Components and the Component Factory in neither assuming nor rejecting component frameworks. In this respect, Catalysis has broader conceptual applicability. On the other hand, Catalysis does not address the technical infrastructural aspects of enterprise systems that are made explicit, albeit only assumed, in the other methods just discussed.

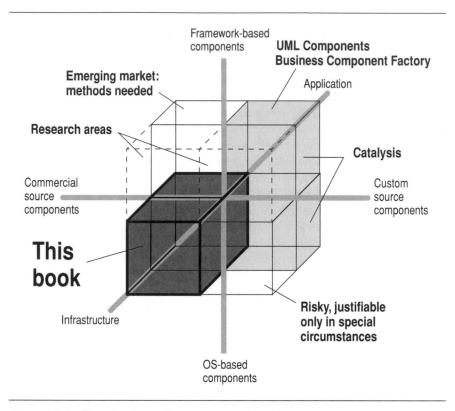

Figure 1-1 The structure of component method space.

The region of framework-based commercial components used for applications (upper left rear of figure) represents an important emerging market. It includes, for example, markets in commercial off-the-shelf Enterprise JavaBeans. Such components are already available in the commercial marketplace as stand-alone components and as product lines of components. While the component framework used in such applications distills away much of the integration complexity that is tackled by this book, the market forces that drive the component market ensures that a considerable residue of mismatch among components will remain. As a result, we expect that engineering methods that address this class of application will need to combine elements described in this book with what is described by Cheesman and Daniels. In any event, work is needed in this area, and soon.

We have dash-outlined the two uncharted regions of space corresponding to framework-based components for infrastructure. There are research projects (sometimes referred to as "programmable middleware") that are under way in this area of space. While these efforts might produce industrial-grade results, these regions are essentially unexplored. Note one area of space that should be avoided at all costs: enterprise infrastructures built from custom software. There may be some justification for this for highly specialized domains, but otherwise there is little justification for avoiding commercial technologies.

The remaining regions of component-method space—applications and infrastructure constructed predominantly from commercial-off-the-shelf (COTS) components—are the subject of this book.

1.3 Process, Method, & Notation Assumptions

While commercial software components pose unique challenges to software engineering, they do not require that we revisit each and every precept of theory and practice. To be sure, certain software engineering practices need to be adjusted, and some outdated notions of software process need to be revised substantially. Some of these adjustments and revisions will not be easy to undertake given how entrenched these precepts have become. Given this challenge, it certainly makes sense to minimize difficulties by starting from a reasonably well-established foundation. Accordingly, we make some assumptions about software development processes as context for the material discussed in this book.

Our first assumption is that all projects use some form of Boehm's spiral development [Boehm 88a] [Boehm+ 00]. Spiral development is characterized by iterative development, with risk analysis at the inception of each iteration. It is important to understand that spiral development is not just best practice, but *essential* practice for building systems from commercial components. Of course, what Boehm actually described was a *metaprocess*—characteristics that any particular software development process must possess for it to be a spiral process. Therefore, it is not sufficient for us to say only that we assume the spiral model, we need to be more specific.

We assume as a starting point the use of the Rational Unified Software Process (RUP), and we use the terminology and idioms of RUP throughout this book. We are well aware of the shortcomings of RUP, and are reminded of a story about President Abraham Lincoln. When an angry congressman insisted that any general would be better than the one Lincoln had appointed, Lincoln responded by saying that he could not appoint *any* general, he had to appoint *some* general. Although RUP is biased toward an object-oriented conception of the world (which is fine if you are doing object-oriented development, of course), and although it is strategically vague in a number of areas, it has several things going for it.

- It is defined.
- It is extensible.
- It supports spiral, iterative, and incremental development.
- It defines a variety of developer roles and their related tasks.
- It does not inhibit the use of components (though it does not address it).

For these reasons RUP provides a good place to start. Of course, this does not require that *you* use RUP. It only means that we find it useful to appropriate RUP terminology and process models as a means to illustrate ideas.

We also have chosen the Object Management Group's Unified Modeling Language (UML) as our notation. Although UML lacks certain features that would make it more effective as an architectural modeling language, we have selected it because it is widely used and should be familiar to most readers.

1.4   Terminology and Acronyms

In the remainder of this book we use the term *component* to mean *commercial software component*. *Component-based development* refers to the practices required to build systems (applications and infrastructures) from commercial software components. This is not to diminish the claims of the other authors cited as to their component orientation. It is, however, an explicit rejection of any claims to the exclusivity of that term.

You will also note that we do not construct many categorical definitions. Of course, it is important to be clear about certain key concepts, and we do (finally) define software component in Chapter 5. But it is difficult to construct airtight categorical definitions. Indeed, it is not even necessary; we can all identify and use money without knowing precisely how to define it.[3] Our preference is to use definitions sparingly, and instead illustrate how the categories are used. This is far more satisfying for the authors and, we expect, for readers as well.

Also, sadly, software engineering and especially the commercial software marketplace generates a seemingly infinite variety of acronyms, nested acronyms, and compound acronyms. Rather than redefine the same acronym in each chapter, we do so only once, and ask you to refer to the glossary for all other uses.

1.5   Summary

Industry is rushing pell-mell to adopt component-based development. But the challenges posed by a large and important class of component-based system, those comprised of commercial software components, have remained unaddressed, or certainly underaddressed. This book establishes the foundations for a methodological response to these challenges.

---

[3] This is an example of the so-called *Socratic fallacy*, which asserts that it is impossible to know whether something is an instance of a property unless one has a definition for that property. Incidentally, Socrates was, in fact, *not* guilty of falling prey to the fallacy that bears his name.

2

The Unfinished Revolution

Would you realize what Revolution is, call it progress; and would you
realize what Progress is, call it Tomorrow.
—Cosette, in *Les Misérables*, by Victor Hugo

We are in the midst of the information technology revolution. This revolution is redefining how software systems are conceived and constructed. Chief technology officers, system architects, and software engineers must adapt to these changing circumstances.

The essence of this revolution is *commercialization*. Peter Drucker, noted sociologist and author, has compared one manifestation of this revolution—the World Wide Web—to the introduction of rail transportation, which is considered by many to be the linchpin of the industrial revolution [Drucker 99]. Alan Greenspan, Chairman of the U.S. Federal Reserve, testified before the U.S. Congress that information technology (IT) is the root and stem of the longest running economic expansion in U.S. history [Greenspan 99]. He also acknowledged, however, that he and other economists are scrambling to understand the implications of the IT revolution on classical economic models and global economic performance.

Greenspan, Drucker, and others describe the IT revolution from lofty perches, but other perspectives are possible. Business executives see the IT revolution in new ways of building strategic plans. Doctors see new ways of diagnosing and treating diseases. Manufacturers see new ways of managing supply chains and controlling inventory. Retailers see new ways to reach consumers. In a process that Greenspan calls "creative destruction," the IT revolution is creating new markets and new jobs at least as quickly as it is destroying others. Throughout every social and economic sector of society, the IT revolution affects each of us in personal and immediate ways.

What form does the IT revolution take for software developers? For us, it takes the shape of a robust and fast-growing market of *commercial software components*— software building blocks that we can use to build larger software systems. To understand the implications of software components on engineering practice, we must first examine the heritage of the current software development regime, which was itself a revolutionary change brought on by the first *software crisis*.

2.1   The First Software Crisis

It is a vast understatement to say that it is difficult to repeatably and predictably develop high-quality software. There are many good computer programs, of course. The problem is that these programs are often the product of a small team (as small as one) of extraordinarily talented software developers. No discipline, as software engineering aspires to be, can rest upon a foundation of a few able craftsmen. Reliance on craftsmen will not suffice as the size of our software systems increase and as these systems proliferate.

This fact was recognized as early as 1969, when NATO called a conference to deal with the software crisis: the persistent failure of system developers to deliver software systems on time, within budget, and of sufficient quality for use [Naur+ 69]. There it was observed that between 50 and 80 percent of projects were never completed or were so far from their claimed objectives that they were considered failures. Of those systems that were completed, 90 percent were over budget by 150 to 400 percent in both time and cost. More recent studies of software project failures are no cause for optimism either.

In the 1960s government and defense agencies were the principal consumers of large-scale information systems. As such, they bore the early brunt of the software crisis. But throughout the 1970s and early 1980s, software systems moved beyond government and became increasingly important for commercial use. As demand for software increased, the effects of the software crisis became more pronounced. Policy makers recognized that software had become vital, not just for the U.S. Department of Defense and other government agencies, but to an increasingly information-driven society. The policy response to the deepening software crisis led, among many other things, to the creation of the Software Engineering Institute (SEI), the first U.S. federally funded research and development center devoted exclusively to software.

We mention the SEI not just out of fealty to our employer, but because it introduced, in 1987, the software capability maturity model [SEI 87a] [SEI 87b], better known as the CMM. The CMM has been called by its advocates "a vision of software engineering and management excellence" [Gibbs 94]. Even its detractors, who use other choice phrases to describe it, acknowledge its profound impact on the the way U.S. industry manages its software development efforts. The CMM has also spawned a European competitor in the form of the ISO-9000 series of quality standards [ISO9000-3 94]. Whatever position one takes regarding the CMM versus ISO-9000, one thing is clear: these software management standards have, for over a decade, established the context for improving the practice of software development. Indeed, to many people, software engineering and software process are one and the same thing. An entire industry has emerged to support the CMM and ISO-9000 models, and process improvement incentives have played a dominant role in defining roles and behavior within software development organizations. The resulting roles and behaviors constitute what we refer to as the *software factory regime*.

2.2   The Software Factory Regime

The software factory regime was born when even large software systems were built one line of code at a time. With some logic, it established roles and behaviors rooted in a manufacturing metaphor, where software processes are analogous to manufacturing processes, programmers are analogous to assembly-line workers, and the ultimate product is lines of code. When viewed in terms of software manufacturing, improvements in software engineering practice are equated with process improvement, which itself is centered on improving programmer productivity and reducing product defects. Indeed, the manufacturing metaphor is so strong that the term *software factory* still denotes the ideal software development organization.

While our use of the term software factory regime is not derogatory, there are parallels between the software factory regime with its equivalent from the French Revolution, *l'Ancien Régime*. Both regimes were firmly entrenched, and

Figure 2-1   *The French Revolution* by Eugène Delacroix

to most people there was no alternative regime in conception or in living memory. Both regimes arose to meet exigent conditions that changed over time. Both survived well beyond the point where their original justification had almost completely eroded. And, both remained propped up by inertia until some singular event laid bare their inability to meet changing circumstances. For *l'Ancien Régime,* this event was the Paris bread riots in the cold, lean winter of 1787. And for the software factory regime?

2.3 The Second Software Crisis

The software factory regime might have resolved the software crisis, or at least have mitigated its worst effects, except for one thing: the unexpected emergence of the microprocessor and its first (but not last!) offspring, the personal computer (PC). The advent of the PC was the equivalent to the Paris bread riots, and was destined to overthrow the software factory regime. Admittedly, the effects of the PC were more slow acting than bread riots, but the end result was just as conclusive in its own way. What were these effects?

The PC generated overwhelming new demand for software. It also moved IT from the back office to the desktop, enabling improved decision making and improving management performance, but also leading to a new class of client/server system that replaced a previous generation of mainframe applications. Demand for software also emerged in new markets such as small business, education, health, personal management, and entertainment.

As computer hardware became cheaper and more accessible, the demands for software increased far more rapidly than our capability to produce it. Since software development is labor intensive, our ability to produce software is constrained by the availability of labor. The Bureau of Labor Statistics predicts 70 percent growth in computer and data processing jobs by the year 2005. Meanwhile, the Department of Education shows that the number of graduates in Computer Science has dropped 43 percent since 1986. In other words, fewer qualified individuals are available to fill an increasing number of positions.

The growing gap between supply and demand has spawned an impressive range of research efforts to find technological "silver bullets." The U.S. government (to say nothing of non-US research) spent hundreds of millions of dollars to find ways to build software systems "better, faster, and cheaper." But while the focused genius of software researchers chipped away at the productivity gap, the chaotic genius of the free market found its own way to meet this demand—through commercial software components. But why software components? Why has the marketplace selected components as the most cost-effective way of meeting consumer demand?

In an article in *American Programmer*, Brad Cox argued that software components enable a packaging of complexity at each link in a chain of commercial transactions, and that this packaging is the essence of all manufacturing commerce [Cox 95]. A more conventional argument is simpler still: you do not need to develop software that has already been developed. Unfortunately, the economics of software reuse, as it applied to the software factory, has always been tenuous. Although estimates vary, reuse experts estimated that a software component had to be reused *two and a half times* to recoup the investment needed to design the component to be reusable in the first place [SPC 94][Weiss 99]. Amazingly enough, achieving even this modest level of reuse in custom software settings proved to be problematic.

The surging demand for software, however, has dramatically altered the economics of reuse. Now, a software component can be reused *thousands of times* once the appropriate market niche can be found. The evidence of a burgeoning market in software components is irrefutable and overwhelming. Today, it is inconceivable to contemplate building an enterprise system without operating systems, databases, message brokers, Web browsers and servers, spreadsheets, decision aids, transaction monitors, report writers, system managers, and a seemingly unending stream of commercial software components. J. Breshahan, in the October 1996 issue of *CIO Magazine,* estimated that as many as two thousand new software components were being introduced into the market *each month,* and that was in 1996, while Web technology was still a relatively new phenomenon [Breshahan 96]!

As many organizations are discovering, that stock and trade of the software factory—control over production variables to achieve predictability, followed by incremental improvement in quality and productivity—is no longer possible. The software engineer no longer has complete control over how a system is partitioned, what interfaces exist between these partitions, how threads of control are passed or shared across partitions, or any number of other critical design variables. In this setting, the traditional methods espoused by the software factory regime—methods that assume control over these variables— are no longer valid. The software factory regime has been overthrown, but by what?

2.4 The Market Regime

Control has passed from the software factory to the *market regime*—component producers and consumers, each responding to marketplace dynamics. The market regime decides which features become available and when, how features are distributed across components, and how long these features are supported. The market regime also determines the interfaces that components support and which standards are adopted. Ultimately, the market regime decides which components thrive, and which are destined for the bit bucket. True, system developers can always opt to build rather than to buy a component. In most cases, however, economic arguments weigh against this alternative. Instead, the only options presented to developers is to choose which commercial components to use, and depending on previous component selections or other factors, even this "choice" may be predetermined.

The ascent of the market regime should be a cause of great optimism. In fact, it has enabled developers to produce larger, more complex, and more functional systems than ever before. However, change brings disruption, and disruption presents both great opportunities and great hazard. Organizations (and individuals) that are prepared for the revolution will thrive in the new regime, while those that are unprepared will fall by the wayside. To justify this strong assertion, however, it is necessary (and high time) to go beyond the metaphors of revolution and examine, in concrete terms, the ways that the component marketplace challenges—and sometimes disrupts—traditional software engineering methods.

SYSTEM ARCHITECTURE REFLECTS TECHNOLOGY MARKET

The large-scale structural aspects of a system—how the system is partitioned into components, what functionality is mapped to these components, and how the components interact—is defined by its architecture. One of the software engineering precepts that has emerged in the last ten years is that most of the quality attributes we associate with systems, such as performance, reliability, and security, derive from its architecture [Bass+ 98]. Attaining these attributes was the primary concern of the system architect. However, as systems become increasingly dominated by commercial components, designers have correspondingly less control over system architecture. The market decides which components are available, and, in many cases, how they interact. Indeed, the large-scale structure of systems reflects the structure of the component market itself, with component topologies often mirrored by vendor alliances. We do not suggest that the architect has no role in component-based systems, but rather that the nature of "architecting" changes under the market regime, and the architect must accommodate these changes.

DESIGN FOR CHANGE

Change is a fundamental fact of life in the component marketplace; without change, the component market collapses. Component vendors make money when customers buy their components or upgrade to new versions of their components. Vendors entice consumers with new features that differentiate their components in the market. Consumers upgrade to gain competitive advantage by using these features, or to prevent competitors from obtaining an advantage. Features that succeed in the marketplace are quickly copied by competitors, forcing a new round of innovation and differentiation. Consumers are often forced to upgrade components whether they want to or not. Attempts to ignore upgrades can be dangerous, as the components that make up a system continue to diverge from each other as they separately evolve, increasing the likelihood of an expensive disruption when the prospect of losing vendor support finally forces component upgrade. Unless an organization is willing to develop disposable software systems, it is better to accept the idea of continuous system evolution than postponing the day of reckoning. Design for change (sometimes called "sustainability") becomes a primary objective for the designer.

DESIGNING SUPPLY CHAINS

Accommodating change means thinking of a system as a set of component *streams* rather than a set of components. Each component stream consists of the current release of the component, a finite sequence of past releases, and an infinite sequence of future releases. Once this mental shift is accomplished, it is not hard to take the next step and substitute component *suppliers* in place of component streams. This is a natural step to take since the likelihood of disruption across component versions is reduced if we upgrade components from the same stream rather than switching streams, say, to an alternative component supplier. In manufacturing, an integration of suppliers is often referred to as a *supply chain*, with suppliers of parts linked to suppliers of subassemblies of parts, and so on, all the way to the top—the end product. This is an apt analogy for component-based systems, with one important caveat: while manufacturers define which components are needed—their interfaces, quality standards, and so forth— in the software world, these details are under the control of the supplier. In effect, the integrated software system becomes part of the component vendor's supply chain, rather than vice versa. This situation is often referred to as *vendor lock*, where the cost of switching suppliers becomes prohibitive, and where designers and maintainers must march to the beat of the vendor's drum.

DESIGN IN THE FACE OF MISFIT

Designers must accommodate two forms of component misfit: *use* and *integration* misfit. A component is *misfit for use* to the extent that it falls short of doing precisely what is needed in any given application. This form of misfit arises from the democracy of requirements that underlies the market regime: vendors campaign to an electorate of *many* systems, not just to *your* system. Differences are bound to arise between what the average system needs from a component and what your system needs. This means that the idea of "getting the requirements right" has to be re-thought: requirements must be conditioned by the components that are available. A component is *misfit for integration* to the extent that it cannot easily be integrated with other components. Integration misfit arises from three causes. First, vendors often have mismatched assumptions about how their components will be integrated, causing components to exhibit *architectural mismatch* [Garlan+ 95]. Second, vendors want to lock in their consumers, so they purposely use their own idiosyncratic approaches to integration. Third, vendors are always trying to innovate, and innovative features by their very nature introduce integration difficulties. The net result of use and integration misfit is that the design process for component-based systems is fairly characterized as a process of achieving fitness for use by removing misfit.

DESIGN TO TECHNOLOGY COMPETENCE

Perhaps the most dramatic evidence of the overthrow of the software factory by the market regime is the current job market for programmers. Demand for developers *with the right skills* has resulted in unprecedented salary gains as well as cutthroat recruiting tactics [NYTIMES 99]. Invariably, these skills are tied to a particular technology, such as Web technology or distributed object technology, or to a particular vendor's component. Developers with these skills have mastered the nuances of a technology area and the lexicon of concepts and features implemented by components within a technology area. Obtaining this kind of mastery is not a trivial undertaking, which is why it is such a valuable commodity. What makes this expertise difficult to acquire is that components are, of necessity, quite complex. This complexity is attributable to two factors. First, the component must package enough complexity to make it worth buying rather than building from scratch. Second, vendors do everything they can to differentiate their components from their competitors'. Thus, knowledge obtained about components does not translate easily to other components, leading to narrow specialization of skills. The important point for designers is that making good design decisions— such as are needed to avoid integration tar pits—requires ready access to the right kinds of technology competence. This kind of dependence on "mere developers" can be unnerving to senior (reactionary!?) designers.

SUSTAINING COMPETENCE

One more aspect of technology competence to consider is the cost of *sustaining* this competence. In the bygone days of the software factory, a programmer's skill was based in programming languages and algorithms, the essentials of which have remained essentially unchanged for 30 years. The component marketplace, however, is driven by change, and the competence needed to assemble component-based systems is a *diminishing*, or *wasting asset:* it loses value with each new component release. In some "hot" technology areas, component competence can have a surprisingly short half-life. As a result, organizations must find a cost-effective way of sustaining competence. Failing this, it will become difficult or impossible to develop new systems, to say nothing of maintaining previously developed systems. However, since it is a rare organization that can afford to sustain maximal competence in all technology areas at one time, competence often must be refreshed "just in time" to make sound engineering decisions. This leads to the next challenge posed by the market regime.

DESIGN AS EXPLORATION

Since sustaining up-to-the-minute component competence at all times is too expensive to be practical, it must instead be obtained *just in time* and *as needed*. This means that designers must embrace the idea that learning about components must occur in tandem with, and in support of, the design process. Of necessity this means accepting the risks of using components that are, in effect, unknown quantities. Indeed, Mary Shaw seems to argue that components of any complexity are inherently too complex to be understood completely [Shaw 96]. Whether she is correct or not (and based on experience, we believe she is correct), the fact remains that, to a large extent, learning about components is a necessary and highly effective form of design risk reduction. The more components there are in a system, the more the design process is characterized by this learning process. In systems that are thoroughly dominated by commercial components (such as the one discussed in Part II of this book) the design process takes on the character of a scientific exploration whose aim is to discover the system that is already implemented by the components that have been selected previously. This is a frightening thought for those who believe that software components are a foundation for a discipline of software engineering, but it is a true state of affairs more often than not.

ACCOMMODATING THE PROCESS SINGULARITY

Looking back over the previous discussion, we have outlined a situation that has rather surreal qualities: design as exploration, system as supply chain, fitness for use as removal of misfit, architecture as market structure, developers as critical design assets. All of this is prelude, however, to the strangest of all challenges of the commercial marketplace, but one that we have witnessed repeatedly: process compression. We have said that components must condition requirements. In effect, this means that detailed knowledge about component implementations must shape requirements, and knowing what to integrate depends on requirements. Making requirements specification and system integration coterminous is the obvious solution. To some extent, this is achieved by spiral development processes without loss of management control. The result compresses the development process, where front-end requirements gathering and back-end integration activities are squeezed into shorter life-cycle intervals, with several of these intervals strung back-to-back over the entire development effort.

The squeezing does not stop here. New component releases occur often enough to introduce a random element to design. The designer must often accommodate maintenance and sustainment types of activities, for example, reintegrating previously established design baselines to incorporate new component releases. Indeed, a system composed of 25 components, with each component vendor producing two releases per year, requires, on average, one maintenance integration per week (for scale, the small subsystem in the case study comprised approximately ten components). Conversely, even after a system has been fielded, evaluating new component releases may mean reassessing system requirements, since, as noted earlier, requirements are often derived from components.

As a result, component-based systems tend to be in all phases of the development life cycle at all times! From inception through retirement, requirements analysis, design, implementation, test, upgrade, and installation all occur simultaneously and continuously. This is what we call the *process singularity*.[1] Given all of this, it is hardly surprising to find as many organizations struggling with the challenges of software components as there are organizations making headway.

2.5   Le Procés c'est mort! Vive le Procés[2]!

An often-overlooked property of revolution is circularity. A revolution, literally, requires that something *revolves* about an axis, and returns to the point of origin. Scientific revolutions, for example, begin in a crisis of "normal" science and return to "normal" science, although based in a new paradigm [Morisio+ 97]. Similarly, political revolutions that begin with one set of social institutions return to institutions that are, in many ways, indistinguishable from the ones they replaced. So it is with software. The software factory may have been overthrown by the market regime, but the overthrow is temporary. In fact, our book, we hope, lays the foundations for a *new* software factory for component-based software engineering.

You might be thinking, "Ah, the forces of reaction are in motion." We assure you that this is not the case. We are, indeed, component revolutionaries. But we are also software engineers, and predictability, repeatability, and "routinization" are hallmarks of all engineering disciplines, and software development processes are a crucial means to these ends. As systems become larger and more complex, greater management and coordination is required, and management processes are needed to make this coordination tractable. Software engineering invariably involves some sort of process control. This is as true for component-based systems as it is for custom software.

But, new engineering problems require new engineering techniques, and new engineering techniques lead to new processes. The old software processes are rooted in one-line-at-a-time development and cannot solve the problems of

---

[1] A singularity arises at the center of a black hole. The laws of physics, as we understand them, do not apply at this point. However, as pointed out by Stephen Hawkings, there is no point speculating on what physical laws exist in a singularity, since nothing that transpires within the boundaries of an event horizon can have any effect on the rest of the universe. Alas, this is not true for process singularities.

[2] *The process is dead. Long live the process!*

the market regime, and do not suit component-based development. In short, the old process is dead, and a new process must be established in its place.

2.6 Summary

The information technology revolution is in full swing. The vast and still growing demand for software that is the result of this revolution has given rise to a robust software component marketplace. Software components, in turn, give rise to the need for new software engineering techniques, and new software processes based in these techniques. At root, these new techniques and processes are needed to accommodate the loss of engineering control over important aspects of system design (partitioning, interfaces, coordination), and to accommodate instability in the component marketplace.

2.7 For Further Reading

Although not directly related to software components, a classic and important book is Thomas Kuhn's *The Structure of Scientific Revolutions* [Kuhn 62], which studies the workings of "paradigm shifts" that underlie scientific revolutions. Although we do not claim that software components represent a fundamental paradigm shift in computing (in the way that, say, biological computing does), the analogy of scientific to technologic revolutions is apt and leads to insights about how software engineering accommodates rapid changes in software technology.

2.8 Discussion Questions

1. Do computer programmers that develop component-based systems have to be more skilled, as skilled, or less skilled than their counterparts who develop custom systems? How about system architects? Project managers? Explain.

2. Do you believe that a commercial market in standard, interchangeable software components is possible? If not, why not? If a component marketplace were feasible, what form would it take? What effect would a component marketplace have on software engineering practice?

3

Engineering Design & Components

Knowing that we have lost control over many factors of engineering to the component marketplace is useful but does not solve the problem. Nor does it serve our purpose to inveigh against component vendors whose products stress innovation at the expense of quality. These vendors, after all, are merely responding to the laws of the marketplace—they do what they need to do to survive.

An engineering approach is needed that accommodates this loss of control. We recommend one approach in this book. Other approaches may be possible, but all such approaches must depart from the usual ways that systems are designed and built. This can cause discomfort to organizations with well-established software development processes. The good news is that however radical these approaches may appear from the perspective of software process, they are not radical from the perspective of traditional problem solving methods, or even traditional software methods. The details of the methods may change, but the essence remains.

3.1 Fundamental Ideas

Engineers are *problem solvers*. Engineering as a discipline (as opposed to an activity) makes problem solving routine, and hence predictable. Over time, some problems have recurred with sufficient frequency that engineering subdisciplines have emerged, such as civil, mechanical, chemical, and electrical engineering. Although each of these subdisciplines may employ different branches of science and mathematics, they are remarkably similar in their overall approach to problem solving. The essence of engineering lies in the nature of this approach.

Take for example a problem that arises in civil engineering, the oldest of engineering disciplines: how to join opposite banks of a river. What does the civil engineer do? First, he (or she) observes that there are several potential solutions. A bridge might be appropriate, or perhaps a tunnel, or perhaps a ferry service would be better still. Next, the engineer must gather numerous facts. How steep are the banks of the river? Are the banks stable? Does the river flood often, and how severely? What kind of geology underlies the riverbed? How much traffic must be accommodated, now and in the future? What kinds of resources are available to the project (time and money)? When enough of these kinds of facts are established, the engineer can select the best general solution. The details of the general solution, for example "suspension bridge," are then made *specific* to the problem at hand and a particular suspension bridge is designed: drawings are made, specifications are set, and the bridge is built.

Granted, this trivializes what civil engineers do, but there is sufficient substance to expose the underlying structure of problem solving in civil engineering and, by extension, other engineering disciplines. Figure 3-1 outlines this structure in three distinct phases, or activities: problem forming, problem setting, and problem solving [D'Ippolito+ 92]. Although there are other ways of characterizing the engineering discipline, this one serves admirably.

- *Problem forming* occurs when a problem (or need) is recognized. The engineer's first objective is to *define* the problem. To do this, the engineer gathers information from many sources to constrain the problem; that is, to help distinguish the real problem from all possible problems. Constraints take the form of physical facts, such as the geology of the riverbed, and requirements, such as the volume of traffic that must be accommodated.

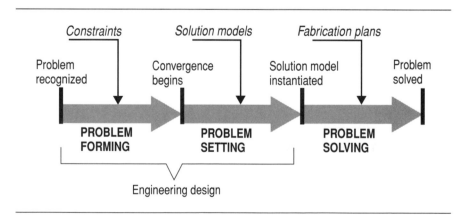

Figure 3-1   The structure of engineering problem solving.

- *Problem setting* occurs when the engineer has the "eureka" moment. At this point, the particulars of a given problem are recognized as a special case of established solutions. The information-gathering activity now gives way to problem setting. Constraints are combined, discarded, and structured in such a way to solve the problem using proven models.

- *Problem solving* occurs when the solution model has been selected and specialized to the problem at hand. Problem solving often involves complex fabrication activities, where design specifications are made real in the physical world. This requires considerable engineering ingenuity, as anyone who is familiar with the history of the Brooklyn Bridge or Panama Canal well knows.

Figure 3-1 makes a further distinction between engineering design, which consists of problem forming and problem setting, and the remaining engineering activities that deal with constructing solutions. This differentiation highlights the sphere of interest of design engineers, who focus primarily on problem forming and problem setting. It also matches nicely with the current emphasis on software methods, which separates specification-forming activities (engineering design) from implementation.

3.2   Impact of Software Components

In the previous chapter, we painted a picture of all advances in software engineering prior to software components with the same factory brush. In fact, genuine and lasting advances in software engineering practice have occurred quite apart from the CMM and its offshoots. Beginning in the late 1960s and continuing to present day, considerable effort has gone into *software methodology*, or the study of methods of constructing software systems

A survey of current software methods would require a book of its own, yet a basic understanding of methods is essential to applying the ideas in this book. Why? Because we do not outline a complete method. Rather, we describe an approach that addresses only those methodological challenges uniquely introduced by software components. Whatever method you are using, in whatever application domain, if you are using commercial software components you will need to extend your current software method with the concepts, techniques, and processes described in this book. An understanding of the structure of modern software development methods will help you to perform this adaptation. We begin by observing that most software methods are concerned with design specifications. In fact, the gross structure of software methods matches up nicely with the syntax of engineering problem solving depicted in Figure 3-1. Many methods adopt the term *analysis* in place of problem forming, and use *design* in place of problem setting. For example, object-oriented analysis/object-oriented design

(OOA/OOD), is sometimes used as a generic term for software method. But the use of analysis and design as *de facto* nomenclature for software methods dates to long before Marca and McGowan's Structured Analysis and Structured Design (SASD) method [Marca+ 87]. Their description only served to canonize a technique that predated object-orientation and already had been in widespread use for many years. In our view, then, software methods describe the practices of engineering design for software engineering.

Many of us, in moments of optimism, believe that software components will contribute to significant improvements in software methods, both from the perspective of intellectual rigor and constructive reality. Figure 3-2 depicts one such optimistic appraisal. It parallels the structure of engineering problem solving depicted earlier, but it substitutes software component terms for their generic engineering counterparts.

- Since components are black boxes, their interfaces are of paramount importance. Interface contracts precisely specify component behavior, and what a component requires to guarantee its behavior [Meyer 00]. An interface may also specify a variety of quality attributes such as performance, memory use, and security. If these specifications are trusted, the properties they describe can help designers structure their problems in the same way that physical constraints help engineers structure their problems.

- Standards such as Sun's EJB and Microsoft's COM+ specify environments for software components. Such standards impose, in effect, an off-the-shelf application architecture on component developers [Seacord+ 99]. As these standards become more robust, and as higher-level and possibly application-specific architectures are defined on top of them, they become proven engineering models for well-specified classes of problem; for example, providing secure, distributed transactions.

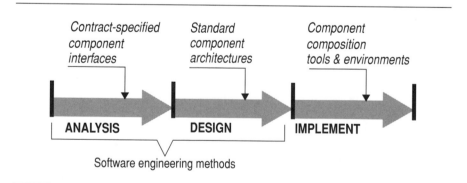

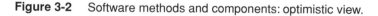

Figure 3-2   Software methods and components: optimistic view.

- Development with software components emphasizes system building through assembly of large-grained building blocks rather than detailed coding. Software development environments that provide a range of tools in support of component composition will greatly increase the productivity of software developers.

There is certainly merit in these arguments. Yet, we know that the market regime imposes a different reality than the idealized one just described. This more pessimistic view is depicted in Figure 3-3:

- In place of contractually specified interfaces, we currently have components whose interfaces are described weakly, at best. Moreover, many of the properties of components that we need to understand are effectively hidden, both by the complexity of the component, and by the fact that we often do not discover *which* property is important until the *lack* (or *excess*) of such a property becomes apparent.

- In place of proven, standard component architectures, we currently have unproven and unstable component *ensembles*. (We will have much more to say about ensembles later; for now it is sufficient to define them as clusters of collaborating components.) The component market produces a variety of such ensembles, each claiming to be better than the others. However, their deficiencies only show up during the implementation phase, well past the point where conventional software methods have terminated.

- In place of high-powered environments that support a compositional metaphor for system development, we have a Babel-like environment of development tools and environments bundled with each component. Development projects must now, more than ever, be multilingual, including all of C, C++, Java, Perl, and SQL, along with a variety of vendor-specific dialects such as JavaScript.

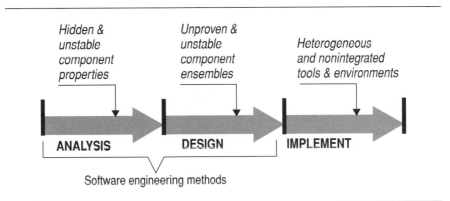

Figure 3-3   Software methods and components: pessimistic view.

This picture is grim, indeed. However, the truth lies somewhere between the optimistic and pessimistic views. It is the nature of things, however, that the qualities expressed in the pessimistic are more apparent in practice, as they are often the most visible cause of failure in development projects. Moreover, in our experience, projects that blindly adopt conventional software methods to component-based development are at great risk of failing.

The question, therefore, is not whether the aggressive use of commercial components is disruptive of established software methods—it emphatically is—but whether we can revise our understanding of software methods to meet these challenges. The answer is yes.

3.3   Designing with and for Components

As we mentioned earlier, this book does not present a complete end-to-end method for building component-based systems. Instead, it outlines only those concepts and techniques that address challenges that are uniquely presented by the use of commercial software components. We assume that you are using some form of iterative or spiral software development process [Boehm 88a] [Cusumano+ 95] [Jacobson+ 99]. While modern software engineering practice has demonstrated that spiral development is a good idea, we assert that it is absolutely essential to component-based development projects. While we do not describe a complete end-to-end software method, the part we do describe nevertheless adheres to two fundamental precepts.

1. Component-based design is a process of exploration, not refinement. Designs are not derived from requirement specifications. Instead, a design manifests constraints imposed by traditional requirements and the capabilities and limitations of commercial components. To the extent that these capabilities and limitations must be discovered, requirements, too, must be discovered, and then design and exploration become indistinguishable. Nevertheless, exploration need not be haphazard; it can be undertaken in a disciplined way to achieve a planned objective.

2. Technology competence is a critical design asset that must be generated just in time, and as a by-product of the design process. This precept assumes that some amount of discovery, and hence learning, is inherent in component-based design. However, it is sometimes mistakenly thought that consultants are a universal salve to the wasting effects of technology change on developer competence. Consultants can help, but they are no substitute for indigenous competence.

As you read this book you may spot other themes, but these two reflect the central theme of this book. The remainder of this chapter provides a high-level survey of the techniques that are described. Each of these techniques is illustrated

The Pros and Cons of Buying Just-In-Time Competence

We claim that technology competence must be generated by a design process. There is another, more time-honored approach: *hire the experts.*

One project we studied that used over 60 components in a worldwide distributed system made good use of this approach. When interviewed, the system architect was adamant that one key to the project's success was the selective use of component consultants. The database consultant, for example, was the very best that money could buy—between five and seven times more expensive than most senior engineers on the project. The consultant was called in sparingly; first, to assist in making early design decisions involving the component, and later, to solve specific problems. Yet when problems did arise he could solve them much more quickly and effectively than the less expensive (but still able) staff engineers. In these situations, hiring an expert, even an expensive expert, can pay off. But this tactic can be overused.

We were called in to help one large commercial enterprise that was having a disastrous time using commercial components. Project after project failed; some quickly, some slowly, but all miserably. A little study revealed why. The information technology staff was familiar with COBOL, RPG, and mainframe-based systems, but unfamiliar with the technologies to be used in the updated systems (CORBA, Web, Java, relational DBMS, message-oriented middleware, public key cryptography, and so on). Rather than start with small and relatively unimportant modernization projects, however, management decided to go after the larger mission-critical projects first. After all, it was these projects that would generate big return on investment from using components. To fill in the competence gaps, numerous consultants were hired, each expert in one or more of the above technologies. They were to act as team leads while overall project management resided with the enterprise.

The problem with this approach, however, was that the consultants had no practical knowledge of the business processes being automated. The necessary creative tension between component capabilities and system requirements was stunted. The consultants often had ulterior motives, such as finding their next job, pushing their company's product, or increasing their company's role in the project. Sometimes honest disagreements arose, too. However, because the project managers were unfamiliar with the components, singly or in ensembles, disagreements between consultants were inexpertly handled, leading to problems, slipped schedules, and bad morale. Clearly, this company had taken the "hire the expert" approach too far.

The lesson is that it sometimes makes sense to hire experts, but that an enterprise must maintain its own indigenous competence. We are inclined to believe that this competence must be at the ensemble level—where the overall system is structured into commercial components, and the components are fit together. That is, an enterprise must "own" the architecture and the competence to sustain it over time.

Kurt

in the case study in Part II. They are, we believe, techniques that are individually useful, but taken together, form the core of a needed extension to traditional development methods.

ENSEMBLES & BLACKBOARDS (CHAPTER 5)

As discussed in the opening chapter, the software industry is finally producing quasi-standard component frameworks. These are, in effect, prepackaged architectures that bundle infrastructure services such as naming, distribution, transactions, security, persistence, and so forth. If, however, these frameworks do not meet your needs, or if you must work with frameworks from different vendors, then you are once again confronted with an infrastructure integration problem.

In the world of infrastructure integration, there are no standard component architectures. Instead, there is a variety of integration patterns that emerge in the market, and vendors to support these patterns. For example, one such pattern consists of a Web browser, HTTP server, CGI script, and relational database management system. There are countless others. We refer to such patterns as *component ensembles*. Picking the right ensemble, and getting ensembles to work with specific configurations of components, is one of the main tasks of the system architect. Indeed, the component ensemble is the basic building block of component-based systems.

It is important that we find a good way to represent component ensembles, but not for the reason you might suspect. We do not represent ensembles as a way to specify a system design, but rather as a way to document assertions about the ensemble that need to be tested. Such representations express something about an ensemble that remains to be discovered, rather than what is already known. We refer to these representations as *ensemble blackboards* precisely because that is where so many of these representations appear—on our blackboards. Nevertheless, although they appear on blackboards, napkins, scrap paper (and, occasionally, in Rational Rose!), there is intellectual rigor in their construction and interpretation.

MODEL PROBLEMS (CHAPTER 6)

While blackboards express something that needs to be discovered, *model problems* are the means by which these discoveries are made. A model problem expresses a design question pertaining to integrating software components in its simplest, most primitive form. A model problem defines a problem that needs to be solved, and defines criteria for evaluating solutions. A model solution is a prototype that answers the question posed by the model problem. A model solution demonstrates that

- A solution that satisfies the evaluation criteria is possible
- No solution can satisfy the evaluation criteria
- A solution that satisfies the criteria is *conditionally* possible

By conditionally possible we mean that a solution may be feasible provided certain other conditions are satisfied. These conditions include a change in the ensemble being evaluated, or a change of contextual assumptions about what is required of the ensemble. Both provisos represent *repair* options. The first repair is a *form* repair, since it changes the form of the ensemble. The second is a *context* repair. Repair is a fundamental activity in component-based design. It reflects an underlying design philosophy of achieving design fit by removing misfit. Without this philosophy, use of commercial components is painful if not utterly impossible.

R³ CYCLE (CHAPTER 6)

Model problems pose design questions. The R^3 workflow (**R**isk analysis, **R**ealize model problem, **R**epair residual risk) ensures that the right questions are posed in the first place. Where model problems ensure that prototyping is ruthlessly efficient, the R^3 workflow ensures that prototypes are developed only where significant design risk exists. The R^3 workflow provides the sole process context for undertaking prototyping activities in component-based design.

Instantiations of the R^3 workflow can be spawned for a variety of reasons. Two are sufficiently important and commonplace to deserve their own names— *repair options* and *contingency*:

- A *repair option* arises if it is unclear which of two or more repairs identified by a model solution should be selected based on existing knowledge. If the repair options are to be explored in parallel, each option is given its own R^3 workflow and managed as a separate subproject of the design effort.

- A *contingency* arises if, for example, there is a design alternative that has both high utility and high risk, versus another alternative that has moderate utility and moderate risk. In this situation, it may pay to adopt the high-risk design provisionally while continuing to develop the moderate-risk option as a contingency, or fallback, position should the high risk option fail.

Contingency planning on large projects is so important that we are tempted to posit the following law of component-based design: the probability of a design failure in a component-based project is inversely proportional to the number of contingency plans available.

DESIGN SPACE MANAGEMENT (CHAPTER 7)

Repairs and contingencies, while necessary adjuncts to a component-based design effort, nonetheless add new sources of complexity to an already difficult activity. Contingencies may have contingencies, and ensembles may be dependent on multiple repairs. In such circumstances, even answering simple questions such as "Is this design feasible?" or even "What is the design?" can be challenging. It is essential that our design notations and our whole approach to managing design specifications adapt to the flux and complexity of component-based development efforts *without* burdening designers with unnecessary documentation requirements.

STORING COMPETENCE (CHAPTER 8)

At the enterprise level, information systems are *eternal*. Numerous projects individually extend, replace, or refine different parts of this eternal system. These projects execute concurrently, and are usually in different phases of their life cycle. In a very real sense, eternal systems are in a perpetual state of design and redesign. Mature IT shops understand this very well, and enforce design constraints in the form of *enterprise architecture* standards. Regardless of whatever other constraints an enterprise architecture expresses, one constraint that should be, and often is, specified is the commercial standards and technologies used to build enterprise applications. As a result, projects use the same components and ensembles on different projects over and over again.

Therefore, at the enterprise level, an important consideration is how competence from previous development efforts can be captured and reused in future development efforts. Blackboards generated by R^3 workflows can be mined and abstracted for future projects. Ensembles provide a useful organizing tool for structuring the mined information, and packaging it in a form that is maintainable and useful for a variety of consumers.

MULTI-CRITERIA EVALUATION (CHAPTER 9) & RISK/MISFIT (CHAPTER 10)

Design decisions usually boil down to *optimization* decisions and *selection* decisions. Optimization decisions involve selection from an effectively infinite, continuous range of alternatives, in which each alternative is the result of a particular configuration of variables. An example of an optimization decision is choosing a setting on a graphic equalizer, a piece of audio equipment that allows amplification of several different ranges of audio frequencies. In contrast, selection decisions involve a usually small, discrete set of choices.

Traditional software design is dominated by optimization decisions, since components and their interfaces can vary in arbitrary ways at the discretion of the designer. In component-based design, however, selection decisions predominate. Selection of components is only the most obvious illustration. Less obvious, but no less important, selection decisions include the choice of which ensembles to use, and which repair strategy to use to remove component misfit. In all cases, the choice of one discrete alternative over others is governed by a number of decision *criteria* (sometimes referred to as *attributes* or *factors*), such as cost, schedule, risk, performance, and so forth. Therefore, a basic understanding of multi-criteria decision making is essential to all designers of component-based systems.

BLACK-BOX VISIBILITY (CHAPTER 11)

No matter how hard you try, and no matter how carefully you plan, things go wrong. Invariably (repeat, *invariably*) an ensemble will behave unpredictably, or just won't work at all, and for no apparent reason. Diagnosing the cause of failure will be difficult because you can't simply throw the system into a debugger—you will not have access to source code for commercial components. Getting component vendors to help is problematic, because they can't help unless they know what is wrong in a more substantive way than "the ensemble doesn't work." Besides, support eats into vendor profit. Therefore, they are disinclined to solve problems unless they know the fault is with their component. As a result, you need to know how to diagnose the causes of failure in systems in which all of the components are, effectively, large, complex, black boxes.

While all of the techniques described in this book are necessary for the design of component-based systems, the techniques for obtaining visibility into black-box behavior that are described in Chapter 11 can save your bacon. This was certainly true of the case study described in this book (Chapter 21 is the most intense illustration of this, but black-box techniques were used in each of the case study chapters, and see Hissam and Carney's article [Hissam+ 99] for a more general discussion of black-box visibility and software maintenance). This is one chapter you should sit down to read with a computer close at hand so that you can try out these techniques.

3.4 Summary

Modern software development methods reflect the structure of traditional engineering problem solving, and the maturation of these methods has contributed significantly to software engineering discipline. However, no method in widespread use addresses the challenges posed by aggressive use of commercial software components. It is possible to augment software methods with the techniques and processes necessary to meet these challenges. These augmentations require a shift in emphasis from that of traditional methods in two ways. First, the more commercial components are used in a system, the more the design effort takes on the character of an exploration. Second, technology competence must be developed by the design process for use by the design process. In brief, generating competence is a principal means of reducing design risk.

3.5 Discussion Questions

1. The characterization of routine engineering presented in Figure 3-1 assumes a steady state—that engineering models already exist. Alternatively, research

engineering is responsible for producing new solution models. Describe a model for research engineering and compare it with the R^3 Cycle. In what ways are they different? the same?

2.   Advocates of formal methods treat software as mathematical objects. In their view, the properties of a system should be proven, not discovered. To what extent does formal specification of software components obviate the need for the R^3 Cycle? Is formal specification of components complementary or antagonistic to the R^3 Cycle?

4

Requirements & Components

with David Carney[1]

The first requirement of a statesman is that he be dull.
— Dean Acheson, American diplomat

... the first requirement for a composer is to be dead.
— Arthur Honneger, French composer

... the very first requirement in a Hospital [is] that it should do the sick no harm.
— Florence Nightingale, English medical pioneer

In the previous chapter, we bypassed a detailed discussion of analysis, focusing instead on design. In this chapter, we take up analysis in detail, for two compelling reasons. The first is that the term "requirements" has been bound up intimately with almost all familiar descriptions of software methodology, and any account of engineering design that we offer must accommodate its importance. More importantly, questions about requirements—What are they? How are they ascertained? How do they govern or constrain the engineer?—traditionally have been central to the design process; therefore, it is fair to ask whether, in component-based engineering design, they still have the same centrality.

We believe that the answers to these questions about requirements are markedly different under the market regime. As with many other aspects of engineering, the presence of components exacerbates a number of familiar problems with requirements, and brings along a few new ones. Note, however, that we make the assertion of *marked difference* with some caution, since we do not mean that the problems of components and requirements are necessarily unprecedented; it is not at all *that* drastic. In any engineering design process, new or old, requirement

---

[1] David Carney is a Senior Member of the Technical Staff at the Software Engineering Institute, Carnegie Mellon University.

trade offs have always been made, requirements have been negotiated, renegotiated, debated, and disputed. Clearly a great many of the difficulties of juggling requirements now encountered in component-based systems were no less present in *l'Ancien Regime*.

In the market regime, however, the central issues of requirements and, more particularly, requirements engineering, are diffused throughout the engineering activity, and it is impossible to consider requirements engineering as isolated from other aspects of the engineering process. For instance, it is arguable that a traditional engineering approach could consider *requirements engineering* as parallel to *problem forming*, and consider it to be a clearly bounded activity. But the presence of components now prevents this approach. The scope of when, where, and how we deal with requirements has been greatly expanded and has become much more pervasive, and our engineering activities must accommodate this change.

We first address the basic question of "What do we mean by requirements engineering?" Then, we consider the common collection of tasks—that is, what a requirements engineer does—for dealing with needs and requirements. We examine those tasks in a traditional vein, since those tasks have not gone away. We then contrast this with the approach that must be taken when designing a component-based system, and how the presence of components impacts managing the system's requirements and creating its design.

4.1   Fundamental Ideas

When we make a brief foray beyond our world of design and engineering, we see that the issue of requirements besets the nonengineer as well: it is surprising how much difficulty can be bound up in such a simple word. One amusing account of this difficulty was made many years ago by the humorist James Thurber, when he described the process by which the editors of *The New Yorker* made their decisions about which cartoons to print.

> They [the editors] do not exactly know what they want. I have in mind one editor who went to F.A.O. Schwartz to buy a toy for his infant daughter, who didn't know what she wanted either, but who wanted something. A saleslady handed him, rather abruptly, a little woolly lamb with a bell around its neck. "Would this help you?" This simple question had a curious effect. The editor began to feel sorry for himself. His own vague yearnings, instead of his child's, became uppermost in his mind. In the end he bought a soft animal, but he never took it home: he set it up on his desk at the office. He doesn't know whether it has helped him or not.
>
> It is much the same with [the cartoons] that are submitted. The personal idiosyncrasies of the picture selectors become mixed up with the ill-defined requirements of the magazine . . . the result is an amorphous

and hazy state of mind out of which it is difficult to fetch up a coherent and succinct answer to the question "What do you want?"[2]

This little anecdote could be descriptive of many systems that have been built over the past decades, and could apply with remarkable accuracy to numerous software projects, successful and otherwise. The problem is partly, as Thurber notes, that people seldom know quite what they want. And they rarely have the ability to translate their needs—unformed, internal, and amorphous— into precise and specific statements that are useful to engineers. But another piece of the problem is that people have the unfortunate habit of changing their minds. It is not uncommon, when people are seeking something new, whether a stuffed animal, a new car, a new skill, or as in our case, a new software system, that desires that were originally thought to be firm and hard can suddenly become soft and mushy, and that some collection of system features that once appeared requisite can suddenly mutate and become negotiable, optional, or even undesirable.

The aggregate collection of tasks for dealing with requirements for software systems is referred to as *requirements engineering*, a term that has been described in various ways. Michael Harrison and Pamela Zave provided a useful definition in an IEEE International Symposium on the topic [Harrison+ 96]:

> Requirements engineering is about the general problem of finding out the needs of the stakeholders and translating these needs into requirements that can be used precisely to constrain or measure the eventual implementation.

A lengthier definition from IEEE's software standards is [IEEE 90]:

> The process of studying user needs to arrive at a definition of system, hardware, or software requirements . . . [where a requirement is defined as] (1) A condition or capability needed by a user to solve a problem or achieve an objective; (2) A condition or capability that must be met or possessed by a system or system component to satisfy a contract, standard, specification, or other formally imposed document; (3) A documented representation of a condition or capability as in (1) or (2).

However one chooses to define requirements engineering, the process involved can range from the haphazard to the disciplined. It is, in fact, the lack of discipline in the area of requirements engineering that has led to the failure of many software systems, and given rise to such clichés as "requirements creep" and "get the requirements right."

Jordon and Davis provides a good description of an ideal engineering approach to requirements [Jordon+ 91]:

> Requirements engineering is the systematic use of proven principles, techniques, languages, and tools for the cost-effective analysis, documentation, and ongoing evolution of user needs and the specification of the external behavior to satisfy those user needs.

---

[2] James Thurber, "Foreword to Fifth New Yorker Album" in *Credos and Curios*. New York: Harper & Row, 1962.

They make the division into three major areas a central element of their definition. *Analysis* is the uncovering, discovery, and elicitation of requirements; *documentation* is the specification or recording of requirements; *ongoing evolution* means that requirements are in constant flux, so that requirements engineering permeates all life-cycle phases.

Jordon and Davis' third characteristic, evolution of requirements, generally has received the least attention historically, and as we assert below, this issue takes on paramount importance in a component-based software development context. Further, we observe how component-based software engineering even affects the validity of the clichés cited above: "requirements creep" is no longer a dreaded condition, and we have made a significant alteration in the advice to "get the requirements right."

4.2   Traditional Requirements Engineering

If we take a customary perspective on building a software system, and assume that the developer has essential control over the code of a system, it is reasonable to expect that *engineered* requirements be subsequently translated into design and, ultimately, implementation. Given this assumption, it is reasonable to assert that a requirement provides a controlling function on the system. The requirement defines a necessary condition; the subsequent design, and still later the implementation, is created in response to the requirement and to fulfill that condition.

In that traditional custom development paradigm, the assumption that requirements were controlling factors was in fact normative. Requirements were elicited and collected from various sources including stakeholder needs and corporate policies. Barring any conflict with other requirements, the existence of a need was generally a sufficient justification for a requirement to be defined. The list of requirements eventually would be considered complete, and the aggregate collection of needs documented in a requirements specification. This document provides a basis for the system design and implementation, or the contractual basis for acquiring a system. This process is illustrated in Figure 4-1.

There are several major challenges for the requirements engineer in the traditional paradigm. The first of these lies in the innocent phrase "barring any conflict with other requirements," which conceals a universe of problems. When eliciting system needs from stakeholders, it is likely that some stakeholders will express needs that cannot be fulfilled. Users might wish for capabilities that are not physically possible, managers might wish for a system costing far beyond the allocated budget, or others may express needs that conflict with equally unchangeable constraints. And even if achievable, the needs of one stakeholder might directly conflict with the needs of others, almost a certainty in a system of any scope and complexity. The requirements engineer's task traditionally has been to negotiate among these alternative ideas about who needs what, and what

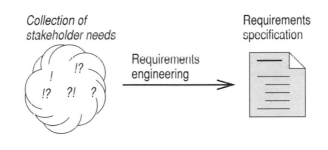

Figure 4-1 Solidification of stakeholder needs in the requirements specification.

is physically or practically possible. The goal of the requirements engineer is refining the list of stakeholder desires into a specification of *nonconflicting* and *attainable* needs—the requirements.

Beyond the agreed-upon requirements, typically there are additional desired goals for the system that are not included in any contractual[3] specification. But they are certainly present; in fact, it is in making such choices (that is, deciding whether a stakeholder's need becomes a real requirement or simply remains a desirable, but noncontractual feature) that the difficulties lie for the requirements engineer. It is, in fact, an easier task to deal with stakeholder needs that are in conflict with unchangeable constraints; these cannot be met by the system at hand, and since such *needs* cannot be satisfied, they are perforce discarded. This overall concept of requirements is illustrated in Figure 4-2.

The second major challenge for the requirements engineer is that, as noted earlier, people's desires are subject to change, whether because time passes or due to other external circumstances. This is why the word "variable" has been added in front of the phrase "desires of stakeholders" in Figure 4-2.

One common instance of this variability occurs when there is a significant time lag between the requirements elicitation and system deployment. Thus, some needs originally declared by stakeholders to be utterly requisite—and that have solidified into requirements—can mutate. For any number of possible reasons, those needs no longer exist, and may even be seen as detrimental. The result is a degree of requirements instability that is almost always detrimental to the development process, resulting in breakage of both design and implementation. When the work has been contracted, the results are potentially even more disastrous since requirements are part of a contractual document that now enforces the creation of a system that its stakeholders do not want. This is a primary flaw in

---

[3] Here we are using this term in a legal sense, rather than a technical sense of contractual interface specification. Even the legal sense should be thought of metaphorically, however, since we mean to include both legal documents governing work that has been contracted, and expectations that have been written down between departments in an enterprise.

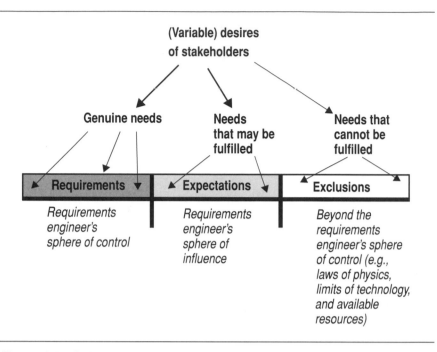

Figure 4-2   Stakeholder desires versus engineering spheres of control.

such development approaches as the waterfall [Royce 70], in which the requirements specification is finalized before any design or development is begun. While attractive in theory, the waterfall approach has been the downfall of many large-scale systems, where finalizing requirements may take months or even years.

To overcome this deficiency, other approaches, most notably the *spiral* approach first developed by Boehm [Boehm 88a] make the assumption that the stakeholders' needs are not well understood at the start of a development program. A system is therefore developed iteratively, as prototypes of the system progress from general functionality (that is, fulfilling only the broadest requirements) through greater and greater degrees of detail. Through this process, the real requirements are uncovered gradually, and risks stemming from too much front-end design are minimized, while at the same time, conflicts between different stakeholders' needs are resolved.

The spiral approach represents a distinct improvement over the waterfall approach. It is significant, however, that both of these still have a strong custom development flavor. The key difference between spiral and waterfall is between singular and iterative discovery of requirements. But in both processes, requirements continue to be interpreted as controlling function, however they are discovered.

Non-Requirements and Virtual Kangaroos

Existing software components often include more functionality than required by the system integrator. For example, a system integrator might use a fairly complex component to perform a relatively simple function in a system. Besides the increased use of resources this might impose (that is, larger image sizes, greater memory consumption) this practice is generally viewed as reasonable. After all, what damage can result from this additional, nonrequired functionality?

An interesting story regarding this practice comes from Dr. Anne-Marie Grisogono, head of the Simulation Land Operations Division of the Australian Defense Science and Technology Organization (DSTO). The Armed Reconnaissance Helicopter mission simulators, built by the Synthetic Environments Research Facility in the Land Operations Division of DSTO, fly in a fairly high fidelity environment which is a 4,000 sq. km. piece of real outback Australia around Katherine, built from elevation data, overlaid with aerial photographs and with 2.5 million realistic 3D trees placed in the terrain in those areas where the photographs indicated real trees actually exist.

To add detail to the simulation landscape, the programmers decided to add animated wildlife, including kangaroos. These kangaroos were created by adapting the code for anti-aircraft-missile-armed infantry detachments. This allowed the detection model associated with the infantry to be used to determine when a helicopter approached, and the behavior invoked by such contact was set to 'retreat.' Replacing the visual model of the Stinger detachment with a visual model of a kangaroo allowed the creation of wildlife that moves away when approached.

These kangaroos behaved as anticipated when tried in the lab—to a point. After initially retreating from the approaching helicopters, these virtual kangaroos re-emerged, firing a barrage of Stinger missiles at the hapless helicopter. The programmers, in this case, had forgotten to remove the weapons and the 'fire' behavior from the adapted infantry components.

There are numerous lessons that can be taken away from this story, but the one we would like to emphasize is that functionality inherent in a component may interact in an unexpected manner with your system. It is important to consider what nonrequired functionality is present in a component being integrated, and if and how this functionality can be disabled or avoided. Another lesson may well be to not antagonize Australia's wildlife.

—*rCs*

4.3   Component-Based Requirements Engineering

The widespread presence of components in the design process creates different circumstances for the requirements engineer. One is the dilution of control, a topic that has been introduced in earlier chapters. A subsequent difference is the competing influence that now exists between the stakeholders' needs for the system and the characteristics of the available components. A direct result of this competing influence is a blurring of the roles of system designer and requirements engineer, and a concomitant mingling of the tasks that each must perform. And finally, any sense that requirements engineering is an early, front-end task is invalidated, and the work of requirements engineering becomes a continuous activity throughout the design and implementation process.

DILUTION OF CONTROL

No engineering discipline has ever exercised total control over its elements; there have always been boundaries of engineering control. Thus, as we have already noted, many unchangeable constraints—for example, the laws of physics present us with certain impassable thresholds or we have a finite amount of resources with which to build a system—can restrict a system's requirements, no matter how great the stakeholders' needs, and no matter how much we are master of its source code. In that sense, requirements engineering in traditional system construction always has had an element of negotiating around immovable obstructions. So the assertion of loss of control in a component-based paradigm is, arguably, no more than an intensification of an existing condition.

But the intensification is a large one, since the presence of components adds a new *source* of control, thus diluting the controlling relationship between the stakeholders' needs and the system's requirements. A component from the marketplace is created independently of any particular system that might subsequently incorporate it. Thus, for a given component, the factors that govern its creation are not some collection of needs for any specific system. Instead, its requirements are the collection of features that its vendor believes will appeal to the widest set of potential customers; those requirements are the aggregate needs of the marketplace, not of any one organization.

Note that not merely the *source* of control but also the *scope* of potential control is altered in this picture; the resulting possibility of instability of system requirements is substantial. The changes that might occur to a component are more than just the component's features and functional workings. The component's vendor makes the ongoing decisions about which features stay and which are removed from future releases. The vendor makes the choices about long-term sustainment, and also makes the critical decision about whether the product continues to exist at all. The vendor has full control over the product's release schedule, deciding when upgrades are released, how often they occur, and how they are licensed.

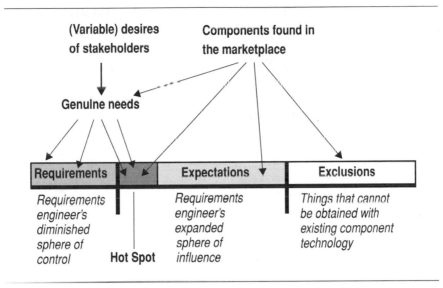

Figure 4-3   Effect of components on spheres of control.

COMPETING INFLUENCES ON SYSTEMS

These independent sources of control exert different, and sometimes competing, influences on the system being designed. The degree of competition varies, but to the extent that a given system makes use of components, there is the potential for at least some conflict, and it is seldom the case that a component vendor modifies a component to meet the demands of a particular system. For the requirements engineer, this means that consideration of a component's properties or characteristics becomes a necessary part of his work, since such knowledge is a necessary part of his negotiating role. Further, while requirements negotiation always has implied flexibility (for example, between alternative stakeholder desires), the need for flexibility is immeasurably greater where components are used.

In effect, the use of components means that the requirements engineer's sphere of influence must expand, while his or her sphere of control diminishes, as depicted in Figure 4-3. The hot spot is that area of overlap between those system features obtained from components that might be either requirements or preferences, depending on which stakeholder has ascendancy on the question. Often such features were identified in the first place because of the awareness among stakeholders of particular component features. This figure illustrates the role that components can play in shaping stakeholders' perceptions about their needs, as well as their role in setting hard limits on what needs a system that uses those components can satisfy.

CONTINUOUS CHARACTER OF REQUIREMENTS ENGINEERING

In a traditional custom development, comparison, negotiation, and instability occur, for better or worse, during the earliest part of system development, and then settle down once the requirements specification is created. Evolution of requirements might lead to a temporary return to the instability of the requirements phase, but would eventually result in a revised requirements specification. The notion of design is, at least at a conceptual level, distinct from requirements elicitation.

However, a subtle result of the relationships shown in Figure 4-3 is that the tasks and roles of designer and requirements engineer have become blurred; these tasks are no longer independent, even conceptually. Instead, they jointly become parts of an ongoing and continuous process of discovery that merges eliciting stakeholder preferences, making design choices, and uncovering risk considerations based on components' properties and vendor circumstances. This merging of tasks and roles is depicted in Figure 4-3 as the dark shaded region that overlaps the requirements engineer's spheres of control and influence. This region is meant to represent those times when a requirements engineer must think like a designer, and when a designer must think like a requirements engineer.

To be sure, the familiar engineering process has always had a degree of instability. The picture we now paint is one in which instability, negotiation, and trade offs still occur, but it is not restricted to an early phase of the development effort, and is not solely the province of the requirements engineer. It is an ongoing condition of component-based system construction. We describe a condition in which, to the extent that commercial components are the basis of system development, it is a direct consequence that the qualities of the component marketplace—instability, frequent change, dependence on component vendors—characterize the way we develop our systems.

There has been little study of this mode of system development, but there is no doubt these changes are occurring. The need for change was forecast within the requirements engineering community when, in an address to the First International Conference on Requirements Engineering in 1994, Clement McGowan made the prediction [McGowan 94]:

> Increasingly, the systems to be built will incorporate . . . component products. . . . If the . . . system will include components . . . then we will do Requirements Engineering differently.

REQUIREMENTS DISCOVERY

As noted earlier, the problems found in component-based systems are not necessarily unprecedented and, from a requirements engineering perspective, we still need to discover what the real requirements are. The novelty now is that the sources that lead us to this knowledge are not restricted to the wants and needs of the stakeholders, but must include the available capabilities of the components we hope to use in our system, as well as data about their vendors. This discovery process is inherently complex, and incorporates several simultaneous activities. Eliciting wants and needs from stakeholders, the traditional province of requirements engineering, is not independent from, but is simultaneous with determining the capabilities of candidate components. And this requires technical discovery of the sort alluded to in the previous chapter, specifically the R^3 workflow.

The net effect of incorporating the R^3 discovery process into the analysis activity is to *borrow* time from development and implementation that would otherwise have occurred during the elaboration phase of the Rational Unified Process, and use this time instead during the inception phase, as depicted in Figure 4-4.[4] Depending on the extent to which components are used, or the extent to which the components that are used play a mission-critical role in the system, more or less time needs to be borrowed. In any case, the added up-front effort requires a heavier investment in system feasibility analysis than might otherwise be the case. That extra expense is more than compensated, we believe, by the reduction in risks originating from masked component deficiencies.

THE REQUIREMENTS CENTRIFUGE

Although requirements discovery necessarily merges elicitation of stakeholders' needs with other activities, the key task of the requirements engineer—determining those properties of the system that are indispensable and nonnegotiable—is still real, and we do not, in Figure 4-3, mean to suggest that his or her role has vanished.

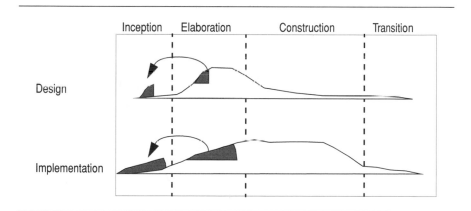

Figure 4-4   Recommended shift in effort in Rational Unified Process.

[4] We have not depicted the effort distribution for requirements, analysis, and test, since the focus of this discussion is only on changes in patterns of investment in RUP. All other investment profiles in RUP remain unchanged by the introduction of component-based discovery into the inception life-cycle stage.

But given its overlap with other roles (for example, those of evaluator and designer), we must consider some different ways that the tasks of the requirements engineer can be accomplished.

One heuristic is that requirements should be minimized. Whereas a stakeholder's expression of need could at one time have been assumed to represent a genuine need, it is critical now to take a much more parsimonious view of stakeholders' needs. We must assume a priori that needs are, in fact, preferences, thereby forcing the genuine needs—those that eventually are considered the requirements—into a restricted set. One reason for this strategy is purely pragmatic: the smaller the number of genuine requirements, the greater the number of marketplace components that meet those requirements. Another reason for the strategy is the reality of commercial practice: even if some component has a near-perfect fit with a complex set of system requirements, the constantly evolving marketplace practically guarantees that the fit will be short-lived.

We suggest that a valuable metaphor to use is that of a centrifuge, which in the physical world separates lighter from heavier matter. Our metaphoric requirements centrifuge operates in much the same way as a physical centrifuge. By applying our requirements centrifuge to some collection of stakeholder desires, only those that are most compelling, most desirable, or absolute (at least to the stakeholders who claim them to be so) move to the outside and become candidate requirements. All other stakeholder needs move towards the center to various locations whose distance from the circumference indicates the strength of preference. This preference is based on a scale going from "really should have this feature" to "nice to have this feature" to "if possible, all else being equal." We illustrate this in Figure 4-5. This centrifuge must operate constantly; as components evolve and change, some needs that were closer to the edge may move

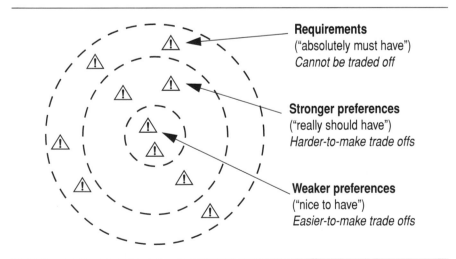

Requirements
("absolutely must have")
Cannot be traded off

Stronger preferences
("really should have")
Harder-to-make trade offs

Weaker preferences
("nice to have")
Easier-to-make trade offs

Figure 4-5   Requirements centrifuge.

towards the center, others may disappear entirely. One interesting result of this view of requirements is that we are no longer seeking to "get the requirements right," as this cannot be done given the unstable commercial marketplace. Instead, we are seeking to "get the right requirements."

Two techniques are particularly useful to achieve this end, both of which are used to support multi-criteria decision making. Multi-attribute utility decision aids (see Chapter 9) define explicit preference hierarchies that allow stakeholders to express preferences as weights, or substitution rates, on specific evaluation criteria. However, great care must be taken to ensure that all evaluated components have been proven to be viable, something that cannot be done, in our experience, without at least some R^3 investment in ensemble demonstration. Risk/misfit decision aids (see Chapter 10) deal effectively with perceived needs that are based in stakeholder perceptions about the benefits of using a particular component. This situation occurs more frequently as end users become more technically sophisticated and know more about the state of commercial software technology. Both techniques provide a quasi-objective structure for prioritizing stakeholder needs that will influence design decisions.

THE REQUIREMENTS PARADOX

By whatever means we do so, we assume that we can separate the *real* requirements (the unconditionally necessary characteristics of the system that are both achievable and nonnegotiable) from every other desirable characteristic of the system. But having done so, the requirements engineer in a component-based paradigm still has a considerable task to accomplish. The remainder of stakeholder needs may be no more than expressions of preference, but they represent a large part, perhaps the majority, of the stakeholders' wants. These preferences will have conflicts, these preferences will have different communities that desire them, and most important, these preferences will be met in varying degrees by the component-based system that will be delivered.

Thus, by following the heuristic that requirements are minimized, this produces an interesting paradox. The requirements engineer now must spend a considerable amount of effort in dealing with nonrequirements. His traditional province—stakeholders' expressions of what they wanted, what they needed, what would make their work improve—deals with those same needs, yet most of these things are now preferences.

4.4 Summary

The use of commercial software components adds new dimensions to established approaches to requirements engineering. Although traditional requirements engineering techniques are still operative, in component-based development efforts the traditional distinctions between requirements engineering and design, and requirements engineering and designer, become blurred. In addition, the formerly discrete requirements analysis activities now take on more of a recurring, or continuing character. Moreover, additional up-front investment in building competence with components and proving component and ensemble feasibility are essential adjuncts to component-based requirements engineering.

4.5   Discussion Questions

1. Has requirements engineering fundamentally changed in the shift from custom to component-based software development? Or is it only the emphasis that has changed?

2. In the modernization of legacy systems, users are often unwilling to relax their requirements to accommodate the use of commercial components that have the potential to greatly reduce system development costs. What processes might be applied to satisfy all the stakeholders in such a situation?

5

Ensembles &
Blackboards

Doubt is uncomfortable, certainty is ridiculous.
—Voltaire

We demand guaranteed rigidly defined areas of doubt and uncertainty.
—Douglas Adams

The previous chapters have outlined the engineering challenge posed by commercial software components and the software engineering methods needed to meet this challenge. This chapter begins a focused elaboration of the techniques that are essential to any component-based software method. We begin with a discussion of component *ensemble*, and its representation as *component interaction blackboard* (or just *blackboard*).

Ensembles are the fundamental units of architectural abstraction in component-based systems. Ensembles allow designers to conceptualize system structure in terms of interactions among component types and instances of those types. They also help designers to identify and reason about those properties of component types and their instances that are critical to specific interactions. Blackboards are representations of ensembles. Each blackboard describes a subset of an ensemble's interactions, and each ensemble is represented by a set of blackboards. Blackboards are expressed as stylized UML collaboration diagrams, although other representational choices are possible. Blackboards express what is known about ensembles, what is desired of them, and, perhaps most importantly, what is unknown about them.

Ensembles and blackboards are the locus of design analysis, process planning, and competence building in component-based projects. They are also the core of our approach to component-based software engineering. This chapter describes what ensembles are, leading ultimately to an ensemble metamodel. We then show how to instantiate this metamodel with blackboards, and illustrate how to use blackboards in the design activity.

5.1   Fundamental Ideas

Since the topic of the book is the engineering design of component-based systems, it should come as no surprise that components figure prominently in our scheme. What may be surprising, however, is that components are not the conceptual focus of the design task. While it is true that a detailed knowledge of specific components is the bedrock of a successful design effort, it is equally true that the design task is to create a system of *interacting* components. Component properties that affect *interactions* between components are of special interest to the designer.

To understand component interactions, it is necessary to define a design abstraction that exposes them. For this purpose we introduce *ensembles*. Informally, an ensemble is a *collaboration*, in the UML sense of that term, of components. In UML, a collaboration:

> defines an interaction, and is a society of roles and other elements that work together to provide some cooperative behavior that's bigger than the sum of all the elements [Booch+ 99].

This explanation is close to what we need. Figure 5-1 depicts a familiar ensemble: a society of components that permits a user to connect to an HTTP server via a Web browser, and to download a Java applet that, in turn, opens a connection to a CORBA server. Thereafter, the applet interacts with the CORBA server to do something interesting. Note that the function of this ensemble is not illustrated. The ensemble might display stock quotes, provide reservation services, or perform any number of other functions.

Although its functionality is not described, the ensemble identifies the *types of components* involved and a *pattern of interaction* among those component types—the canonical definition of architectural style [Bass+ 98]. The ensemble

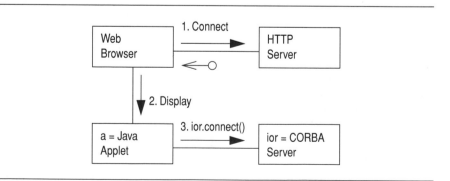

Figure 5-1   A simple ensemble.

also defines a reusable design pattern for a well-bounded part of a system [Gamma+ 94]. In fact, a component ensemble lies somewhere between architectural style and design pattern, with a scope slightly narrower than the former and slightly broader than the latter.

While Figure 5-1 conveys useful information, it falls short as a design representation—it is simply too ambiguous about too many things. For example, does Figure 5-1 suggest that all Web browsers support Java applets? Is there anything required of a Web browser for the applet to open a connection to a CORBA server? Are there any properties of the interactions themselves that must be understood; for example, quality of service requirements? Do any of these interaction properties depend on component properties; if so, which component properties? This type of design information requires a richer conceptual vocabulary and notation than is depicted in Figure 5-1.

5.2   The Ensemble Metamodel

The following sections introduce the vocabulary of ensembles and describe their representation in UML. We begin by defining "component" and build from there to a complete ensemble metamodel. We then describe component blackboards, which instantiate the ensemble metamodel.

COMPONENT

There is no concept in software engineering that is more protean than *component*. This is understandable when we study the term's Latin roots—*com*, meaning "together," and *ponere*, meaning "to put." Exactly what is put together depends greatly on one's point of view. More specifically, it depends on the analytical approach used to differentiate what lies within the problem space (the task of analysis) and solution space (the task of design).

Fortunately, a *rough* consensus of software component has emerged. We say "rough" because there remains significant subtlety in the details. For example, some assert that the concept of component is meaningless without an associated concept of *component standard* with which the component must be in compliance [Cheesman+ 00]. Other widely used criteria define a component as *binary*, independently *deployable* (and conversely, *substitutable*), and *contractually* specified [Szyperski 98]. Much of this subtlety is of deep concern to research, where such fine distinctions are often significant. But for practicing software engineers, a more intuitive and inclusive definition is needed. Accordingly, we strip the concept to its essentials, and only include those qualities that bear on the challenges posed by commercial software components.

Definition: Commercial Software Component.

A commercial software component is a unit of software implementation that

- Is produced by a vendor who sells the component or licenses its use to profit from that sale or license
- Is released by its vendor in binary (that is, compiled) form
- Provides an interface that supports third-party integration with other components

While it is practically impossible to develop perfect categorical definitions for concepts of any complexity, definitions should classify correctly most things of interest. The above definition correctly classifies most of the components that interest us, with the possible exception of a grey area known as *open source software*.

Open Source Software: The Other Commercial Software

It would be a mistake for us to write a book about building systems from commercial software components while discounting all other types of components from which systems can be built. This book is about what developers and integrators have to deal with when software components are acquired from an outside source. Software that is purchased from the commercial marketplace has characteristics that can make it more difficult to integrate, especially when things go wrong or there is a mismatch between that which you need the component to do and what it actually does. This stems from the fact that commercial components are black boxes.

Open source software is certainly another viable and competitive source of software components from which to build systems. Open source software components are not black boxes at all, the source code is there to see by all. But does having the source mean having the keys to the kingdom? It depends on which kingdom you intend to rule.

Good or bad, commercial software vendors do things to protect the intellectual property embodied in their components. Such things may include undocumented functionality, hidden features, unknown pre- or post-conditions, deviations from supported protocols, environment-specific differences, use of deprecated functions (within the component or environment), lack of designs and specifications, and the keys to the kingdom: the unpublished software blueprints (source code). As a consequence, it becomes difficult to integrate a component and learn its behavior.

If integrators around the world had a nickel for every time they said "If I could only see (or have) the source code, I could . . ." world hunger could have been eliminated by now. Certainly, if we could look at the software source code for the components that we need to integrate, we could discover platform-specific differences, uncover pre- and post-conditions, expose hidden features and undocumented functionality, and eliminate deprecated functions.

True, with the source code it is possible (and highly probable given enough time) that specific behavioral nuisances can be tracked down and discovered in a manner that does not require extensive black-box visibility techniques, some of which are discussed in this book. Further, repair methodologies for overcoming misfit take on a new cost equation, as having the source gives the integrator another avenue for making a repair—that is, to make the change directly in the source! All of this bodes well for open source software.

But does having the source code make up for having poor documentation? Does it make up for not having the designs and specifications that went into the building of the software? Some would say, emphatically, that it does— what better documentation can exist other than the source code! In fact, Linus Torvalds, creator of the wildly popular Linux Operating System, an open source software product, has been quoted as saying, "Show me the source." If this were the case then there would be no need for UML, there would be no need for use cases, sequence diagrams, and so forth, there would be no need for ensembles and blackboards (the subject of this chapter), and, for that matter, there would be no need for /* */ and // (that is, code comments—tell that to my college lab instructor).

Absolutely, having the source code is great! Bring it on! But know that you (the architect, the integrator, the designer, or someone you hire) are going to be spending time and effort gaining and storing competence in that open source software component not only at the use and integration level of the component, but also at the source level (hey, it's there, why not read it; there's no documentation, right?). But don't spend too much time reading it, because in a few weeks, if not days, another version is sure to hit the newsgroups and web sites, so don't get too comfortable with version 5.0.12 beta!

This brings me to my last point. The commercial marketplace is driven by its own motivations such as time to market, competition for new markets, and out-pacing the competition, that makes commercial software components complex, idiosyncratic, and unstable. Like commercial software, open source software has its own motivations, which cause open source software to exhibit the same marketplace behavior (that is complex, idiosyncratic, and unstable). And the result of these motivations is, that as integrators we are faced with components that we are forced to understand, many choices (between like components), and frequent updates.

And just like commercial software, open source software is driven to create components that are not trivial, but complex enough to warrant their creation. If they were not complex, why would we not simply build the component ourselves? Perhaps we want to use and gain from the expansive experience base of open source software developers that went into the component's development, test, and use. And that might be true, but not every open source development activity can expect to get the same caliber of talent from project to project. So, if the component is complex enough to warrant its acquisition from an external source (rather than create it in house), then competence in the component will have to be achieved regardless if it is open source or not.

As such, open source software components do not alleviate the need for the management of the design space and the integration complexities that we see with commercial components. This is not to say that open source software components are just like commercial software components in every way, but, more succinctly, open source software is the same from the perspectives that matter in this book—that of the architect, design engineer, or integrator forced to build a system from components which he has little insight and control over.

—shissam

QUASI-COMPONENT TYPES: TECHNOLOGIES AND PRODUCTS

The definition of component is not of much utility in and of itself: we need an additional classification scheme to partition the universal set of commercial software components into meaningful subsets, where these subsets contain components that share one or more properties. Such subsets can be arranged in an arbitrarily complex taxonomy, and, in principle, an infinite number of taxonomies is possible. In practice, though, only two classifiers have proven to be useful: *technology* and *product*.

Technology.   A component technology contains the set of all components that have comparable functionality. For example, *relational database technology* refers to all components that implement the functions that the software industry has come to associate with relational database management systems. The criteria that define a technology are often quite vague, and care must be taken to define meaningful categories. For example, *middleware technology* is too broad. On the other hand, *message-oriented middleware* seems about right.

Product.   A product contains the set of all components provided by a particular vendor that satisfy the technology criteria. For example, Oracle DBMS product might refer to all relational database management systems, current and obsolete, sold by Oracle. The category could be narrowed, for example Oracle 8.0+/Unix might refer to all Oracle DBMS products, version 8.0 or more recent, that run on any Unix platform. While the criteria that specify a technology might be vague, the criteria for a product must be more precise. Still, one should define product criteria in such a way to classify more than one component, since many vendors offer the same versions of products on different platforms, or very similarly featured products on the same platform.

Figure 5-2 illustrates the general idea of component classifiers. The set S of all components is partitioned into two technologies $T1$ and $T2$, which are further partitioned into products P1 through P5. Each product classifies some number of components, which are depicted as black squares. Clearly, the same component can be classified under different technologies, and, in reality, the component marketplace is not so neatly hierarchical as depicted. However, the way we classify

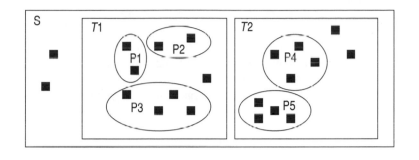

Figure 5-2 Component classifiers.

components is driven more by the kinds of decisions that we need to make than by any compunction on our part to define some objective "truth" about the technology marketplace; that would be a pointless and, ultimately, futile endeavor.

COMPONENT INTERFACE: PROPERTIES AND CREDENTIALS

The definition of component as an implementation with an interface is more subtle than it appears. Most readers probably interpreted "interface" to mean *application programming interface* (API). This is understandable and wholly consistent with the everyday use of that term in software engineering and, in fact, in UML. Regardless of convention, an interface is much more than an API. Nowhere is this concept more important to understand than in component-based development.

As David Parnas succinctly observed many years ago, a component interface is a *specification of assumptions* that a client may make of any component that implements that interface [Parnas 71].[1] Unfortunately, only a relatively small subset of these assumptions—or rather, the component properties on which these assumptions rest—can be specified in an API. Of course, we are not the first to observe this fact, and programming numerous language extensions have been proposed and used as remedies.

For example, language extensions exist that permit the specification of behavioral properties of components as pre- and post-conditions. However, for many other important properties, there are no widely used notations. For example, each operation defined on an API may have an associated quality of service such as average response time and average completion time; or, the component as a whole may exhibit a variety of properties, such as reliability, start up cost, and memory or processor use. At best, such properties are documented as comments

---

[1] Parnas was concerned with the partitioning of systems into modules rather than components, but this distinction (to the extent that it even exists) is inconsequential for the purpose of this discussion.

in the API or in manuals. More typically, such properties are wholly unspecified. All such properties, no matter how obscure, are a source of inter-component dependency.

Worse still, the set of all such properties can be impossibly large for the components used to build real systems. Traditional notions of interface specification such as API, even APIs enriched with formal annotations, are inadequate to this challenge. There are bound to be a large number of properties that are left unspecified. In practice, then, component interfaces must include APIs along with an additional mechanism to document such properties as they are discovered. For this purpose Mary Shaw suggested the practical and useful idea of *credentials* [Shaw 96].

Definition: Credential.

A credential is a triple <property, value, howVerified>, where *property* is the name of the component property, *value* is the value of this property for a particular component, and *howVerified* is the means that have been employed to obtain this value.

Are You Sure?

Almost nothing can be known with absolute certainty. There are a number of well known "facts" that were taught to us all as school children that we now know not to be facts at all—for example, that Saturn is the only planet in our solar system with rings and that Mercury always keeps one face to the sun.

Since we cannot know things with absolute certainty, it is important that we know the degree of certainty with which we do know something. The level of certainty we have in a fact becomes an attribute of the fact. These attributes can then be associated with the fact to form credentials. But how do we know something with any degree of certainty? Certainty is a belief. Absolute certainty (or as close as we can get) can only be achieved through logical deduction based on a set of axioms. For example, there are a set of mathematical axioms first suggested by Peano in 1889 that define the progression of natural numbers [Gries 93]. Based on these axioms, we know with absolute certainty that $6 + 3 = 9$—but only because we have provided the universe within which this statement is true, by specifying the initial axioms. To quote Albert Einstein, "As far as the laws of mathematics refer to reality, they are not certain; as far as they are certain, they do not refer to reality."

In the physical universe, facts are more elusive and must be ascertained through experimentation and observation. However, experimentation and observation are both imperfect and subject to failure. Experiments can return incorrect results if not controlled properly and observation often depends on the use of instruments that may malfunction. In any case, information acquired through experimentation usually can be accepted with a high degree of certainty, especially when the results have been verified independently.

Certainty in software systems leads to a curious middle ground between an artificial, mathematical universe defined by axioms and the physical universe only knowable through experimentation and observation. Small programs can be proved correct through the application of formal methods. In formal methods we define a number of axioms that we hold to be true; for example, that the statement $a = a + 1$ will increase the value of the variable a by one. We can then examine a sequence of these statements and define a mathematical expression that describes the end-state of the system after these statements have been executed. This statement can then be proven to be true using mathematics.

Large software systems, however, effectively protect themselves from analysis by formal methods by their size. As a result, large software systems take on the characteristics of physical systems. This is especially true of black box components, whose source codes cannot be examined directly. The best we can hope with these components is to learn facts about them gathered through experimentation and observation, with the associated reduction in certainty that these processes entail. Statistical testing [Trammell 95], mutation testing [Offutt+ 95], and sampling are all examples of testing techniques that use experimentation and observation to learn about software components.

Another interesting characteristic of certainty is that it is based on personal belief. One individual can be certain of a fact while another individual remains unconvinced. Certainty, then, must be measured relative to a single individual. In the context of a component-based software engineering effort this is preferably the lead architect of a software system. How certain an individual can be of a given fact is dependent, not only by how the information was determined, but also by the credibility of the information source.

rCs

An example of a credential might be `<throughput, 85Kbits/Sec, benchmark>`, which states that the throughput property of some component has a specific value that has been obtained by a benchmark. Naturally, it is possible to be more precise, for example, to describe the benchmark used. By introducing knowledge as an additional attribute of a `<property, value>` pair, Shaw exposes the distinction between truth and knowledge, or what a component *really does* versus what we *think* it does. How knowledge about component properties is obtained affects the trust we have in this knowledge. We trust something we have seen more than hearsay, for example. As the design process unfolds, we require more detailed and trusted knowledge about component and ensemble properties, and so an explicit indicator of how we came by knowledge of a component property becomes quite useful.

A credential, therefore, is a statement of something we know about a component. But how do we describe properties whose values we do not know? In place of a credential, we need something else that expresses a quantum of knowledge that we wish to obtain. Naturally we have to have an a priori idea of what we need to know before we can express the need to know it. In practice, what we need to know is expressed in terms of attributes and their values. Does a component possess a particular attribute? If so, what is the value of that attribute? This is similar to the idea of a credential, except it describes something we need to know rather than something already known. This is an important distinction, worthy of its own place in an ensemble metamodel.

Definition: Postulate.

A postulate is a triple `<property, value, howToVerify>`, where *property* is the name of the component property that the component is thought to possess, *value* is a possibly undefined value of this property for a particular component, and *howToVerify* is the means *that will be used* to obtain this value.

Figure 5-3 is the first step on the path to define a metamodel for component ensemble. An ensemble includes things with properties, with those properties described as credentials. For simplicity we have not included the differentiation of credential from postulate. We defer that to the complete metamodel. There are three kinds of things with properties: components, products, and technologies. Products and technologies are set abstractions that contain components. They are *roughly* analogous to the idea of *class* or *type* in programming languages. Therefore, credentials associated with technologies and products ultimately apply to the components they classify.

The stereotype `<<ensemble>>` is used to reinforce that it is a metamodel that is being described rather than a model of any particular system. Thus, we use a stereotyped class to represent a component rather than using UML notation for component.

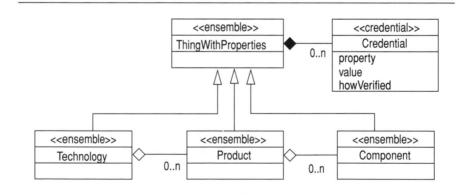

Figure 5-3   Ensemble credentials.

INHERITANCE STRUCTURE

Given the definition of *technology* and *product* classifiers, it might seem more natural to make *product* a subclass (or subtype) of *technology*. After all, these classifiers defined a hierarchy of sets, which is perfectly consistent with subclassing. The *technology* and *product* subclasses do not live up to the full rigor of type semantics, however. The difficulty that arises is what to do in the case of the three-legged elephant? That is, if elephants are classified as a subtype of four-legged mammals, how does one classify a particular elephant born with only three legs?

These types of exceptions frequently arise in the component marketplace. For example, returning to Figure 5-2, suppose we asserted a set of properties X on technology $T1$, meaning that all products, and hence all components, of $T1$ support all properties $x \in X$. In general, there must be some such set of properties, or else it would be nonsense to assert the existence of the technology in the first place. Similarly, there must a set of properties Y that distinguishes product P1 from $T1$, and possibly distinguishes P1 from other products contained in $T1$. But what if there is some property $z \in X, z \notin Y$? In short, what if P1 is a three-legged elephant? Should z be demoted from a property of the technology to a property of products, even though it is possessed by all products in $T1$ except P1? Should subclassing semantics be loosened to permit P1 to be an exception? What if it is thought that future versions of P1 will incorporate z?

Sadly, the commercial marketplace is too chaotic to conform to the mathematical rigor of subclassing or subtyping. The boundaries between products and technologies, and indeed between technologies themselves, are constantly shifting. In the component marketplace, the exception is often the rule. As a result, we decided on the subclassing strategy reflected in Figure 5-3. We also include the injunction that you not treat these abstractions as dogma, but adopt a practical approach to their use.

INTERACTIONS

Components have many properties, and hence many possible credentials. One property of a component is its price, and it is entirely reasonable to have a price credential. As important as price is, however, it is not the concern of ensembles.

Here we are interested in the properties of components that pertain to how they fill a particular role in a system, that is, how they *interact* with other components. Indeed, component interaction is the particular purview of the system designer. For example, designers are responsible for ensuring that systems achieve desired quality attributes such as security, availability, and responsiveness. These and other quality attributes are inherently interactional. Indeed, it is impossible to think about what these quality attributes might mean in a way that is divorced from component interaction.

Although quality attributes are interactional, they depend on component properties. Ultimately, all interactions depend on the components that participate in the interaction. For example, a designer may desire that interactions between two components remain confidential. To achieve this confidentiality, the designer might require that each component use a particular encryption algorithm. In this illustration, a desired quality attribute, confidentiality, is translated into a required component property, data encryption.

All of the statements we wish to make about interactions in a component-based system are of this sort: some desired interaction property X requires that components possess properties Y and Z. In effect, such statements constrain the components participating in the interaction. It is important to note, however, that not every desired interaction property refers to a quality attribute. Quite often, designers struggle just to get components to work together at all. In such cases the desired interaction property is "can be integrated." Designers of component-based systems must be satisfied with such small victories more often than we like.

Definition: Constraint.
A constraint denotes a property of a component interaction, and identifies the component properties that this interactional property depends on.

We represent interactional properties and their dependence on component properties as *constraints*. Informally, constraints express facts about relations among credentials. Quite often these statements take the form of predicates—statements about things that are, or must be made to be, true. When constraints are applied to the credentials of technologies or products, they are either universally or existentially quantified. That is, the constraint asserts that all components possess certain properties, or that some component possesses these properties, respectively.

As with credentials, a constraint can express something we know or something we need to discover. This introduces a distinction between a constraint and a postulated constraint. Also, again with similar logic to credentials, expressing a constraint as a postulate suggests that we need to obtain knowledge. As with credentials, therefore, constraints have an associated knowledge attribute that describes how the truth validity of the constraint has been, or needs to be, established.

THE ENSEMBLE METAMODEL

When we introduced the concept of ensemble earlier in this chapter, we defined it in terms of a UML collaboration. We can now refine this definition, and also define a metamodel for ensemble that supports a design representation for ensembles—blackboards. This is not too different from the original UML definition of collaboration. In place of UML "society of roles and other elements" we use technologies, products, and components. Also, a UML collaboration is said to define an *interaction*, whereas an ensemble defines a *set* of interactions. This is a subtle distinction best explained by the ensemble metamodel, depicted in Figure 5-4.

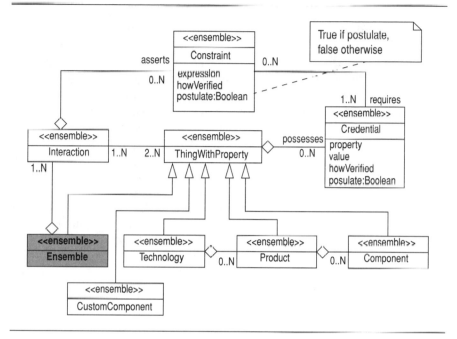

Figure 5-4   Ensemble metamodel.

Definition: Ensemble
An ensemble is a set of interactions among technologies, products, and components that cooperate through these interactions to provide some useful and predicted aggregate behavior.

Consistent with the prose definition, the metamodel defines an ensemble as a composition of one or more interactions, where each interaction is an N-ary association between anything that can possess properties, that is, technologies, products, and components. Observe also that Ensemble (shaded to make its identification easier) is a subclass of ThingWithProperty. Therefore, an ensemble may also have properties and may interact with other ensembles.[2] Also, we have added CustomComponent to the metamodel. This models software that implements the application-specific ligaments in an ensemble. The Java applet in Figure 5-1 exemplifies a custom component. It is often necessary to introduce one or more custom components to properly describe the interactions in an ensemble. The ensemble metamodel also reflects the distinctions between things we know (credentials and constraints) from things we need to know (postulated properties and postulated constraints).

---

[2] The metamodel allows ensembles to interact with technologies, products, and components. A simple UML object constraint language (OCL) constraint would avoid this possibility, but it is not shown.

5.3 Modeling Ensembles with Blackboards

We have defined what ensembles are, but not how they are represented or the role these representations play in the design process. Note that we are careful to use the term "representation" rather than "specification." We do so because blackboards contain a mix of credentials, postulates, constraints, and postulated constraints. This touches on a recurring theme of this book: the more a system depends on commercial components, especially components in innovative technology areas, the more the design activity resembles a journey of exploration rather than a problem solving activity. In such an exploration, ensemble representations demarcate the known from the unknown—the areas of design risks. An ensemble representation is not unlike a map possessed by a fourteenth century explorer. It is partly conjectural, and contains, in analogous form, a mix of established geographic fact, inaccuracies, misconceptions, and myths.

> **Definition: Blackboard.**
> A blackboard is an instantiation of the ensemble metamodel for a subset of interactions within the scope of an ensemble.

By intent, blackboards are constructed to expose areas where we need better understanding. These are the "rigidly defined areas of doubt and uncertainty" referred to in the epigraph to this chapter. These areas of doubt and uncertainty are the signposts for the exploration needed to reduce design risk. Having undertaken such explorations, some information contained in the instigating blackboard may become outdated, not unlike the parts of maps decorated with sea serpents and other misconceptions of antiquity.

Of course, explorers didn't throw away their maps on discovering an island archipelago in place of a nest of sea serpents. Instead, they revised their maps accordingly to accommodate their newly acquired knowledge. In the same sense, we treat ensembles and their representations as instruments of the discovery process. A by-product of this process is a representation of useful knowledge about the ensemble, in the form of component credentials and interaction constraints.

BLACKBOARD AS COLLABORATION DIAGRAM

Blackboards are instantiations of the ensemble metamodel, and are represented as UML collaboration diagrams. However, blackboards are not literal instantiations of the ensemble metamodel. Such a literal interpretation would be too clumsy and artificial. Instead, we use a diagrammatic notation that is simpler and far more intuitive. Whatever rigor is lost by this decision is more than made up for by ease of use.

Figure 5-5 is a blackboard for one of the simplest ensembles possible—one that involves just two technologies, Web browser and HTTP server. The name of

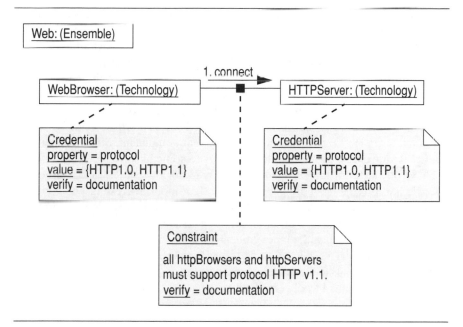

Figure 5-5   Blackboard for Web.

the ensemble is the name of the instance of class *Ensemble,* in this case, Web. Similarly, the objects in the collaboration are instances of the classes found in the ensemble metamodel. By convention, we do not show the connections between the ensemble object and all of the interactions within the ensemble. The ensemble object is virtually connected to all interactions.

We represent instances of *Interaction*[3] as small, solid boxes that act as junctions between two or more components. This representation can be supported by UML tools that allow alternative visual depictions for stereotyped classes. If your tool does not support this feature, you need to model interactions of three or more components using a literal instantiation of Interaction. There is only one interaction modeled in the Web ensemble, called connect.

Constraints and credentials are expressed as UML annotations rather than class instantiations. There is no loss of precision involved in this. In fact, we gain some generality. It is often convenient to refer to UML classifiers (other than credentials) in the specification of interaction constraints. UML annotations allow us to do this. Constraints and credentials are introduced by the keywords *Constraint* and *Credential,* respectively. To distinguish the postulated versions of each we attach the "?" character as a suffix to the keyword. Thus, *Credential* refers to a

---

[3] We use uppercase letters, for example as in Interaction, to denote elements of the metamodel.

property known through a specified verification procedure, while *Credential?* refers to a property that must be verified. The analogous convention applies to constraints. In the Web blackboard depicted in Figure 5-5, a constraint is associated with the connect interaction. Since the interaction involves technologies, the constraint must be quantified. The constraint asserts that all Web browsers and HTTP servers support version 1.1 of the HTTP protocol specification.

The constraint is expressed in terms of two credentials; each asserts that its respective component possesses a property called *protocol* whose value is a set of versions of the HTTP protocol supported by that component. Since neither credential is suffixed by "?" the credentials refer to something we know. Moreover, we have obtained this knowledge by having read documentation to that effect.

Figure 5-6, the signedApplet ensemble, is a more interesting and complex illustration. It introduces a bit more formality into the representation. First, we permit ourselves the luxury of an ensemble namespace. Thus, we introduce the name d to stand for digitalSigner in credentials and constraints. The namespace is especially useful if we decide to use a somewhat more formal notation for describing credentials and constraints. For this purpose we use UML OCL.

Two components have been added to the Web ensemble: applet and digital-Signer. The applet is custom code that ties together the interactions in this ensemble. A credential asserts that all HTTP browsers have a verification function that verifies the digital signature of an applet. As before, this knowledge was obtained by reading documentation. Note that the API to the verify function is not at issue. It might well take additional or different parameters, as might the sign function asserted as a credential for digitalSigner. Three component interactions are enumerated:

1. Offline signing, an interaction between digitalSigner and applet. Note that this is not the sort of interaction you would find in a UML collaboration.

2. Connect, an interaction between a Web browser and HTTP server which downloads a digitally signed applet to the browser.

3. Display, an interaction between the Web browser and the applet that displays the applet. Note that we have not bothered to instantiate a metamodel interaction, since there are no constraints here.

The constraint associated with offline signing serves to define the structure of a digitally signed applet, that is, as a pair consisting of the applet and its computed digital signature. It defines a logical type that is used by other constraints. We could have modeled the offline signing as a three-way interaction among applet, signedApplet, and digitalSigner. However, this would have obscured the fact that the signed applet is a data item of an interaction rather than a participant in that interaction.

The constraint associated with connect poses a question: does there exist any signing component ds that will work with all browsers? That is, can all browsers verify the digital signatures produced by ds? This is not a constraint that applies only to digitalSigner components, even though the primacy of the

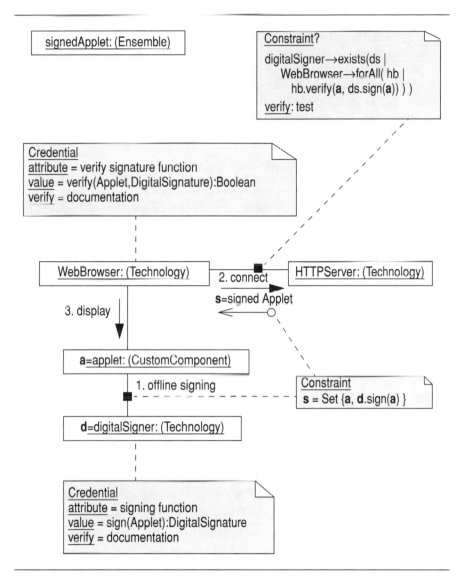

Figure 5-6   Blackboard for signed Applet.

existential quantifier might suggest that is the case. For the constraint to be satisfied, all conditions must be satisfied, including conditions placed on WebBrowser
components. Note that the global namespace simplifies the navigation logic in the
OCL expression. Without this simplification, applet would need to be referred to
by the path expression through the Web browser. OCL purists may object to our
shortcut, but we've never encountered difficulties interpreting these expressions.

The illustration also shows that constraints, like credentials, can be characterized by an acceptable form of evidence (knowledge). That is, even though the signing and verifying functions may have been verified by reading documentation, the constraint on the connect interaction poses a question about the interworking of these functions. A demonstration of this interworking requires its own evidence. In this case, the verification procedure for the constraint is more rigorous than that used for credentials. This is often the case.

QUANTIFICATION AND COMPONENT BINDING

At first glance, the convention of associating credentials and constraints with sets of components presents certain difficulties. For example, the constraint in Figure 5-6 involves existential and universal quantifiers. But to what set of components does this expression apply? If we have not bound a real set of components to digitalSigner and WebBrowser, then the expression cannot be evaluated. That is, we cannot tell if a digital Singer component exists that meets this constraint until we have looked at all candidate digital signing components. What if, for practical reasons, we only examine a small subset of digital signing components, and from this nonrepresentative set, reach the wrong conclusion? What if the set of signing components changes over time? Will we know to reevaluate the constraint?

These are all reasonable questions, but we do not provide answers until we discuss the bind relation in Chapter 7. For now, we simply note that a blackboard is not a statement about global truths about all products and technologies in the market. Instead, it is an outline of what is currently known about how the ensemble works, what is needed if the ensemble is to work, and what still remains to be discovered about the ensemble.

For example, in Figure 5-5, credentials assert that all Web browsers and servers support (at least) HTTP v1.0 and HTTP v1.1. This expression cannot be literally true unless we examine each and every HTTP server and Web browser. That, of course, would be nonsensical. Instead, we interpret these credentials as statements of what must be true of all *real* browsers and servers, where *real* means nothing more than "browsers and servers that we would be interested in using in this ensemble."

Statements such as those found in the blackboards above express design intention. For the signedApplet ensemble to work (as defined), at least one digital signer must exist that will work with all Web browsers in the system. Depending on when this statement is made, there are two distinct interpretations.

- If the statement is made prior to selecting, or even identifying, specific digital Signer and Web browser components, then the credentials and constraints are interpreted as criteria that must be satisfied by some future selected components. All components that satisfy these criteria are considered to be *feasible* alternatives with respect to the interactions specified in the blackboard.

- If components have been selected already, then the credentials and constraints are interpreted as normative conditions that must be satisfied by the ensemble. If the previously selected components do not possess the requisite properties, then it is the ensemble that is infeasible.

This discussion of feasibility, especially what it means to be a feasible component, is crucial to understanding how to make component selection and design selection decisions in component-based systems. We return to this topic in greater depth in later chapters on managing the design space and multi-criteria evaluation.

5.4 Summary

Ensembles are the central architectural abstraction for component-based design. As a design abstraction, ensembles lie somewhere between architectural style and design pattern. Each interaction within an ensemble depends on one or more component properties. Discovering these properties, and ensuring that all selected components exhibit these properties, greatly reduces overall design risk.

Since there are bound to be many unknowns, we need a design notation that exposes areas of uncertainty. For this purpose, we have introduced the use of ensemble blackboards and credentials. A blackboard is an instantiation of the ensemble metamodel. In blackboards, components and their interactions are annotated with credentials and constraints. Constraints identify what is required of components for an interaction to work, and accordingly are defined in terms of relations among component credentials. Constraints and credentials are predicates on interactions and components, respectively, where their truth value has been established previously as validated or still remains to be validated.

Blackboards demarcate areas of certainty from uncertainty. Therefore, they are instrumental for undertaking focused design exploration. As a by-product of these explorations, critical component properties and unexpected interactions are often discovered. This leads us to further investigations and, ultimately, to a proper understanding of what is needed to make ensembles work properly.

5.5 Discussion Questions

1. Microsoft's Office Suite allows documents of one type to be embedded in another, for example an Excel spreadsheet can be embedded in a Word document. Construct a blackboard to describe how this happens. What did you discover?

2. If you were to construct a handbook of ensembles, analogous to Gamma et al.'s handbook of design patterns [Gamma+ 94], how would it be organized? Would the ensembles refer to components, products, technologies, or all three? Can you estimate the cost of keeping this handbook up to date? How might you think of this cost in terms of investment potential?

6

Model Problems

A man of genius makes no mistakes. His errors are
volitional and are the portals of discovery.
—James Joyce, *Ulysses*

The dynamics of the component market practically guarantee that engineers will be (at least in part) unfamiliar with the capabilities and limitations of software components individually and, especially, in ensemble. Such knowledge gaps mask the presence of component misfit, and can result in an overly optimistic appraisal of the feasibility of an ensemble. Simply put, there is a direct correlation between the magnitude of this knowledge gap and project risk. Unfortunately, the old adage applies: you don't know what you don't know.

So, how are risks exposed? How and where does one look to discover the unknown? Our experience is emphatic on this point: hands-on experimentation, that is, prototyping, is needed. It is often the only way that engineers and designers can acquire the competence needed to spot technical risks, and to develop quickly the know-how to resolve these risks. However, although prototyping is necessary, it can be time consuming and expensive. To be effective, prototyping must be ruthlessly efficient. We must build prototypes only when needed. Even then, the prototypes must be lean and sharply focused. In short, we need an optimized process for discovering technical risks and their mitigations.

6.1 Fundamental Ideas

Prototyping is a fundamental technique of software engineering, having been canonized by Boehm's Spiral Model [Boehm 88a] and presently incarnate in various industrial-strength software processes [Cusumano+ 95] [Jacobson+ 99]. In spiral process models, a project is conceived as a series of iterations over a prescribed development process. Usually, each iteration (except the last, of course) produces at least one product, a *prototype,* that is further refined by succeeding iterations.[1]

Spiral development is an excellent approach for managing software projects, especially those that make heavy use of commercial software components. However, a closer look at the concept of software prototype reveals a variety of interpretations beyond that found in spiral development. Table 6-1 shows one such interpretation. It differentiates the *motivation* for prototyping (left column) from *consumers* of prototypes (top row). The intersection represents the form of prototype that satisfies a motive when presented to a consumer. Customers are the usual targets of prototypes. What distinguishes component-based projects is the importance of recognizing the designer as a consumer of prototypes.

Ultimately, all prototyping is motivated by the desire to reduce risk. For example, the development team might want to reduce the risk that a customer will be unsatisfied with the interface of an application. As a result, the team builds a series of interface prototypes through a rapid application development (RAD) process. These prototypes are designed to elicit interface (or other) requirements from end users. On the other hand, there is much less motivation to build RAD prototypes for the designer. Thus, we designate the intersection of "elicit" and "designer" as "not applicable."

As shown in Table 6-1, there are three primary motivations to build prototypes for designers. The first, familiarization, is for the designer to develop a basic level of competence in a component, or in an ensemble of components. For this purpose, we suggest developing *toys,* a term that is not meant here to be pejorative of this form of prototype.

Having obtained basic competence, the designer may have specific questions about how a component should be used, or whether an ensemble satisfies specific evaluation criteria. Generally speaking, such design questions can be approached *experimentally,* beginning with a hypothesis of the form "components *A* and *B*

Table 6-1   Forms of Prototype

	Consumer	
Motive	**Designer**	**Customer**
Familiarize	Toys	N/A
Experiment	Model problems, black-box visibility	N/A
Persuade	Model problems, black-box visibility	Marketing demo
Elicit	N/A	Rapid application development (RAD)
Develop	N/A	Spiral prototypes

[1] It might be argued that we are conflating spiral and iterative development. A pure spiral development approach uses risk analysis to determine what needs to be done in the next iteration, and, perhaps, how it will be done (that is, what process will be used).

can be used to achieve objective *X*." This hypothesis (if stated correctly) possibly can be refuted by the construction of an experiment. For this purpose, we suggest the use of *model problems*.

The third motivation for building prototypes for the designer is *persuasion*. Design decisions may be advocated by project members who possess deep technical knowledge about the features of one or more components. Risk/misfit requires these advocates to justify their feature advocacy in terms of risk reduction. This can be a significant hurdle (indeed, that is the point!), and is, by its nature, conservative. On the other hand, sometimes features can be good, and the designer may wish to encourage "out of the box" thinking by project members. The designer may give the advocates an opportunity to prove their case. Again, we suggest model problems as a disciplined way of doing this.

The experimental evidence produced by model problems (and black-box visibility) are intended for designers. Consequently, this evidence can be detailed and raw; for example, memory dumps, call traces, traces of network traffic, inspection of specific memory locations, and so forth. Designers almost never require advanced graphical interfaces for their prototypes. In fact, constructing "pretty" prototypes for designers usually shows that something has gone wrong in the development process—usually confused thinking about the purpose of the prototype—and that resources are being wasted.

6.2   The Role of Toys

Watch any child and it is immediately evident that play is a natural condition for people. It is a fundamental way that we learn about the world around us, and our places within it. Referring to someone as being childlike is often high praise. It refers to a quality of mind that is inquisitive, flexible, unaffected, unselfconscious, and, ultimately, hungry for knowledge. In a word: *playful*.

Sometimes play is achieved entirely in the world of imagination. Sometimes play is facilitated with toys. Toys are nothing more than the instruments with which we explore the world. Of course, we must be mindful not to venture too far into the meaning of play and toys—this is not, after all, a book on cognitive psychology. For the purpose of this book, a toy is an instrument with which to explore the design space in a particular development effort (that is, design options, tradeoffs, contingencies) in a low- or no-risk setting.

INSTALL IT

First, obtain the component (or components), and install them in your playpen—your personal testbed. If at all possible, do not delegate this step to a system administrator. You can acquire a great deal of useful knowledge in the installation process. For example, are there configuration options? Do these options influence

Enterprise JavaBeans: Just the Essentials

Enterprise JavaBeans (EJB) is a specification developed by Sun Microsystems in conjunction with approximately forty independent software vendors. EJB is part of Sun's Java 2 Enterprise Edition (J2EE). Overall, J2EE is Sun's attempt to demonstrate that Java technology is a viable choice for implementing server-side functionality for large, mission-critical enterprise information systems.

EJB developers write business logic as Enterprise *Beans.*[†] Enterprise Beans are components that are deployed into EJB *servers.* EJB also has containers that execute in servers, but for our purposes we can lump container and server together. EJB servers provide a runtime environment for Enterprise Beans, managing when they are created, activated, deactivated, cached, and deleted. EJB servers also provide a number of important services to Enterprise Beans, including transactions, naming, security, and persistence.

There are two classes of Enterprise Beans defined in the EJB 1.1 specification: Session Bean and Entity Bean. Session Beans are used to export services to clients; each Session Bean can be connected to, at most, one client at a time. Session Beans come in two varieties: stateless and stateful. Stateless Session Beans do not maintain conversational state for the client during a particular session. Stateful Session Beans, in contrast, maintain client-specific state for the duration of a session. Entity Beans are used to model business objects; conceptually, they correspond to data in a persistent repository such as a relational database or file, but they may actually refer to data held by other applications, non-relational databases, files, and so on. The EJB server manages the flow of data between Entity Beans and relational database. Many clients (most often these are Session Beans) can share a single Entity Bean.

[†] Enterprise Beans have nothing in common with JavaBeans, other than their common heritage in Java and the use of the term "Bean" to denote the component.

the functional or nonfunctional properties of the component? How hard is it to install? What kinds of resources are needed (disk space, virtual memory, real memory)? Does it depend on other components? If so, how are these dependencies bound? In the case of especially complex components, you may need the assistance of an expert system administrator; for example, where configuration options refer to networking services or operating system kernel patches. Even in this situation, consider sitting alongside your administrator through the installation process.

IMAGINE THE SIMPLEST SPANNING APPLICATION POSSIBLE

This step requires a bit of study. By "spanning application" we mean an application that touches (or "spans") as many features of the component as are interesting to the toy builder. Note that the application may have nothing at all to do with the real applications that you are developing. Indeed, it probably should be far removed from the real application so you can resist the temptation to design real-world complexities into your toy. We reserve these complexities for model problems, which are discussed later. So, by *simplest* spanning application, we mean one which covers the largest set of relevant features with the least amount of application (or "semantic") complexity.

How do you discover the features of a component? More particularly, how do you decide which features are interesting and hence worthy to be included in one or more toys? There is obviously no cookbook answer to this, and a facility for finding features and constructing the simplest application is something that will come with time and practice. Here are a few good ways to start:

- Examine any demonstration programs that come with the installation. Indeed, you really should install and run these demonstrations to ensure that you have properly installed the component. (There is nothing so frustrating as working for days to get a seemingly broken toy to work only to discover that you haven't properly installed the component!)

- Skim through the component documentation and work through any tutorials provided with the component. It may be useful to attend training courses, but this is often quite expensive. The expense may be worth it, however, if this is the only practical way to get management sanction to build toys.

- Look for white papers or case studies that describe applications built using the component. These resources often can give you clues about design patterns involving the component, or heuristics about how to use the component in different settings. This last point in particular helps with the process of imagining what your toy application should do.

Let us illustrate the main ideas using Enterprise JavaBeans (EJB). What sort of EJB toy should we build? Given that the case study describes a system that retrieves image data from a data server, it makes sense to build an application that retrieves data.[2] But we needn't introduce all of the complexity involved with handling very large slugs of data (for example, gigabyte images) or other messy details. Instead, the toy we build is remarkably simple: it is an application that maintains a set of `<key, value>` pairs, where key and value are ASCII strings. Figure 6-1 depicts the essentials of this toy. Do not be deceived by the apparent simplicity of this toy. While it is possibly the simplest EJB toy that can be constructed that uses both types of enterprise beans, there is quite a lot going on, as you will discover by implementing this application. For example, Figure 6-1 does not show the variety of interfaces involved—each bean must implement both a remote interface and a home interface in addition to its bean interface. Nor does it show the steps involved in deploying the bean from the development environment

---

[2] There is no contradiction between this and the earlier injunction to keep toys separate from application. The *spirit* of that injunction is to keep the real-world complexities of your application domain separate from the toy. There is nothing wrong with using knowledge about your intended application domain as a source of inspiration.

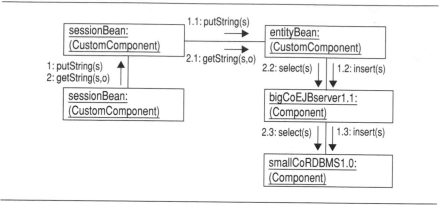

Figure 6-1   A Simple EJB toy.

to the EJB server, or any of the code generation steps involved in deployment. Nonetheless, the illustration does convey a key property of toys: minimal application complexity and maximum feature coverage.

IMPLEMENT THE TOY

It is in implementation that the lion's share of competence is generated. There is no secret to implementing toys. It is just like any other programming assignment, except in this case, *you* are the customer. In fact, it pays to treat yourself as a customer. Consider doing the following:

- Establish a development schedule and stick to it. Be realistic, but be dedicated. You honor your commitments to your customers—why treat yourself any differently?

- Document the product. In this case, however, the product is not the toy, but the *competence* generated by building the toy. Keep a diary, and take good notes. Be neat. Put the notes in a binder. This is a valuable asset.

Above all, adopt a reflective attitude in your development. Be persistent in asking yourself questions: Why am I doing this step? Are there other ways to do this? What is this tool doing? Could I do it manually? Where are the intermediate products produced by the tool? What is in them? And so forth.

REPEAT {OBSERVE, MODIFY} UNTIL SATISFIED

As you might have guessed, reflection is one form that your play will take, but it is not the only form. After building a toy, it only makes sense to play with it, too. And the way to play with the toy is to modify it to do different things, use different features, or use the same features in a different way.

Indeed, the form your competence takes after building the initial toy is likely to be a set of questions about the component. If you have kept good notes you already will have developed a list of questions, and you probably have an idea of how to prioritize these questions. That is, which answers do you need for your project? Do the answers to some questions depend on the answers to other questions? Take the time to develop a learning plan. What form might this learning plan take for the EJB toy? Consider doing the following (or, better still, make up your own list!):

- Does the EJB server support distributed transactions? Change the toy to manage triples `<key, string1, string2>` with string1 and string2 stored in different installations of Oracle, and one entity bean per database. Were you successful? Why or why not?

- Is the server's transaction implementation sound? Add transactions to the deployment descriptor and modify your enterprise beans to run through a long delay. Kill the server in mid-transaction. Observe the database. What is the result?

- Will enterprise beans developed for one vendor's EJB server port to another vendor's server? Get an evaluation copy of another EJB server, and try to deploy your toy. What happens?

It might be possible to fill an entire book with these kinds of EJB experiments, all centered on the trivial toy sketched in Figure 6-1. At some point, however, there will be a noticeable diminution of return on investment (that is, competence generated per hour spent) from building toys. Quite often this point is reached within a week or two. Depending on the complexity of the component, this might vary a little in either direction, but not by much. Therefore, it is important to know when to stop, which leads to the last step.

THROW IT AWAY!

Unless you plan to implement your own EJB server, or start a career as an EJB consultant, you will probably find that within a week or two you have obtained a basic level of competence in EJB. Any further effort will be directed at exploring advanced features and dark recesses of EJB.

When you reach this point, stop and—pay attention now—you must *throw away* all your toys. You have outgrown them. There is a tremendous temptation to continue playing with these toys. Even worse, you may be tempted to use these toys in an application. This may sound impossibile. But if you have taken your play seriously, you will have become quite attached to your toys. Remember what the Buddha says: all possessions transmit pain. Trust us. Throw your toys away before you (or your management) decide to ship them to your customer.

Throw away your toys, we say again. But keep your notes!

6.3   From Toy to Model Problem

Having introduced the Buddha, it might seem as if our intention is to create a software developer's Nirvana on earth, each developer with their own playpen, and with a superabundance of time devoted to play. This is not the case. Fortunately, there is no contradiction between building and playing with software toys and the hard realities of tight budgets and even tighter schedules of software development projects. The trick is to build and play with toys within a specific design context, and to use the competence developed to answer specific design questions. Seen in this light, building toys is really an investment in reducing project risk.

A toy that is situated in a specific design context is called a *model solution*. A description of the design context is called a *model problem*. A model problem may have any number of model solutions. How many model solutions are developed depends on the severity of the risk described by the design context, and the relative success of the model solutions in addressing this risk. Figure 6-2 illustrates the structure of a model problem,[3] as described below. Note that we are being a bit "fast and loose" with our use of UML in Figure 6-2. The model solution is modeled as a single component. In practice, it is usually a collaboration of components. We are also presenting the structure of a model problem as a collaboration

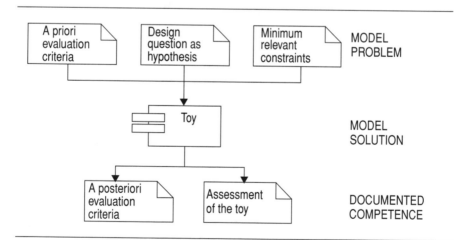

Figure 6-2   Structure of a model problem.

[3] By convention, we have come to describe the entire structure <model problem, model solution, documented competence> as a "model problem." This usually does not cause confusion, since if we wish to refer to the description of the design context (defined as the "model problem" earlier) we most often refer to something specific, for example a particular evaluation criterion, the design risk, or a constraint.

of UML annotations and UML components, which is a bit strange. Our purpose, though, is to develop your intuition about model problems rather than about UML, so please forgive our "apostasy."

- The *design question* is the initiating element of the model problem. It refers to an unknown that is expressed as a (possibly refutable) hypothesis. For example, if it is unknown whether components A and B can be integrated, this question might be expressed as the hypothesis "components A and B can be integrated."

- The *a priori evaluation criteria* describe how it will be determined that the model solution supports or refutes the hypothesis. It might be sufficient, for example, to observe some specific behavior of the ensemble containing components A and B from the above hypothesis. The hypothesis and evaluation criteria are usually defined in tandem. Difficulty in defining evaluation criteria usually points to a problem with the experimental hypothesis.

- The *minimum relevant constraints* specify the fixed (that is, inflexible) part of the design context that governs the implementation of the model solution. These constraints might include things such as platform requirements, component versions, and business rules. You should minimize the constraints imposed on the model solution. Anything beyond the bare minimum may result in an unnecessary falsification of the hypothesis.

- The *model solution* is a toy that is situated in a design context. Specifically, it is a minimal spanning application that uses only those features of a component (or components) that are necessary to possibly falsify the hypothesis.

- The *a posteriori evaluation criteria* most often include all of the a priori criteria, plus criteria that are discovered as a by-product of implementing the model solution. Remember, the purpose is to generate the component competence needed to answer design questions. You should expect to discover new criteria as your competence increases.

- Finally, there is the *evaluation of the model solution* against the a posteriori criteria. This evaluation is more than a statement of "hypothesis sustained" or "hypothesis refuted." If the hypothesis is refuted, the evaluation might also document modifications to the model solution or design context (which now uses the a posteriori criteria in place of the a priori criteria) that may possibly result in a sustained hypothesis.

This description fairly exudes the formality of a laboratory setting, down to the developers wearing starchy white lab coats. This, in fact, is a false image when we consider the crush of events in any real development effort, especially one involving many commercial components with all of the attendant market events. Nevertheless, this is not an excuse to be sloppy in the construction of model problems. In practice, some evaluation criteria or constraints remain implicit, especially if the model problem is just one in a sequence of previous model problems. However, you should understand the essentials of the model problem before embarking on the model solution.

With that caveat in mind, an illustration is in order. The workflow in Figure 6-3 demonstrates how to proceed. Returning to the earlier EJB toy, imagine that the ultimate application supports distributed data management, and that databases are hosted on several host servers. Moreover, data relationships span these databases, meaning that updates must also span these databases. Thus, there is a hard requirement for distributed transactions with two-phase commit. With this scenario in mind, the model problem might unfold as follows.

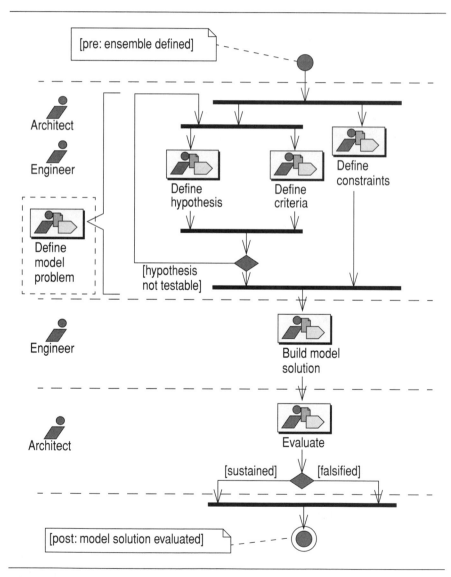

Figure 6-3   Model problem workflow.

HYPOTHESIS

The design question is whether a distributed, two-phase commit protocol is supported by EJB. But that is far too loose: does this mean supported by the EJB specification? All EJB servers (that is, EJB technology)? All versions of a specific vendor's implementation of EJB (that is, EJB product)? Or perhaps the concern is with a particular version of this EJB product? To tighten this up, we might state the hypothesis as follows: BigCompany's EJB server version 2.6 fully supports two-phase commit distributed transactions.

A PRIORI EVALUATION CRITERIA

Next, evaluation criteria must be defined. How could the above hypothesis be falsified? At least two aspects of distributed transaction support might be falsified. First, that a transaction successfully updates two databases running on different hosts. Second, that a transaction successfully rolls back when required, resulting in no changes to either database. These criteria are deemed sufficient[4] to test the hypothesis, and ultimately are described more fully as a test plan that, in effect, constitutes the experimental protocol.

IMPLEMENTATION CONSTRAINTS

Some implementation constraints are already apparent in the hypothesis. Other constraints include the database vendor, the versions of the database, platforms, and so forth. An additional constraint is that the model solution must use the EJB *container-managed persistence* option rather than custom (that is, hand-crafted) data management. It is possible to include such constraints in the hypothesis. In some cases, it is difficult to decide between these options.

MODEL SOLUTION

During implementation we discovered that the BigCompany EJB server does not use JDBC 2.0.[5] Instead, it uses an earlier version of JDBC for its container-managed persistence. This makes it impossible both to use container-managed persistence (a constraint placed on the model solution) and to achieve distributed transactions (the hypothesis). However, the database does provide its own, non-standard API for distributed transactions. Using the vendor-supplied API and

---

[4] As always, the threshold for what constitutes "sufficient" largely depends on the magnitude of the risk associated with the model problem. For a mission-critical application, far more robust and stringent evaluation criteria would be defined than appears in the text illustration.

[5] **Java Database Connect**, a quasi-standard API for Java to relational database access. Support for distributed transactions was introduced in JDBC 2.0.

custom, rather than container-managed persistence, makes distributed transactions possible. However, the performance of these distributed transactions is highly unsatisfactory.

A POSTERIORI EVALUATION CRITERIA

Two previously unforeseen evaluation criteria surfaced from the model solution. The first criterion, in hindsight, was sufficiently obvious to have been spotted earlier: EJB vendor support for JDBC 2.0. Do not become demoralized or embarrassed by such discoveries. They are an inevitable part of learning. Besides, in a real project involving a variety of new components, such oversights are to be expected. In an important sense, model problems serve as a useful "cross check" for developing evaluation criteria and assessing components. Missing the second criterion, performance of distributed transactions, is also forgivable (unless you are a database specialist). You may or may not have to quantify what is meant by "acceptable" performance. In any event, this criterion also helps define a successful demonstration of BigCompany's support for distributed transactions.

EVALUATION

The model solution falsifies the hypothesis: it is impossible to use BigCompany's container-managed persistence to implement distributed transactions with two-phase commit, since the container uses a version of JDBC that lacks this feature. However, by waiving the implementation constraint concerning container-managed persistence (that is, a context repair), it might be possible to sustain the hypothesis. But this can only happen if we exclude performance issues. If performance is important, that is, if this is a design constraint that cannot be waived, then the hypothesis conclusively has been falsified: the ensemble has been proven infeasible for the project.

6.4 Finding the Right Model Problems

The above illustration demonstrates the concepts involved in building toys and model problems. Yet, it is undeniably simplistic. In practice, it is usually unnecessary to employ the full experimental and process rigor of model problems just to build competence in a single component. Rather, the full utility of model problems is realized when the design space is much larger and amorphous. These situations arise when a collection of complex or unfamiliar components must be formed into an ensemble. Often, one or more components is an unknown quantity. Even with perfect knowledge of all components, it is still likely that they might be combined in multiple ways. Such a design problem can be thought of as an *L x M x N* selection problem:

- L represents the number of component technologies that might be relevant to solving the design problem.
- M represents the number of component product choices within each component technology.
- N represents the number of distinct component ensembles.

Designers are faced with a daunting, risk-fraught challenge when, as in the case study described later in this book, *L, M,* and *N* are large and, worse still, if they are also unstable. In such situations, you must adopt an orderly and sustainable process for obtaining situated, just-in-time competence. In this way, you can explore the design space in a cost- and risk-effective way. This is the motivation underlying the R^3 process, for **R**isk analysis, **R**ealize model problem, and **R**epair residual risk. The workflow for this process is outlined in Figure 6-4.

The entry conditions for the R^3 workflow are that an ensemble has been identified and one or more design goals have been assigned to it. These may be functional and nonfunctional goals. They provide a starting point for defining fruitful model problems. The exit conditions are that the feasibility of the ensemble has been defined, and, if infeasible, a (possibly empty) set of repairs has been identified. Ensemble feasibility is defined in one of three ways:

- A *feasible* ensemble satisfies the design goal with an acceptable level of risk.
- An *conditionally feasible* ensemble can satisfy the design goal only if it is susceptible to an identified repair.
- An *infeasible* ensemble cannot satisfy the design goal under any circumstances.

Observe that the repair set includes changes to the design goal (the ensemble *context*) as well as changes to the ensemble. Since it is assumed that the customer of the R^3 prototypes (indeed, the entire R^3 workflow) is the designer, any repairs involving the ensemble (its mechanisms) can be approved or rejected within the workflow itself. On the other hand, context repairs might involve resetting customer expectations, redefining requirements, or other courses of action that are not usually left to the sole discretion of the designer. This is what it means for an ensemble to be conditionally feasible—it is feasible if and only if the stakeholders of the process *within which R^3 is executing* agree to the repair provisos.

The R^3 workflow itself is straightforward if you understand the structure of model problems and ensemble blackboards. The first activity, risk analysis, begins with modeling the ensemble. Given the design goal, the modelers produce one or more blackboards that specify execution threads through the proposed ensemble. Demonstration of these threads either satisfies the goal directly (if it is a functional goal), or defines the conditions under which satisfaction of the goal can be analyzed or otherwise tested (if it is a nonfunctional goal). If the engineers have adequate knowledge of the components, or prior experience with this

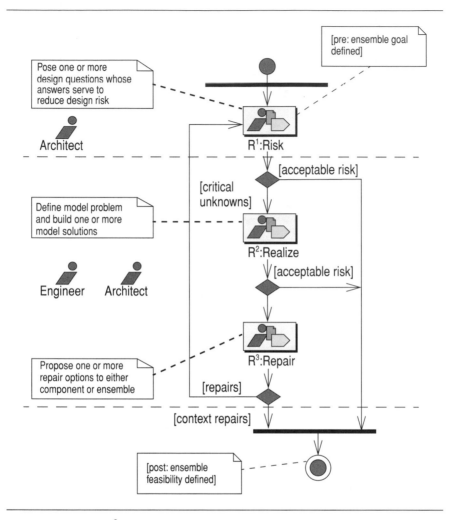

Figure 6-4 The R^3 discovery workflow.

ensemble, the model will be fairly concrete, perhaps to the point where analysis alone is sufficient to determine the feasibility of the ensemble.

The modeling effort becomes more difficult, however, when component or ensemble competence is lacking. Competence gaps are manifested in two ways.[6]

1. There are gaps in the specification of component interactions, or some key properties of these interactions are unknown.

---

[6] Note that these cases are not mutually exclusive, and indeed the existence of one is a strong predictor of the existence of the other, regardless of whether the designer immediately recognizes this fact.

2. More than one collaboration model is identified, and it is not evident which (if any) model might best satisfy the design goal.

We deal with the first case here. We address the second case in the discussion of contingencies later in this chapter.

RISK ANALYSIS

Risk is inherently associated with uncertainty. A hole in an enterprise's firewall is not a risk per se. Instead, the risk is a *function* of the *probability* that the hole will be exploited, a cost *estimate* to the enterprise should it be exploited, the *probability* of the exploitation being detected, an *estimate* of the benefit the intruder might obtain from being successful, and an *estimate* of the cost to the intruder of being caught. As you can see, risk analysis can become quite involved, and it often deals with multiple levels of uncertainty.

This distinction between uncertainty and certainty is important to understand the R^3 workflow. We often hear developers assert that the inability to integrate two components is a risk. This inability is *not* a risk, even if (and especially if) we know with *certainty* it would cause the project to fail. On the other hand, it *would* be a risk if we only *suspected* this inability, or if we were certain of it but only *suspected* that there were workarounds (repairs).

Thus, when confronted with a collaboration blackboard that has interaction (or other) gaps, each such gap is *prima facie* a risk. There is a probability that what is unknown may have an adverse consequence. Naturally, this is vacuously true in the general case. Where collaboration blackboards are concerned, however, at least the unknowns are highly localized. That is, we can point to and describe what we do not know. Nevertheless, it is often difficult to assess the criticality of a gap. All we can suggest is that more experienced designers and engineers are typically better at making these assessments than novices. Experience, after all, does count for something.

REALIZE MODEL PROBLEMS

Assuming that at least some of the gaps discovered from the collaboration modeling exercise are deemed risks, we define one or more model problems to remove the unknowns, using the workflow defined in Figure 6-3. We define a falsifiable hypothesis for the unknown quantity. We also define evaluation criteria and other constraints to complete the experimental protocol. Next, we implement and evaluate one or more model solutions. When all of the model solutions have been evaluated, we aggregate the results and determine if enough is known to render judgement about the ensemble.

At this point we have two options. First, enough may be known to render a judgment in favor of an ensemble. Since we never claim to know everything about an ensemble (it saves us future embarrassment to admit this up front), we assert that the ensemble presents an acceptable level of risk. Second, we may only have discovered more unknowns as a result of our efforts. This is to be expected when the components and ensembles are complex, at least in initial iterations of the R^3 workflow. Or we may have discovered enough about the ensemble to reject it. Even in this case, it often pays not be too hasty. Whether we have more unknowns or are inclined to reject the ensemble, the next step is repair analysis.

REPAIR ANALYSIS

As was noted in the earlier description of model problems, an ensemble often fails to satisfy one or more evaluation criteria. Yet, several repair options may suggest themselves almost as a direct consequence of the failure. In the repair analysis step, these repair options are made explicit, perhaps as blackboards, and are prioritized according to their feasibility. It is also not unusual for the analysis to introduce new repair options to the model solution.

At this point, an important decision must be made. It is evident (if we are at this spot in the R^3 workflow) that the ensemble is still deemed excessively risky. Now we must decide whether to continue exploring design options, or whether to terminate the workflow. Continuing the exploration involves investing more time and money to learn about the repair options. Terminating the exploration means accepting whatever repairs seem most promising, and proposing to the stakeholders any context repairs that are needed.

We must make this decision by assessing the overall level of residual risk that remains in the ensemble after repair, estimating the cost of continuing the exploration, and considering other project management factors.

6.5 Repair and Contingency

A close look at the R^3 workflow reveals something that might seem a bit odd: why does the workflow return to risk analysis? After deciding that an ensemble is sufficiently risky to warrant further exploration, is it then possible for a risk analysis step to reach the *opposite* conclusion? What is going on here? The answer can be found in the dynamics of how we evaluate model solutions, and how we identify repairs for any deficiencies found in evaluation.

First, evaluation and repair analysis both generate alternative repairs, especially in early iterations of the R^3 workflow. The repair alternatives that emerge during the evaluation of a model solution focus on the direct causes of ensemble failure. For example, workarounds for the lack of a two-phase commit in an EJB server's persistence mechanism failure might be immediately evident. Repair analysis, however, tends to have a broader focus. For example, doing away with EJB altogether might be proposed as a repair. In both cases, it is best to focus on generating repair alternatives and not on performing detailed risk analysis.

Second, the identified repair options may, in fact, represent alternative ensembles (that is, alternative designs). The ramifications of these alternatives may ripple beyond the ensemble that triggered the R^3 workflow. A decision not to use EJB, for example, requires the use of an alternative form of transaction monitor. This, in turn, might require a redesign of other parts of the system that were formerly "distant" from the initial ensemble, or, as in this EJB illustration, require a different paradigm for structuring and deploying business logic.

From the preceding discussion two observations can be made:

1. The R^3 workflow generates many design options, and care is necessary to avoid distraction and fragmentation. While the designer must be open to radical alternatives, a conservative approach is needed, especially as the project proceeds and design commitments build on previous commitments.

2. When the exploration of a design alternative is demanded by circumstance—whether it is a radical design alternative or a fallback alternative—create a separate sandbox where you can explore the alternative independent of the status quo design alternative.

The parallel investigation of design options leads to the concept of *design contingency*. A design contingency, as its name suggests, enables the designer to respond to events that may or may not occur. A design contingency is a design option involving distinct component ensembles. For example, they may contain different products or technologies, different collaboration models, or they may support different design goals. A *process contingency* is a design contingency that is supported by its own instantiation of the R^3 workflow. Not all design contingencies imply process contingencies.

Ensembles are the unit of design abstraction in a component-based system. Process contingencies are the unit of process management. Each process contingency simultaneously a) fleshes out the details of a design for part of a system, b) reduces design risk for a part of a system, and c) invests in developing the personal component competence of project engineers.

6.6 Summary

Toys and model problems enable project members to acquire component competence just in time to make good engineering decisions. Indeed, it is difficult to find a more efficient mechanism to build this competence. However, if the design of component-based systems is about learning, it is equally about exploring. As more is learned about the components and their collaborations, new and better ideas about how to use these components arise, leading to new and different designs. Conversely, residual pockets of ignorance often intrude on our ambitions at precisely the worst time. The (usually inscrutable) component market can also spring surprises, both pleasant and unpleasant. Design and process *contingencies* are the technical and managerial mechanisms, respectively, for sustaining the exploration process and for ensuring that it delivers a working system that provides value to its customers.

6.7   For Further Reading

In this chapter, the R^3 process and model problems has been described in terms of competency building and risk reduction. Another, equally valid way of thinking about these is as a problem-solving approach. For another perspective on problem solving, see G. Polya's classic *How to Solve It* [Polya 45].

6.8   Discussion Questions

1. Is there any value in separating design constraints from hypothesis in the description of the design context of a model problem? What (if any) different roles are played by these two specifications?

2. What sorts of criteria would be useful to determine whether to launch a process contingency? To what extent can this decision be based solely on objective criteria?

3. Are the techniques described in the chapters on MAUT and Risk/Misfit pertinent to the evaluation of model solutions? Why or why not? If so, in what way?

7

Managing the Design Space

Here lyeth muche rychness in lytell space.
—John Heywood (1497?–1580?)
from *The Foure PP*

In an article titled "My Accordion's Stuffed Full of Paper," Dave Brown made a wonderful observation on the relationship between design documentation and comprehension of a design problem [Brown 84]. What he observed was the "accordion effect." Initially, a design problem is thought to be simple—the accordion is closed. Upon further study, however, hidden complexity emerges—the accordion expands as more complexity is discovered. After still more study, the designer experiences an "aha" that shows the problem to be simple after all—the complexity collapses as extraneous details are discarded, and the accordion is closed. If the design process has generated reams of documentation, however, the documentation *becomes its own source of complexity.* Sometimes, this extra complexity inhibits the psychological "aha." The accordion cannot be closed because it is stuffed with paper!

One remedy is to minimize design documentation. Some approaches to software development are extremely liberal in applying this remedy [Cusumano+ 95], although it might be argued that even a remedy can be its own ill if taken too far. Metaphors aside, commercial components present special challenges because the accordion effect occurs repeatedly. Component interactions thought to be simple are discovered to exhibit mysterious mismatches. Opaque component behavior makes diagnosis of mismatch a complex undertaking. Eventually, the cause of the mismatch is discovered, and the problem becomes a simple matter of repair. If nothing else, the approach taken to producing and managing design specifications must not stuff our accordions full of paper. More generally, though, our approach to managing the design space must meet a wide range of challenges posed by component-based development.

- The design process involves exploration, and hence learning. Design documents must be "lightweight." It simply does not make sense to invest too much in documenting something that is poorly understood and likely to change.

- The component market is dynamic, with new component features leading to new patterns of interaction. Design documents must be modular and disposable so they can be as easily maintained as the systems they document.

- Component-based design is not a linear elaboration of requirements to implementation. Instead, designers allocate repairs and contingency plans to parallel design threads. Design documents must reflect the relationships among design threads, because the by-products of these threads are interdependent.

- Experience is the best teacher; prior experience, reflected in design documents, can be reused. However, designs are situational and, because of market dynamics, the value of documentation diminishes over time. Design documents must be extracted from their situation, and abstracted to allow reuse of stable knowledge.

This chapter defines an approach to component-based design documentation that satisfies the first three criteria. The next chapter takes up the last criterion on reuse of prior experience.

7.1   Fundamental Ideas

While the blackboard is a central design artifact of the design process we prescribe, no one blackboard completely describes an ensemble. Recall that an ensemble defines a pattern of interactions among components. These interactions may be grouped into subsets. For example, in the applet ensemble[1] found in our case study, identification and authentication (I&A) comprise one set of interactions. User authorization comprises another. It is often useful to create blackboards for each such *coherent* and *separable* pattern of interaction. The criteria for coherent and separable are not always clear, yet assigning specific patterns of interaction to their own blackboards makes the design documentation easier to read and maintain since changes are usually restricted to these subsets.

One consequence of this approach, however, is that the design process generates a (potentially large) number of blackboards. We need a management structure to help us:

- understand how blackboards relate to one another,

---

[1] An applet is a Java program running in a Web browser's Java virtual machine (JVM). A servlet is a Java program running in an HTTP server's JVM.

- know which blackboard contains the information that is needed, and
- ensure that information contained in different blackboards is consistent.

Such a management structure must make explicit the relationships between ensembles, between ensembles and blackboards, and between blackboards. In Section 7.2 we set the stage by briefly returning to ensembles and blackboards. In Section 7.3 we discuss, in detail, ensemble and blackboard relations, their semantics, and their management.

7.2   Ensembles, Blackboards, Relations

Let's assume we are going to develop a simple system comprising a Web browser, an HTTP server, and Java technology. Is there an ensemble here? If so, what is it? These questions are not as innocent as they appear.

To begin, we propose that there is not one, but two ensembles implied by these technologies (Figure 7-1). The applet ensemble situates Java technology on the browser side, while the servlet puts it on the server side. We justify this distinction because the same technologies are used to implement different patterns of interaction. In this example, there are significant qualitative differences between these ensembles with respect to performance, scale, security, and other quality attributes.

Questions immediately arise, however. For example, how are the applet and servlet ensembles related *to each other*? We might assert that they are related by

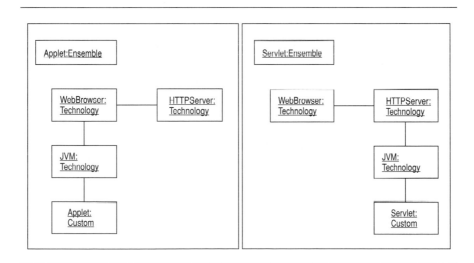

Figure 7-1   Two ensembles?

virtue of being design alternatives. That is, a designer could choose to implement the application as either an applet or a servlet. We might also assert that they are related by virtue of a common ensemble parent, say Web ensemble. Both assertions are valid. In fact, they are not mutually exclusive. They do, however, have different underlying premises:

- The ensembles are design alternatives *if they are units of composition*. That is, we select the applet ensemble to implement one part of a design, while we select the servlet ensemble for another part. In some cases, the ensembles we select must work together, or be composed.

- The ensembles have a common ancestor *if they are types*. Because they are types, various type relations might hold, for example subtyping. That is, ensemble *B* is a subtype of ensemble *A,* if *B* further constrains *A* in a way that does not contradict any constraints defined by *A*.

Both of these express useful points of view. However, we must be careful when treating ensembles as types. For example, what if we wanted an ensemble that used servlets *and* applets? It is natural to think of such an ensemble as subtyping both applet and servlet ensembles. But how will the subtype relation be defined? There is no ensemble interface, in the usual sense, upon which to hang axioms. Using state machines or process algebras might be possible. But these approaches are vulnerable for the very reason we use blackboards in the first place: we do *not* fully understand, and therefore *cannot* formally describe, the behavior of complex commercial components. For all these reasons, we tend to avoid the "ensemble as type" premise.

A blackboard models a subset of component interactions that lie within the scope of an ensemble. However, if a blackboard describes only a subset of component interactions, might it not include only a subset of components? Where does the *complete* specification of the ensemble exist (if it exists) that describes *all* of the components and their interactions? The answer lies in the relationships among blackboards. Since each blackboard describes a subset of the components and interactions within the scope of an ensemble, a specification of that ensemble can be found in the *aggregation* (*not* to be read as *composition*) of its blackboards. This is simple and acceptable for all practical purposes. It does, however, exact a price. It means that we must abandon the idea of an objectively complete specification, since we could always choose to include or exclude any particular blackboard, or add further detail to existing blackboards, depending on how much we need to learn about the behavior of components. But even if we compromise the ideal of completeness, we need not compromise on consistency or, more importantly, utility.

7.3   Ensemble Management

Ensembles are modeled as UML packages, and blackboard views as collaboration diagrams within these packages. Beyond this, a variety of relationships arise among ensembles and blackboards. These must be managed if the design process is to remain under control. We describe the relations that compose the design space in three ways. First, we describe them informally to provide an intuition about their meaning and their connection to the design process. Second, we describe them more formally. Last, we describe, and illustrate, how they are modeled as UML blackboards.

NOTE: Readers uninterested in the formal treatment of the design space may skip the sections titled "formalization." This material is included for those who wish to develop automated tools or further formalize and extend our ideas.

Table 7-1 summarizes the concepts, relations, and predicates that are the constituents of the component-based design space.

Table 7-1   Summary of Design Space and Its UML Representation

Fundamental Ideas	UML Representation
Ensemble and ensemble refinements	UML package and subpackages, respectively.
Alternative ensemble refinements	Blackboard of a meta-ensemble whose name is *Contingency*, which contains only ensembles and their associations. Primary alternatives are represented as associations of type *primary*, and contingent alternatives by associations of type *contingency*.
Fundamental ensemble feasibility predicate	An annotation on ensembles in the contingency blackboard, with the keyword "feasible" equivalent to "true," "not feasible" equivalent to "false," and "feasible?" equivalent to "unknown."
Alternative ensemble remedies	Blackboard of a meta-ensemble whose name is *Contingency*, which contains only ensembles and their associations. Active remedies are represented as associations of type *repair*. Passive remedies are represented as annotations using the keyword "wait."
Ensemble aggregation	An ensemble view whose name is *Manifest*. Contains all technologies, products, components, and their credentials, found in any view of the ensemble.
Binding	Associations between technologies and products, and between products and components, represent product and component bindings, respectively.
Binding predicate	UML annotations on technologies or products found in Manifest, with the keywords "bound" equivalent to "true," and "unbound" equivalent to "false."
Qualified binding predicate	Same as with binding predicate, with the addition of an expression that can be applied as a predicate to candidate products and components.
Ensemble view	Blackboard of an ensemble subset whose name denotes the pattern of interaction modeled by the blackboard.

NOTATIONAL CONVENTIONS

In the following discussion, we denote an ensemble as $e \in E$, where E is the set of all ensembles in a design. We treat e as a set $e = T_e \cup P_e \cup C_e$, where T_e, P_e, and C_e are the sets of technologies, products, and components within the scope of e. Where it will not result in confusion, we simply use T, P, and C. The symbols $\cup$ and $\cap$ denote set *union* and *intersection*, respectively. The symbols $\subset$ and $\subseteq$ denote *proper subset* and *subset*, respectively. The expression $r(e_x, e_y)$ refers to a relation r, with ensembles e_x and e_y participating in a relationship denoted by r. The expression $p(e)$ refers to a predicate p applied to ensemble e. The symbols $\wedge$ and $\vee$ are logical *and* and logical *or*, respectively. The expression $p(x, y) \equiv q(x, y) \vee r(x, y)$ denotes the relation p that may take the form of relation q or r. We occasionally denote variables in relations by means of the universal quantifier $\forall$ and the existential quantifier $\exists$. For example, the expression $\forall (c \in C) \exists (p \in P) \bullet b(p, c)$ states that for all components c there exists a product p such that p and c are in the relationship b.

ALTERNATIVE REFINEMENTS

Intuition.   An ensemble may have two or more competing and mutually exclusive *refinements*. Given our earlier reservations concerning the treatment of ensembles as types, we use the term *refinement* informally. For example, the applet and servlet ensembles in Figure 7-1 could have been an alternative refinement of a more general Web ensemble. The blackboard for the Web ensemble would comprise a Web browser and Web server, but not Java technology.

The designer eventually must choose either the Web ensemble or one of its refinements. However, there may be many reasons to defer making this selection. Perhaps the applet ensemble is preferred, but its feasibility has not been demonstrated with respect to some criteria. The decision to choose the applet ensemble might be made *contingent* on the results of further investigation. Of course, there may be any number of contingent alternatives. It is also often useful to distinguish one alternative as *primary*. This represents a tentative commitment to a design alternative. This commitment may be overturned after investigating the contingent alternatives.

Primary should not be interpreted as *preference*. For example, a primary refinement might be a low-risk ensemble that is known to be feasible, while a contingent refinement might be preferred but have unknown feasibility. In this scenario, the high-risk ensemble might be preferred but still not be primary.

Formalization.   The *alternatives* relation $a(e, e_y)$, for ensemble e with alternative e_y, models contingency planning. The alternatives relation is composed from two more primitive relations, $a(e, e_y) \equiv p(e, e_y) \vee c(e, e_y)$. The *primary* relation $p(e, e_y)$ asserts that e_y is the primary refinement of e. The *contingent* relation $c(e, e_y)$

asserts that e_y is a contingent refinement of e. The following restrictions apply to the construction of $a(e, e_y)$:

1. An ensemble has *at most* one primary refinement.

2. An ensemble may be its own primary refinement, that is, $p(e, e)$.

3. An ensemble may have zero or more contingent refinements.

4. An ensemble can *never* be contingent on itself, that is, $c(e, e) = \emptyset$.

The alternatives relation does not introduce any feasibility dependencies. That is, an ensemble remains feasible even if all of its alternative refinements and primary refinement (assuming $p(e, e) = \emptyset$) are infeasible. (See the later discussion of the fundamental ensemble predicate.)

Representation.   The alternatives relation is modeled as a blackboard that contains only ensembles. However, these ensembles do not interact in the way typical of blackboards. Instead, their associations model design alternatives. The name of this ensemble (really, a meta-ensemble) is *Contingency*. Figure 7-2 illustrates the alternatives relation for the Web ensemble, `Web::Contingency`. In this illustration, the applet and servlet ensembles are both refinements of the Web ensemble, but the applet ensemble is the default choice.

THE FUNDAMENTAL ENSEMBLE FEASIBILITY PREDICATE

Intuition.   Ultimately, the designer must select and compose ensembles that are appropriate for a design problem. Selection is the predominant mode of design

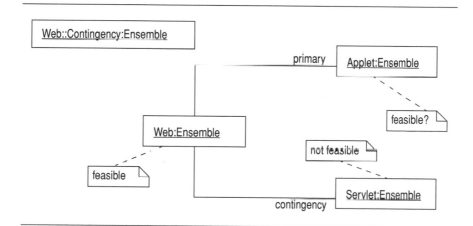

Figure 7-2   Primary and contingent ensembles.

decision making in component-based systems.[2] It applies equally to the selection of components and to the selection of ensembles. Prior to selection, we must eliminate *infeasible* alternatives, so that an alternative can be selected from the remaining viable alternatives based on *preference* rather than necessity. The designer must define feasibility criteria, and from these judge the feasibility of ensembles.

Formalization.   A feasibility predicate expresses a design judgment about the suitability of an ensemble to a particular design problem. We represent design uncertainty using three-value logic :

$$\text{ensemble feasibility} = f(e) \equiv true \lor false \lor unknown$$

which requires that we know, for every ensemble, whether it is feasible (true), infeasible (false), or has unknown feasibility (unknown).

Table 7-2 provides the truth table for three-valued logic. This truth table is used in later discussions.

Representation.   The feasibility predicate is modeled as an annotation on ensembles found in the Contingency blackboard. The keyword *feasible* is interpreted as *true*; *feasible?* is interpreted as *unknown*; and *not feasible* is interpreted as *false*. By convention, unannotated ensembles have *unknown* feasibility. Figure 7-2 illustrates these annotations. Usually, a judgment of not feasible is accompanied by an annotation describing unsatisfied feasibility criteria. As shown in the case study, the feasibility predicate expresses judgment. A significant part of component-based design is deciding how much investment is required to change a value of *unknown* to *true* or *false*, and how much evidence is required to make this change.

Table 7-2   Three Value Logic

p	q	$p \land q$	$p \lor q$
0	0	0	0
0	?	0	?
0	1	0	1
?	0	0	?
?	?	?	?
?	1	?	1
1	0	0	1
1	?	?	1
1	1	1	1

[2] We note again, for emphasis, that the class of components that are the subject of this book are commercial components; that is, components that preexist the design problem, exist independent of the design, and cannot be changed to accommodate the design.

ALTERNATIVE REMEDIES

Intuition.   The feasibility of an ensemble often depends on one or more remedies.[3] For example, consider the case when two components use inconsistent protocols. In this situation, the ensemble comprising these two components would be infeasible. However, there may be a variety of ways to remove the protocol mismatch. *Active* remedies are under the control of a development project. Developing a protocol bridge illustrates an active remedy. *Passive* remedies depend on market events. Waiting for a new release of a component illustrates a passive remedy. A remedy is a special case of contingency where the feasibility of an ensemble depends on the feasibility of the remedy. In contrast, the feasibility of an ensemble does not depend on the feasibility of a contingency.

Formalization.   The *remedy* relation $s(D_e, e_x)$, for an ensemble e with a set of deficiencies D and remedy e_x, describes remedies. Like the alternatives relation, it is composed from two primitive relations, $s(D_e, e_x) = r(D_e, e_x) \vee w(D_e, e_x)$. The relation $r(D_e, e_x)$ asserts that e_x is an active remedy for the deficiencies D of ensemble e. The relation $w(D_e, e_x)$ is a passive remedy.

The feasibility of e depends on the feasibility of e_x. This relation is useful because an ensemble e can be *conditionally feasible* even if it exhibits deficiencies that would otherwise render it infeasible, that is, $f(e) = false$, provided that each deficiency has *at least* one repair for that deficiency. Or, more formally, $\forall (d \in D) \exists (e_x \in E) \bullet (r(d_e, e_x) \vee w(d_e, e_x))$. Building from the truth table shown in Table 7-3, we can express this dependency in logical terms as a refinement of the feasibility predicate:

feasibility of ensemble e is $f(e) \vee (f(e \cdot s(D_e, e_x)) \wedge f(e_x))$

where $f(e_x)$ is the feasibility of the remedy, and $f(e \cdot s(D_e, e_x))$ is the feasibility of ensemble e *after* the remedy $s(D_e, e_x)$ has been applied. This last term is crucial since the feasibility of an ensemble might depend on an arbitrary number of remedies. For example, assume e has two deficiencies, one of which will be remedied by e_x and the other by e_y. In this situation, $f(e) = false$—it cannot be feasible because it needs two remedies. Now, assume that we know that $f(e_x) = true$, that is, this repair is feasible. Even so, this is not sufficient to establish that e is feasible; we must wait until it has also been established that $f(e_y) = true$. Until then, we must consider $f(e, s(D_e, e_x)) = unknown$. The remedy is feasible, but its application to the ensemble is not definitive. Considering repair e_x only, the contingent feasibility of e is therefore:

$f(e) \vee (f(e \cdot s(D_e, e_x)) \wedge f(e_x)) = false \vee (unknown \wedge true) = unknown$

Contingent feasibility is a powerful concept that allows us to reason precisely about complex dependencies among ensembles and remedies.[4] Using simple

---

[3] We use the term remedy and repair synonymously throughout the book.

[4] The authors are indebted to Santiago Comella-Dorda for clarifying these ideas.

rewrite techniques, it is possible to assess the feasibility of an ensemble that may have multiple levels of remedy. It is also possible, and in many cases highly desirable, to define several remedies for each deficiency. This situation can also be modeled using the refined feasibility predicate.

Representation.   The remedies relation is modeled as part of the Contingency blackboard, since remedies and alternatives are complementary relations. Figure 7-3 extends the previous illustration by introducing two deficiencies on the primary ensemble. Deficiencies are expressed as annotations; they describe the particular ways an ensemble fails to satisfy its feasibility criteria. Two remedies are prescribed, an active remedy for one deficiency and a passive remedy for the other. If either repair proves infeasible, then the applet ensemble is infeasible. However, in this example, even if both remedies are feasible the applet ensemble is only conditionally feasible. Deficiencies only catalog the known limitations of an ensemble. There may be other feasibility criteria that remain untested and hence other deficiencies that may be discovered.

Note that our modeling conventions are not uniform for active and passive remedies. This is because active remedies almost always take the form of an ensemble refinement (when they do not take the form of a relaxation of feasibility criteria). On the other hand, market events tend to be more varied. It would be artificial to model an anticipated bug fix from a vendor as an ensemble refinement. In some cases, the anticipated market event can be quite vague; for example, confirmations of a rumor that a vendor is introducing a new product line. For these reasons, it is simpler to model passive remedies as annotations.

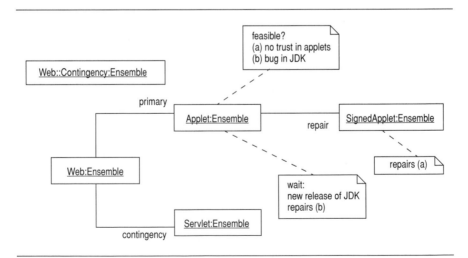

Figure 7-3   Active and passive remedies.

COMPONENT BINDINGS

Intuition. Our proposed design representation would be seriously deficient if it didn't answer the question, "what components does this ensemble comprise?" This simple question has more nuance than might be expected. For example, the *real* question might be about products rather than components. This question might be asked by someone negotiating license agreements. So, we need to distinguish bindings of components to products from bindings of products to technologies.

A different nuance arises where a technology has not been bound to a product because an ensemble is intended to work with all products in a technology. This might arise where a technology has industry standard interfaces. An analogous situation arises where a product has not been bound to a component because the ensemble is intended to work with all versions of the product; that is, with all components in the product line. Conversely, the absence of bindings could reflect binding decisions that have yet to be made. So, we also need a way to distinguish an overt binding decision from a nondecision.

Sometimes it is also useful to qualify a binding decision. For example, rather than explicitly binding a component to a product, we might define a rule for binding components, such as "more recent than release v3.5." An analogous qualification might apply to the binding of products to technologies; for example, "only products that support X.509v3." A qualified binding is therefore a special case of an overt binding.

Formalization. The bind relation $b(x, V) \equiv b(t, P_t) \vee b(p, C_p)$, where $t \in T$, $p \in P$, $P_t \subseteq P$, $C_p \subseteq C$, and $V \subseteq (P_t \cup C_p)$ expresses which products are bound to which technologies, and which components are bound to which products. The bind relation has already been defined as the aggregation associations between these classifiers in the ensemble metamodel (see Figure 5-4).

The *binding predicate* $\forall(x \in T \cup P) \bullet b(x)$ is defined for each technology and product in an ensemble, where $b(x)$ = *true* if no *additional* bindings are permitted on a product or technology, and *false* otherwise. The predicate has different interpretations, depending on whether x has been bound to any products (if x is a technology) or components (if x is a product). Table 7-3 gives the interpretation of the binding predicate under different circumstances.

Table 7-3 The Binding Predicate

	$b(x)$ = *true*	$b(x)$ = *false*
$V = \varnothing$	An ensemble is feasible for all possible bindings.	No binding decisions have been made.
$V \neq \varnothing$	An ensemble is feasible only for $b(x, V)$.	An ensemble is feasible for $b(x, V)$, but more, untested, bindings are possible.

The *qualified binding predicate* $\forall (x \in T \cup P) \bullet b(x(r))$ associates a binding rule *r* with technologies and products. This predicate is interpreted as applying the binding rule as a predicate of the elements of an unbounded set of products (when $x \in T$) and components (when $x \in P$). If the predicate is true, then the element is bound to *x*. A qualified binding predicate can be defined in conjunction with the bind relation, but must not result in a contradiction.

Representation.   The set of binding relations associated with an ensemble are modeled in a blackboard of the ensemble called *Manifest*. Figure 7-4 extends the Web illustration to illustrate these ideas. The manifest contains technologies, products, and components that appear in *any* blackboard for that ensemble. The manifest blackboard does not model interactions, however; it only models bindings.

The binding predicate is expressed as a UML annotation. The bind relation is expressed as associations from technology to product, and from product to component.[5] In the illustration, the Web ensemble has two technologies, WebBrowser and HTTPServer. WebBrowser has been bound to two products, Microsoft's Explorer, and Netscape's Navigator. The binding predicate for WebBrowser has the value *unbound*, meaning that more bindings are possible, but it is not certain that the Web ensemble will be feasible with Explorer components. Explorer is not bound to any components, but its binding predicate is *bound*.

This states that the ensemble is feasible with all versions of Explorer (or, more accurately, no version of Explorer will render the ensemble *infeasible*). Navigator has a qualified binding that asserts that the ensemble is feasible with all Navigator components more recent than version 4.7. HTTPServer has been bound to a particular product, but its binding predicate is *bound*. In this case, the

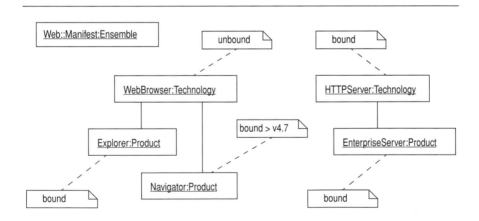

Figure 7-4   Web ensemble bindings.

[5] These are instantiations of the aggregation associations defined in the ensemble metamodel.

ensemble is declared to be feasible *only* with respect to Enterprise Server, and to be feasible with respect to all versions of Enterprise Server.

VIEW

Intuition. Several blackboards are necessary to describe nontrivial ensembles adequately. Each such blackboard describes a subset of an ensemble's components and interactions. It is a good idea to give the view a distinguished name so that it can be referred to in the contingency diagram. Sometimes, it is useful to describe an ensemble completely in one blackboard. In this case, the name of the view is the name of the ensemble itself. We often refer to this as the *grand unified blackboard*.

Formalization. The view relation $v(e, e_x)$ where $T_x \cup P_x \cup U_x \subseteq T \cup P \cup U$, expresses the relation between ensembles e and the views e_x that define them. Note that a more complete formalization of $v(e, e_x)$ would include interactions as well as components. However, the given formulation is sufficient to express the main ideas of a view.

Representation. Each view is represented in a blackboard of an ensemble whose name denotes the subset of components and interactions modeled in that view. Figure 7-5 illustrates the I&A view of the Web ensemble.[6] It describes only those interactions of the Web ensemble that are required to understand identification and authentication. If a grand, unified view is created for an ensemble, that

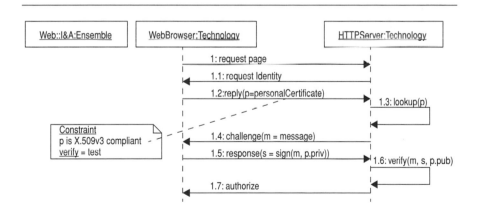

Figure 7-5   Web ensemble I&A blackboard.

[6] It is always acceptable to express a blackboard as a UML sequence diagram, since interaction diagrams and sequence diagrams are semantically equivalent.

is, a blackboard that includes all components and their interactions, its name should be that of the ensemble it describes.

AGGREGATION

Intuition.   Each view describes a set of interactions, with *credentials* and *constraints* describing aspects of components and interactions, respectively. An aggregate view of the constraints and credentials is as important to the designer as is the manifest of components. The aggregate view can be used to gauge the impact of introducing new components. In particular, new components must possess specific credentials to satisfy specific constraints.

Formalization.   The aggregation relation $g(e_m, E_x)$, where e_m is the manifest for e, E_x is the set of views on e, and $T_m \cup P_m \cup C_m = T_x \cup P_x \cup C_x$. We assume that credentials are aggregated along with technologies, products, and so forth.

Representation.   Aggregated credentials are represented as component annotations in the manifest blackboard. Since the manifest does not model component interactions, constraints are implicit in the credentials. Figure 7-6 illustrates view aggregation. Credentials introduced in the Web::I&A ensemble are transplanted into its manifest.[7] The credential is extended to include a reference to the blackboards whose interactions depend on the credentials.

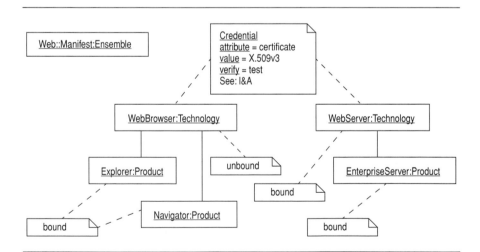

Figure 7-6   Blackboard aggregation.

---

[7] Only the constraint was illustrated in Figure 7-5.

Each ensemble refinement has its own manifest. It is a matter of convention whether a refinement manifest includes only those technologies, products, components, and interactions introduced by that refinement, or whether it includes all technologies, products, and so forth found in the refinement. If information is distributed across manifests, then credentials inserted into an ancestor manifest are extended to include a reference to the refinement and its blackboard whose interactions depend on the credentials. In the case study, we treat each refinement as a self-contained specification, and so include all technologies, and so forth in each refinement manifest. This makes it convenient to locate information pertinent to an ensemble, but also adds considerable complexity to the problem of maintaining consistency among blackboards.

7.4 Component & Ensemble Composition

Existing methodologies tend to emphasize custom specification and implementation of components, but component composition is what component-based development is really all about. Each blackboard contains information about the component interactions that, in effect, define what it means for components to be composed. The bulk of this book elaborates the processes and techniques to make component composition rational and repeatable, so we will not belabor matters with a discussion of component composition. But *ensemble* composition is another matter entirely!

In principle, ensemble composition should be indistinguishable from component composition. After all, commercial components may well be ensembles themselves, implemented by components that are invisible to us. From the vendor's point of view, our component is their ensemble. So why shouldn't we treat ensembles as if they were components? If anything, their composition should be easier, since many of the details of ensemble implementation are available to us.

One possible objection is that an ensemble does not satisfy our definition of component. However, recall that a component is, at root, an implementation with an interface. A composition of components, each of which is an implementation, will itself be an implementation. But what about the ensemble interface? This can be provided using the idea of gateway interfaces defined by Herzum and Sims [Herzum+ 00]. That is, for each ensemble that we wish to compose, we develop a custom gateway component. This gateway defines an interface for which the ensemble is the service provider, and which other components (or ensembles) use to obtain services. The gateway component simply routes service requests to the appropriate ensemble component.

While this idea might work for functional (for example, business) components, things are not nearly so simple for infrastructure components. To illustrate, we introduce the public key infrastructure (PKI) I&A ensemble, shown along with the Web I&A ensemble in Figure 7-7. The Web I&A ensemble has an

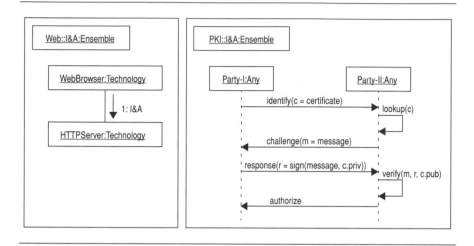

Figure 7-7   Two primitive composable ensembles.

atomic interaction between browser and server to perform I&A. The details are left unspecified because the interaction can be implemented using different technologies. The PKI I&A ensemble shows how I&A is performed using digital certificates. Now it should be apparent that the Web I&A ensemble illustrated in Figure 7-5 was an implicit composition of Web and PKI technologies.

Instead of beginning with the implicitly integrated ensemble in Figure 7-5, what if we began with the more primitive ensembles depicted in Figure 7-7? What would we need to know to compose Web::I&A and PKI::I&A, and what form would the composition take, that is, how would it be specified?

First, it is clear that no simple gateway interface to the PKI I&A ensemble will suffice. This might be sufficient for a password-based I&A mechanism, but as you can see, a PKI-based mechanism requires a more elaborate two-way interaction between parties. Instead, we need to recognize that WebBrowser can play the role of Party-I, and HTTPServer the role of Party-II. (Or is it that Party-I can play the role of WebBrowser, and Party-II that of HTTPServer?) We must be sure that it is acceptable to replace the unidirectional interaction in the Web I&A ensemble with the bilateral PKI interaction. We must also specify a mapping between ensembles.

It is certainly possible to answer these questions—and in fact we do that *to some extent* in Chapter 8. However, it should be clear that ensemble composition introduces challenges quite distinct from those of "simple" component composition. In fact, the subject is a matter of research (see [Allen+ 97] for example). While progress is being made in compositional reasoning, more work is needed.

7.5   Repository Structure

We have, so far, focused on blackboards, and the naming conventions for the ensembles and meta-ensembles they specify. It is equally important to define conventions for organizing blackboards in a design repository. Different schemes are possible, and much already has been implied in the previous discussion. Figure 7-8, which continues from the previous illustrations, shows one possible repository structure. As noted earlier, ensembles are modeled as packages, and their refinements as sub-packages. The manifest, contingencies, and views are blackboards contained within an ensemble package.

At this point, we should mention the dark side of UML, at least as it's applied here. We are using collaboration diagrams, primarily, to model ensembles. For this reason we must model technologies, products, and components as UML *objects*, because only objects have behavior and can therefore take part in collaborations. In our method, however, technologies, products, and components have both the behavioral aspects of objects, and the specification aspects of classes. If we modeled technologies and so forth as UML classes, we could take advantage of tool-provided consistency management. This is convenient when a specification (such as a class) is found in many diagrams. However, we would

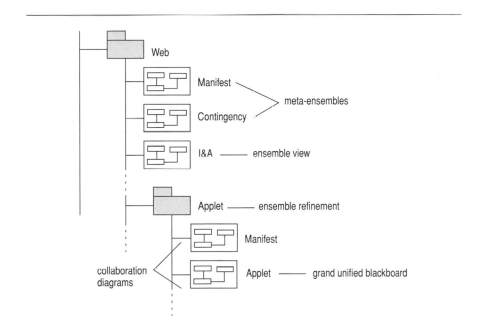

Figure 7-8   Blackboard repository structure.

lose the ability to describe collaborations, which is central to the idea of ensemble. Modeling technologies and so forth as UML objects allows us to specify collaborations. At the same time, it introduces issues of consistent naming conventions and consistency management.

We have decided to model blackboards as collaborations, and technologies and so forth as UML objects. The ensemble manifest is our compromise with UML. The manifest is the repository of definitions about components, credentials, and constraints. Developers must keep the manifest current with the design.

7.6   Summary

One of the major challenges of component-based development is keeping track of many low-level details. For example, feasibility of a design might depend on several repairs, each of which involves detailed implementation. Design contingencies arise as a natural response to uncertainty. When contingencies are combined with repairs, the effect is often analogous to juggling one too many balls. Part of the difficulty is that software engineers did not make these kinds of dependencies explicit. In this chapter, we introduced UML conventions to make these dependencies explicit.

It is fair to ask whether the conventions we describe also satisfy the criteria of being *lightweight* and *modular*. Modularity is inherent in the use of blackboards to model ensemble views. New views can be added and old ones removed without disturbing other views. Whether the notation is lightweight is a matter of perspective. It is not as lightweight as not documenting ensemble dependencies. On the other hand, if we assume that it is valid and useful to make ensemble dependencies explicit, then our suggested notation does so without much extra baggage. The case study provides an extensive illustration of the notation, and we let the notation speak for itself.

7.7   Discussion Questions

1.   Extend the ensemble metamodel to incorporate the relations and predicates discussed in this chapter. What distinguishes these extensions?

2.   Can the revised ensemble feasibility predicate (including the remedy relation) be a basis for automated composition of ensembles?

3.   Assuming your project has contingencies and remedies, how would you answer the question "what is the current design of your system?"

8

Storing Competence

All experience is an arch to build upon.
—Henry Brooks Adams (1838–1918)
from *The Education of Henry Adams*

Ensemble blackboards serve multiple purposes. First, as the case study demonstrates, they help to chart a design effort, and to demarcate what is known from what is still to be discovered. Second, as with any design documentation, they support system maintenance. For example, blackboards capture assumptions about component features, and how these features are used for component integration. But there is a third purpose as well. Blackboards represent stored competence. However, the value of this stored competence is only realized if it can be used to minimize R^3 cycles. That is, there is less need for contingencies and competence-generating R^3 workflows if there is sufficient on-hand component expertise, or if this expertise can be produced quickly using documented prior experience.

While it is possible to reuse the blackboards produced by previous projects *as is*, this may not be cost effective. Experience richly demonstrates that extra effort is required to make any software artifact, whether it is code or documentation, reusable. So, developers must invest effort at the expense of a current project for a potential return on a future project. Incentives can ensure that this additional effort is undertaken. However, this will not ensure that the *right kind* of effort is undertaken.

8.1 Fundamental Ideas

To store competence effectively, we must be guided by principles that distinguish the one from the many—what is particular to one project from what is applicable to a variety of projects. The process of making these distinctions is called *ensemble deconstruction.*[1] Two forms of deconstruction are required to make the blackboard

---

[1] Decontextualization may be more accurate, but is too ugly to be tolerated.

by-products of R^3 reusable. *Design* deconstruction extracts ensembles from application-specific designs, and then situates them in a reference design. *Binding* deconstruction horizontally slices ensembles into blackboards exclusively comprising technologies, or products, or components.

ENSEMBLE DECONSTRUCTION

Design Deconstruction.   The repository structure illustrated in Figure 7-8 does not depict the context of the Web ensemble. This ensemble is just one of several, and possibly dozens, used in a moderately complex system. We could impose an all-encompassing structure for managing all UML artifacts, including blackboards, but this would not be in the spirit of our approach. Specifically, our method can be used to extend existing methods to deal effectively with commercial components. It would be inappropriate to define an ensemble-centric project structure when, in some cases, component integration is just one aspect of a project. Instead, we expect that a project's repository structure will mirror the application architecture, with ensembles located within the systems or subsystems they contribute to implementing.

However, let's assume that projects will not be using a standard, application-specific software architecture. While establishing such a standard is a good idea, we cannot propose one here. Such a standard depends on many organization-specific factors. We can, however, define a logical architecture that provides an innocuous, if not very detailed, scheme to organize ensembles and their blackboards for later reuse. Our approach is quite similar to those of Herzum and Sims [Herzum+ 00], and Cheesman and Daniels [Cheesman+ 00], both of which organize component-based systems according to a layered reference architecture.

Figure 8-1 illustrates one possible reference architecture. Others are possible. The illustration shows how the Web, servlet, and applet ensembles used in Chapter 7 would be situated in this reference architecture. The illustration also suggests that ensembles also may be deconstructed into smaller, separately selectable ensembles. This was done when we extracted the PKI I&A ensemble

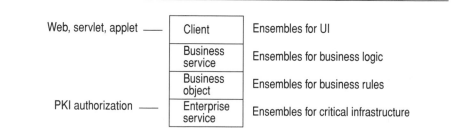

Figure 8-1   Logical reference architecture.

from the Web I&A ensemble. Whether this latter form of deconstruction is war-ranted varies across organizations. For example, the extent to which projects are free to combine ensembles or vary from enterprise standards is a factor that might influence whether this form of deconstruction will be cost effective. We return to the reference architecture later in this chapter.

Binding Deconstruction.   As our full-fledged case study shows, binding deci-sions are not made in lock-step fashion. It is seldom the case that we can select all technologies, then all products, and finally all components. Instead, some binding decisions are made early; others are made, then retracted; and still others are not made until late in the design. As a consequence, blackboards have a mix of tech-nologies, products, and components. Sometimes, this mix reflects conscious decisions not to make a binding, for example, a product with no component bind-ings but a binding predicate = *bound*. Often, it simply reflects the state of the design at the time the blackboard was constructed. Binding deconstruction seeks to normalize blackboards to uniform levels of abstraction. Blackboards compris-ing only technologies (and their interactions) are called *reference ensembles*. Blackboards comprising only products and technologies with qualified bindings are called *supplier ensembles*. And blackboards comprising only components and products with qualified bindings are called *configuration* or *assembly ensembles*.

Information in higher-level ensembles is more abstract, and is therefore more stable than lower-level ensembles. Test this theory against the ensembles in Figure 8-2. A description of how things work at the DB assembly level is going to change more quickly than its analogous description at the reference level. For

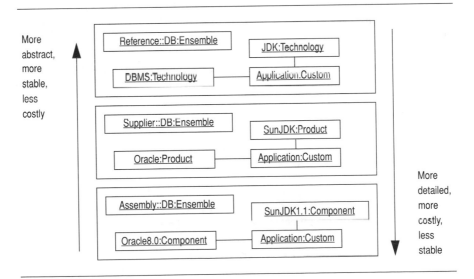

Figure 8-2   Layers of ensemble abstraction.

example, Oracle might release a new implementation of a JDBC driver that has new features. This may change assembly-level interactions, but these changes probably will not have any impact at the supplier or reference levels. Chances are, you can say something about how the ensemble works at the reference level without knowing how it works at the assembly level. Because they are more stable and abstract, reference ensembles are less costly to develop and sustain than assembly ensembles. On the other hand, they provide less value to developers who must understand, in detail, how an ensemble works.

However, not every developer needs to know the inner details of an ensemble. Moreover, such details are not necessarily appropriate at each phase of the development project. By factoring ensembles into different levels of abstraction, we can package them for different classes of consumer.

8.2 Packaging with Ensemble Handbooks

We can extract additional value from blackboards by distinguishing different classes of blackboard consumer. Ensembles and components are alike in that the type of expertise required to implement an ensemble (or component) is not usually the same type that is required to use it. This is especially true where ensembles implement infrastructure services. Application developers need to know which ensemble to use and how to use it, but not necessarily the details of how it works. The process of making blackboard information useful to different classes of consumer is called *ensemble packaging*.

With a modest investment, a repository of ensembles can be packaged as a design handbook that combines multi-criteria decision aids, prose, and blackboards. The subject of software engineering handbooks is bound up with the broader issue of how a true software engineering discipline can be established. For the present, we have limited our attention to a design handbook based in ensembles, and strictly qualify what we mean by design handbook. In brief, a handbook of component ensembles should:

- Help designers select appropriate ensembles.
- Identify ensemble dependencies for the purpose of ensemble composition.
- Be modular, easy to maintain, and current with the component market.

Working with a local industry partner, we developed an experimental handbook, called the Generic Enterprise Ensemble (GEE), to test the feasibility of building an ensemble handbook. The content of the GEE was derived from the case study described later in this book.

Contingency diagrams were mined for design alternatives. Contingencies (both contingent and primary refinements) are hedges against risk, or as speculative but promising lines of investigation. Just because a designer must choose one branch of a contingency tree does not mean that he or she might not have chosen otherwise. In other circumstances—in a project more or less averse to risk—alternatives that were cast aside might have been preferred. Therefore, what was learned about discarded design alternatives can be put to good use in later projects. This approach also improves the cost effectiveness of the method we describe in this book, which is an essential way to approach component-based development whether competence is captured and stored or not.

While a contingency indicates a design alternative, it might not be clear what design problem was being addressed. Moreover, it might not be clear what criteria were used to select an alternative, whether these criteria were purely situational (applications requirements), or intrinsic to the ensembles (lack of feasibility in the most extreme case), or both. If the blackboards were developed with reuse in mind, then some of these details may have been deposited for later mining. Otherwise, context clues and project retrospectives (always a good idea) may be all that is available.

In any event, for there to be design alternatives, there must be a design question with multiple possible answers. In the GEE, these questions were denoted as flex points, and their answers as design options.[2] To develop the GEE, the first step was to deduce (or remember) what this question was, and to give it a name. The name given to the flex point was abstracted from contingencies. Each named flex point was then situated in the reference architecture depicted in Figure 8-1. A fragment of the GEE that corresponds to the illustrations from Chapter 7 is depicted in Figure 8-3. In this fragment, the decision to use a servlet, applet, or Java application is expressed as a decision about how content is delivered to the client program. Thus, although an HTTP server might be deployed on a business

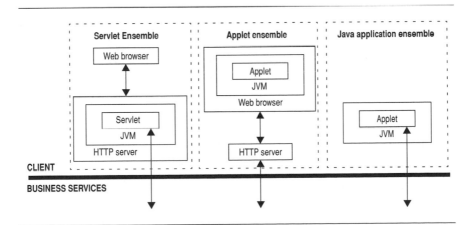

Figure 8-3   Content delivery flex point.

---

[2] We originally used the term *flexion* to denote fillers of flex points. This term was more consistent but usually evoked a quizzical expression.

server machine, the logical role it plays is presentation and dialog management. However, what the flex points are called, and how they are situated in a generic design, is less important than the use of consistent conventions.

Note that we have abandoned UML and blackboards to depict the flex point. While packaged design competence might be useful to a variety of decision makers, not all of them are versed in UML. Besides, notations that are more compact and intuitive than UML are possible, and might help consumers obtain the gestalt of a flex point. UML was not designed to support quick, high-level comparisons of design alternatives. Whether our notational conventions served this end is open to debate. It is safe to say, however, that UML will not be the final word on design notation. What matters at this level of abstraction is clarity and consistency.

In the GEE, each flex point was limited to a one-page summary which contained a graphical depiction of the design options (Figure 8-3), a description of their strengths and weaknesses, and the circumstances under which each alternative would be appropriate. We also included a multi-criteria table of comparisons in the one-page write-up. It reflected the design decision underlying the flex point rather than generic criteria. For example, criteria for the content delivery flex point included security, performance, ease of administration, flexibility, and robustness. Figure 8-4 shows the layout of the Client Locale design option.

Each design option in a flex point was indexed to a reference blackboard and accompanying documentation, where more detail about the ensemble would be provided. The reference ensemble acted as a container for one or more implementation ensembles. At the time the GEE was constructed, we had not yet distinguished assemblies from supplier ensembles. We also did not fully apprehend binding relations and the binding predicate. As a result, implementation ensembles in the GEE contained a mix of technologies, products, and components.

Figure 8-5 depicts the overall structure of the GEE Handbook. The key idea was to present the most stable design information "higher-up" in the handbook structure, with less stable information directed toward the leaves. We did this by using reference ensembles for each design option, and used these to classify one or more implementation ensembles. The result is modular and supports our maintainability objectives. The result also has the "feel" of an engineering design handbook, as (admittedly) vague as that sounds.

However, we have only discussed how the handbook is structured to support ensemble selection and handbook maintenance. The complement of selection is composition, and it, too, must be addressed. In fact, ensemble selection and composition are linked. Unless a system can be constructed from just one ensemble, a prospect that is hardly conceivable, several ensembles must be selected. If several are selected, then it is likely that some of them must be combined. We already have (briefly) alluded to some thorny theoretical issues of ensemble composition in Chapter 7. Our approach to ensemble composition in the GEE is pragmatic but not wholly satisfactory—each one-page write-up includes a "see also" reference.

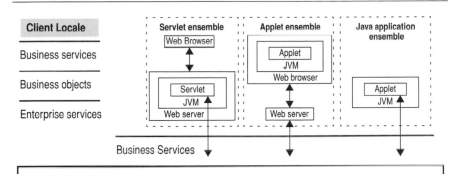

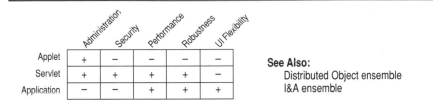

Figure 8-4   Illustration of GEE flex point.

8.3   Automation

We also experimented with a more ambitious approach to ensemble selection and composition via the GEE roadmap. The roadmap is a decision tree for selecting a consistent set of ensembles. What made the attempt ambitious was the GEE configurer, a tool to support the roadmap in the style of a *wizard*.[3] The motivation of the wizard was to deliver to application developers a "starter kit" of components, sample programs, test data, and documentation that was tailored to a selection of

---

[3] This also allowed us to refer to the tool as "GEE-Wiz."

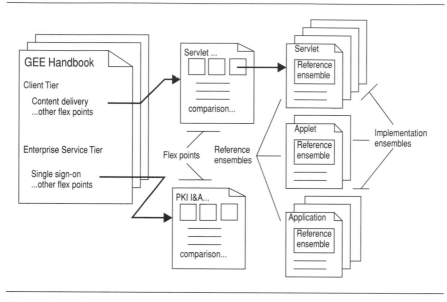

Figure 8-5   Structure of an ensemble handbook.

ensembles. To do this, we bundled each ensemble with an implementation of a simple, canonical use case. The GEE wizard would construct a deployable configuration of components and documentation as the user made ensemble selections. Upon completion, the GEE wizard would deploy the results to a designated location.

The GEE configurer was only marginally successful. While it was certainly feasible to deploy a starter kit for a set of selected ensembles, the real need was for a tool to compose ensembles in the manner discussed in Chapter 7 with respect to the Web I&A and PKI I&A ensembles. This is a promising avenue for research.

8.4   Summary

Blackboards are the products of competence-generating processes such as R[3]. These blackboards are valuable assets that can be mined using techniques such as design and binding deconstruction. Mining is just the first step, however. To obtain maximum value from these assets, they should be packaged in a way that makes them informative as well as easy to use and maintain. We briefly described our experiences developing such a handbook, and described one possible structure for a handbook of component ensembles.

8.5 Discussion Questions

1. Project idea: construct an ensemble handbook from the case study.

2. Is it feasible to develop an industry standard handbook of ensembles? If so, what would it contain, and how would it be organized? If not, why not?

9

The Multi-Attribute
Utility Technique

*The affairs of life embrace a multitude of interests, and he who reasons in
any one of them, without consulting the rest, is a visionary unsuited to
control the business of the world.*
—James Fenimore Cooper

Organizations that want to use commercial software components often focus on
component evaluation first. This certainly makes sense—what good are commercial components if you consistently choose the *wrong* ones? Yet, as we illustrate
in the case study, component selection is just one kind of design decision that
must be made that concerns the use of components. Moreover, component selection cannot be separated cleanly from these design decisions.

Nevertheless, the most popular technical processes used to select components involve multi-criteria evaluation. One form in particular is perceived as a
"best practice" in software engineering—the *multi-attribute utility technique*
(MAUT). MAUT provides a rich and well-established framework for making
component selection decisions. Although we assert that you should *never* make
component selection decisions based on MAUT analysis alone, there are two reasons why the technique is nonetheless of fundamental importance to component-
based development. First, the theoretical model underlying MAUT is an important foundation for design processes dominated by selection rather than optimization. Second, it is a form of decision analysis that you probably have already
used, or will surely encounter in practice. For these reasons, it pays to have a
solid grounding in the theory and practice of MAUT.

9.1   Fundamental Ideas

Most of us are unaware of the processes involved in making day-to-day decisions. For truly important decisions, however, we often employ some form of decision making technique. We might, for example, develop a list of pros and cons for accepting a new job, or make a list of the features of our ideal house.

Formally, such techniques are referred to as *decision aids*. A decision aid can be a simple device to help you remember the attributes of various options. For example, rather than specifying the features of an ideal house, we might keep track of the features of each house we visit. Some decision aids also include a *decision procedure*. For example, the late President Richard Nixon was known to draw up lists of pros and cons for important decisions, and to decide based on which list was longer. In this case, a crude but simple decision procedure might be to select the alternative with the longest list.

Decision procedures are based on some underlying theory of what contributes to good decisions. Obviously, some theories are better than others. The ancient Greeks used sheep as decision aids, and auspices as their decision procedure, on the theory that this approach provided insight into the will of the gods. Most of us would consider Nixon's technique to be more palatable than fried sheep parts, but this is perhaps unfair bias. Both decision aids, however, served the same purpose: to help the decision maker obtain *insight* into the decision at hand. This is a crucial point. The decision aid does not produce decisions—it offers assistance to the decision maker.

Within the past forty years or so, tremendous strides have been made in elaborating a coherent theory of decision making. Early pioneering work by Herbert Simon provided a rational basis for making strategic business decisions where the outcome depended on multiple, often competing, factors. The general term used to denote the overall theory was multi-objective, or *multi-criteria,* decision making. Although it originated in business theory, multi-criteria decision making was later applied to the making of public policy and a variety of other applications—including component evaluation.

The premise of multi-criteria decision making is deceptively simple. It involves selecting between alternative courses of action, where the *merit* of each can be expressed as a (possibly large) number of discrete factors, or criteria, each of which contributes to the outcome. Each criterion can then be analyzed separately in terms that are pertinent to that particular criterion; for example, cost, safety, fairness, and usability. A decision procedure *aggregates* these separate analyses into a measure of merit for each alternative course of action. The decision maker then selects the alternative that has the best overall merit. Decomposing a decision into multiple criteria provides insight into the factors that contribute to a good decision, while the decision procedure helps manage diverse and highly technical data.

An enormous body of theory and literature has flowed from this theory of decision making. Of the many multi-criteria decision techniques developed, MAUT is by far the most popular. We should be careful to note that MAUT is not a single technique, but rather an approach to producing mathematical models of decisions. Its premise is that each criterion can be modeled in terms of its contribution to the utility of an outcome. For example, the techniques developed by Edwards and Newman [Edwards+ 82], [Kontio 95], and [Saaty 90] are all distinct techniques, yet each firmly adheres to the utilitarian philosophy underlying MAUT.

There are three useful ways of thinking about MAUT: as a mathematical modeling tool, as a technique for systematically decomposing decision factors, and as a process. We examine each in turn.

A MATHEMATICAL VIEW OF MAUT

All decisions ultimately involve selecting one course of action from a set of possible alternatives. We might be, for example, choosing one car from a set of cars. The mathematical view of this decision in MAUT is succinctly (if too simply) expressed in Eq. 9-1, *the basic MAUT Equation*, where U_Y is the overall or *aggregate utility* of some alternative Y; for example, the red Corvette Stingray at Conway's used car dealership. Utility is a measure of goodness, or fitness for use, and a higher value of U_Y indicates a better alternative. U_Y is an *aggregate* measure of utility because it comprises the utility of a (possible large) number of distinct *attributes*. The term $w_i a_i$ is how we model these attributes, where a_i represents a measure of utility for some particular attribute i of alternative Y (say, fuel efficiency), and w_i represents the weight, or priority, of this attribute relative to all of the other attributes (say, not very important).

$$U_Y = \sum_i w_i a_i$$

Eq. 9-1

The basic MAUT equation is really a template for a variety of mathematical formulae, and various MAUT techniques interpret these symbols differently. For example, they differ in whether they use weights, and, if so, what their scale is and how they are computed. MAUT techniques also differ in how they express the utility of attributes and in the form of aggregation used—it is not always a simple sum, as might be inferred from Eq. 4-1. At least two attempts have been made to develop a framework of MAUT techniques that allow separable selection of these and other variations [Morisio+ 97][Roy 91].

Decision theorists and specialists argue the nuances of their particular approaches to the basic MAUT equation, and fisticuffs have been known to break out over the merits of ratio scale versus interval scale for weights. For the practical software engineer, however, these distinctions are quite beside the point. What does it really mean for attribute a_i to have an importance (weight) of .023 while attribute a_{i+1} has an importance of .120? Can the precision of weights to the thousandths have any real meaning when we consider that a major challenge is even figuring out what a system's requirements are in the first place? Also, weights represent *tradeoffs*—in MAUT terminology *substitution rates*—for utility values. Thus, the above hypothetical weights suggest that we are willing to trade (or substitute) .023/.120 units of a_i utility per 1 unit of a_{i+1} utility. Does any practicing software engineer believe that design or implementation tradeoffs can be made with this level of precision?

We aren't suggesting that weights are meaningless. Weights can be used to understand differences in the perspectives of various stakeholders, and especially to identify conflicting priorities. Weights can also help us to prioritize attributes. The crucial point to keep in mind is that the mathematical accoutrements of MAUT serve only one purpose: to help the decision maker express judgments about the decision at hand—and judgment is not a matter of precision. The moment you start haggling over several hundredths of a unit of weight, or, worse still, interpret the aggregated utility U_Y as an inherent truth, then you have been seduced by the false precision of MAUT.

On the other hand, we can employ the mathematics of MAUT to perform quantitative analysis in support of subjective decision making. Of particular importance is sensitivity analysis, which is used to validate the stability of a decision model with respect to its assumptions (that is, criteria weights and measures). For example, the decision maker may consider whether a slight change in the weight of one attribute would result in a different ranking of alternatives. Sensitivity analysis allows a decision maker to explore a variety of these "what if" scenarios, and to obtain deeper insight into the decision factors than could ever be obtained by using the basic MAUT equation only to generate numbers. Commercial decision support packages often provide a quite sophisticated battery of tools for performing sensitivity analysis and for visualizing the results of this analysis. Besides being useful in their own right, these tools are often fun to use.

A HIERARCHICAL MODEL VIEW OF MAUT

The mathematical theory underlying any particular MAUT technique is probably of more interest to the technique's designer than to decision makers. Instead, decision makers are more likely to see MAUT as an exercise in decomposing a decision into its constituent parts, ultimately producing a hierarchical *preference structure*, the principal artifact of MAUT.

Figure 9-1 illustrates a preference structure. A top-level decision is decomposed into three objectives (or criteria), one of which is further decomposed. Concretely, our decision might be to select the best family car, and our top-level objectives might be to select the best car with respect to fuel *efficiency*, *safety*, and *style*. Perhaps "safety" is a bit too vague for us, so we further decompose this into three different safety objectives: *front* impact, *side* impact, and *rear* impact safety. We might decompose side impact into *front-seat* versus *rear-seat* safety.

The KAI Compiler

A system integrator recently performed a thorough evaluation of C++ compilers for the Sun Solaris platform. The evaluation method was not an application of MAUT but followed a well-defined series of steps including:

1. Establish/refine selection criteria
2. Quick-look paper analysis of candidates
3. Gather test programs
4. Acquire evaluation products
5. Perform tests and gather test data
6. Document results

The stated criteria included C++ ANSI standard compliance, Standard Template Library (STL) support, Oracle 8 support, configuration management tool compatibility, incremental compilation, and vendor support. Candidate products included the Sun SPARCompiler C++, Rational Apex IDE, and the Kuck & Associates, Inc. (KAI) compiler. The evaluation showed that these three products were evenly matched on most criteria with the greatest deviation in support for the C++ ANSI standard. This criterion was considered important because the project had selected C++ as a development language and the ANSI standard provides the definition of the language.

At the conclusion of the evaluation, the KAI compiler was selected as the C++ compiler for the Sun Solaris platform as it came closest to implementing the C++ ANSI standard. Unfortunately, the C++ ANSI standard does not standardize the representation of symbols in object files and shared libraries. As a result, it is not possible to link object files and libraries compiled with the SPARCompiler, the predominant C++ compiler on the Sun Solaris platform, using the KAI compiler without first demangling the names. This problem was both detrimental to the project's ability to integrate new components and pervasive, as it affected nearly every component that had to be integrated—reoccurring with every release of each component.

What makes compliance to the ANSI C++ a poor criterion in this case is that no real advantage is gained by selecting a compiler that closely supports the C++ standard. In theory, the selection of a compiler that most closely implemented the standard would allow for greater portability and minimize the risk of vendor lock. In practice, if no other compiler implemented this standard in the same way, conformance to the standard was irrelevant!

The wrong product was selected in this case for several reasons. First, the initial criterion was ill-considered and poorly weighted. If someone had asked what the risk was of not using an ANSI C++ compliant compiler, this evaluation criterion may have been eliminated (see Risk/Misfit in Chapter 10). Likewise, if the C++ compilers under evaluation had been evaluated in conjunction with other components under evaluation in a component ensemble, the difficulties imposed by C++ name mangling would have been readily apparent (see Ensembles and Blackboards in Chapter 5).

—RCS

Note that safety and fuel efficiency are likely to be competing objectives: heavier cars are probably safer but less fuel efficient. We are, therefore, unlikely to find cars that optimize both of these criteria. Because of this tradeoff, it would be useful if we could determine which of these objectives is more important. Toward this end we have numerically prioritized each objective in the hierarchy. Each priority reflects the importance of a particular objective. Note that as illustrated, the priorities for all siblings at any point in the hierarchy sum to 1. This is not implied by the basic MAUT equation, but it is often convenient. The decision aid depicted in Figure 9-1 is called a *preference structure* because it reflects the decision maker's (or other stakeholders') preferences.

The preference structure is a powerful tool for obtaining insight into a decision. It allows decision makers to decompose a decision until its fundamental, nondecomposable qualities are exposed. This decomposition also helps decision makers understand their preferences, since they can usually assign priorities to sibling criteria in a preference structure. For example, referring again to Figure 9-1, the decision maker might assert that safety is twice as important as style and efficiency. On the other hand, it is unlikely that a decision maker could deduce the effective priority of the criterion "rear seat impact safety." It is not .50 as you might guess from the illustration, but rather .0825. This magic number is obtained by multiplying the priority of rear seat impact safety with the priorities of its ancestors. We refer to this as the *effective* priority of this criterion because it is this that is used in the basic MAUT equation. We think the relative, sibling-level priorities convey more insight than the effective priorities. It also allows decision makers the option of sub-aggregation—that is, comparing alternatives with respect to subsets of criteria.

While the priority structure provides insight into a decision, it is nearly worthless as input to a decision procedure without well-defined *utility functions*. Formally, a utility function converts measures of effectiveness into units of utility. A utility function defines the map from criterion-specific units of measurement

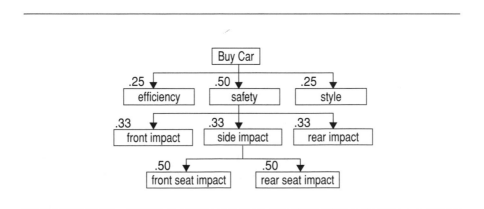

Figure 9-1   Preference structure.

(the domain) to units of utility (the range). Informally, *each leaf* of the priority structure identifies something that must be measured. Since each criterion (each leaf) may measure something different about an alternative, different utility functions are needed. For example, efficiency may be measured in interval units of *miles per gallon*. Style might be measured in ordinal units of *sedan* or *coupe*. These measures must be converted to abstract units of utility—U_Y in the basic MAUT equation.

Let's take efficiency as a concrete example. For this particular criterion, we must find an appropriate unit of measure—for example, miles per gallon (mpg) for city and highway driving, averaged. We can define arbitrarily complex utility functions. However, simple functions usually suffice and are easier to understand. In this example, we define a simple linear function. It asserts that a car that gets 15 mpg or less has no utility, while any car that gets more than 30 mpg is of highest utility. We have arbitrarily[1] defined an interval scale for utility from 0 to 100, with 0 for minimum utility and 100 for maximum utility. We might have chosen another scale, for example 1 to 10. The scale used is less important than the fact that all criteria must be mapped to the same scale. We must also state that utility values have a *floor* of 0 and a *ceiling* of 100. Without this stipulation, the ideas of priority and utility would become hopelessly blurred.

Figure 9-2 depicts the resulting utility function $u_{eff}(x)$, for converting x miles-per-gallon fuel efficiency to a utility value. The graph to the left might be convenient for picking off utility values for various miles-per-gallon efficiencies. However, the equation to the right is easier to use in the long run and is not too difficult to derive (this is one advantage of defining simple utility functions). Once we have this utility function, we can consistently compare the utility of alternative cars with respect to efficiency. Without it, our decision procedure has an air of arbitrariness, even randomness.

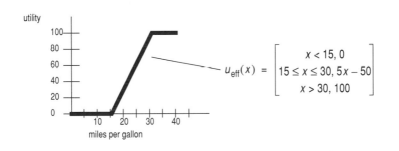

$$u_{eff}(x) = \begin{bmatrix} x < 15, 0 \\ 15 \leq x \leq 30, 5x - 50 \\ x > 30, 100 \end{bmatrix}$$

Figure 9-2   A simple linear utility function.

[1] The selection of a utility scale is not quite as arbitrary as we suggest. However, a discussion of these subtleties belongs more properly in a book devoted to multi-criteria decision making.

This illustration shows how an attribute with an objective measure (miles per gallon) could be expressed in terms of utility. Judgments based on attributes with objective measures are said to be repeatable, or essential, since they do not depend on subjective assessments. Some attributes, however, lack objective measures, or their objective measurement might be too difficult or costly to obtain. In the automobile illustration, *noise level* and *steering responsiveness* are criteria that might have objective measures, but in all likelihood are measured using subjective judgment. Even in these cases, however, the judgments must be expressed on the 0...100 utility scale. These criteria do not, however, yield repeatable judgments. Whether repeatability is important or not depends on the circumstances of the decision. In general, repeatable judgments are preferred to nonrepeatable judgments.

The process of decomposing a decision into its constituent criteria and priorities is a natural one that is readily mastered. True, there are some subtleties; for example, how to avoid having too many criteria, or sibling criteria in the hierarchy that have radically different scopes, or the consequence of criteria with overlapping scopes. There are also many subtleties involved in defining utility functions, and in selecting criteria that can be defined by utility functions. Awareness of these and other subtleties comes with time, study, and practice.

A PROCESS VIEW OF MAUT

Effective use of MAUT requires facility in the human processes involved in constructing decision aids in addition to the underlying theory. Figure 9-3 gives a skeletal outline of the basic MAUT workflow. Three elements of a canonical MAUT process are worth discussing: objectify the decision, set evaluation goal, and the iteration from sensitivity analysis to criteria and preference definition. Let's begin, however, with an apparently strange assertion: that decision making is not in the scope of MAUT, and is therefore not part of the decision aid. (In Figure 9-3, the region in gray highlights that portion of the process which produces a decision aid.)

This assertion is easy to understand if we remember that MAUT produces *decision aids*, and that a decision maker may use *multiple* decision aids. For example, MAUT might be used to rank alternative components. However, the decision maker also might be prototyping with one particular component, and conducting a formal market analysis of the vendor of some other component. By keeping decision making outside the scope of MAUT, we avoid treating MAUT as an end in itself. We also avoid the trap of becoming engrossed by the MAUT decision procedure—that is, assigning greater meaning to the utility score U_Y than is reasonable. At the risk of repeating ourselves, MAUT does not generate answers. It helps the decision maker obtain insight into factors that govern a particular decision. We now return to discuss the three elements of the process for building and using MAUT decision aids.

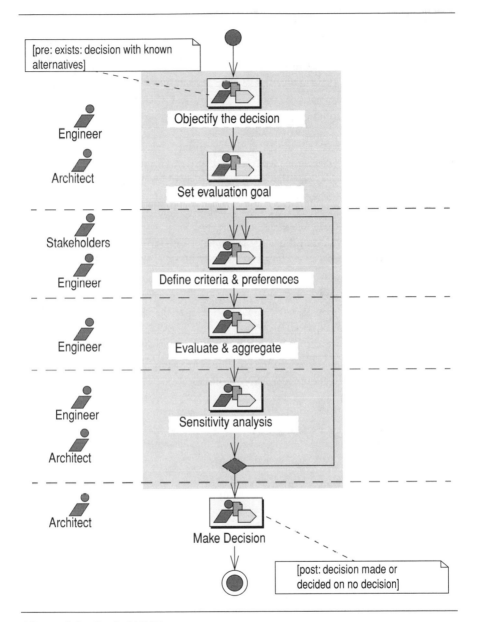

[pre: exists: decision with known alternatives]

Engineer

Architect

Stakeholders

Engineer

Engineer

Engineer

Architect

Architect

Objectify the decision

Set evaluation goal

Define criteria & preferences

Evaluate & aggregate

Sensitivity analysis

Make Decision

[post: decision made or decided on no decision]

Figure 9-3   Basic MAUT process.

Objectify the Decision.   As strange as this may sound, we have seen numerous MAUT evaluation efforts hampered by a failure to identify the decision that must be made. Identifying the decision means more than identifying the fact that we want, for example, to buy a car. It is just as important to identify which options are available—buy the Stingray, the Porsche, or the used Chevy Malibu. Without these alternatives, there can be no decision. What is more, confusion about which alternatives are "on the table" means confusion in the MAUT analysis. It is also important to identify the stakeholders of a decision. In particular, we must identify the key stakeholder—the decision maker. We have actually seen evaluations conducted where the evaluator could not identify the person (or persons) responsible for making the decision! In such a situation, MAUT cannot be effective.

The bottom line is that we must be clear about what decision is being made and by whom. At the same time, we must not underestimate how difficult it is to obtain this kind of clarity, especially in large software projects.

Set Evaluation Goal. MAUT is a very flexible technique, and it can be used in a variety of ways. Deciding how MAUT will be used, *setting the evaluation goal*, is as important as defining the decision. Decision makers have different styles. The decision analyst has to accommodate these idiosyncrasies if the decision aid is to have maximum impact, and hence value. The decision itself may require a different way of using MAUT. Table 9-1 illustrates a variety of evaluation goals, what they mean and when to use them. This list is not exhaustive. It is meant to illustrate the variety of ways that MAUT can be used. Selecting the appropriate model (the evaluation goal) requires experience and tact.

Table 9-1 Sample Evaluation Goals

Goal	Description	When to Use
Classify	Define categories of alternatives, for example "desirable," "acceptable," and "undesirable." Place each alternative into exactly one category.	When the utility value of alternatives cluster in distinct regions, or where the decision maker likes some ambiguity.
Choose	Define two categories: "best" and "rest," and place at most one alternative in the "best" category.	When the decision maker likes simplicity and prefers to focus on the leading candidate only.
Sort	Place each alternative in its own category, ranked from best to worst.	When the decision maker likes detail, or likes to discover patterns or categories.
Describe	Do not categorize alternatives by utility alone, but describe them according to their most pronounced features.	When the decision maker distrusts numerical decision methods, or is better with words than numbers.
Threshold	Select some aggregate utility threshold that defines an acceptable alternative and then evaluate alternatives one at a time until an acceptable one is found. Discard the other alternatives.	When the decision maker cannot, for some reason, support a detailed examination of all options but will accept a "first fit" (as opposed to "best fit") alternative.
Concept	Don't examine any alternatives, but develop criteria that would describe an ideal alternative.	When the decision maker has trouble identifying alternatives (defining the decision).

Process Iteration and Sensitivity Analysis. Earlier, we discussed using sensitivity analysis to determine the stability of a decision aid. This analysis might include changing the preferences of criteria to see if they affect the ordering of alternatives. The objective of this analysis is to validate a model. If rankings are sensitive to small changes in assumptions, the model may not be valid. However, as this analysis does not include stakeholders, it is not considered an iteration of the MAUT process.

On the other hand, sensitivity analysis can play a significant role in reconciling stakeholders who have strongly conflicting points of view. Imagine that two groups differ about the importance of a criterion. One way to resolve the conflict is to argue about it and then, ultimately, average the two preferences. This, however, is guaranteed to satisfy no one. A better way is to flip a coin and select one group's preferences. This guarantees support from at least half of the stakeholders. You won't necessarily lose the support of the other half (although they may initially be quite suspicious) since their own preferences are plugged into the decision aid during sensitivity analysis. At this point, it is possible to see whether the difference in preference has a material bearing on the decision. Quite often, the change in priority does not affect the ranking of alternatives. In this fashion, sensitivity analysis reduces conflict, while also providing process iteration as different stakeholder perspectives are reconciled.

The important point is that insight is not always acquired in a linear fashion, and sensitivity analysis may trigger the need to reconsider preferences, change scores, and add or remove criteria. Iterative development is important even in decision theory!

9.2   Evaluating Components with MAUT

This has been a necessarily terse overview of a rather large and diverse topic. We hope the discussion has revealed some of the positive aspects of MAUT—its underlying mathematical foundation, the way it exploits natural cognitive functions such as problem decomposition to obtain insight, and the straightforward processes for performing MAUT-based evaluations. It should come as no surprise that MAUT lies at the heart of many component evaluation techniques used in the software industry.

However, MAUT is deficient in a number of ways when it comes to dealing with the realities of building systems from commercial software components. These deficiencies, which we discuss below, do not invalidate MAUT for component selection decisions. However, they do severely limit the effectiveness of MAUT analysis. As a consequence, one of two things happens in practice. First, the decision maker does not recognize the limitations of MAUT, and makes selection decisions based solely on MAUT analysis. Only later is it discovered that MAUT failed to highlight, and indeed could not highlight, some critical criterion which rendered the component unfit for use. Second, the decision maker does recognize the limitations of MAUT, and therefore completely discounts the analysis, or worse, coerces the technique to validate selection decisions made previously, possibly without the use of any formal decision aid.

In the next chapter we suggest a third option: augment MAUT with other techniques that address its limitations.

LIMITATIONS OF MAUT

Independent Component Selection Decisions.   MAUT assumes that we can select the fittest component from every category of component that contains alternatives. In the real world, this is not an adequate theory. Component selection decisions are most definitely not independent of each other. Instead, as we illustrate in the case study, component selection decisions are often based on intricate dependencies among components.

This means, in practice, that the notion of "best of breed" integration is inherently flawed: it is a bad design strategy to select the "best" components in each class independently of each other and hope that they will work together. Instead, we need to think of component selection in the context of *ensembles*. In other words, designers need to select components that work well together, regardless of whether each component is the "best" (by some measure) in its category. The selection decision, to the extent that it exists, is a selection among alternative ensembles.

All Alternatives Must Be Feasible.   MAUT rests on one particularly critical assumption: all the alternative courses of action are *feasible*. MAUT helps decision makers decide which alternative is *preferred*. Each criterion in a MAUT model expresses a preference, not a requirement. What *weight* should be assigned to a requirement? The idea of a "must have" criterion simply makes no sense in most applications of MAUT.[2]

In practice, this means that MAUT should be deferred until you have identified a number of feasible component (or ensemble) alternatives. Premature use of MAUT is the mistake we have enountered most frequently.

Component Adaptation Is Not Factored Into Evaluation Criteria.   Utility functions in MAUT express fitness for use with respect to a single criterion. However, this notion of a utility function is too static. In real design processes, there is considerable give and take between requirements, design, and components.

---

[2] Some MAUT techniques have been developed that express the idea of "must have" criteria as vetoes—see the recommended further reading section at the end of this chapter for more details.

While MAUT utility functions provide a measure of fitness for use, they do not accommodate the possibility of increasing fitness through adaptation of the component, the design, or the system requirements.

In practice, MAUT criteria are interpreted in a normative fashion; that is, as requirements that a component must satisfy. This becomes more and more irrelevant in the face of practical tradeoff decisions that must be made in the design process. An adaptation of MAUT, Risk/Misfit, extends the idea of utility function to these kinds of tradeoffs. We discuss Risk/Misfit in the next chapter.

Utility Functions Are Not Always Easy to Come By.   Our example of utility function worked quite nicely for automobiles. However, software is a newer invention and is less well understood. A convincing demonstration of this can be found in any book on software measurement (see [Fenton 93] for example). How do we measure the quality of software components? What are the units of measure for a criterion such as "ease of use"? Quite a lot of good thinking has gone into this topic. There are standard quality models [Boehm+ 78] [IEEE 89], and some agreement on what different quality attributes mean. But there is little agreement on how to measure these attributes. Even if we decompose ease of use into "learnability," "error handling," and "convenient menus," we still will be at a loss to *measure* these attributes.

In practice, MAUT decision aids tend to include criteria that cannot be measured. These criteria raise obvious questions about consistency of judgments across different components, and repeatability of the judgments across different evaluators.

BEYOND MAUT: RISK/MISFIT, MODEL PROBLEMS, ENSEMBLES

Design, in general, is the process of identifying and selecting from alternative courses of action. These decisions are often referred to as tradeoff decisions, since each option, presumably, optimizes one set of design criteria at the expense of another; for example, performance at the expense of security. It would seem that MAUT would be ideally suited for making just these sorts of decisions. All it requires is that we identify the alternatives, define fitness criteria, and define measures for these criteria.

As we have discussed, however, commercial software components require us to extend our repertoire of evaluation techniques. For example, we need to discover system requirements and concepts of operation that make a design amenable to commercial software components. We also need to discover systematically the properties of software components Part II of this book demonstrates this extended notion of evaluation and the associated repertoire of techniques that support it.

9.3 Summary

MAUT is a flexible and powerful tool for supporting multi-attribute decision making. Since most component selection decisions are based on a number of different factors, MAUT should be an ideal fit for component-based software engineering. However, MAUT is, at best, only one of several techniques that are needed to make sound component selection decisions. Some of these other techniques are discussed in detail in the following chapters and illustrated in Part III of this book.

9.4 For Further Reading

Readers interested in a more formal treatment of multi-criteria decision making should consult the family of MAUT techniques called ELECTRE [Roy 91]. Also interesting is an evaluation process that includes the design of the evaluation technique itself from a toolkit of building blocks [Morisio+ 97]. Both of these papers are a bit theoretical, but still accessible.

Readers interested in practitioner-oriented component evaluation processes based in MAUT should consult Kontio's OTSO (Off-The-Shelf Option) [Kontio 96][Kontio 95]. This technique is particularly strong in its disciplined handling of utility functions and in the treatment of measurement conversions between component attributes and utility.

No practitioner of MAUT analysis can be taken seriously if he or she is not familiar with Saaty's Analytic Hierarchy Process (AHP). Saaty's book is the most authoritative and complete [Saaty 90], but Min [Min 92] and Hong and Nigam [Hong+ 81] provide case studies of using AHP for selecting software components. However, Belton demonstrates that AHP is not the best approach in all situations [Belton 86].

9.5 Discussion Questions

1. Evaluation criteria in MAUT can be considered a map from system needs to component features, and the MAUT utility function can be considered a quantification of a "gap" between needs and features. Should an analyst start with system needs and then find component features that support these needs, or start with component features and find which needs they satisfy? What are the pros and cons of both approaches? Which approach occurs more frequently in practice?

2. A consultant explains that he or she wants to use an evaluation technique that weights each component feature according to whether it is a "must have" feature, which is weighted as 5; a "desirable" feature, which is weighted as 3; and a "nice but non-essential" feature, which is weighted as a 1. Dozens of criteria will be used, but the distribution of weights across the criteria is uncertain. Your task is to convince your project manager to fire this consultant based on the demerits of this weighting scheme. What is your argument?

3. We have asserted that the inclusion of "mandatory" criteria is inconsistent with MAUT theory. However, absolutes are always dangerous when applied to MAUT. Devise a scheme that allows mandatory and preference criteria to be mixed. Hint #1: Make sure that preference criteria cannot be substituted (mathematically) for mandatory criteria. Hint #2: Introduce a minimum utility threshold and relate this to the number of mandatory criteria present.

10

Risk-Misfit

Pessimism is only the name that men of weak nerves give to wisdom.
—Mark Twain

Risk/Misfit is a decision aid that exposes and quantifies, in terms of cost and risk, tradeoff decisions pertaining to the use and repair of components. We developed Risk/Misfit as a result of observing how component selection decisions were made in practice. In particular, we observed a disjunction between two evaluation processes: one overt and one covert. The overt process was invariably based in MAUT, often in response to a policy about how component selection decisions must be made. The covert process, on the other hand, usually involved prototyping and hands-on work by project engineers. More often than not, the covert evaluation process was the basis for selection, while the overt process was given only pro forma consideration or, in some cases, manipulated to support decisions that were already made.

Naturally we have great empathy for these covert evaluation processes. In fact, this book attempts to make these processes overt and standard practice. There is, however, no need to "throw the baby out with the bath water." In some situations, the structural and intellectual rigor of MAUT can make a positive contribution to component selection. Risk/Misfit is rooted in MAUT. You can use it in the style of MAUT, or, alternatively, use it to understand the implications of one or more component repair options. Risk/Misfit can be applied at the component level, or at the ensemble level.

10.1 Fundamental Ideas

First we show that Risk/Misfit is a consistent interpretation of MAUT, putting us on solid theoretical footing. We define and illustrate a workflow for using Risk/ Misfit to select a component repair. We then extend the workflow to address component selection. Last, we discuss our experiences with Risk/Misfit, and point out problem areas and potential pitfalls in its use.

THE UTILITY/RISK COMPLEMENT

In component evaluation, the best alternative is that which is, overall, most "fit for use." The basic MAUT equation, described in Chapter 9, can be used to quantify fitness for use: $U_Y = \sum w_i u_i$ where u_i represents an evaluation criterion against which some alternative may be measured. Thus, U_Y is an expression of fitness for use, and higher values for u_i signify greater fitness for use with respect to particular criteria. Risk/Misfit is also concerned with fitness for use of components but instead of expressing fitness, Risk/Misfit expresses its *complement*, or what naturally, if awkwardly, might be called *mis*fitness.

Figure 10-1 presents a geometric interpretation of MAUT. When properly constructed, it accurately depicts the generality of the basic MAUT equation. A measure of utility for each criterion u_i of some component Y has been assigned to spokes in a Kiveat diagram, with the vertex representing a utility of 0 and the points on the circumference representing a maximum utility value of 100. With this geometric setup, we can define the aggregation function of the basic MAUT equation as a calculation of the area of the shaded region. This area essentially quantifies the fitness of Y. Since the maximum value of this area has been bounded (the utility of each criterion lies in the range 0...100), we can always derive the unshaded area of misfitness from the area of fitness, and vice versa. Thus, misfit is the complement of fit, at least in this formulation.

But how does one express and, ultimately, quantify misfit? Designers are comfortable expressing misfit as *risk*. That is, if a high level of fit is a harbinger of good things, then a high level of misfit must be a harbinger of bad things—in a word, *risk*. Risk/Misfit equates misfit with risk, hence the name of the evaluation

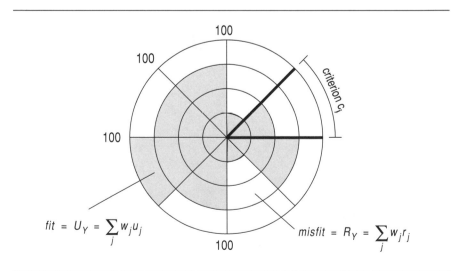

Figure 10-1   A geometric interpretation of MAUT.

technique. On the right of Figure 10-1 we have adapted the basic MAUT equation for Risk/Misfit by substituting risk R in place of utility U. Since R_y can be derived from U_y, as explained above, we are safe in saying that Risk/Misfit is derived from MAUT.

REPAIR STRATEGY AS RISK MITIGATOR

The shift from utility to risk has an interesting consequence. It allows Risk/Misfit to expose, and to help designers explore design alternatives. In the conventional world of risk management, all risks can be mitigated [SEI 96]. One might naturally wonder if this also holds true of risks that express misfit between a component and its use context. Can misfits be removed in an analogous way that risks can be mitigated? It turns out that removing component misfit is one of the principal activities of component integrators. We often hear how components were "wrapped," or "glued," or any number of other verbs. Each term reflects the same basic activity: transforming a component that was previously misfit into one that is fit.

MAUT evaluation techniques do not typically consider removal of misfit. That is, the utility of a component is assessed "as is" with respect to a criterion. MAUT does not consider how utility might be improved through modification of the component. Risk/Misfit, on the other hand, allows the evaluator to consider one or more *repair* strategies that might remove misfit, and thereby reduce the risk of using a component (or, conversely, to improve its utility).

Figure 10-2 is an abstract fragment of a Risk/Misfit decision aid that assumes a top-level goal of selecting a component. As with MAUT, it specifies and arranges criteria in an arbitrarily deep hierarchy. Criteria that are not decomposed into subcriteria (that is, criterion-1.1, criterion-1.2, criterion-2, and criterion-3) represent measurable features. Each such subcriterion may have one or more repair options defined. These repair options represent ways to reduce misfit if, for example, a component does not satisfy a criterion. The designer must select a

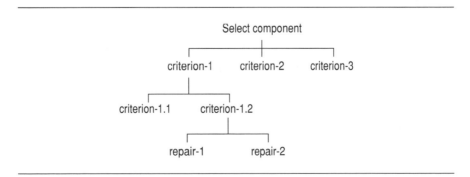

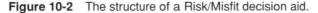

Figure 10-2   The structure of a Risk/Misfit decision aid.

repair option for any criterion with one or more repairs. Only then can a measure of misfit be assigned to that criterion. Thus, Risk/Misfit involves two classes of selection decisions: selecting repair options and selecting components.

It may seem that repair options apply only to components, but this is not true. A misfit indicates a lack of fit between a component and its use context. It follows, then, that the misfit could be removed by changing either the component or the *component context*. The component context includes the requirements of a system and the architecture of that system. But is it appropriate to change requirements or architecture as a result of a component evaluation? The answer is (as we discuss next), "it depends."

NORMATIVE AND FORMATIVE EVALUATION WITH RISK/MISFIT

MAUT typically is used as a *normative* instrument. That is, evaluation criteria are defined according to a set of system requirements. These criteria are the *norms* that must be satisfied. Utility U_Y of some component Y is like a test score. There is no flexibility or negotiation between component capabilities and system requirements. You can readily imagine situations in which a rigorously normative approach is justified—in safety-critical systems, for example. In our experience, however, the use of commercial software components in such systems is the exception rather than the rule.

In contrast, the use of commercial components in enterprise information systems is not just typical, but absolutely essential. For this class of system, the scope of automation of business processes is often defined in terms of what can be achieved within time and budget constraints. Commercial components can also shape business processes. Consider, for example, the rush by many enterprises to embrace Web technologies. In these situations, commercial software components can and do play a formative role in the design of systems. But what do we really mean by *formative* evaluation?

Intuitively, formative evaluation is the converse of normative evaluation. Normative evaluation holds requirements constant. It implies that reducing misfit implies changing a component. In contrast, formative evaluation holds components constant. It implies changes to requirements, instead. Normative evaluation starts with requirements and determines how well component features satisfy these requirements. Formative evaluation starts with component features, and seeks to determine which requirements these features satisfy.

Figure 10-3 shows the converse relationship of formative and normative evaluation as a function of time and commitments. As a project proceeds, decisions are made that lead to design commitments. These commitments can be broken, but as this generally leads to pain and suffering, these reversals are not taken lightly. It is best to use formative evaluation early in the project, when the number of commitments made is low, and when the lack of commitments makes normative evaluation problematic. Formative evaluation helps to firm up requirements. As

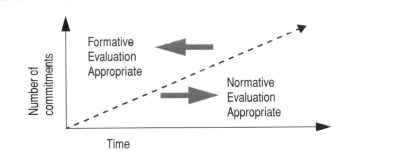

Figure 10-3 The formative/normative continuum.

time passes and commitments accumulate, formative evaluation becomes less appropriate. In later phases of the project, requirements firm up and technical certainty settles in. At this point, normative evaluation becomes more appropriate. At the extreme, normative evaluation is a form of acceptance testing confirming that components meet the exact requirements framed through an earlier design activity.

Designers cannot afford the luxury of exclusively normative or formative evaluation. Both are necessary. There are bound to be requirements that cannot be dismissed. There are also component features that can introduce significant value with little or no cost, although that value might require increasing the scope of the system. The trick is to avoid overemphasizing one form of evaluation at the expense of the other. Overemphasizing normative evaluation limits opportunities to use commercial components. Overemphasizing formative evaluation risks a dangerous infatuation with component features at the expense of good judgment.

Risk/Misfit can be used in a normative or formative fashion. While this is also true of MAUT in general (it is only tradition that leads to the exclusively normative use of MAUT), Risk/Misfit provides safeguards against irrational attachment to technology features.

10.2   Feature and Repair Analysis

This section illustrates Risk/Misfit by elaborating an evaluation criterion for a hypothetical component. We have purposely oversimplified some of the technical aspects of the component and alternative repair strategies. Figure 10-4 outlines the generic Risk/Misfit workflow. The workflow is annotated to show the correspondence between the workflow and the illustration.

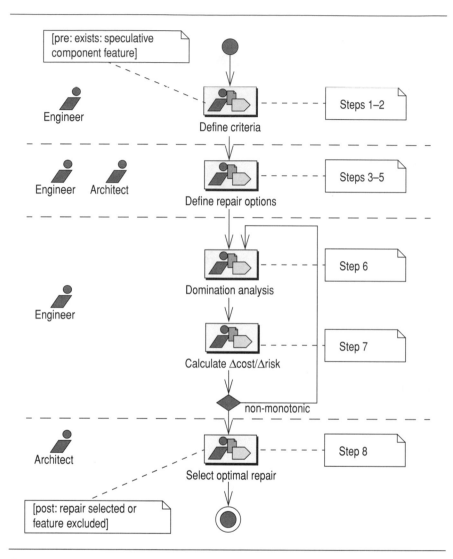

Figure 10-4   Repair analysis in Risk/Misfit.

STEP 1: CONSTRUCT FEATURE/RISK CRITERION MAPPING

The first step is to identify evaluation criteria. These criteria map between measurable features of a component to design requirements.[1] To begin, itemize the relevant features of a component. In some cases, you should take a systematic

---

[1] A mapping of component features to design requirements should be made in all applications of MAUT to component evaluation. Unfortunately, this mapping is left implicit in many cases, which tends to give MAUT evaluations a sense of arbitrariness.

approach for itemizing features. This is a good idea, for example, if you are developing criteria against which several components will be assessed. Reference models [ECMA 91] or component comparison checklists are a good place to start if a systematic approach is needed. Alternatively, a more limited approach may be sufficient. This is often the case where the evaluation is intended to increase confidence in a tentative selection decision, or to provide additional insight into how best to use a component. In these cases, vendor literature, such as reference manuals, advertising glossies, or even user-group bulletin boards may be sufficient.

The illustration centers on a load-balancing feature provided by a component (or class of components). The component accepts some parameterized number of connections. When this number is exceeded, a new run-time instance of the component is launched, possibly on another machine in the network.

To transform this feature into an evaluation criterion, map it to some system requirement. The source of the requirement can be previous design commitments, or perhaps a bona fide system requirement. Regardless of source, we construct the criterion mapping as a risk statement that states the potential negative consequence if a component does *not* possess a feature:

Feature	Risk
New server instances are created for N+1 connections.	System response time significantly degrades at peak load.

The deduction of this risk may appear obvious. However, real design issues lie just below the surface. For example, will adding server instances improve overall system performance? Is there an anticipated usage profile? Are peak loads predictable? What is the intensity of these loads? What is the required average response time? How much degradation under peak load is acceptable? The risk stated above does not expose these details, but it provides a basis for asking these questions. In this sense, the process of forming criteria in Risk/Misfit requires the active participation of the system designer. Even though a technology expert might be able to deduce the purpose of a component feature and create a risk statement such as above, the designer needs to understand the implications of the risk. The net effect—and this is one objective of Risk/Misfit—is to directly involve the system designer in the evaluation activity, and to make both the process and the artifacts of formal evaluation useful to the designer.

A word of caution is in order. Components may have many features, and you need a measure of restraint when defining criteria. Too few criteria can leave important design assumptions hidden, but too many criteria reduce the benefit-to-cost ratio of Risk/Misfit and can alienate the designer. The analyst (or designer) must focus on component features (hence criteria) that reflect important design decisions. The trick is to identify these criteria. The use of nonstandard component features is often a good means of identification. These often imply a hidden tradeoff between system functionality and openness to component substitution. Another good source of key criteria are those that bear on component integration, as these often have structural ramifications in a system design.

In short, the evaluator often plays the role of a gadfly—asking irritating questions (in the form of "what risk does this component feature address?") and looking for hidden and often inconsistent design assumptions. But this role can sometimes wear thin on your colleagues. (Socrates, for example, was known among his contemporaries as "the Gadfly" for being a bit too effective in asking difficult questions, and we know what his fellow Athenians did to him.)

STEP 2: QUANTIFY THE RISK

Unless there is an objective way of measuring risk (which is unlikely), you will use a subjective approach. However, this is not a problem if you remember that Risk/Misfit, like MAUT, is used to obtain insight into decision factors rather than mathematical certainty. With this in mind, how might risk be quantified to obtain insight into the decision at hand? One technique is to start qualitatively. For example, one dimension might categorize risks according to their impact on cost, schedule, and function. Another dimension might introduce a coarse notion of risk magnitude; for example, negligible, moderate, and severe. Combining these dimensions produces the risk taxonomy is shown in Table 10-1. Other risk taxonomies are possible, and you can use Risk/Misfit with any of these. For example, the risk taxonomy developed by the SEI [SEI 94] would serve the purpose, as would others.

In this illustration, the hypothetical designer decides that degraded performance at peak load constitutes a severe functional risk (SF) to the system:

Feature	Risk	Max Risk
New server instances are created for N+1 connections.	System response time significantly degrades at peak load.	**SF**

Note that this risk specification may also help the analyst and designer prioritize the evaluation effort. This illustration works depth-first through a single criterion. In practice, several criteria may be elaborated simultaneously to the level of detail that includes maximum risk. The designer may then choose to focus only on criteria that surpass some predetermined risk threshold. It is important to work out these issues prior to a Risk/Misfit evaluation.

Table 10-1   Risk as a Function of Risk Factor and Severity

	Negligible (N)	Moderate (M)	Severe (S)
Cost (C)	Negligible cost risk (NC)	Moderate cost risk (MC)	Severe cost risk (SC)
Schedule (S)	Negligible schedule risk (NS)	Moderate schedule risk (MS)	Severe schedule risk (SS)
Function (F)	Negligible risk to system function (NF)	Moderate risk to system function (MF)	Severe risk to system function (SF)

STEP 3: IDENTIFY REPAIR OPTIONS (RISK MITIGATION)

Having identified a significant functional risk, the designer may wish to identify repair options. Note that a repair option may be appropriate even if we know that a component possesses a feature. As alluded to earlier, the feature may be non-standard. This alone is cause for concern—what happens if the vendor chooses not to support this feature in future releases, or if the vendor goes out of business? Repair options for nonstandard features provide designers with fallback options for such cases. They can also justify (or refute) the use of these features.

Sometimes, repair options are used to develop criteria for a class of components. In this case, we must assume that at least some members of a class of components do not support a specified feature. Otherwise, this criterion would not be a distinguishing trait of at least some components, and therefore would not be included in our criteria. Nevertheless, repair options usually vary from component to component. Thus, this step usually depends on identifying a deficiency of a particular component, or deciding to investigate alternative ways of *not* using a particular component feature (Table 10-2).

In this illustration, the designer has decided that there are four viable repair options. Option R1 extends the component through a wrapper—a front-end to the component that performs rudimentary connection management. The wrapper intercepts all calls to the "wrapped" component. When the number of connections on the component exceeds a set limit, the wrapper spawns a new image of the component. Option R2 pays the vendor for custom enhancements. A discussion of the perils of this repair strategy is a topic in its own right. The illustration reflects only that it can sometimes be a viable option. Option R3 mixes vendor enhancement and custom development. In this case, the vendor agrees to provide a "plug-in" interface for a connection management component, but the integrator must develop this component. Option R4 waives the "requirement" for uniform performance at peak load. Note that this is not the same thing as doing nothing or ignoring the risk. Waiving the requirement is an overt repair strategy that applies to the system rather than to the component. Option R5 purchases additional

Table 10-2 Feature with Repair

Feature	Risk	Max Risk	Repair	Residual Risk
New server instances are created for N+1 connections.	System response time significantly degrades at peak load.	SF	R1: Custom wrapper	NC + NS
			R2: Vendor enhancement	NC + NS
			R3: Vendor plug-in interface	NC + NS
			R4: Accept degraded performance	SF
			R5: Bigger iron (i.e., faster CPU, more memory, higher bandwidth networks)	MC

computer resources so that adequate performance can be guaranteed under anticipated maximum system loads.

The designer or analyst assigns each repair option a measure of effectiveness, expressed as *residual risk*. A repair strategy may reduce risk (for example, from severe to negligible), transfer risk from one category to another (for example, from cost to schedule), or both. However, risk is seldom completely eliminated. In the illustration, custom wrapping, vendor enhancement, and vendor plug-in all transfer functional risk to a combination of cost and schedule risk. At this level of detail, it is impossible to distinguish among the effectiveness of these options. Indeed, it is not even clear that the combination of two negligible risks has a lower risk magnitude than a severe risk. This ambiguity does not necessarily need to be resolved, but we do so later for the sake of completeness. Option R4 does not mitigate any risk, so the maximum risk remains as the residual risk. Option R5 mitigates the functional risk with a moderate increase to cost.

Not all risks require repairs. A risk without repairs might signify that the maximum risk impact is not significant enough to warrant even the investigation of repair (in which case the criterion should be removed from consideration as it is unimportant). It might also signify that there are no feasible repairs. In both cases, the value of the residual risk is equal to the original (unrepaired) maximum risk impact. Lastly, it might signify that a feature is mandatory, and no repair is allowed. However, such mandatory requirements do not fit Risk/Misfit any more than they fit MAUT.

STEP 4: QUANTIFY MAXIMUM AND RESIDUAL RISK

In many situations risks can be treated *qualitatively*. In some situations, however, we have to adopt a *quantitative* treatment. In particular, a numerical representation of risk is needed if qualitative treatment does not distinguish between repair options, or if we need an aggregate measure of maximum or residual risk for a component. In the illustration, we require a function to map the two-dimensional risk taxonomy in Figure 10-1 (the domain) to some numeric scale, say, a simple interval scale (the range). As is often the case, the KISS[2] principle should be kept in mind when defining this function.

The function shown in Figure 10-5 satisfies the property of simplicity by mapping all risks of negligible magnitude to the interval 0...33, all moderate risks to 34...66, and all severe risks to 67...100, regardless of the risk factor (function, cost, or schedule). Sometimes, more complex functions are in order. This is appropriate under special circumstances, for example, if a richer risk taxonomy than in Table 10-1 has been used. In the illustration, the designer assigns values to maximum and residual risks within the constraints defined in Figure 10-5. This results in the criterion shown in Table 10-3.

---

[2] Keep it simple, stupid.

$$f(factor,\ magnitude) \rightarrow \begin{bmatrix} 0 \le f(\_,\ N) \le 33 \\ 34 \le f(\_,\ M) \le 66 \\ 67 < f(\_,\ S) \le 100 \end{bmatrix} \quad \begin{array}{l} \text{for N negligible risk, M moderate risk,} \\ \text{and S severe risk.} \end{array}$$

Figure 10-5   Converting from qualitative to quantitative treatment of risk.

It is often false economy to skip the qualitative treatment of risk and head straight for the quantitative treatment. Remember, the objective of Risk/Misfit is to generate insight, not answers. The conversion of risk to a numeric magnitude is required for aggregation, whereas the risk taxonomy expresses meaning. It is also easier to quantify a risk once you have classified it using a semantically rich taxonomy.

STEP 5: ESTIMATE REPAIR COST

At this point, you have assigned a measure of effectiveness to each repair strategy by specifying how much risk it mitigates. We are not yet able, however, to select the optimal repair strategy. We do not know the cost of the repairs. Although custom wrapping (R1) seems to be a good option, it may be substantially more expensive than simply buying excess hardware (R5). What we need is an estimated cost for each repair (Table 10-4).

Risk/Misfit provides an effective framework for including cost in an evaluation. For various reasons, it is difficult for decision makers to assign a monetary value to utility. How much is good performance worth in terms of dollars? On the other hand, estimating repair costs is, or should be, a straightforward task. The cost/risk technique used in Risk/Misfit adapts a technique described by Edwards and Newman [Edwards+ 82].

Using software cost-estimation models the designer has determined that the cost to develop a custom wrapper is $95,000. The component vendor is willing to add the load-balancing feature for $50,000. The vendor is also willing to provide

Table 10-3   Quantified Unrepaired and Residual Risk

Feature	Risk	Max Risk	Repair	Residual Risk
New server instances are created for N+1 connections.	System response time significantly degrades at peak load.	98	H1: Custom wrapper	5+5=10
			R2: Vendor enhancement	15+15=30
			R3: Vendor plug-in interface	10+10=20
			R4: Accept degraded performance	98
			R5: Bigger iron	35

Table 10-4   Repair Cost Estimate

Max Risk	Repair	Residual Risk	Est. Cost
98	R1: Custom wrapper	10	$95,000
	R2: Vendor enhancement	30	$50,000
	R3: Vendor plug-in interface	20	$55,000
	R4: Accept degraded performance	98	$0
	R5: Bigger iron	35	$175,000

a plug-in interface for only $10,000. This, combined with a $45,000 cost to develop the plug-in component, results in a total repair cost of $55,000. The hardware vendor is convinced that the new class of server machines will solve all possible performance problems, for a mere $175,000.

The only cost estimation question of any complexity is what to do with option R4. It waives the requirement for predictable performance at peak load. Is there a hidden cost to this in terms of lost revenue or angry customers? There might well be; but for our illustration, we assume that this is an unknown. The designer might need to return to this question if R4 looks like the best repair option, but let's assume this situation will not arise.

STEP 6: DOMINATION ANALYSIS

We simplify the analysis by removing repairs that will never be selected. This process is called *domination analysis*. Informally, alternative A dominates B if A is at least as good as B with respect to all criteria, and better than B with respect to at least one criterion. In this situation, we can eliminate B, since it can never outperform A.

Domination analysis would be a complicated affair if we had a large number of alternatives or a large number of criteria. This is not the case with Risk/Misfit, for two reasons. First, there are only two criteria: cost and risk. Second, there are not likely to be a large number of repair options. Thus, domination analysis usually can be done by inspection, as in the illustration in Table 10-4. R5 has a

Table 10-5   Domination Analysis

Max Risk	Repair	Residual Risk	Est. Cost
98	R4: Accept degraded performance	98	$0
	R2: Vendor enhancement	30	$50,000
	R3: Vendor plug-in interface	20	$55,000
	R1: Custom wrapper	10	$95,000

higher residual risk and higher cost than R1. In this case, we can eliminate R5. No other alternatives are dominated.

The remaining options now exhibit a useful property: alternatives that have lower residual risk also have higher cost. (If this property is violated it means that there are still dominated alternatives present.) We have reordered the options from least to most expensive (Table 10-5).

STEP 7: CALCULATE COST-TO-RISK RATIO FOR EACH REPAIR

Choosing to accept degraded performance leaves significant risk, but nothing is spent for the repair. If we select vendor enhancement, we reduce risk from 98 to 30, but increase cost from $0 to $50,000. Thus, choosing vendor enhancements is appropriate if we are willing to pay the cost of vendor enhancement to achieve the reduction in residual risk offered by this enhancement. This is expressed as the ratio of increased cost to reduced risk:

$$\frac{cost(R2) - cost(R4)}{risk(R4) - risk(R4)} = \frac{\$50,000}{68} = \$735/risk$$

Similarly, selecting the vendor plug-in and developing a plug-in component means paying the difference in cost between vendor enhancements and the plug-in strategy:

$$\frac{cost(R3) - cost(R2)}{risk(R2) - risk(R3)} = \frac{\$5,000}{10} = \$500/risk$$

But there is something funny about this result. Domination analysis produced criteria that obeyed an ordering property; lower residual risk implied higher cost. This is a useful property that should also hold when we compute the $\Delta cost/\Delta risk$ ratio. A little study reveals why this property has been violated. For a very modest increment in cost, the plug-in strategy results in a substantial reduction in risk. This means that the option with the lower $\Delta cost/\Delta risk$ ratio (in this case, R3) is superior to the previous option (R2). We should remove the previous option and recalculate the $\Delta cost/\Delta risk$ ratio:

$$\frac{cost(R3) - cost(R4)}{risk(R4) - risk(R3)} = \frac{\$55,000}{78} = \$705/risk$$

We have made the same calculations for all repair options, in each case producing a cost-to-risk ratio to express the added cost increments attendant with further risk reduction. The result is shown in Table 10-6.

The cost-to-risk ratio provides the basis for selecting a repair strategy. Specifically, if we could assign a dollar value V to each unit of risk, then we could select the repair option according to three simple rules. If $V \leq \$705$, then the designer should accept degraded performance. If instead $\$735 < V \leq \$4,000$, then purchasing the vendor plug-in and custom component is appropriate. Last, if

Table 10-6   Cost/Risk Ratio

Max Risk	Repair	Residual Risk	Est. Cost	ΔCost/ ΔRisk
98	R4: Accept degraded performance	98	$0	$0
	R3: Vendor plug-in interface	20	$55,000	$705
	R1: Custom wrapper	10	$95,000	$4,000

$V > \$4,000$, then custom wrapping is the way to go. It all hinges, of course, on the value of V.

STEP 8: ASSIGN A DOLLAR VALUE TO RISK AND SELECT REPAIR

You might ask the decision maker straight off, "what is a unit of risk worth to you, in dollars?" Chances are, this will not produce the desired answer. Instead of this direct approach, you might pose the following scenario. Suppose you offer to sell the decision maker a magic wand that could eliminate all peak-load performance risks. How much would the decision maker be willing to pay for this wand? If the decision maker would pay $120,000, then the cost basis for a unit of risk is $120,000/98 = $1225/risk. That is, it is worth $120,000 to reduce the risk from its maximum of 98 to its residual of 0. (This is a *magic* wand, after all.)

The decision maker may not appreciate the magic wand test, or perhaps you do not trust that the answer reflects the true cost basis for risk. In this case you may need to hunt around for additional data points. Although we have only elaborated one criterion, others may serve the purpose. One criterion might be that a component has a number of sample programs. This feature might be justified by the cost and schedule risks of learning how to use a component. Although the absolute risk might be small for this criterion, the decision maker might still estimate how much developing such sample programs, and thus reducing the small risk, would be worth. The point is, several data points can be obtained to determine a cost basis for units of risk.

Once you have obtained a cost basis for risk, you can select the repair option using the algorithm described at the end of step 7. If the cost basis for risk is $1,225/risk, then vendor plug-in provides the best cost-to-risk ratio.

10.3   Component Selection

We have come a long way. But for all of our effort, we have only selected a repair strategy for a single evaluation criterion. The same techniques must be applied to each criterion that has repair options (the cost basis for risk can be reused across criteria, of course). But what happens if a component selection decision must be made in addition to repair selections? That is, what if there are several components, each with repair options? We can use the same technique that we used to select repair options to select components. This workflow is depicted in Figure 10-6, which requires just a little explanation.

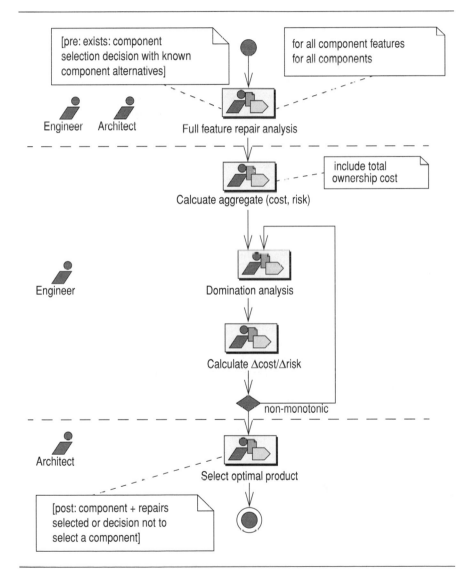

Figure 10-6   Component selection in Risk/Misfit.

Figure 10-1 introduced a modified form of the basic MAUT equation that is suitable for Risk/Misfit: $R_Y = \sum w_i r_i$ where R_Y denotes the overall risk (or misfit) of alternative Y and $w_i r_i$ denotes the weighted risk (or misfit) of criterion i. However, the techniques used to select a repair option do not follow this model. An accurate model[3] is:

$$R_Y = \sum_i \rho(r_i, c_i)$$ where ρ is a function of residual risk r_i and the cost c_i of obtaining this level of risk for criterion i.

This accurately reflects the structure of evaluation criteria after repairs have been selected for each criterion. That is, after all such repair options are selected, each *criterion* has a residual risk. Residual risk is equal to the maximum risk if no repairs have been specified, or equal to the risk remaining after repair. Each criterion also has a repair cost. Repair cost is zero if no repair is specified, or some other cost (possibly zero) corresponding to the cost of the repair.

The function ρ is still to be defined. As written, it maps the risk and cost tuple (each criterion) to something suitable for aggregation. There are a number of options for ρ. For example, ρ might disregard residual risk so that, presumably, the component requiring the least repair cost would be selected. Alternatively, we might disregard cost. In this case, the component presenting the least residual risk is selected. Or perhaps ρ would express the cost/risk ratio. Each of these options, and perhaps many others, might be feasible under different circumstances.

But not so fast! The attentive (or skeptical) reader may have observed that there are additional cost factors associated with commercial components. These cost factors include license fees, support contracts, training, additional documentation, and additional system administration. There is no generally accepted formula for computing these overall costs, but there is general agreement on their name: *total cost of ownership*, or simply "TCO." We can capture total cost of ownership while still preserving the analogous treatment of components and repairs for ρ selection. We'll do this by introducing an artificial feature called "TCO," and assign to this feature a repair cost equal to the total cost of ownership, with no residual risk. It is surprising but true that total cost of ownership is generally not considered in published component evaluation techniques.

10.4   Why Risk/Misfit?

Risk/Misfit helps designers of component-based systems avoid common pitfalls: the bandwagon effect, featureitis, and buried design.

---

[3] Note that we have removed the weighting factor w_i from this equation. Our reasons for doing so are explained in Section 10.5 where we discuss our experiences using Risk/Misfit.

BANDWAGON EFFECT

One of the motivations for using commercial components is to stay current with software technology. "Cutting edge" technologies attract attention because they promise a competitive advantage in functionality, performance, or robustness. In some cases, adopting a new technology is driven by well-considered business cases. In other cases, it is a defensive reaction to a perception that competitors may be better positioned to exploit a new technology. E-commerce over the Web illustrates both motives.

Unfortunately, the breadth of change in software technology over the past several years convincingly demonstrates that developing expertise in even a few technology areas is an expensive proposition. Sustaining this expertise across the full range of technologies used in modern enterprise systems is hopeless for all but the largest corporations. Thus, while consumers may be aware of the promise of new technologies—trade magazines and marketing hype assure us of this— they are not always aware of the subtle complexities of these technologies, or the boundary between hype and reality. Designers need a technique to focus on the details of a component or technology that go far beyond bandwagon hype.

Risk/Misfit does this by shifting the MAUT focus from utility to *risk* as a measure of fitness for use. Risk/Misfit, then, is useful for exposing the pros and cons of jumping on the bandwagon. (Bear in mind, not all bandwagons are headed for the cliff.)

FEATUREITIS

It is often said that a little knowledge can be a dangerous thing. This is certainly true in the case of commercial technologies. There, a little knowledge often leads to *featureitis*. Unlike the situation where advocates jump on a bandwagon without knowing where it is going, featureitis results from a narrow but intense infatuation with particular component features. The problem arises when this narrowly focused knowledge is not balanced against overall system goals and objectives.

Risk/Misfit decreases the risk of featureitis by requiring that you justify the use of features in terms of the risks that arise from *not* using these features. This discipline spotlights where expertise has become advocacy. In a more positive vein, this discipline helps build a balanced and rational technical and business case for adopting technologies.

BURIED DESIGN

Sometimes, critical design decisions are waved off as "implementation detail." This is especially common in component-based systems, and it is not hard to see why. Components can be quite complex. The probability that a system architect (who is often quite senior and concerned with a range of high-level concerns) has mastered this complexity becomes vanishingly small as the number of components used increases. This is a dangerous situation, especially where featureitis and the bandwagon effect are operating. We need a technique to expose design decisions that are buried as implementation decisions. Most of these buried design decisions involve adapting components to remove misfit, or endowing them with new features. These adaptations may have architectural implications.

Risk/Misfit exposes these kinds of architectural implications by associating, with each feature, one or more repair options. These repairs represent different ways of adapting a component to remove misfits. In this way, Risk/Misfit exposes these adaptations as part of the overall component selection process.

10.5   Experiences with Risk/Misfit

Risk/Misfit has a number of uses beyond those implied by the above illustration. We have found it to be a flexible tool with several applications:

- Select a component using a best-fit or first-fit evaluation strategy. As implied by the extended illustration, Risk/Misfit may be used analogously to other MAUT techniques for simple component selection. Risk/Misfit is superior to traditional MAUT when it comes to first-fit selection. Its focus on risk rather than utility makes a stronger case for component feasibility.

- Select an adaptation strategy for a best-fit or first-fit component, or for a component that has already been selected. Risk/Misfit is superior to MAUT in its handling of design trade-offs involving different ways of improving component "fit." These alternatives can be incorporated into component selection or applied to previously selected components.

- Explore integration misfit among components or classes of components, and prioritize investigation of repair strategies. Risk/Misfit can be useful as a tool for exploring the design space. In particular, the discipline of expressing risks and mitigations quickly reveals knowledge lacunas that must be filled by model problems or other activities. The risk magnitudes even suggest how much effort to expend on these investigations.

- Force component, vendor, or technology advocates to justify their advocacy with respect to alternative design approaches. This motivation was, in fact, the progenitor of Risk/Misfit. All too often, major design decisions were made by technologists who were extremely knowledgeable about one or more components, and extremely articulate in their advocacy. But for all their expertise, their overall judgment was clouded by bias. Risk/Misfit can expose and remove this kind of bias.

- Document trade-off analysis leads to component selection and adaptation as part of an overall component-based design record. The decision aid produced by Risk/Misfit documents design trade-off decisions. The rationale for component selection is cast in terms of design risks which may change over time. The adaptation strategies may likewise change as new component versions are introduced by vendors. Risk/Misfit can serve as an important touchstone in the face of these changes.

We have used Risk/Misfit in all of the above ways. We have been particularly successful in using Risk/Misfit to force designers, or more particularly contractors and consultants, to justify their advocacy for a particular component or technology. There are, however, situations in which use of Risk/Misfit can be problematic. The first concerns the fact that Risk/Misfit excludes weights on criteria. The second concerns a more subtle issue involving use of component-specific evaluation criteria.

AVOIDANCE OF WEIGHTED CRITERIA

The single aspect of Risk/Misfit that raises the most objections is that it does not include the use of criteria weights. The problem with weights is that their implications are quite subtle. As discussed in the previous chapter, weights imply a substitution rate that, in effect, models a quantitative tradeoff among evaluation criteria. In practice, no such precision exists, especially where the criteria bear on component integration. More fundamentally, though, weights are incompatible with a quantification of risk—or, put another way, are redundant with risk. A criterion that is important to address is important precisely because it introduces significant risk. While it might be possible to construct a meaningful interpretation for a criterion that has low risk but high importance, no such interpretation is immediately obvious. Assuming such an interpretation is possible, the basic Risk/Misfit equation could well be extended to include weighted criteria.

PER-COMPONENT CRITERIA

There is, however, one subtle pitfall that needs to be understood to be avoided. Straightforward use of Risk/Misfit produces evaluation criteria that differ across each alternative component. This is natural since different components support different features, and may therefore require different integration approaches and repair strategies. This is not problematic per se, especially when Risk/Misfit is used for exploring the design space. However, using per-component evaluation criteria makes component selection problematic for the following reason: each component exhibits a different scope; that is, a different set of features, and therefore a different set of responsibilities within a system.

Thus, a component that exhibits substantially more overall risk and repair cost may also exhibit substantially greater utility than all other alternatives. Referring to the geometric interpretation of MAUT and Risk/Misfit in Figure 10-1, we can say that risk R and utility U are complementary for two alternatives X and Y if and only if, $R_X \geq R_Y \rightarrow U_X \leq U_Y$. A component that simultaneously has higher risk and higher utility violates this axiom. Thus, if we really want to use Risk/Misfit for component selection using per-component criteria, then we should also use a conventional MAUT technique to quantify utility as well as risk. However, we have not explored this combined use of Risk/Misfit and MAUT, so this remains an open area for investigation.

10.6 Summary

Risk/Misfit requires us to justify the use of particular component features according to the design *risk* that arises from *not* using these features. For each such design risk, we identify one or more design alternatives *not* involving the use of that feature. For each such design alternative, a cost/risk analysis is conducted. We can then select the best alternative, whether it involves using the feature or not.

Risk/Misfit is a reinterpretation of MAUT that makes it suitable for selecting components, selecting alternative designs, or selecting a component adaptation to improve the fit between a component and its use context. The use of risk instead of utility loses none of the generality of MAUT, but introduces a significant shift in perspective. This shift makes it easier and more natural for the designer (the targeted decision maker) to define and quantify (in terms of cost and risk) tradeoffs involving the use of component features.

Risk/Misfit is a set of techniques and not a process model. Not all Risk/Misfit techniques are applicable in any given situation. The order in which Risk/Misfit techniques are applied may vary, and some techniques may be applied in parallel and even then only partially applied.

10.7 For Further Reading

G.A. Hazelrigg has also attempted to apply MAUT to decision support in engineering design activities [Hazelrigg 99], although this approach, in contrast to Risk/Misfit, places MAUT at the center of an engineering design process, while Risk/Misfit is intended to be just one of several design decision aids.

10.8 Discussion Questions

1. As illustrated in this chapter, Risk/Misfit defers questions of total cost of ownership (TCO) to component selection. Should TCO be considered at the repair level? For example, is there a TCO of custom wrapping when we

consider that the wrapper may need to be tested and possibly modified for each new release of the wrapped component?

2. In many cases, the selection of one component adaptation strategy implies a selection of others. This suggests that criteria are not independent but interdependent. Does this present a challenge to Risk/Misfit? If so, how might the challenge be addressed? If not, why not?

11

Black Box Visibility

In theory, there is no difference between theory and practice.
But, in practice, there is.
—Jan L.A. van de Snepscheut

There is an unavoidable truth that accompanies the use of commercial software components: individual component evaluation cannot identify all of the potential integration issues, no matter how extensive an assessment is performed. As the number of components increases, the likelihood that all component interactions can be fully understood decreases. Unknown or poorly understood component interactions can lead to system failures, and the cause of the failure, once identified, may not always be correctable.

The source of the difficulty is obvious: the integrator has limited visibility into commercial software components and no control over their operation. Component documentation is nearly always incomplete, often inconsistent, and not always provided in sufficient detail. A system integrator must therefore rely on keen diagnostic skills and a good general knowledge of underlying technologies to gain an "inside the black box" perspective. In this chapter, we identify some of these diagnostic skills, introduce techniques, and demonstrate tools that you can use to gain insight into black box components.

11.1   Fundamental Ideas

System failures occur for many reasons. In custom software development, you can usually identify the source of a failure by stepping through the source code until the failure occurs. Debugging becomes a different, and much more difficult, activity when source code is unavailable. Even the basic meaning of "debugging" is changed. Debugging no longer centers on finding code defects, but focuses on observing the behavior of large, opaque components and making inferences from that behavior.

Regardless of the actual cause of failure, the person debugging the system is not the person who created the components but rather the integrator of components developed elsewhere. The integrator is therefore unfamiliar with the assumptions that underlie the component implementation, nor does the integrator have access to source code or detailed design documents. Thus, the debugging activity is different from traditional source code debugging. Even the outcome of debugging is different, since it is not to repair source code but rather to determine if and how unexpected component behavior can be reconciled with the desired behavior of the whole system.

The systematic approach for diagnosing and correcting failures in a component-based system is essentially that of the classic scientific method shown in Figure 11-1 of observation, hypothesis, and prediction [Toulmin 87]. A hypothesis is formed based on one or more observations. To test that hypothesis, an effect is predicted as a result of a given stimulus. An experiment is then designed to test the prediction. Results from the experiment either support or contradict the hypothesis. If the hypothesis is not supported, refinement of the hypothesis and subsequent experimentation is needed.

This method, having proven itself over many centuries, is equally valid today in software engineering. For instance, a problem report (that is, the observation) indicates that a sorting routine fails whenever the nth element is added to a list. An initial assumption (the hypothesis) is that the list is bounded by a hard-coded fixed limit; the prediction is that a review of the source code will reveal a constant that dictates the list's upper boundary. If, in the ensuing review (that is, the experiment) no such constant is located, the hypothesis must be refined and other debugging activities begun.

If we substitute a sorting *component* for source code, a more indirect approach is needed to refute hypotheses. We again start with the simple hypothesis that the implementation has some hard-coded upper limit for the length of an input list; only this time, we need to design a more elaborate experiment. We might input a series of lists of varying length and content to the component. Regardless of list length or the content of the sorted items, we expect this sort to fail when the input list exceeds the same fixed number.

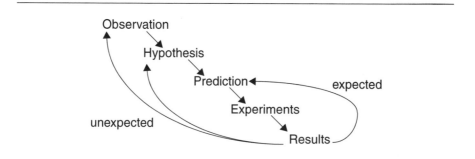

Figure 11-1   The scientific method.

For discussion, let's assume that this does not occur—that, instead, the sort fails on different numbers of items. This would refute our initial hypothesis, so we would need a new, possibly more complex, hypothesis. We might observe that the input list with items requiring large amounts of storage fail more quickly than lists with smaller items. According to our new hypothesis, the component is pre-allocating a fixed buffer for the elements it sorts. As a result, a list consisting of larger items should cause the buffer to fill more quickly. This hypothesis predicts a constant ratio between the size of sorted elements and maximum size of a sorted list. We can then run a series of tests to verify this hypothesis. Should the results refute our hypothesis, we would need to devise a new hypothesis and experiment.

Notice the different approaches used when source code is available versus component debugging. When source code was available it was a fairly straight-forward process to determine if a constant upper bound was the cause. If this was not the cause of the failure, code profilers, static and dynamic analyzers, and other techniques could be used in successive tests to determine the cause of the problem. In the case where source code is not available, the integrator must manipulate the environment in which the component operates to observe cause and effect. This requires considerable imagination and skill on the part of the component integrator. Indeed, the need to enlist the scientific method is in no small part why debugging component-based systems has such a strong affinity with what Kuhn refers to as "science as puzzle solving" [Kuhn 62].

Given the necessity of observation and the fact that the source code is often not available, other techniques for gaining visibility must be found. The following sections describe mechanisms for providing this visibility.

11.2   Opportunities for Visibility

Every software component exists in a context. This context includes the *services* on which the component relies and the services that the component exports for other software components to use. Software components access the services of other components through *interfaces*.

It is sufficient here to define an interface as any point where data or control extend beyond a component's boundary. While it is not possible to provide a comprehensive list of all existing interfaces, it is possible to enumerate the *classes* of interfaces that exist between component boundaries:

- Network services, both physical (for example, Ethernet) and logical (for example, TCP/IP);
- Hardware services such as device drivers and computer peripherals;
- Operating system services such as file I/O and process creation;

- Runtime services such as garbage collection, thread management, and event management;
- Component services directly accessible from the component's own API.

Interfaces provide the means for observing component behavior, and these observations can be used to refute[1] hypotheses about component implementation. Several such interfaces are illustrated in Figure 11-2, each of which may serve as a basis for lab experiments. Most interfaces can be exploited given the availability of adequate reference materials. Further, many interfaces satisfy published standards that can be consulted.

Note, however, that different interfaces may support different kinds of observations, and hence may require different laboratory techniques and experimental apparatus. Often, but not always, the apparatus used to gain visibility at an interface depends on some mix of operating system, hardware, protocols, programming language, and application programming interfaces.

There are four common techniques used to exploit an interface and gain visibility into a commercial software component:

1. Probing: examining the state of a component at runtime or postmortem;

2. Snooping: observing the behavior of two or more communicating components;

3. Spoofing: deceiving a component by impersonating a communicating peer or interposition between two or more components;

4. Static program analysis: examining the contents, structure, and logic of an executable file image.

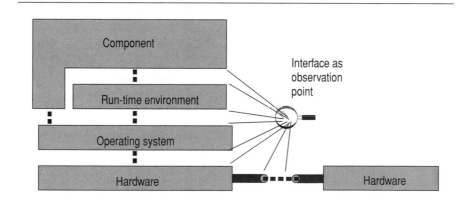

Figure 11-2   Exploitable interfaces.

[1] Strictly speaking, science progresses through refuting rather than proving hypotheses. As we will see, however, some visibility techniques, especially disassemblers and decompilers, allow us to relax this puritanical view of the scientific method when applied to debugging.

We examine each of these visibility techniques in detail in the remainder of this chapter.

11.3 Probing

Probing is used to observe an individual component as opposed to interactions among components. The techniques and tools used to probe software components reveal parent–child relationships, thread performance, user stack, resource use, signal and event disposition, message queues, system calls (including parameters, and return and error codes), and open files.

Probing tools are usually specific to, and distributed with, operating systems. For example, the UNIX utilities *ps* and *truss* are preinstalled with the Sun Solaris operating system. Likewise, the utilities *Process Viewer* and *Spy/Spy++* are installed with the development environment for Microsoft's Windows 95/98/ NT operating systems.

Sample Tools Used for Probing on POSIX-Based Systems

ps: prints information about active processes.
trace, truss: executes a specified command and produces a trace of the system calls it performs, the signals it receives, and the machine faults it incurs.
crash: used to examine the system memory image of a running or a crashed system by formatting and printing control structures, tables, and other information.

Sample Tools Used for Probing on Microsoft OSs

PsList: view process and thread statistics on the local system, or a remote one, with this POSIX 'ps'-style tool.
Process Viewer: displays detailed information about processes running under Windows.
IROTVIEW: displays information about ActiveX and OLE objects currently existing in memory.
HandleEx: describes files, registry keys, and other objects that processes have open, or which DLLs they have loaded.
WinObj: a 32-bit Windows NT program that uses the native Windows NT API to access and display information on the NT Object Manager's name space.
PMon: a Windows NT device driver/GUI combination that logs and displays all process activity on a Windows NT 4.0 system.

Here is something you can try under Sun Solaris to gain insight into the *login* process:

1. Using the *ps* command, locate the process ID of the Internet daemon, *inetd*

```
ps -ef | grep inetd
 UID    PID PPID  C  STIME TTY   TIME   CMD
 root   147   1   0  Aug 26  ?   0:01   /usr/sbin/inetd -s
```

2. Trace the process flow of the *inetd* service (process ID 147) using the *truss* command and watch what happens when someone logs in. Save the output to a file to prevent the results from scrolling off the screen—for example, the following command saves the results to `login.txt`.

```
truss -o login.txt -f -t"fork,exec,setuid,read,write"
   -p 147
```

3. From another window, use *telnet* to connect to the computer on which you are running *truss*, and log in.

4. Stop tracing and examine the results contained in the saved file. The results should appear similar to the results shown below (some details have been eliminated for brevity). If you examine your results carefully you should find your password!

```
                                                        return
line command                                            code
  1:  fork()            (returning as child ...)     = 147
  2:  execve("/usr/sbin/in.telnetd", .., ..)  argc = 1
  3:  execve("/bin/login", .., ..)                   argc = 6
  4:  write(1, " l o g i n :  ", 7)                   = 7
  5:  read(0, " s h i s s a m\n", 1024)              = 8
  6:  read(4, " r o o t : B d P y R b X".., 8192)    = 989
  7:  write(2, " P a s s w o r d :  ", 10)            = 10
  8:  read(4, "\n", 1)                                = 1
  9:  setuid(4207)                                    = 0
 10:  write(1, " L a s t   l o g i n :  ".., 54)      = 54
 11:  execve("/bin/tcsh", .., ..)                    argc = 1
 12:  write(17, " r e : s h i s s a m % ", 12)        = 12
```

We can learn something about the way inbound network log-in services are handled and what happens when a user connects and logs in to a computer by examining the output from the *inetd* service trace. First, we can see that the *telnet* daemon server (*in.telnetd*) is not launched until the service is requested. Second, we can see that the *login* program is launched by *in.telnetd* on line 3 and that the user name and password are not collected by the *telnet* daemon, but by *login*. An interesting observation here, with security implications, is that the user name and password are passed in the clear. Another interesting system call is made on line 9 to `setuid()`, just prior to passing control to the command shell. The `setuid()` call sets the effective user ID to the user logging in. If this call were omitted, the user would be logged in with root permissions. This information has been used by hackers to gain root permission to UNIX systems.

This example shows how it is possible to discover details about components by probing. Without access to source code, we identified the sequence of system calls, including parameters and return codes, invoked by a program running under Sun Solaris.

11.4 Snooping

Snooping can provide insight into interactions between components by allowing an observer to examine communication between components. This communication is not limited to software component interfaces, but includes hardware interfaces as well. In fact, snooping can occur wherever data and control extend past a component boundary, including: intercomponent communication across process and processor boundaries; parent/child communication; remote procedure calls; client/server communication; and dynamic data exchange. Additionally, snooping is not limited to network traffic over Ethernet; FDDI (Fiber Distributed Data Interface) and other protocols can be snooped on physical transport layers such as RS-232 and SCSI.

Like probing tools, most snooping tools are specific to an operating system and runtime environment. Some snooping tools, such as line monitors and protocol analyzers, can be used regardless of the platform. The high cost of this equipment may be difficult to justify if its sole purpose is to gain insight into commercial software components. On the other hand, this equipment is often available in labs that perform hardware integration.

Perhaps the most common snooping tool is *tcpdump*. This tool has been ported to nearly all modern operating systems that support the TCP/IP protocol. Many variants of this program exist for different operating systems including *etherfind* for SunOS, *snoop* for Sun Solaris, *WinDump* for Microsoft's Windows 95/98/NT, and *sniffit* for Linux. These are powerful tools that allow you to see the details of the underlying network protocols across which software components communicate. If these programs are unavailable for your computer, try searching software archives or use a Web-search engine to locate a *tcpdump* variant for your system.

In the probing example in the previous section, we noted that the user name and password appeared in clear text during execution of the *login* program. If a third party could discover the user name and password combination, he or she could gain unauthorized access to the system. It is possible that the *telnet* client and the *telnet* server daemon will protect this information. We could not determine this during our probing session, since we were only examining system calls on the host system. However, by observing the conversation between the *telnet*

Sample Tools Used for Snooping on POSIX-Based Systems

tcpdump, etherfind, snoop, sniffit: capture and inspect network packets.

ipcs: report inter-process communication facilities status.

ttsnoop: interactively monitors ToolTalk message traffic, pattern matching, and client function calls.

Sample Tools Used for Snooping on Microsoft OSs

DDESpy: allows you to view information about the status of dynamic data exchange (DDE) conversations, included with Microsoft Visual Studio *winsock* tool.

Filemon: a GUI/device driver combination that monitors and displays all file system activity on a system. It has filtering and search capabilities for examining how applications use files and DLLs, or tracking down problems in system or application configurations. Under Windows NT/2K *Filemon* can also be used to monitor named pipe activity.

Regmon: a Registry spying utility that watches and displays information on system-wide registry accesses as they occur.

Portmon: a GUI/device driver combination that monitors and displays all serial and parallel port activity on system.

MTS Spy: attaches to MTS processes and captures information such as transaction events, thread events, resource events, object, method, and user events.

client and the *telnet* daemon, we can learn if the user name and password can be read by an eavesdropper:

1. Using the *snoop* command under Sun Solaris, establish a point-to-point snooping session between the workstation running *telnet* and the log-in server:

```
snoop -x 54 labpc.sei.cmu.edu apollo.sei.cmu.edu
Using device /dev/le (promiscuous mode)
```

The *snoop* command generates a great deal of information so it is a good idea to save this output to a file for later review.

2. Use *telnet* to connect to the server and log in.

3. Search the output for the strings used in the *login* process. Your output should appear as follows (again, details have been removed for brevity):

```
Packet 1: apollo -> labpc TELNET R port=2785
  0: 0d0a 0d0a 5375 6e4f 5320 352e 360d 0a0d    ....SunOS 5.6...
 16: 000d 0a0d 00                                 .....

Packet 2: apollo -> labpc TELNET R port=2785
  0: fffb 01ff fb03 fffd 016c 6f67 696e 3a20    .........login:
```

```
Packet 3: labpc -> apollo TELNET C port=2785 shissam
   0: 7368 6973 7361 6d0d 0000                       shissam...

Packet 4: apollo -> labpc TELNET R port=2785 Password:
   0: 5061 7373 776f 7264 3a20                       Password:

Packet 5: labpc -> apollo TELNET C port=2785 my1paSS
   0: 6d79 3170 6153 530d 0000                       my1paSS...
```

We can see the communication exchange in the *snoop* output: the server "says" something and the client "responds." In the first two packets, our server prompts the client to log in. This is the same login: prompt we saw in the trace of the *login* program when we ran the *truss* command on the internet daemon in the previous section. Although most of the data that appears in the network packets is understandable, there is a sequence of data in Packet 2 fffb 01ff fb03 fffd 01 that is not easily decoded. By reading the specification for the *telnet* protocol[2], you can decode this sequence as part of the *telnet* protocol (a series of escape sequences). Packets 3 through 5 complete the initial log-in sequence. It is during this exchange that we can see the user name and password passed in the clear between the *telnet* client and server.

There are a few things that you should learn from this example, beyond the fact that *telnet* is not secure. First, understanding the interactions between components may require more than one tool and more than one technique. In this example, we used both probing and snooping techniques to determine that *telnet* is insecure. Second, diagnosing a problem or understanding an interaction often requires knowledge about the underlying protocols. Access to protocol documentation and specifications is needed to understand the semantics of component communication. In cases when this documentation is unavailable or ineffective, a significant amount of guesswork is required, as well as experiments aimed just at understanding the protocol.

11.5 Spoofing

The tools and techniques discussed so far have been nonintrusive—discounting the Heisenberg uncertainty principle.[3] Spoofing, like snooping, can yield insight into a component's interfaces and behavior. Unlike snooping, spoofing allows

---

[2] J. Postel. Apr-03-1972. (Updates RFC0158) (Updated by RFC0435) (Also RFC0139, RFC0158)

[3] In 1927, Heisenberg formulated what is popularly referred to as the uncertainty principle: we cannot know both the *momentum* and *position* of a particle. The more precisely we determine one, the less we can know about the other. Similarly, you cannot observe a component's behavior without affecting its behavior. Interaction with monitoring tools, by necessity, must use computer resources and alter the behavior of the component being observed.

you to become an actor in a system; for example, to interpose yourself between two components.

Spoofing methods are not always specific to any particular operating system but it is difficult to find any tool that is common to all of them. SATAN (Security Administrator Tool for Analyzing Networks) is a security analysis tool that is also considered a spoofing tool. SATAN is designed to assess the vulnerability of a system by stressing many of the well-known interfaces and services common to POSIX-based and Microsoft operating systems. It works by acting like a would-be hacker and attacking potentially vulnerable areas of a system. In contrast to the broad concern of SATAN, spoofing tools developed for gaining insight into component-based systems are more likely to be more narrowly focused.

An easy interface to spoof is the interface between a Web browser and an HTTP server. These two software components communicate using HTTP, a TCP/IP-based protocol. In the following illustration we show how to spoof an HTTP server into thinking it is communicating with a Web browser:

1. Using the *telnet* command, connect to any HTTP server:

```
telnet www.netscape.com 80
Trying 205.188.247.66...
Connected to vwww-va2.netscape.com.
Escape character is '^]'.
```

2. From *telnet*, type an HTTP command requesting a document with a name you do not expect to be found. You must enter a carriage return (↵) twice as required by the HTTP specification

```
GET /myfavorite.html HTTP/1.0↵
↵
```

3. Observe the response from the HTTP server

line response

```
1:    HTTP/1.1 404 Not found
2:    Server: Netscape-Enterprise/3.6 SP1
3:    Date: Sat, 18 Sep 1999 01:10:26 GMT
4:    Content-type: text/html
5:    Content-length: 207
6:    Connection: close
7:
8:    <TITLE>Not Found</TITLE><H1>Not Found</H1>
      The requested object does not exist on this
      server. The link you followed is either outdated,
      inaccurate, or the server has been instructed
      not to let you have it.
```

The response from the HTTP server is fairly straightforward. Line 1 contains the HTTP response code, 404, or the infamous "not found" message. Lines 2–6 contain the MIME response header providing server and content information, and line 8 contains the HTML content. This is precisely the data that any Web browser receives when requesting an invalid document from an HTTP server.

Try repeating this procedure, but this time request a document that you know is on the HTTP server (GET / HTTP/1.0 is a universally accepted HTTP request) and compare the HTTP response code and the MIME response header with that seen earlier.

These examples illustrate how programs like *telnet* can be used immediately to masquerade as a different program, such as a Web browser. However, *telnet* cannot be used in every case: the component protocol may be binary (which is difficult to enter at a keyboard), the protocol may be complex, or the nature of the diagnosis might be repetitious and may need to be performed over long periods of time. In these cases, it may be necessary to develop scaffolding using higher level programming and scripting languages to spoof the component under investigation. We can duplicate the earlier spoofing illustration, for example, using the Perl scripting language to automate our masquerading Web browser. The simple Perl script shown in Figure 11-3 is designed to report the total time elapsed to connect, request, and respond with the HTTP server.

Spoofing a commercial software component requires imagination backed by in-depth knowledge of the interfaces and protocols used by the component. However, spoofing can provide a tremendous return on the initial investment of time and effort. Specifically, spoofing can produce:

- A deeper understanding of the component interface and its use of underlying protocols, leading to further insights into how to integrate the component.

- Example programs and harnesses that can be used to test the component, and possibly other components, for needed functionality.

```
#!/usr/bin/perl -w
use IO::Socket;
$then = time;
$remote =
  IO::Socket::INET->new
  (Proto => "tcp",
  PeerAddr => "www.netscape.com",
  PeerPort => "80");
unless ($remote) { die "cannot connect" }
$remote -> autoflush(1);
print $remote "GET / HTTP/1.0\n\n";
while ( <$remote> ) { ; }
$now = time;
print "Access time was ", $now - $then, " seconds\n";
close $remote;
```

Figure 11-3 Simple Perl Web browser.

- The ability to isolate failures to a single component in a multi-component system.

11.6   Static Program Analysis

Probing, snooping, and spoofing focus on the dynamic or runtime behavior of a component. This section describes tools used to determine a program's contents, structure, and logic by examining its executable file image. These range from simple programs, such as the UNIX *strings* utility that can extract ASCII strings from a binary image, to decompilers that can reconstruct the original program source. These tools have no logical equivalent in custom software development, since there is no need to reconstruct program logic when the source is available.

BINARY VIEWERS AND EDITORS

There are several simple but effective tools for viewing and editing the binary form of the component. Besides the bits to bytes representation dictated by the machine architecture, binary viewers and editors ignore any implied or explicit record formats. Programs such as *od* typically found under POSIX-based operating systems, *hexdump* available under Linux, *Hexedit* available for Microsoft's MS-DOS, and *HEdit* for Microsoft's Windows NT/95/98 are examples of binary viewers and editors. Some of these tools, specifically *Hexedit* and *HEdit*, allow users to modify binary files. An example of a hexadecimal and ASCII dump produced by *hexdump* is shown in Figure 11-4.

```
hexdump NervousText.class
00000000: CA FE BA BE 00 03 00 2D 00 99 08 00 5D 08 00 64
J~:>...-....]..d
00000010: 08 00 65 08 00 66 08 00 95 08 00 96 07 00 61 07
..e..f........a.
    :
000002A0: 74 3E 01 00 04 43 6F 64 65 01 00 07 48 6F 74 4A
t>...Code...HotJ
000002B0: 61 76 61 01 00 0F 4C 69 6E 65 4E 75 6D 62 65 72
ava...LineNumber
000002C0: 54 61 62 6C 65 01 00 12 4C 6A 61 76 61 2F 6C 61
Table...Ljava/la
    :
```

Figure 11-4   *Hexdump* output of `NervousText.class`.

Sample Binary Viewers/Editors on POSIX-Based Systems

strings: find printable strings in an object or binary file.

od: generates, by default, an octal dump of a file.

hexdump: *hexdump* is a utility filter which displays the files in a user specified format, hexadecimal, by default.

Sample Binary Viewers/Editors on Microsoft OSs

Hexedit: *hexedit* is a Curses-based Hex editor.

HEdit: a hexadecimal editor for binary files. It displays the contents of any binary file, including text files, in the hexadecimal format with the corresponding ASCII characters for readable symbols in a separate pane.

The file shown is `NervousText.class`—the compiled, executable form of the *NervousText* applet, a Java demonstration applet delivered with Java Software Development Kit (JDK). This applet can be found under the directory `demo/applets/NervousText` and executed using the *appletviewer* program, also included in the JDK. The output of this applet, shown in Figure 11-5(a), consists of the string "Java Development Kit 1.2" moving about in a nervous fashion.

The output from *hexdump* consists of three fields: the hex offset into the file, the sequence of bytes found at that offset (also in hex), and the ASCII representation of the bytes. In the `NervousText.class` file, the string `"HotJava"` can be found at offset `0x2AC`. To see how this string is used in this applet, remove the line beginning with `<param name=text ...>` from `example1.html` in the *NervousText* directory and re-run the applet. The applet should now appear as shown in Figure 11-5(b).

```
cd c:\jdk1.2\demo\applets\NervousText
appletviewer example1.html
```

(a)   (b)

Figure 11-5   Execution of *NervousText* applet.

To significantly change the default behavior of the *NervousText* applet, we need to have its source code. However, simply changing the string that *NervousText* displays in the absence of the `<param>` tag could be accomplished without having access to the source code. Using the binary editor, *HEdit*, on the class file `NervousText.class`, locate offset `0x370` and replace `"HotJava"` with a different string of the same length (7 bytes). Figure 11-6 illustrates the use of *HEdit* to replace `"HotJava"` with `"SEI CMU"`. After the modified file is saved and closed, re-run the *NervousText* applet. The string `"SEI CMU"` now appears dancing nervously in the window.

This simple technique works only when the size of the file is not modified. Indeed, "hacking" binary code can result in any number of subtle consequences. For example, if you insert bytes to extend the length of the string, the JVM generates a class format exception resulting from an illegal constant pool type. The constant pool is a table of structures representing various string constants, class and interface names, field names, and other constants within the class file structure and its substructures. The error occurs because we attempted to expand this constant into the start position for the next constant in the table. Since the ASCII character entered is not a valid constant pool type (these are restricted to values between 1 and 12 corresponding to types such as integer and string) the resulting exception occurs. To extend a string successfully, all the offsets in this table would need to be adjusted—making this method of modifying the class file rather inefficient, to say nothing of dangerous. Of course, the string easily can be shortened by padding it with null characters. For Java classes, manipulating string and numerical constants is perhaps the extent to which this technique can be applied practically. It also may be possible to change the bytecodes used to encode operations, but because of the difficulty, this should be considered a measure of last resort.

We actually have used this technique when, just prior to a demo, we discovered that an object that was displayed in "green" should in fact have been displayed in "red." As the demo was deployed on a demonstration machine, and the Java

---

Hedit NervousText.class

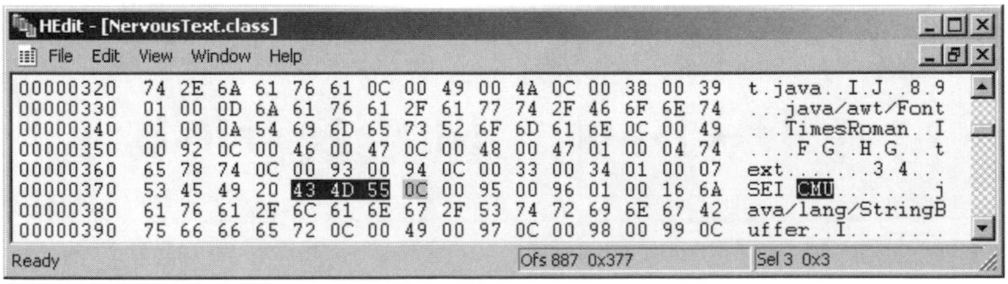

Figure 11-6 HEdit editing session on `NervousText.class`.

development environment was not available, we edited the binary class to make this modification. We are not particularly proud of this story, and we are not advocating that developers edit binary code. In our case, this was only a last resort. In general, binary editing should be used only to confirm some hypothesis about a component so that a vendor might make an appropriate repair. This stipulation becomes more pertinent when we use more powerful tools for reconstructing program logic from raw binary: disassemblers and decompilers.

DISASSEMBLERS

Unlike generic binary editors such as *hexdump*, disassemblers understand the internal format of the binary file provided as input. Disassemblers are generally targeted to a specific computing architecture such as SPARC, i386, or Motorola architectures. Disassemblers have knowledge of the operations supported by the computing architecture (for example, op codes, register size, and byte order). Some disassemblers are also targeted to a specific language. For example, Sun's JDK comes complete with a Java class file disassembler, *javap*.

In the previous section, we discovered that the applet *NervousText* looks for a parameter called `text`. Any value assigned to `text` is the value displayed by *NervousText* when it executes. We could see this by looking at the applet tag in the HTML file (that is, `example1.html`). We also learned that in the absence of the `text` parameter, *NervousText* displayed the string `"HotJava"`. From this behavior we should deduce that within the applet there should be a logic test for this parameter. However, it is difficult to ascertain if and where this test occurs by reading the bytecodes contained in the class file. Another approach is to disassemble the *NervousText* applet using *javap*.

The results of disassembling the *NervousText* class file are shown in Figure 11-7. In the disassembled output, a reference to `"HotJava"` is found within the applet's `init()` method (near bytecode offset 18). Also in `init()` is the `"text"` string just prior to a call to the `getParameter()` method (in the instruction at bytecode offset 4). Recall from the previous example that `"text"` is the name of the parameter found in the `<param>` applet tag. By interpreting the generated pseudo language we can see where the method is called to retrieve a value for the parameter text that is stored in the field `banner` (bytecode offset 7). We can see a test for null, `ifnonnull`, and a jump past the code segment that puts the string `"HotJava"` in the same `banner` field (bytecode offset 14). It is fairly clear from analyzing the disassembled class file that a test does occur in the applet initialization method.

Even with disassemblers, interpretation can still be a laborious process. Further, the reassembly of the disassembled component may be impossible, preventing modification or extension of the program logic (again, for testing purposes only). This is where a decompiler comes in handy.

```
% javap -c NervousText
       :
Method void init()
   0 aload_0
   1 aload_0
   2 ldc #6 <String "text">
   4 invokevirtual #32 <Method java.lang.String
       getParamter(java.lang.String)>
   7 putfield #26 <Field java.lang.String banner>
  10 aload_0
  11 getfield #26 <Field java.lang.String banner>
  14 ifnonnull 23
  17 aload_0
  18 ldc #1 <String "HotJava">
  20 putfield #26 <Field java.lang.String banner>
  23 aload_0
       :
```

Figure 11-7   Disassembled *NervousText* applet.

DECOMPILERS

Decompilation is the process of reconstituting a software component's source code from its executable form. Decompilation is the Holy Grail of software component visibility since, once source code is available, the problem of diagnosing and correcting component behavior is reduced to one of software development. Although decompilation is not new, the effectiveness of decompilers is limited by the amount of information lost in the compilation process [Cifuentes 94][Cifuentes+ 95]. Java, on the other hand, has a rich semantic bytecode representation that makes decomposition feasible. A number of Java bytecode decompilers are available, including *DeJaVu*, *Jad*, and *Mocha*.

We applied the Java decompiler, *Jad*, to the binary code for the *NervousText* applet. The results are shown in Figure 11-8. Even if you are not familiar with Java, you should have no trouble in reading this code. Moreover, once you have the reconstituted source code you can make arbitrarily complex modifications. We have used decompilation to debug a vendor-supplied component that handled public and private keys (refer to Chapter 14 for more details on public/private key infrastructure). In this case, we determined that the component was testing for object equality rather than content equivalence. After reconstructing the source, we implemented the correct equality operation, and thereby proved to ourselves and, more importantly the vendor, the source of the error. Our bug fix found its way into a future release of this component.

```
jad NervousText.class
    :
public void init()
{
    banner = getParameter("text");
    if(banner == null)
        banner = "HotJava";
    int i = banner.length();
    bannerChars = new char[i];
    banner.getChars(0, banner.length(), bannerChars, 0);
    threadSuspended = false;
    resize(15 * (i + 1), 50);
    setFont(new Font("TimesRoman", 1, 36));
    addMouseListener(this);
}
    :
```

Figure 11-8   Decompiled *NervousText* applet.

Sample Disassemblers

javap: java class file disassembler included with the Sun JDK.

dis: object code disassembler utility under UNIX.

IDA Pro: a multi-processor, multi-OS, interactive disassembler for Ada from DataRescue.

Windows Source, Sourcer: two products from V Communications that work in tandem to produce commented disassemblies of Windows executables, dynamic link libraries (DLLs), device drivers, 32-bit virtual drive drivers (VxDs) and OS/2 files.

Sample Decompilers

jad: the fast Java decompiler, free for noncommercial use.

SourceAgain: commercial Java class decompiler from Ahpah Software, Inc.

DeJaVu: available as part of the Object Engineering Workbench from Innovative Software.

WingDis: a Java decompiler available from WingSoft.

Mocha: *Mocha*, the first and most widely known Java decompiler can be freely obtained over the Web although it has not been supported since the death of its creator, Hanpeter van Vliet in 1996.

11.7 Summary

Components pose a significant challenge for software developers accustomed to the feeling of omniscience that accompanies owning source code. Component integrators instead face complex and often inscrutable components, and the need to uncover their mysteries through experimentation. Coping with this challenge requires that integrators possess the qualities of ingenuity, persistence, and well-developed problem solving skills. Integrators also require considerable expertise in operating system tools, network protocols, and a variety of reverse engineering techniques.

Although we have presented a range of techniques in the guise of debugging, these techniques are more properly tools of discovery. This discovery process lies in the nether region between scientific method, old fashioned debugging, and plain old hacking, but it is an integral part of designing component-based systems, and will remain so until computer scientists can describe adequately all of the necessary properties of components in a formal interface specification.

11.8 Discussion Questions

1. Unfortunately, *telnet* has been used in the past to hack into systems by exploiting the *sendmail* program and the *login* program. Is the use of *telnet* to obtain visibility into commercial software components different from these cases of hacking? Why or why not?

2. The simple Perl Web browser shown in Figure 11-3 does not indicate to the HTTP server which specific Web browser it is. How would you modify that script so that the HTTP server would be spoofed into believing the Perl browser is a version of Internet Explorer or Netscape Communicator? How would you confirm you successfully spoofed the HTTP server?

PART TWO

CASE STUDY

*I pass with relief from the tossing sea of Cause and Theory to the firm
ground of Result and Fact.*
—Winston Churchill

12

The DIRS Case Study

The bravest are surely those who have the clearest vision of what is
before them, glory and danger alike, and yet notwithstanding,
go out to meet it.
—Thucydides

This chapter introduces a case study based on our own experiences. The project, the Distributed Image Retrieval System (DIRS), began in March 1997. Therefore, many of the technical difficulties that are the grist of this case study have since been addressed by component vendors, and may therefore appear anachronistic. However, as the reader might expect, market dynamics ensure an ample supply of new difficulties. The details of the problem may change, but the essence remains. Our involvement with DIRS actually predates March 1997, but work performed during this period best illustrates the practices and techniques described in this book.

As the name implies, DIRS is an image storage and retrieval system. Images are stored on optical platters using a commercial component. The index to this data is stored in a relational database. Figure 12-1 shows some of the major components of the system. In March of 1997, DIRS was operational at 36 separate locations within a large, loosely coupled organization.

The version of the DIRS software deployed in 1997 was principally implemented in C++ and used software components that were proprietary to the system integrator. All in all, the DIRS system was a good example of a deployed prototype—its architecture had never been particularly well defined, and little attention had been paid to ensuring that DIRS could be adapted to new user needs or new technologies. Requirements and implementation both had been developed incrementally over a period of years, and the resulting system was extremely fragile, and therefore difficult and expensive to modify.

In March 1997, the DIRS management embarked on an ambitious system re-design and modernization effort. As in similar efforts in other organizations, a heavy reliance on commercial components figured prominently in the design strategy. The project was determined to base their overall design on such emerging

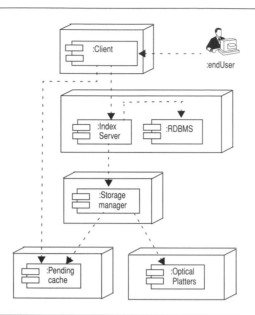

Figure 12-1   Legacy DIRS system.

technologies as Web browsers and HTTP servers, Java, CORBA, and public/ private key cryptography. However, neither management nor development team had significant experience with these technologies in isolation and still less experience in their integration.

The DIRS management engaged us to improve the ability of the design team to evaluate commercial components, and to improve the connection between component evaluation and system design. The main objectives of our work were to introduce practices that would:

- Reduce the risk inherent in using emerging and still-unstable component technologies by helping the development team obtain relevant "just-in-time" expertise.

- Ensure that a design emerged that made maximum and effective use of components while preserving fall-back positions in case of component failures.

- Expose trade-off decisions to scrutiny; for example, the use of vendor-specific component features versus generic features.

While we provided some guidance to project management, we primarily worked with the development team. Before too long, we were fully integrated with the design team.

12.1   Sources of Complexity in DIRS

At a glance, DIRS appears to be a relatively simple system. However, in addition to its functional requirements, DIRS had to scale up to:

- Allow reading and writing of very large image data
- Support a large number of local and geographically dispersed users
- Support many simultaneous transactions
- Support an open-ended variety of image formats
- Enforce multiple levels of secure access and confidentiality
- Provide adequate, interactive-speed performance
- Ensure ease of maintenance and upgrade.

Another source of complexity was that DIRS had to accommodate a variety of site-specific business processes. For example, some locations using DIRS expected configuration management for images to be delivered as part of the system. Other locations expected to use external configuration management tools. In addition to functional variations, each site had incorporated idiosyncratic and frequently inconsistent conventions for managing data. For example, image and index data was inconsistently defined at each site. Worse still, image names encoded information about the location of an image on optical platters. As a result, a DIRS user looking for a particular image could not find it without knowing its location. This had not been a major source of complexity for the original system. However, as part of the modernized system, DIRS required interoperability between installations. This "requirement," incidentally, was a direct consequence of the fanfare associated with commercial components and their application to enterprise-level Web "Intranets" and "Extranets."

12.2   A False Start

The management response to the need for a replacement system was to initiate a major rewrite of the now-overtaxed DIRS system. The new effort was intended to be a complete replacement of the existing system. Since the legacy relational database scheme was not normalized, a complete redesign of the relational database was undertaken. The new database modeled all key business processes and system management information in addition to providing the index of images stored on optical mass storage devices.

Although this effort represented a direct and honest approach to solving the DIRS problem, it failed for a practical reason: there were insufficient resources, both in time and money, to support this complete rewrite. For example, the revised DIRS database scheme required a rewrite of all DIRS applications. Thus, after significant effort, and despite considerable consternation on the part of development and management teams, DIRS found itself in a still more critical situation than it had been in before the redesign began.

12.3   Regrouping: The "DeepWeb" Approach

The DIRS management convened a workshop to identify alternative courses of action. The overall goal was to resolve the dilemma of the need to provide users with better services, and the reality that the existing system could not accommodate the needed changes within the strictures of time and budget. Six major design alternatives emerged from this workshop. One of these, later known as "DeepWeb," was selected. DeepWeb had three major premises:

1. There are many more consumers of information than suppliers, and therefore DIRS should focus its attention on making data consumption easier.

2. Web browsers and HTTP servers would provide low-cost, flexible, distributed, and "open" access to central DIRS resources.

3. A middleware-based integration infrastructure allows a group to deploy an initial DIRS Intranet using existing functionality. It would also allow management to replace legacy code gradually with commercial components.

These premises appealed to a wide range of stakeholders. Moreover, the arguments were strengthened by a number of circumstances. The Intranet argument, for example, resonated well with the browser and "thin client" bandwagon that was careening through the IT landscape. The promise of low-cost distribution, network computing, and "write-once-run-anywhere" applications were intoxicating to managers beleaguered by excessive maintenance costs.

The argument to focus on data consumers rather than suppliers also found fertile ground. The project had, for various reasons, focused primarily on the needs of data administrators rather than users. This focus was not conducive to building broad-based user support for the system. Such support would be vital in building a case for a continuation of the DIRS project.

The middleware strategy is best described as an attempt to build the component-based equivalent of a "Potemkin Village." Legacy spaghetti-code was to be hidden behind a more modular, component-based interface. Once this interface was complete, parts could be replaced by commercially available components without disrupting DIRS client programs.

These arguments and the DeepWeb approach carried the day. As a result, the DIRS project team embarked on an effort that represented a dramatic departure from their experience.

12.4   Implications of DeepWeb

DeepWeb required an architecture that supported existing as well as replacement functionality. Moreover, an a priori constraint had been imposed that "Web" technologies including Web browsers and HTTP servers, Java, and CORBA would play a pivotal role in this architecture. The HTTP-based intranet would provide client access to application servers, while CORBA would handle server-to-server communication and wrapping of legacy components.

Figure 12-2 depicts the architecture defined as a starting point for DeepWeb. It describes the state of the DIRS design at the start of our involvement with the project. DeepWeb assumes a three-tiered architecture that distributes system functionality across front-end (client), middle, and back-end computers. The middle tier supported business logic processing. This design does not specify the mechanisms used to communicate between the client and the middle tier, and between the middle and back-end servers, but it does suggest that there is no direct communication between the client and back-end servers.

From a project perspective, DeepWeb required an alternative management approach. In place of longer running assignments with broadly defined statements of work, management shifted to short-term, sharply focused iterations. This introduced a sense of urgency on the part of the development team and pushed them to "show results" at the end of each short-term development cycle.

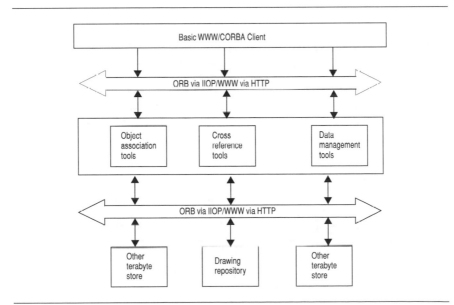

Figure 12-2   Initial DeepWeb architecture.

Web Browsers: Universal Paradigm or Siren's Song?

Not since the advent of software development toolkits has a technology captured the imagination of the software development community like browsers. Browsers provide the interfaces for an increasingly broad range of applications, from Internet sites intended for entertainment to large, enterprise information systems. While browsers have done a great deal to encourage the development of distributed systems, one has to wonder—at what cost? Has the rabid expansion of Internet browsers into all manner of distributed applications gone beyond the limits of good sense?

Ulysses and the Sirens by John Waterhouse, 1891.

An often applied rationale for the use of browser-based interfaces is that end users are accustomed to using them. This is only one of many misconceptions about browsers including:

- Browser applications are inherently "cross-everything" applications.
- Browsers simplify the development of any distributed system.
- Browser-based systems are always easier to install and upgrade.
- Browsers have robust and well-considered security models.
- Poor performance in browsers is a result of network latency.

A browser-based design may be appropriate if the requirements of the system conform naturally to a browser infrastructure. For strictly hypertext systems, Internet browsers are an ideal solution. However, a browser-based design is not appropriate when the desktop client has a large, complex user interface and requires access to local machine resources, or when performance or security are critical issues.

The use of a browser-based infrastructure will influence and limit the overall architecture and design of your distributed system. As such, it is critical that this is an informed, considered decision.

— rCs

While laudable, this did not match well with the overall DeepWeb strategy that focused on establishing an architectural infrastructure for migrating from existing functionality to better capabilities. Decisions frequently arose that involved choosing between a design path that would result in immediate and easily demonstrable progress, and one that had better long-term implications but was not easily demonstrable to end users. On the whole, this produced a healthy level of creative tension in the project and quite a few spirited design meetings.

Confounding this pressure to "show results" was the general lack of familiarity of the project team with the capabilities and liabilities of the underlying component technologies, and the implications of even the most obvious architectural alternatives these technologies presented. Just as serious was the fact that these underlying technologies were still emerging and were therefore quite unstable. This instability was a two-edged sword: successive releases had more capability, but their quality was always suspect, often for good reason.

12.5 Commitments

By June of 1997 a number of decisions had been made that would strongly influence ensuing efforts. In Chapter 9 we noted that accumulating decisions require an increasingly normative approach to component selection. In the next two sections, we summarize key decisions and their normative implications.

STRATEGIC DECISIONS

Incremental Development.   An incremental development approach was adopted, which was a radical departure for the development team. Operationally, the goal was to deploy new functionality every 90–120 days. The project took this approach to deliver functionality more quickly while still reducing development risks.

Componentization.   The redesigned system would encapsulate functionality into replaceable components. These components would be implemented as CORBA servers, with their interfaces fully described in the CORBA Interface Definition Language (IDL). This preliminary step was necessary to eventually replace legacy code with commercial components. The use of CORBA would expedite the transition from the existing two-tiered client/server model to a three-tiered architecture.

Web Technology.   The design would use Web technology to support current users and to expand the DIRS user base. Web models for distribution, installation, and upgrades would minimize client disruption. Browser-based interfaces would provide users with a familar interface and make DIRS more "user friendly."

Commercial Components.   The design would use commercial software components wherever possible, especially to implement the DIRS infrastructure. The management believed that components would boost developer productivity and improve system functionality at the same time. Limited time and budget reinforced this belief.

Evolution.   DIRS was a large system, with many users and evolving requirements. The design had to accommodate new users, new types of image data, new business processes, and new patterns of integration with other external (non-DIRS) systems.

Standards-Based Architecture.   The redesigned DIRS system would employ solutions based on industry standards wherever possible and practical. The design team hoped that using real and de facto standards such as HTTP, IIOP, and JDBC would make components more replacable. The team also hoped to use supporting tools, methods, and products developed around these standards.

TECHNOLOGY SELECTION

In addition to the strategic decisions mentioned above, the design team made a number of preliminary product and technology selections, as shown in Figure 12-3. Although no formal evaluation had yet been performed, the design team presumed

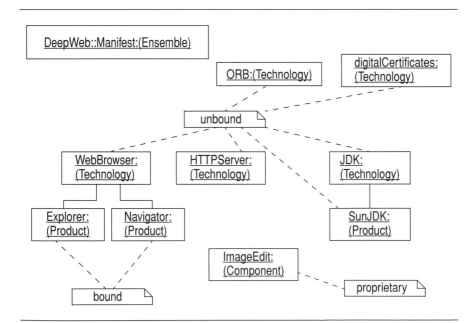

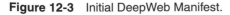

Figure 12-3   Initial DeepWeb Manifest.

that each technology would play a specific role in the redesigned DIRS system. For example, the design would use CORBA to integrate legacy C++ applications, HTTP servers and Web browsers would deliver content to the end-user, Java applets would provide dynamic content within the browser, applets would be digitally signed to establish trust, and JDBC would be used to communicate with a relational database management system such as Oracle.

It was at this point that we entered the picture, and it was on this path that the design team now embarked, possibly without an entirely clear vision of the future, but one, we hoped, that was not overly optimistic.

12.6   Deceptive Simplicity

Functionally, DIRS is quite simple. In one generic use case, users query for an image, the image is transferred to their workstation, they edit the image, and submit the updated image back to the system for subsequent quality assurance steps. The security requirements are not atypical for information systems, and do not seem at first glance to be overly challenging:

1. Authorization—only authorized users are allowed to update and retrieve images.
2. Auditing—all updates and retrievals are tracked, and can be reviewed later.
3. Confidentiality—all data exchanged between users and DIRS must remain private.

This seemed simple enough. Authorization is basically a business logic function applying a user's access rights to an asset (in this case, an image). If the user has the right to read an asset, retrieval is allowed. Further, if the user is permitted to write, then an update is allowed. Auditing (another simple security concept) is a business logic function which makes a record each time a user accesses (reads and/or writes) an asset. And finally, confidentiality is the application of a mechanism to keep information private between two parties, in this case between a user and the system. However, the complexity hidden in the above generic use case becomes more apparent when we consider the preliminary technology commitments. Before discussing these complexities, we review the major commitments (refer to the manifest in Figure 12-3):

- Both Netscape Communicator and Microsoft Internet Explorer would be supported as the primary client interfaces to DIRS.
- DIRS would use ImageEdit for image editing and quality assurance. The user community was already trained to use this component, and this was the only component capable of editing the size and format of DIRS images.
- Since Web browsers already supported digital certificates for identifying users, the design team wanted to make use of certificate-based mechanisms for "single sign-on" security services.

We can now construct a technology-specific instantiation of the generic use case described above. A user contacts the DIRS system with a browser. An HTTP server authenticates the user and grants permission to retrieve and possibly edit images. Images are then confidentially and reliably transmitted over a wide-area network (WAN) for editing by ImageEdit. The modified image is then returned to the DIRS system using the same reliable, confidential connection. Still sound simple? Perhaps, until the following details are considered.

THE HTTP SERVER AUTHENTICATES USERS

The design team had not selected an HTTP server, but the team was leaning toward the Netscape Suitespot Web Server since it was already under a corporate licensing agreement and available at little to no additional cost. Which authentication mechanism? Given the strong desire to use certificate-based mechanisms, public key infastructure (PKI) seemed to be the best choice. But this only resulted in further questions: Would the same certificate-based identification and authentication mechanism work with both Navigator and Explorer? Would DIRS be able to interchange Netscape's Suitespot with another HTTP server should it become impractical to use Suitespot? This ensemble is illustrated in Figure 12-4. (We have simplified the blackboard by having all three certificate sources share the same credential. Strictly speaking, this is a modeling "no no.")

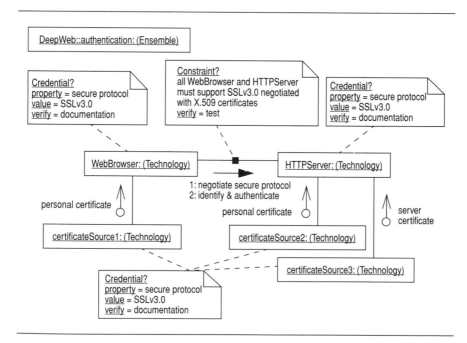

Figure 12-4   Blackboard for authentication.

We explore the questions posed here in depth in the chapters on the basic Web ensemble (Chapter 13), the application of certificate technology (Chapter 14), and finally the application of certificate technology and the basic Web ensemble in a secure environment (Chapter 17).

VERY LARGE IMAGES

Images on DIRS were typically 10–200 megabytes. The legacy system used a proprietary application protocol over TCP/IP. The image travels from the image store to the client workspace over a local area network (LAN). A wide area network (WAN) environment is much more challenging, though, with respect to performance, reliability, and security. Which application protocol should serve large images? Should those images be pulled by the client, or perhaps pushed by servers (for security reasons)? Figure 12-5 captures the ensemble for large image transfers. Chapter 18 specifically looks at the performance issues surrounding the transfer of large images over a WAN using a variety of protocols.

CONFIDENTIAL DATA TRANSFER

How should DIRS achieve confidentiality? A variety of mechanisms could be used, such as encryption or privately operated networks. However, encrypting data on a public WAN seemed to be the most cost-effective mechanism to secure server and client transmission. Which encryption would be used? Would the encryption be implemented in software, hardware, or both? How long would the data need to remain private? How much overhead for encrypting and decrypting

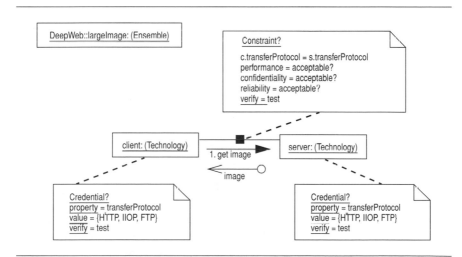

Figure 12-5   Blackboard for large image ensemble.

would users tolerate? To some extent, these issues are implied in the authentication ensemble in Figure 12-4.

Issues of confidentiality appear throughout the case study, but the most relevant are addressed in Chapters 14, 15, and 17. Issues of confidentiality were sufficiently complex and important to justify our investigating a variety of design alternatives, including hardware-based support for confidentiality (Chapter 20) and the development of a custom ensemble (Chapter 19).

RELIABLE DATA TRANSFER

Although it was understood that the underlying transport mechanism would be TCP/IP (a reliable protocol), what application protocol would be used? How would that application protocol be integrated seamlessly so that data transfer happens transparently to the user? Would the protocol be HTTP, FTP, IIOP, or something else? HTTP is pervasive in Web-based content delivery. However, the size of the byte stream for these images and the question of MIME conversion brought into question the reliability and performance of HTTP. File Transfer Protocol (FTP) has been proven and has withstood the test of time for moving vast amounts of data over WANs, but is typically used as an interactive protocol. FTP can be automated, but it does not present a convenient abstraction for programmers. IIOP, on the other hand, is easier for developers to use, but there were questions about its maturity, and about the quality of commercial object request brokers (ORBs). As with questions about confidentiality, we chose to combine reliability with the large image transfer ensemble (Figure 12-5). Chapter 18 examines three of the possible values for the transfer protocol (that is, HTTP, FTP, or IIOP).

AUTHORIZATION OF RIGHTS

Who is permitted to read and/or write? It was clear that mechanisms for identification and authentication would have to be tied to authorization logic to permit the business logic to control access. Where would the authorization codes and access control lists be stored? Would administration be centrally managed or distributed? The authorization ensemble is illustrated in Figure 12-6. We look at the authorization constraints in secure Web ensemble in Chapter 17, and in the concluding chapter of the case study, Chapter 23.

EDITING IN IMAGEEDIT

The system was required to maintain support for the legacy image editor ImageEdit. It was too costly in terms of retraining and user satisfaction to do otherwise. What would be the programmatic interface between a Web browser and ImageEdit?

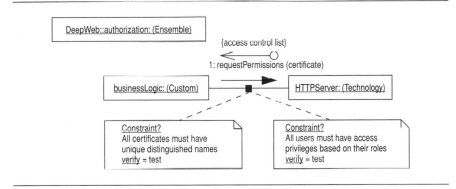

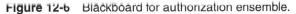

Figure 12-6 Blackboard for authorization ensemble.

Would the browser simply launch the ImageEdit in the same manner it launches JPEG viewers? Would the browser try to "object embed" (that is, plug-in) ImageEdit into the content delivered via HTML? How would the browser hand off the image to ImageEdit? Are there viable commercial alternatives to ImageEdit that work in a browser's environment? The ImageEdit ensemble is shown in Figure 12-7. We look at the integration issues surrounding ImageEdit (essentially launching external applications) in Chapters 13, 17 and 23.

USER CHOSEN WEB BROWSER

DIRS users would be permitted to use either Netscape Communicator or Microsoft Internet Explorer to connect to the DIRS server and interact with the forms, Web content, and images provided by the DIRS server. Would there be

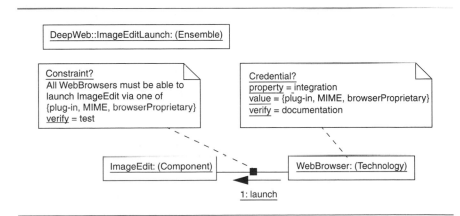

Figure 12-7 Blackboard for ImageEditLaunch ensemble.

applets involved? Would these applets behave in the same manner in the two browser environments? What are the differences between the browsers available and they way they handle HTML content? We explore what it means to be browser independent throughout the case study, but most specifically in Chapters 13, 15, 17, and 23.

12.7 Summary

The DIRS project, a distributed image retrieval and storage system, is used for the case study discussed in this book. The modernization effort adopted commercial components. Even though the technical details may be different, the challenges confronting the DIRS project typify the same challenges faced today by projects that aggressively use commercial software components.

12.8 For Further Reading

An in-depth discussion of technical issues relevant to incorporating Web technology as part of a component-based system is described in Seacord and Hissam's "Browsers for Distributed Systems" [Seacord+ 98]. This paper was, in fact, inspired by our involvement with the DIRS project.

12.9 Discussion Questions

1. Was the choice of a Web-based design an appropriate one for this system? What are the advantages and disadvantages of this approach over more traditional clients?

2. Taken as a whole, were the strategic decisions helpful or hurtful to the future of the project? How might these decisions be changed, and what would be a predictable consequence?

13

Applet Ensemble: The Opening

> *No plan of operation can extend with any prospect of certainty, beyond the first clash with the hostile main force. Only a layman can pretend to trace throughout the course of a campaign the prosecution of a rigid plan, arranged beforehand in all its details and adhered to the last. All successive acts of war are therefore not pre-meditated executions but spontaneous acts guided by military tactics.*
> —Field Marshal Helmuth von Moltke, "the Elder"

This chapter describes the initiating design question. It identifies a main design thread, along with a more promising but speculative contingency plan. The case study describes an attempt to demonstrate the viability of this contingency plan.

13.1   Where are We?

The close of Chapter 12 posed a number of questions about how to transform the unstructured manifest depicted in Figure 12-3 into something more tangible. At root, each of these questions tries to clarify the implications of a number of prior technology commitments.

During the earliest stage of the design, two overall approaches surfaced. The first approach used HTTP server scripting to produce dynamic Web content and to act as a gateway interface between browsers and back-end DIRS services. The second approach used Java applets running in browsers to communicate with DIRS services. Each approach had its strengths and weaknesses:

- The HTTP server scripting approach promised to be easy to implement, at least in the early stages. On the other hand, there were concerns that the approach would lock the project into a proprietary scripting language. This was dangerous considering how fast that segment of the technology market was changing. There were also worries about the long-term maintainability of this approach.

- The applet approach promised to be a flexible way to deliver applications to geographically distributed users. This design also made fewer commitments to vendor-specific features of either Web browsers or HTTP servers. On the other hand, there were serious concerns about the performance and security attributes of this approach.

After much gnashing of teeth, the project architect committed to the server-side approach, while initiating exploration of the feasibility of the applet approach. If its feasibility could be demonstrated before the server-side approach had progressed too far, a switch-over could be effected without impact to the overall project schedule. There was, after all, considerably more development on other aspects of DIRS. The case study begins in earnest from the situation depicted in Figure 13-1. The main design branch was the Server-Side JavaScript (SSJS) ensemble, while the main contingency was the applet ensemble.

13.2   Risk Analysis

Our exploration of the feasibility of the applet ensemble initiates an R^3 discovery cycle (Risk analysis, Realize model problem, Repair). At this point, so little was known that almost everything presented risk. Would the applet take too long to download? Would it introduce security risks? Could a solution be implemented that worked on both Microsoft and Netscape browsers? How would images be transferred from the image store to the applet? In the aggregate, these unknowns presented an unacceptable level of risk. It would have been impractical to attempt to answer all of the above questions at once. Besides, there were many more questions, as well. To begin, we posed the following design question: Does there exist an applet ensemble that works with Netscape and Microsoft browsers, and that allows users to connect to DIRS and to download an image into a third-party image viewing component?

This question is interesting for the issues it does not address—security and performance. In fact, it only asks for a demonstration of the most basic form of

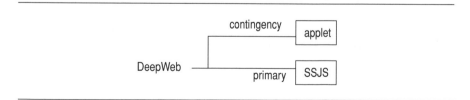

Figure 13-1   Main design path and contingency plan.

feasibility: an existence proof that a collection of components can, in fact, be integrated to achieve a modest objective. With the above question in mind, we moved on to realize a model problem (the second R in R^3).

13.3 Model Problem

We decided to define and implement a use case for retrieving an image from the repository. We did this for several reasons. First, retrieving images is a key capability of the system. Second, image retrieval involves components in all three tiers of the DIRS architecture. Third, the problem was simple to model and communicate. However, there were also several drawbacks. This problem did not, for example, model the transactional properties of the system, but the model problem was deemed sufficient to answer the motivating question, and any further effort would have been inappropriate.

Implementing the image retrieval model solution required that we consider components in all three tiers of the architecture. The middle tier included a component representing the business rule interpreter (BRI). The BRI encapsulated DIRS business rules, supported connections with multiple, simultaneous clients, and coordinated data flow throughout the system. The back-end server contained a component representing the storage manager (SM). This component maintained the actual image files. The client, middle tier, and bottom tiers of the architecture were all hosted on separate platforms. A high bandwidth LAN connected the client to middle tier, although we also considered a low bandwidth WAN. The middle tier to lower tier connection is guaranteed to be a high-bandwidth LAN connection.

After brief discussion, three major options presented themselves, as depicted in Figure 13-2. Each model solution provided an alternate approach for implementing control flow and data flow. In all three, control flow is via the IIOP connections. Our interest in data flow is principally with image retrieval, as movement of images is essential to both the model problem and the actual DIRS system. Additionally, the size of image files stored in DIRS could be extremely large—on the magnitude of 10–200 megabytes. As a result, handling these images is a critical, if not overriding consideration. Each design alternative uses the same components, but in a different way. The first ensemble transfers images over IIOP connections between the client and the BRI, and between the BRI and the SM. All communication in this solution travelled through the BRI. There was no direct connection between the client and the SM. The second ensemble uses HTTP to transfer image files directly from the storage manager to the client. The third ensemble transfers images directly from the storage manager to the client over IIOP.

The indirect IIOP ensemble (1) had deficiencies that were readily apparent: it required images to be transferred twice—once between the SM and the BRI

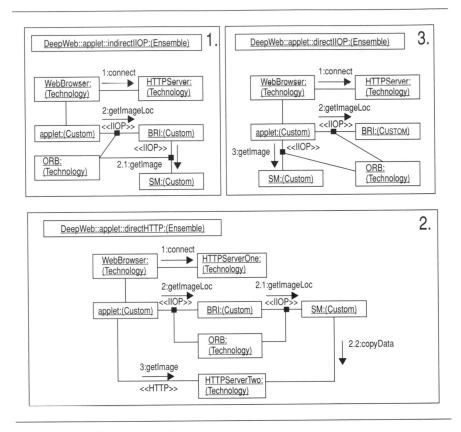

Figure 13-2   Three ensembles.

and again from the BRI to the client. This was unacceptable, due to the potential size of these images and the performance overhead of transferring images a second time. On the other hand, recently we had developed an application using this ensemble to transfer small images. Thus, we were confident that we could produce another implementation. This ensemble could become an interim solution should one of the remaining ensembles appear to be promising but only conditionally feasible. In a sense, then, the indirect IIOP option was a contingency within a contingency.

Before proceeding, we worked with the architect to develop evaluation criteria. That is, how would we know that an ensemble is feasible? We agreed that retrieval of an image from an image store would constitute success, at least at this stage of the design. Then, again working with the architect, we settled on implementation constraints, mainly concerning selection of components.

Java applets were developed using version 1.1.3 of the JDK and OrbixWeb 2.0.1 for communicating with CORBA servers on the middle tier and back-end servers. We often refer to Java applets that communicate with CORBA servers as *orblets*. These orblets were to run on versions 3.0 and 4.0 of the Netscape Browser, and versions 3.0 and 4.0 of the Internet Explorer Browser. The client platform operating system was Windows NT 4.0. The BRI and SM servers were coded in C++, compiled with the SPARCompiler C++, and run on Solaris 2.5. Implementing C++ required installing an additional compiler and dusting off our C++ manuals. We felt this small, but additional, effort enabled us to more closely model the DIRS system. (After all, when looking for a reliable trail guide it is best to find someone who has been down the same trail, and as recently as possible.) Both the BRI and SM used Orbix 2.2 to communicate with each other and the client. Version 2.0.1 of the Netscape FastTrack Server was the HTTP server.

Some of these component selections were consistent with those made for the main design thread (see Figure 13-1), while others were intentionally varied to build team competence in the event that a switch-over would be required.

13.4   Model Solutions

We decided to skip implementing the indirect IIOP ensemble. Prior experience convinced us that this design could be implemented. Therefore we didn't feel this effort would be justified. Instead, we focused our attention on the two remaining ensembles.

MODEL SOLUTION WITH DIRECT HTTP ENSEMBLE

Figure 13-3 shows a deployment diagram for a model solution developed with the direct HTTP transfer ensemble.

The UML sequence diagram shown in Figure 13-4 provides a detailed description of the interactions among components in the solution. The end user first opens the main DIRS HTML page using a browser. The browser contacts the HTTP server that downloads the page content including a Java applet. The applet is loaded into the JVM in the browser and passes control to the applet. The applet uses the CORBA bind operation to bind to the BRI, which in turn binds to the SM. Control returns to the end user who can now request the location of the image by interacting directly with the applet running within the browser. The applet contacts the BRI with this request, which is forwarded to the SM running on the back-end server. The SM returns a URL for the image to the BRI that constructs a new HTML page containing a link to this URL. The URL for this newly constructed page is returned to the applet. The applet sends a request to the browser to display the new HTML page (effectively terminating the applet's existence). The new HTML page containing a link to the image on the storage manager is displayed in the browser. The end user can now select the link to view the image.

Web Browser Evaluation and Risk/Misfit

One of our early interactions with the DIRS design team centered on Web browser evaluation. Prior to our involvement, the design team had a long list of what were deemed essential browser features. Unfortunately, there were no browsers available on the market that possessed all of these features, nor was it clear which features were essential and which were merely desirable. There was considerable controversy, for example, over whether the browser required an on-board JVM of version 1.1 or better, and there were the usual squabbles over whether Netscape Navigator or Microsoft Explorer or both should be supported.

To help matters along we introduced the use of Risk/Misfit, and began by defining the objective of the evaluation. We defined two objectives for the evaluation:

- The evaluation criteria should be satisfiable by Explorer and Navigator, as these possessed (at that time) over 90% of the browser market.

- The evaluation criteria would identify only those browser features that the DIRS design would depend on; DIRS would depend on no other browser features.

Each browser feature that had been identified as "essential" had to be justified in terms of the design risk that would arise without that feature. The aim of this was twofold. First, it forced feature advocates to use constructive rather than categorical arguments to justify their advocacy. Second, it surfaced and documented design assumptions that were held by different members of the design team. Sometimes these assumptions were in conflict, and clarifying the risk statement helped to resolve these conflicts. One other benefit of this approach was that, having identified design risks associated with the absence of features, the design team was provoked into imagining possible mitigators to the risk. In effect, these mitigators expressed design options for DIRS that did not depend on so-called essential features. In fact, the design team discovered that the only truly essential features were those for which no risk mitigation (called "repair" in Risk/Misfit) could be conceived. Thus, building Risk/Misfit evaluation criteria had the effect of identifying those features that defined minimum satisfaction criteria for browsers to be considered "feasible," while all other features expressed mere preference.

A fragment of the resulting evaluation criteria is shown in Table 13-1. Note that we had adapted Risk/Misfit for the purpose just described, and so, at this point, repair cost and residual risk were not yet a concern. Observe, though, that the criteria include something not discussed in the Risk/Misfit chapter: a specification of how a misfit will be detected. Such modifications to Risk/Misfit or any other technique described in this book are encouraged, provided they are sound, in addition to being expedient.

—shissam

Table 13-1   Web Browser

Support Feature	Risk	Mitigator	Assessment Technique	Feature Description
HTTP/1.0 persistent connections	Performance overhead	Use HTTP/1.0 and "cookies"	Product literature	The server can keep a connection with an HTTP/1.1 client open for more than a single request.
Plug-in support for editors	Loss of support for 45 million stored images	None	Model problem	Specify other data and object formats that are supported by the browser.
Object Signing	Loss of authentication and integrity checking	Use 3rd-party security COTS and added integration effort	Model problem	Support of object (applet or ActiveX) signatures with manual and/or automatic acceptance/denial of download of object based on signature.
SSL v3.0	Unencrypted data can be disclosed; also no indication of loss of data integrity	Revert to SSL v2.0	Model problem	The server can communicate using the SSL version 3 protocol.

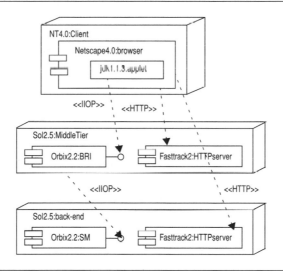

Figure 13-3   Deployment view of Direct HTTP Ensemble.

The implementation went well until we needed to generate a request to the browser to open the new page. At this time, we did not have any experience communicating from the applet to a browser. Luckily, we acquired a copy of the book *Java Network Programming* by Rusty Harold [Harold 97] and learned about the `showDocument()` method in the `java.applet.AppletContext` class. On page 131 of this book we discovered that:

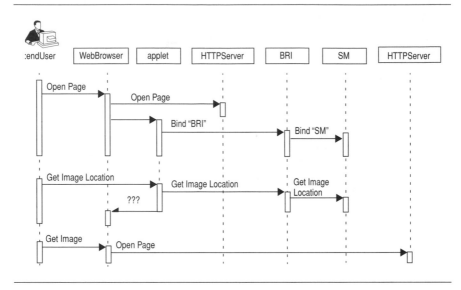

Figure 13-4   Direct HTTP Ensemble sequence diagram.

This method shows the document at URL u in the `AppletContext`'s window. It is not supported by all web browsers and applet viewers, but it is supported by Netscape and HotJava.

We added a call to the `showDocument()` method from the applet to display the HTML page in the browser. As promised, this worked with Netscape Navigator, but it was not known to work with Internet Explorer. By using Netscape Navigator to implement the browser component, we had proved, at a minimum, that one implementation of the ensemble was possible. However, we had not satisfied the evaluation criterion that the solution work with both Navigator and Explorer. This was an important criterion, since the DIRS user community used both browsers. After implementing the model solution, we modified our blackboard as shown in Figure 13-5.

The first and most obvious change is that technologies have been replaced with components. CORBA has been replaced with Orbix 2.2, used to enable communication with the legacy C++ servers and OrbixWeb 2.0.1, used to enable communication with the Java applets within the browser. The interaction between applet and BRI is associated with both ORBs since it involves different implementations of the CORBA standard, albeit by the same vendor. The diagram also includes a credential for the show document method. Its equivalent on Explorer was only a postulate.[1]

---

[1] A later version of Microsoft IE did, in fact, support the show document method.

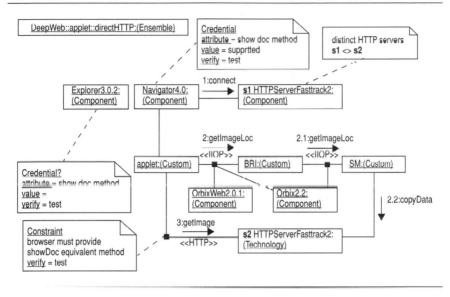

Figure 13-5   Revised Direct HTTP.

Without the show document method we would have to abandon this ensemble. When dealing with emerging technologies, the critical role played by low-level component features may not be apparent until implementation time, which is what makes early prototyping so important. In our experience, model problems are the most efficient way of implementing these prototypes.

MODEL SOLUTION WITH DIRECT IIOP ENSEMBLE

The second model solution we implemented used the direct IIOP ensemble. This model solution used the same components employed in the direct HTTP transfer solution except it did not require an HTTP server on the back-end. We originally intended to deploy this model solution as depicted in Figure 13-6.

We did have some apprehensions about implementing this ensemble. The model solution requires that a Java applet, running within a browser on the client platform, directly calls remote methods on both the BRI server running in the middle tier and on the SM server running on the back-end. However, for reasons of security, the JVMs within both the Netscape and IE browsers prevent an applet from connecting to a second machine. To circumvent this restriction, a little creativity was required. We created a second "helper" applet that is loaded with the HTML page generated by the BRI and served up from a HTTP server on the back-end platform. So we needed a second HTTP server after all! Figure 13-7 shows the sequence diagram for this model solution. (The second HTTP server is not shown, to make the diagram easier to read.)

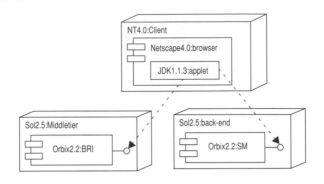

Figure 13-6 Deployment view of Direct IIOP Ensemble.

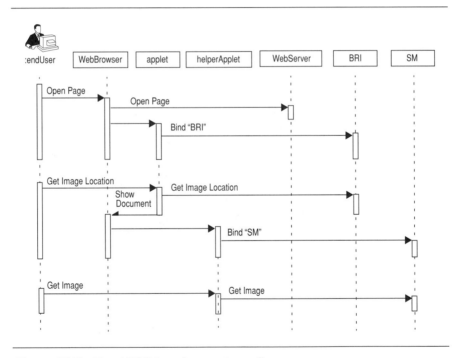

Figure 13-7 Direct IIOP transfer sequence diagram.

As in the direct HTTP transfer ensemble, the end user opens the main DIRS page with the browser. The browser contacts the server that downloads the page content including a Java applet. The applet is loaded into the browser JVM and control is passed to the applet. The applet uses the CORBA bind operation to bind to the BRI. Unlike the direct HTTP transfer solution, the BRI no longer binds directly to the SM. Control is returned to the end user who sends a request for the image location to the applet. The applet forwards this request to the BRI that constructs an HTML page containing a second, helper, applet. The location of the image is included in the new page as a parameter to the helper applet. When control is returned to the applet, it calls the show document method as in the direct HTTP transfer solution. The new page, including the helper applet, is loaded by the browser and control is passed to the new helper applet that binds to the storage manager. The end user now sends a request to the helper applet to retrieve the image, which is forwarded to the SM. The SM converts the requested image into a sequence of bytes, or *octets* in CORBA terminology, and returns it via IIOP to the helper applet running within the browser.

Figure 13-8 shows the revised deployment diagram for this model solution. This is a good example of how actual experience gained from implementing model problems can alter a design. As suggested by von Moltke, in the epigraph that opens this chapter, it is impossible to predict the utility of a plan or design beyond the initial phases. This makes it incumbent on the designer to insist on increasingly stringent proofs of design feasibility.

EXTENDING THE SANDBOX

We succeeded in transferring an image from the storage manager to the client in the direct IIOP transfer ensemble, and, by logical extension, in the indirect IIOP ensemble as well. However, we have come short of a full solution in both cases. The image data is stored as a byte array within the JVM and cannot be directly displayed. We still need to get the image data out of the JVM and into the third-party image viewing component. Although other commercial image viewers were available, they did not support some of the nonstandard image formats used by DIRS. The image viewer is invoked on a command with an argument specifying

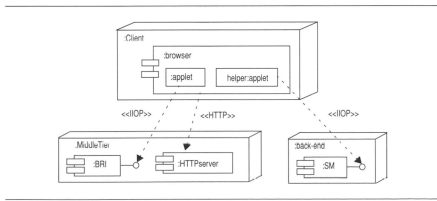

Figure 13-8   Revised direct HTTP transfer abstract model solution.

the location of the file containing the image to be viewed. To invoke this image viewer from our thin client we had to:

1. Write the image data to a temporary file on the client platform.
2. Launch an external application on the client platform.

Unfortunately, these are both privileged operations under Java. To prevent downloaded applets from malicious behavior, version 1.1 of the JDK, operating in a browser environment, enforces a security mechanism known as the *sandbox*. An applet running in a sandbox is restricted from performing operations that might compromise the security of the platform. The sandbox, for example, restricts reading or writing files on the local file system.

The options available in 1997 for allowing applets to operate outside of the browser sandbox were extremely limited. Netscape provided the Netscape capabilities classes that allowed an applet to operate outside of the sandbox. The capabilities classes added facilities to refine the control provided by the standard Java security manager class. These classes could then be used to exercise fine-grained control over an applet's activities outside of the sandbox.

A full discussion of the use of digital certificates and security is contained in the following chapter, but a brief introduction is required here. Access control decisions boil down to who is allowed to do what. In the capabilities model, a principal represents the "who," a target represents the "what," and the privileges associated with a principal represent the authorization for a principal to access a specific target. Using digital certificates, the *principal* is represented by a signing certificate while the *target* is one or more system resources, such as files stored on a local disk. The capabilities classes make it possible to determine whether any given principal (that is, signing certificate) is allowed to access the local system resources represented by a given target. The answer is expressed by a *privilege*, which states whether access is allowed and, if so, for how long.

We extended our IIOP transfer solutions to use the Netscape capabilities classes to write image data out to a temporary file and invoke an external application to view them. Additionally, we used the capabilities classes to circumvent the restriction that a Java client could only communicate with the host from which it was downloaded. The capability of connecting to multiple hosts also eliminated the need for an additional helper applet to communicate with the SM.

Unfortunately, the capability classes also had drawbacks. Since they are proprietary, we could not use them in non-Netscape browsers, for example, Microsoft Internet Explorer. The revised blackboard for the Direct IIOP ensemble, illustrated in Figure 13-9, shows that applets must be digitally signed (refer back to Figure 5-6 for the details of the signed applet ensemble). It also clearly indicates, via a postulated credential on Explorer 3.0.2, that it is uncertain whether Explorer provides an equivalent feature. As will be seen when we resume the case study narrative in Chapter 15, this postulate introduces a whole range of rather complex issues pertaining to interoperability of digital certificates.

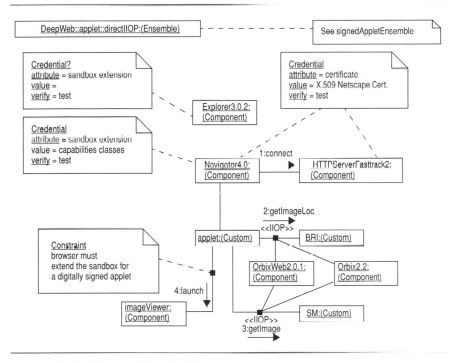

Figure 13-9   Revised Direct IIOP.

13.5 Evaluation

We had completed two model solutions but had obtained decidedly mixed results. On the one hand, the Direct HTTP Ensemble proved feasible (we had, by this time, verified that Explorer supported the show document method). This was good news except for the fact that this ensemble, shown in Figure 13-4, is too complex for the simple function it performs. There also remained questions about how to manage error propagation considering the fact that distinct control and data channels are used. Another detail concerned finalization of the retrieval scenario. Specifically, data on the second Web server should be deleted immediately upon retrieval; this involves one more interaction, and still more complexity.

On the other hand, the Direct IIOP solution was simple and elegant. Unfortunately, our model solution relied on proprietary Netscape interfaces. Since the model solution did not work with both Navigator and Internet Explorer, this ensemble was, at best, only conditionally feasible. It had failed to satisfy the evaluation criteria established for the model problem. However, we already had in mind several repair strategies and were not ready to concede defeat. We had heard rumors of a product from JavaSoft called Java Protection Domains that promised to be a portable alternative to Netscape's Capability Classes, and we were willing to wait on this market event while continuing to explore the ramifications of this ensemble. (Persistence is an important quality when building component-based systems. Optimism also helps.)

Figure 13-10 depicts the situation in terms of contingency management. Work was proceeding on the main design option, while more work remained to prove that the applet ensemble was a viable alternative. The direct HTTP ensemble was feasible, but ungainly. We were suspicious that anything that ugly could be correct. Therefore, we considered its feasibility to be unproven. The direct IIOP ensemble was the favorite, but it was infeasible without repair. Java Protection Domains, we thought, would repair the Navigator dependency, and accordingly we decided to "wait" on its release from Sun Microsystems. This did not mean, however, that further repair options were foreclosed.

Figure 13-11 summarizes what we discovered in a fragment of the manifests associated with the direct IIOP and direct HTTP ensembles. Roll-up diagrams like this are exceedingly useful as the number of components and potential ensembles explodes.

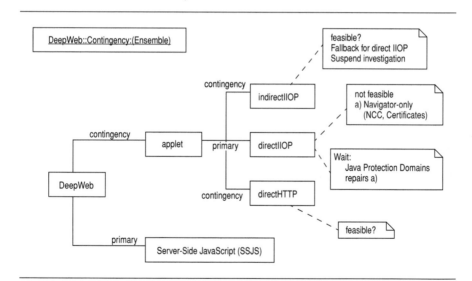

Figure 13-10   DeepWeb contingency.

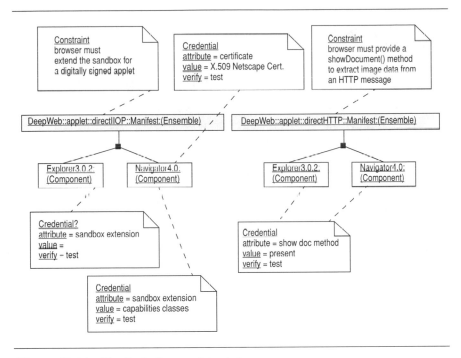

Figure 13-11   Manifest after model solutions.

13.6   Summary

This chapter illustrates our approach to the design of component-based systems. The design space is partitioned into branches corresponding to a main design option (the trunk) and one or more contingencies. Each contingency may itself be partitioned, recursively, with effort allocated to each design option. Model problems are used to guide the exploration of contingencies. In this chapter, the design question for one model problem was defined: were there any applet ensembles that would work with both Internet Explorer and Netscape Navigator? Three ensembles were specified, two of which were realized as model solutions.

The model problem and their solutions significantly extended our knowledge of the design space. We discovered problems that revised our initial ideas about how these ensembles worked. However, as is the norm for any field of exploration, we were left with more questions. Was there a mechanism that can be used to provide fine-grained access outside of the sandbox that would work with both Netscape Navigator and Microsoft Internet Explorer? Would the transfer of images over IIOP be the most efficient mechanism? We explore these questions, along with others, in the remaining chapters of this part of the book.

13.7 Discussion Questions

1. Direct transfer of images over HTTP appeared to provide adequate performance. What are the arguments for and against this abstract model solution?

2. Late selection of products that implement technologies provides additional time for evaluation and experimentation through model problems. Early selection of a product helps to solidify the design and provide focus to the development. Discuss other advantages and disadvantages of these conflicting approaches. When is one approach better than the other?

14

Public Key Infrastructure

Anyone who considers arithmetical methods of producing random digits is, of course, in a state of sin.
—John von Neumann (1903–1957)

Securing software systems is a common theme for many of the case studies in the book, so some knowledge of this field is necessary. This chapter is a primer for the security concepts and technologies referenced throughout these chapters. If you understand software system security, then proceed with the remainder of the case studies. If not, you may wish to read this chapter as it will help you to understand the remaining case studies.

Security can mean different things depending on the system, the data, and associated risks. It is possible, though, to discuss security more precisely in terms of the *attributes* a secure system should possess. Although experts disagree over the number of attributes and their definition, the seven attributes discussed below offer a reasonable approximation for nonexperts. To describe these attributes, we use an analogy of conducting commerce at a local store:

1. Someone making a payment requests a signed receipt so that, later, the recipient of the payment cannot deny receiving it. This is *nonrepudiation*.
2. Things that are said and done are held in confidence; for example, credit card numbers and what is purchased are generally not on display for others to see. This is *confidentiality*.
3. The product or service being delivered is received as intended. The item has not been altered between the time it was purchased and the time the customer takes possession. This might actually start from the time the article was manufactured (for example, tamper-resistant packaging). This is *integrity*.
4. We have confidence that we are dealing with the intended business. If we purchase a hamburger from a place called "McDonald's" and it has golden

arches, we believe it is *the* McDonald's, and not some impersonator. This is *assurance*.

5. We know when the place of business is open. It has posted hours, and it is open for business during those hours. This is *availability*.

6. The business and its contents are protected from unauthorized intruders through alarm systems, locks, and barred windows. This is *physical security*.

7. The business can track who comes and goes, and can recall that information. The store may have a security camera, for example. This is *auditing*.

Not all of these attributes are needed for a system to be "secure." In some cases, a subset of these attributes is sufficient. For many mission-critical systems, however, all of these attributes are relevant. Moreover, these attributes are inter-independent. Auditing does not depend on assurance, for example. However, it may be important that the audit record has integrity, so that we know it has not been modified.

In the remainder of this chapter, we discuss the mechanisms for ensuring three security attributes that are of particular relevance to the case studies in this book—*nonrepudiation*, *confidentiality*, and *integrity*. The mechanism we discuss is usually referred to, in the aggregate, as Public Key Infrastructures (PKI). After discussing the principles of PKI, we discuss how it is used to achieve the above three security attributes.

14.1   Fundamental Ideas

To understand PKI's use in securing software systems, it is helpful to examine its underlying technologies. We begin with background on cryptography, and then discuss the foundation of PKI—public/private key cryptography. We then discuss various applications of public/private key cryptography: digital signatures, secure hashing, and digital certificates. After this brief introduction to PKI technology, we return to nonrepudiation, confidentiality, and integrity.

CRYPTOGRAPHY

Cryptography is an algorithmic process of converting a plain text (or clear text) message to a cipher text (or cipher) message based on an algorithm that both the sender and receiver know, so that the cipher text message can be returned to its original, plain text form. In its cipher form, a message cannot be read by anyone but the intended receiver. The act of converting a plain text message to its cipher text form is called enciphering. Reversing that act (that is, cipher text form to plain text message) is deciphering. Enciphering and deciphering are more commonly referred to as *encryption* and *decryption*, respectively.

There are a number of algorithms for performing encryption and decryption, but comparatively few such algorithms have stood the test of time. The most successful algorithms use a *key*. A key is simply a parameter to the algorithm that allows the encryption and decryption process to occur. There are many modern key-based cryptographic techniques [Schneier 96]. These are divided into two classes, symmetric and asymmetric (also called public/private) key cryptography. In symmetric key cryptography, the same key is used for both encryption and decryption. In asymmetric key cryptography, one key is used for encryption and another, mathematically related key, is used for decryption.

Symmetric Key Cryptography. The most widely used symmetric key cryptographic method is the Data Encryption Standard (DES) [NIST 93]. Although published as long ago as 1977 by the National Bureau of Standards (reprinted in Beker and Piper [Beker+ 82]), DES has not yet been replaced by any other symmetric key approach. DES uses a fixed length, 56-bit key and an efficient algorithm to quickly encrypt and decrypt messages. DES can be implemented easily in hardware, making the encryption and decryption process even faster. In general, increasing the key size makes the system more secure. A variation of DES, called Triple-DES or DES-EDE (encrypt-decrypt-encrypt), uses three applications of DES and two independent DES keys to produce an effective key length of 168 bits [ANSI 85].

The International Data Encryption Algorithm (IDEA) was invented by James Massey and Xuejia Lai of ETH Zurich, in Switzerland, in 1991 and is patented and registered by the Swiss Ascom Tech AG, Solothurn [Lai 92]. IDEA uses a fixed length, 128-bit key (larger than DES but smaller than Triple-DES). It is also faster than Triple-DES. In the early 1990s, Don Rivest of RSA Data Security, Inc., invented the algorithms RC2 and RC4. These use variable length keys and are claimed to be even faster than IDEA. However, implementations may be exported from the U.S. only if they use key lengths of 40 bits or less.

Although symmetric key cryptography works, it has a fundamental weak spot—key management. Since the same key is used for encryption and decryption, it must be kept secure. If an adversary knows the key then the message can be decrypted. At the same time, the key must be available to the sender and the receiver and these two parties may be physically separated. In essence, symmetric key cryptography transforms the problem of transmitting messages securely into that of transmitting keys securely. This is a step forward, because keys are much smaller than messages, and the keys can be generated beforehand. Nevertheless, ensuring that the sender and receiver are using the same key and that potential adversaries do not know this key remains a major stumbling block. This is referred to as the key management problem.

Public/Private Key Cryptography. Asymmetric key cryptography overcomes the key management problem by using different keys for encryption and decryption. Having knowledge of one key, say the encryption key, is not sufficient to determine the other key, the decryption key. Therefore, the encryption key can be made public, provided the decryption key is held only by the party wishing to receive encrypted messages (hence the name public/private key cryptography). Anyone can use the public key to encrypt a message, but only the recipient can decrypt it.

James Ellis, Malcolm Williamson, and Clifford Cocks first investigated public/private key cryptography at the British Government Communications Headquarters (GCHQ) in the early 1970s [Ellis 87]. The first public discussion of public/private key cryptography was by Whitfield Diffie and Martin Hellman in 1976 [Diffie+ 76].

A widely used public/private key algorithm is RSA, named after the initials of its inventors, Ronald L. Rivest, Adi Shamir, and Leonard M. Adleman [RSA 91]. RSA depends on the difficulty of factoring the product of two very large prime numbers. Although used for encrypting whole messages, RSA is much less efficient than symmetric key algorithms such as DES. El Gamal's is another public/private key algorithm [El Gamal 85]. It uses a different arithmetic algorithm than RSA, called the discrete logarithm problem. An extensive discussion of public/private key cryptography, including much of the mathematical detail, can be found in the book, *Public Key Cryptography* [Salomaa 96].

ENCRYPTION USING PUBLIC/PRIVATE KEY CRYPTOGRAPHY

The mathematical relationship between the public/private key pair permits a general rule: any message encrypted with one key of the pair can be successfully decrypted only with that key's counterpart. To encrypt with the public key means you can decrypt only with the private key. The converse is also true—to encrypt with the private key means you can decrypt only with the public key.

The decision as to which key is kept private and which is made public is not arbitrary. In the case of RSA, the public key uses exponents that are relatively small (in comparison to the private key) making the process of encryption and digital signature verification (discussed later) faster.

Figure 14-1 illustrates the proper and intended uses of public/private key cryptography for sending confidential messages. In the illustration, a user, Bob, has a public/private key pair. The public portion of that key pair is placed in the public domain (for example, in a Web server). The private portion is guarded in a private domain, for example, on a digital key card or in a password protected file. For Alice to send a secret message to Bob, the following process needs to be followed:

1. Alice passes the secret message and Bob's public key to the appropriate encryption algorithm to construct the encrypted message.

2. Alice transmits the encrypted message (perhaps via e-mail) to Bob.

3. Bob decrypts the transmitted, encrypted message with his private key and the appropriate decryption algorithm.

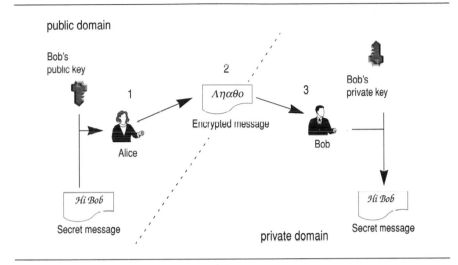

Figure 14-1   Proper encryption using public/private key cryptography.

Bob can be assured that Alice's encrypted secret message was not seen by anyone else since only his private key is capable of decrypting the message (that is, confidentiality).

Since we know that a private key can also be used to encrypt messages, Bob technically could respond in secret to Alice's original message by using the same public/private key pair as illustrated in Figure 14-2. In this scenario:

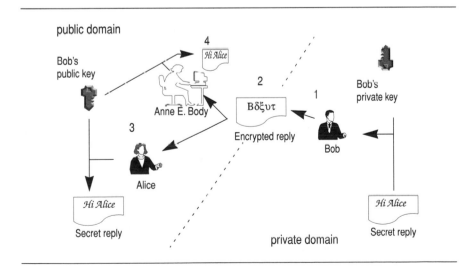

Figure 14-2   Improper encryption using public/private key cryptography.

1. Bob passes the secret reply and his private key to the encryption algorithm to construct the encrypted reply.

2. Bob transmits the encrypted reply to Alice.

3. Alice decrypts the transmitted, encrypted reply with Bob's public key and the decryption algorithm to read this reply.

Unfortunately, Bob's message is not confidential because anyone with access to the encrypted reply and Bob's public key (which is in the public domain) can decrypt the reply and see the text of the message. However, if Alice had her own public/private key pair, then Bob and Alice could communicate confidentially. In this case, Bob would send messages encrypted with Alice's public key (which only Alice could decrypt by using her private key), and Alice would send messages to Bob encrypted with Bob's public key (which only he could decrypt using his private key).

DIGITAL SIGNATURES AND PUBLIC/PRIVATE KEY CRYPTOGRAPHY

It is true that anyone can read a message encrypted with a private key. On the other hand, the receiver knows who the sender was. For example, in Figure 14-2, Alice knows that the message came from Bob because Bob's public key can *only* decrypt a message encrypted *using Bob's private key*! At the expense of confidentiality, Bob let Alice know that the reply was actually from him. This property of public/private key cryptography is used in *digital signature* technology.

A digital signature is typically computed using two inputs: 1) some artifact such as a message, document, or file; and 2) a private key of a public/private key pair. A digital signature is a sequence of numbers that is statistically unique because the inputs to the signing algorithm (message and key) are sufficiently random. Figure 14-3 shows the basic steps required for Bob to sign a message, and for Alice to verify this signature:

1. The message is reduced, by way of a cryptologic hashing algorithm, to a hash value (a number based on the message).

2. The hash value is encrypted using the private key (in this example, Bob's private key) to generate an encrypted hash value otherwise known as the digital signature.

3. Bob sends the original message and its digital signature to the intended recipient (in this example Alice).

4. Alice generates the hash value of the message received using the same hash algorithm used by Bob.

5. Alice decrypts the digital signature (the encrypted hash value) using Bob's public key to recover the hash value originally computed by Bob.

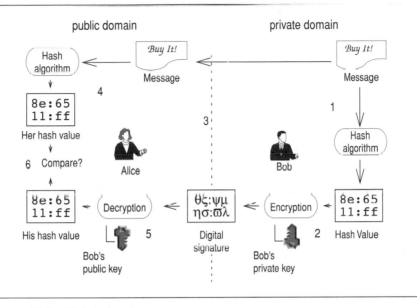

public domain   private domain

Figure 14-3   Digital signatures.

6. Alice then compares the hash value she computed with that recovered from Bob's digital signature and compares them to determine if the message was that originally sent by Bob.

As a result of Step 6, Alice knows that the message came from Bob (but see the discussion on "Whose Public Key Is That Anyway?" below), and that the message was not altered or damaged during transmission. If the hash values do not compare, Alice should question both the integrity of the message (that is, was it damaged during transmission?) and the authenticity of the sender (that is, did it actually originate from Bob?).

SECURE HASHING

Generating a hash value for a digital signature is simply a performance optimization (but an important optimization). It would be possible to send a plain text message and an encrypted version of the message. The recipient could decrypt the encrypted message and compare it with its counterpart to see if they matched. In this approach, Alice can still make the same assertions about the message as she can in the algorithm outlined in Figure 14-3. But, applying a hash function improves performance and throughput. The hash value is typically smaller, in total number of bytes, than the original message, and is usually a fixed length. This is true for the two popular secure hashing algorithms MD5 [Rivest 91] or SHA-1 [NIST 95]. These algorithms are called "secure" in the sense that they have been mathematically proven, based on the size of the hash value (128 bits for MD5 and 160 bits for SHA-1), to have two key properties:

1. Any change in the input, or message, has a high likelihood (approaching absolute certainty) of producing a different output, or hash value.

2. The likelihood that two messages have the same hash value (called a hash collision) is vanishingly small.

The performance cost of computing, encrypting, and decrypting a hash value is low compared to the cost of encrypting and decrypting an arbitrarily large message. Further, including a digital signature (encrypted hash value) in the message has little impact on the overall size of the message. Given the fixed size of the digital signature, designers and engineers can predict impact on performance and throughput.

WHOSE PUBLIC KEY IS THAT ANYWAY?

Throughout this discussion, the underlying premise was that Alice knew that the public key she possessed belonged to Bob's public/private key pair. But how did she come to possess this knowledge? She might, in fact, have been *tricked* into thinking this was true. Without the ability to undeniably connect a public key to an individual, Alice cannot be certain that Bob was the one to see her message (in Figure 14-1) or that a message received was actually from Bob (in Figure 14-3). This is the role performed by digital certificates (also known as digital IDs).

DIGITAL CERTIFICATES

Digital certificates, or just certificates, are computer-based files or structures used to convey information about a user for identification purposes [Gerck 97]. Certificates are based on the ITU-T Recommendation X.509 [ITU-T 97]. There are a number of different certificates (called *end-entity* certificates) defined in the X.509 specification:

- *Personal certificates* represent individuals, and are typically used to secure e-mail and access to web servers.
- *Server certificates* indicate that a server belongs to the company it claims to belong to.
- *Developer certificates* are used by developers to sign software or other objects.

A certificate binds an identity (a name) to a public key. The certificate includes the name of the person (for example, Bob), their public key (for example, Bob's public key), and a digital signature sealing the data. This information can be verified (authenticated) by validating the digital signature.

Similar to the signature and stamp of a notary public, the digital signature is added by a trusted third party known as a *certificate authority* (CA). Certificate authorities confirm the relationship between identities and their public keys. Certificate authorities also publish public keys that then verify end-entity certificates. This process uses the public key of the authority that issued the certificate to validate the digital signature.

So, how do you get the public key of a certificate authority? In addition to end-entity certificates, the X.509 specification defines *certificate authority certificates*. These special certificates identify third-party organizations entrusted to validate the identity of individuals requesting end-entity certificates. Similar to end-entity certificates, CA certificates contain a name (the name of the authority), a public key, and a digital signature sealing the data. CA certificates are critical in obtaining end-entity certificates and close the circle of trust.

Obtaining a Digital Certificate.   Certificates are obtained by sending a request to a certificate authority. Information about an individual (for personal certificates) or a site or company is sent to a CA along with a public key. The package sent to the CA is called a *certificate signing request* and is also defined in the X.509 specification.

Upon receiving the request, the CA validates the contents through a process defined and published by the authority. The authority validates the digital signature placed on the signing request to ensure that it is a valid public key (that is, it is part of a public/private key pair). Ultimately, confidence in the certificate is based on the trust you place on the certificate authority's assurance mechanism.

If the information contained within the certificate request is recognized as genuine, the authority generates the requested certificate. In addition, the authority *chains* their certificate to the new certificate. This allows an individual receiving the certificate to identify the authority that issued it, and to consider this information when deciding to accept or reject the certificate. Figure 14-4 illustrates the general process.

As this discussion demonstrates, the mathematical sophistication of PKI ultimately rests on a foundation of public trust. That is, we trust that a public key belongs to a particular individual, and this trust is vested in one or more authorities. Alice believes she possesses Bob's public key because she trusts the authority that told her so.

CERTIFICATE AUTHORITIES AND TRUST

Presenting a certificate is not that different from presenting a photo ID. In most cases, we can trust the person presenting the photo ID because we can match the image on the photo ID with the person. We can also read other identifying information from the photo ID such as a social security number, employee number, or home address and compare that information with other sources.

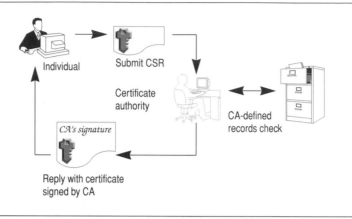

Individual Submit CSR

Certificate
authority

CA-defined
records check

CA's signature

Reply with certificate
signed by CA

Figure 14-4 Generalized certificate generation process.

However, we seldom blindly trust just any photo ID. Like certificates, photo IDs can be created by anyone. However, we are more likely to trust a driver's license or a passport because they are created by a third party. Specifically, we trust that these issuing parties have no vested interest in falsifying the documents and that the processes used in verifying the information are sound. Further, these IDs may include countermeasures against forgery such as holograms, checksums, use of special paper, or electromagnetic signatures.

Similarly, you trust certificate authorities to issue certificates, much as the government is trusted to issue passports. And who exactly gives these organizations their authority? The answer is that you do. You entrust certificate authorities in the same manner you entrust a credit card company, a bank, or any other institution. This may be based on their size, predominance in the marketplace, alliances with other trusted institutions, or, perhaps, because they are the only game in town. We trust the information contained within the certificates because we trust the processes followed by the certificate authority to verify that information and because we believe that the authority has no interest in falsifying certificates.

An alternative to using a commercial certificate authority is to use an enterprise certificate authority. An enterprise authority creates and signs certificates for use within a closed community, such as a corporate-wide intranet or a specific WAN application, such as a virtual enterprise. It usually follows the same processes as a commercial certificate authority. In other words, it should test for the accuracy and validity of each certificate request presented. For example, the enterprise authority might have operational procedures to check with the organization's security or human resources office to validate that the requestor is a current employee. The enterprise authority also maintains the list of all valid and revoked certificates and renewing certificates.

14.2   Nonrepudiation

Nonrepudiation is the *inability* to disavow an act. In other words, evidence exists that prevents a person from denying an act. For example, you log in to a computer system by presenting a user name and password. Most software applications consider this sufficient evidence to permit access, but could it be proved (for example, in a court of law) that it was really *you* that was logged in? You could argue that someone else obtained your password, possibly using one of the snooping and spoofing techniques discussed in Chapter 11. Now, suppose that a computer system requires a fingerprint or retinal image to gain access. Contesting the fact now becomes more difficult.[1]

Systems that use mechanisms for nonrepudiation are more secure than those that do not. The mechanisms supported in PKI, specifically public/private key cryptography, digital signatures, and certificates, provide a basis for nonrepudiation.

PKI IN IDENTIFICATION AND AUTHENTICATION

Identification and authentication (I&A) schemes based on user names and passwords are quite susceptible to compromise. Such approaches only require you to provide something you *know*. But what you know (for example, a password) can sometimes be learned by others. Stronger schemes typically require two elements, something you have (for example, an ATM card) and something you know (for example, your PIN). Impersonation is now more difficult since two elements are needed, not just one. Having either element in isolation is not enough to gain access.

PKI mechanisms used for I&A follow this basic approach of something you have and something you know. The "something you have" in this case is the private key. The private key may be stored in a smart card or in a local file on your computer. The "something you know" may be a PIN for the smart card or a password to unlock the file. Figure 14-5 illustrates the use of PKI for I&A:

1. A user (for example, Bob) connects to a Web server or intranet service (for example, AB's server) requesting a service. In response, the server requests user identification and authentication by offering Bob a challenge.

2. Bob, supplying a password only he knows, accesses his private key to digitally sign the challenge using a digital signature algorithm.

3. Bob identifies himself by sending his digital certificate and authenticates himself by sending a digitally signed response back to the server challenge.

4. The AB server may obtain another copy of Bob's certificate from a trusted source, such as a directory server it maintains or that is maintained by a certificate authority, for the purpose of comparison.

---

[1] Unless, of course, you happen to be missing an eye or a finger.

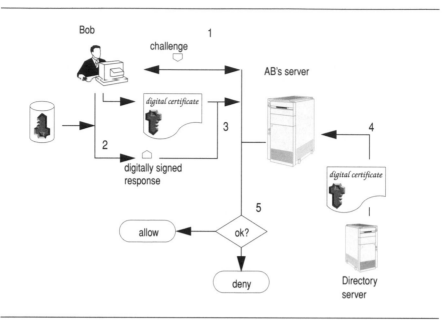

Bob

Figure 14-5   PKI in I&A.

5. The AB server checks the validity of Bob's certificate and the digitally signed response to the challenge presented in step #1. If these checks succeed, Bob is allowed to access the AB server, and if not, Bob is denied access and the connection is terminated.

In this scenario, the AB server performs a number of steps to check the validity of the certificate. First, it checks that the certificate presented has been issued by an authority that it trusts. Second, it verifies the digital signature on the certificate (as shown in Figure 14-4). Third, it ensures that the certificate has not expired or been revoked by the CA. And finally, the AB server optionally might compare the certificate presented with one already on record (as illustrated in the example step #4 for Figure 14-5).

Checking the validity of the digital signature applied to the challenge (as illustrated in step #2 in Figure 14-5) is straightforward and follows the same general mechanism as shown earlier in Figure 14-3. The only difference is that the server generates the message to be signed. The message is typically a pseudo-random number, sometimes based on values that both the user and the server know.

Given that all of these checks pass, the server has strong evidence that the user (for example, Bob) is who he says he is based on the following facts:

1. The certificate is from a trusted source.

2. The certificate is authentic.

3. The digital signature of the challenge is valid (that is, the signer has the corresponding private key).

4. The certificate is listed as one that is valid for access.

It would be difficult for Bob to deny that someone else accessed the AB server and subsequently was identified and authenticated (given that he did not give out his password and leave his machine unattended and available).

14.3   Confidentiality

Confidentiality assures that unintended third parties cannot view information sent between two communicating parties. Encryption is the most widely used mechanism for providing confidentiality over an insecure medium.

On the whole, systems that use encryption to achieve confidentiality are more secure than those that do not. As discussed earlier, symmetric and asymmetric encryption are the basic mechanisms for providing confidentiality. The downside to symmetric encryption is key management (that is, both communicating parties must have the same key to successfully decrypt encrypted messages). While asymmetric key encryption solves the key management problem, encryption and decryption degrade performance. One solution is to use both symmetric and asymmetric key encryption to provide confidentiality without compromising performance.

PKI IN SECURE SESSIONS

Normal communication between a client, such as *telnet* or a Web browser, and a server, such as a Web site, is unencrypted. In fact, we demonstrated in Chapter 11 just how easy it is for someone to eavesdrop on (snoop) these communications. Passing private information over an unsecured communication channel puts that information at risk, allowing the unscrupulous to learn credit card numbers, social security numbers, and military and industrial secrets. Encryption does not prevent someone from snooping the communication channel, but it does make the data that they see unintelligible.

There are a number of competing and complementary standards which use encryption (for example, symmetric, asymmetric, or some combination thereof) to achieve confidentiality over an insecure communication medium such as the Internet. The Secure Sockets Layer (SSL), developed by Netscape Communications Corporation, uses a combination of symmetric and asymmetric encryption for achieving confidentiality between a client and server [Hickman 95]. Figure 14-6 illustrates the concept behind SSL.

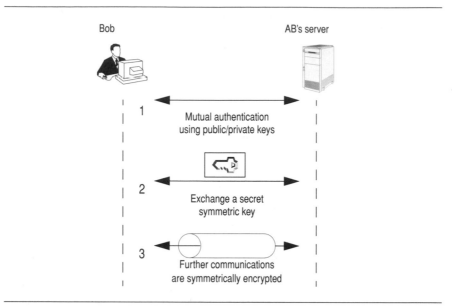

Figure 14-6   PKI in secure sessions.

1. The client (in this case Bob) and the server (for example, AB's server) *mutually* authenticate each other using the I&A mechanism discussed in Section 14.2. Each peer (that is, client and server) now has the other's public key.

2. The two peers agree on a secret key, using each other's public keys and asymmetric encryption to exchange secret data and formulate a session key. The session key becomes a one-time secret key used in an agreed-upon symmetric encryption algorithm (for example, DES, RC4, and so on).

3. Any further communication initiated by one peer is encrypted using the symmetric key before it is transmitted; the receiving peer then decrypts the incoming transmission so that it can be understood.

There are two principal benefits of using a combination of asymmetric and symmetric encryption. First, the key management problem (typical of symmetric encryption) is solved. Public/private key encryption uses seed-data between the client and server to negotiate a symmetric key, authenticating each other during that process. Second, the relatively slow performance of public/private key encryption is solved by using symmetric key encryption for the bulk of the communication. In addition, under SSL, the secret symmetric key is used only for that session. Once either the client or the server ends the session, that key is discarded. SSL combines the ease of key management inherent in public/private key encryption with the speed of symmetric key encryption.

The Internet Engineering Task Force (IETF) is attempting to introduce an international standard, based on SSL 3.0, called Transport Layer Security (TLS).

A Request for Comments on the TLS Protocol Version 1.0 was issued in January 1999 [IETF 99].

14.4 Integrity

Integrity is knowing that the message you receive was exactly what was sent. Integrity is an important attribute in commerce and elsewhere. Tamper-resistant packaging is frequently used in many of the products we use today such as over-the-counter medication. We can also identify tamper-resistant packaging going back hundreds of years, when wax and personalized stamps were used to seal letters between kings and between lovers. If a vassal receives a letter sealed with the king's signet, he can be fairly certain the letter comes from the king and the words in the letter convey the king's wishes. If, on the other hand, the wax seal is broken on an order to attack the enemy, then the wise warrior questions the validity of the command. In fact, the letter may have been altered to read "attack" when the original might have said "stay put." Tamper-resistant packaging is just as important in the software systems that are in use today, as it was hundreds of years ago.

Today, we commonly download Web content that executes on local workstations. Knowing that the content has not been surreptitiously modified is critical if you are to trust the content. If the content is from a trusted source[2] and it is unmodified, your confidence in that content is higher, because the content has integrity. If the content is from an unknown source or you cannot tell if it has been modified, the content cannot be trusted. PKI mechanisms such as digital signatures and certificates help maintain the integrity of exchanged products and services.

PKI IN OBJECT AND CODE SIGNING

PKI also plays an important role in securing dynamic Web page content. Dynamic content (for example, scripting, plug-ins, or Java applets) includes instructions that are executed by your browser or computer that potentially can cause damage. To ease the fear of executing unknown computer codes, content providers have begun to digitally sign their content and code so that you can decide whether or not to permit it to execute. This is called *code signing* (also referred to as object signing).

Code signing is the process of digitally signing computer codes or Web content prior to delivery. Upon receipt of the signed content, you can identify the content provider by verifying the digital signature. If the contents have been damaged, or

---

[2] The issue of whether to trust a content provider is outside of the scope of PKI.

Key Size Does Matter

Using encryption algorithms for confidentiality can be effective. However, the effectiveness of the algorithm is based on two factors: the strength of the algorithm and the size of the key(s). The encryption algorithms discussed in this chapter are all relatively strong and have been discussed at length in mathematical and computer journals. Their Achilles' heel is the key itself. Small keys are more susceptible to attack than large keys. However, while large keys are more secure, they require more computational power.

Cryptographers, hackers, and others have demonstrated the weaknesses of encryption algorithms hobbled by small keys. Using sophisticated but inexpensive hardware and software, they solve encrypted puzzles in shorter and shorter amounts of time even though these puzzles use ever larger keys.

These cryptographic puzzles were solved by a brute-force attack of the key space. The program executing this attack tries the first possible key and all subsequent keys until the correct key is identified. In 1999, nearly 245 billion keys per second were achieved at peak performance in the 56-bit challenge (row 3 of Table 14-1). Based on 1999 performance, the entire key space for a 40-bit key could be searched in nearly 4 seconds, where in 1997 it took 3.5 hours to search a subset of the key space. However, if the key size is increased to 168-bits, then it would take 4.4×10^{19} years to perform the same exhaustive search of 100% of the keys (NB: our sun is approximately 4.5×10^9 years old!).

These experiments underscore the importance of selecting the proper key size when using encryption for confidentiality. The longer the information needs to remain private the larger the key size required. Information that is not as critical, or is only critical for a short period of time, can be encrypted using a smaller key. The rule of thumb then, is to select the key size that is appropriate for the lifetime of the data to be protected.

—shissam

Table 14-1   Time to Crack by Key Size

Key Size	Number of Keys	Time to "crack"
40-bit	1,099,511,627,776	3.5 hours on 1/28/1997
48-bit	281,474,976,710,656	313 hours on 2/10/1997
56-bit	72,057,594,037,927,936	22 hours on 1/19/1999
128-bit	340,282,366,920,938,463,463,374,607,431,768,211,456	not yet
168-bit	374,144,419,156,711,147,060,143,317,175,368,453,031,918,731,001,856	not yet

perhaps altered by an unscrupulous hacker, the digital signature on the content is invalid. Further, if the digital signature verifies, but the content provider's certificate, or the authority that issued the provider's certificate cannot be verified or trusted, the content should be questioned.

The use of packaging, digital signatures, and certificates for code signing produces a tamper-resistant package that both the consumer and the publisher can trust. The general process for code signing is illustrated in Figure 14-7.

1. Alice, using her private key, packages her code content and her certificate and applies a digital signature.

2. The digitally signed package is placed in the public domain for others to access. In this case it is placed on AB's Web server.

3. Bob, accessing information from AB's Web server, downloads the digitally signed package and verifies the signature on the package to determine the integrity of the contents.

The digital signing and verification techniques used above are the same as shown in Figure 14-3. For Bob to verify the signature placed on the package, Bob has to trust the authority that issued the publisher's certificate to Alice. Further, Bob has to determine if he trusts Alice as a software publisher, and if the contents of the package can be verified to match the signature placed on the package.

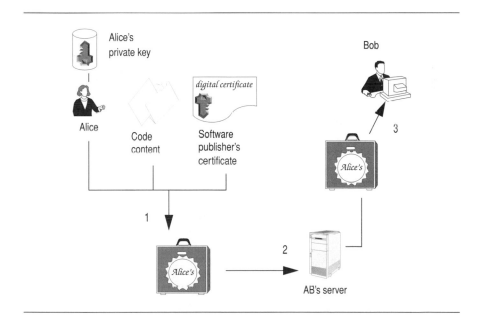

Figure 14-7   PKI in code signing.

14.5   Summary

Nonrepudiation, confidentiality, and integrity can all be achieved through the use of a Public Key Infrastructure (PKI). PKI uses digital certificates to identify individuals and organizations in cyberspace. Our trust in these certificates rests on our trust in the authorities that issue these certificates.

The following chapters build on the basic security concepts described in this chapter as we continue the narrative of our work on the DIRS project.

14.6   For Further Reading

A good, general introduction to cryptography for data security can be found in [Denning 83]. For a more general, but rather mathematical, description of cryptography and cryptanalysis see [Bauer 97] or, for public-key cryptography in particular, see [Salomaa 96].

One of the most authoritative and comprehensive books in the field is *Applied Cryptography: Protocols, Algorithms, and Source Code in C* by Bruce Schneier [Schneier 96]. It not only describes all the cryptographic techniques and algorithms that you are likely to come across, but also relates them to the real world, contains the source code for nine of the algorithms, and has a bibliography with over 1,600 references.

For digital signatures and their associated infrastructure, see [Ford+ 97]. *Web Security & Commerce* by Garfinkel and Spafford [Garfinkel+ 97] tackles the problem from the other side, explaining the risks and what can be done to minimize them.

14.7   Discussion Questions

1. Is trust essential to security?

2. We have discussed the application of PKI in ensuring nonrepudiation, confidentiality, and integrity. Can PKI also be used to provide assurance and availability? How would this be implemented?

15

A Certificate Odyssey

The thing's hollow—it goes on forever—and—oh my God!—it's full of stars!
—Dave Bowman in Arthur C. Clarke, *2001: A Space Odyssey*

This chapter resumes the case study narrative that was suspended so that we might introduce the fundamentals of public key cryptography in Chapter 14. The following discussion offers a dramatic illustration of how component selection decisions are governed by mutually constraining influences, with each selection decision seemingly dependent on other selection decisions. Quite often there is no *top* in the resulting decision lattice. Instead, detailed investigative work is necessary to untangle the knot of mutual dependencies.

15.1 Where Are We?

At the conclusion of Chapter 13 we had implemented a model solution using the direct IIOP ensemble. The solution required use of the Netscape capability classes and Netscape certificates to allow a signed applet to launch an external image viewer. The dependency on the Netscape capability classes and Netscape certificates constrained our solution to work only with Netscape Navigator. However, since the evaluation criteria for the model problem stipulated that model solutions must support at least Netscape and Microsoft browsers, we were forced to admit that the direct IIOP ensemble was not yet proven to be feasible. At the moment we were waiting on an anticipated market event—Java Protection Domains. Java Protection Domains had been presented at the leading Java conference (JavaONE) by Sun. If delivered, this product would provide a portable alternative to the Netscape capability classes—greatly improving the feasibility of the direct IIOP ensemble.

Although we were waiting on a market event, this did not mean that we were stymied or that we needed to remain passive. Much was entailed by the introduction of certificates and signed applets, and there was much to learn. Our immediate objective was to understand the degree of selection freedom available to us with respect to different certificate technologies. A secondary concern was to understand what sort of technical infrastructure would be needed to administer and sustain a public key infrastructure.

15.2   Exploring Certificate Space

1997 was an interesting year for Web technology. The browser war between Microsoft and Netscape alliances was raging, and a new front had been opened in the PKI arena. Every day, it seemed, brought new product announcements, vendor claims and counter-claims, few victories for the systems integrator, and many setbacks. The direct IIOP ensemble put our design effort at ground zero in this conflict.

Our immediate task was to determine the degree to which the direct IIOP ensemble could be realized with different vendor components, and, conversely, the degree to which we would be *locked into* particular vendor offerings. To obtain an answer to this question it was first necessary to define the design context in which selection decisions would be made. First, there was the question of which components to consider. Second, there was the question of which component interactions governed the use of these components.

COMPONENT CHOICES

Figure 15-1 depicts the component options that lie at the intersections of a technology by product matrix. We refer to this as a *binding box* since the components

	Javasoft	Microsoft	Netscape
Web browser	HotJava	Internet Explorer	Navigator
Web server	~~Java Web server~~	~~Internet Information Server (IIS)~~	Enterprise server
X.509v3 signing	Java certificate	Authenticode certificate	Netscape certificate
Signing tool	Javakey	Signcode	Signtool
Certificate manager	Javakey	CertMgr	Certificate management server

Figure 15-1   Component binding box.

may be bound to the more generic technology and product classifiers that are found in ensemble blackboards. As can be seen, Java Web Server and Internet Information Server have both been eliminated as viable Web servers. This decision had been made by the DIRS architect largely due to platform and performance considerations. The remaining technologies and products concern object signing. Three different varieties of signing certificates are included: Authenticode, Java, and Netscape certificates. All three of these were advertised as being X.509v3 certificates. The "v3" part of the X.509v3 standard, however, defines a standard way of introducing nonstandard extensions. Invariably, vendors take advantage of any such extension mechanism to differentiate their products in the marketplace. Differentiation, in turn, normally serves to limit interoperability. We had yet to discover whether there were significant differences among these forms of certificate, but we suspected the worst.

ENSEMBLE CONTEXT

The applet ensemble (both direct IIOP and direct HTTP variants) is a composite of several interactions. These can be thought of as distinct ensembles, or as blackboards that describe a subset of the interactions composed by the applet ensemble. In the discussion that follows, they are treated as distinct ensembles, since they seem to have independent identity, but this is probably a matter of taste. The applet ensemble is a composite of three ensembles:

- Identification and authentication
- Object signing
- Secure session

Why these three? Because they are fundamental to how the applet ensemble must work in DIRS. Users must be identified and authenticated—that is a requirement of the system. Secure sessions are an implied requirement, since data must be kept confidential and data integrity must be guaranteed. Object signing, as was discovered in Chapter 13, is not so much a requirement as it is a necessity imposed by the technologies being used: only applets trusted by the browser are allowed to launch an external image viewer and open connections to remote servers, and the browser uses object signing to establish trust. Each of these fundamental interactions is discussed in turn, with particular emphasis on issues pertaining to the use of certificates.

IDENTIFICATION AND AUTHENTICATION

The manner in which the applet ensemble (both the direct IIOP and direct HTTP variants) performed identification and authentication (I&A) was of critical importance because we expected to use this capability of Web browsers and servers *out of the box*. It was our intent to piggyback off of a robust single sign-on

I&A capability to implement secure sessions and user authorization in a way that was transparent to the end user.

The Web authentication ensemble was briefly discussed in Chapter 12. The blackboard depicted in Figure 12-4 combines *two* interactions: one interaction for I&A—in practice these go hand-in-hand—and one for the negotiation of a secure session. The blackboard depicted in Figure 15-2 differs from the one in Figure 12-4 in two important ways. First, in place of technologies there are products. Second, postulates have been replaced by credentials and constraints. So the blackboard asserts something that is known to be true of the products included in the ensemble.

Considering products first, DirectoryServer, a Netscape product, replaces the server-side certificate sources from Figure 12-4. As already mentioned, the DIRS project had more or less committed to using Netscape products on the server-side, mostly due to platform considerations. On the browser-side, the certificateSource from Figure 12-4 has been removed altogether since the source of certificates is

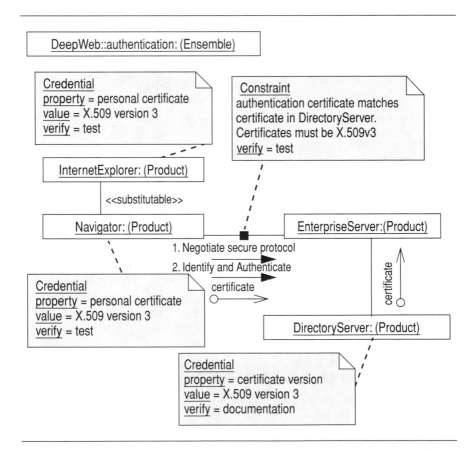

Figure 15-2   Web authentication blackboard.

the browser itself rather than a separate server. There are two browser products shown, and they may be used interchangeably, as the UML substitutable stereotype on their association indicates. That is, both browsers satisfy the ensemble constraint.

The constraint indicates that a user must present a certificate to be identified and authenticated, and that the Web server will see if a "matching" certificate can be found in DirectoryServer using an algorithm analogous to that described in "PKI in Identification and Authentication" in Chapter 14. If all of these checks pass, the server considers the client to be authenticated, checks what resources the client is permitted to access according to the server's access control lists (ACLs), and establishes a session for that user. If the answer to any of the questions is "no," the user is denied access to the server. As seen in a later chapter, the investment required to obtain this knowledge would yield a good return.

In summary, the direct IIOP ensemble and direct HTTP ensemble satisfy the multi-browser requirement with respect to the I&A interaction, and there was no need at this point to eliminate any component choices from the binding box.

OBJECT SIGNING

The principles behind object signing were described in "PKI in Object and Code Signing" in Chapter 14. Software objects are signed using *developer certificates,* which assert that the software object comes from a known source. Considered from the most generic perspective, object signing involves an interaction (and hence an ensemble) among the objects to be signed, a signing tool, and certificates. For DIRS, a more specific ensemble is required, where Java applets are substituted for generic objects, and Web browsers and servers are introduced to make explicit the context in which the signed applets will be used. A blackboard for this ensemble was shown in Figure 5-6. Java applets are signed using a signing tool such as *signtool*[1] or *javakey.*[2] The parameters to the signing tool include the applet to be signed, the developer's certificate, and the developer's private key. The signed applet can then be deployed to a Web site, downloaded to a browser, and recognized as being from the developer who signed the applet.

Since the direct IIOP ensemble was already constrained to use Netscape Navigator, it made sense to start with Navigator as an initial selection, and to discover any component incompatibilities entailed by that decision. Component vendors seldom list incompatibilities with other products. However, there are often clues regarding compatibility issues. Sometimes this is as simple as identifying components that are *missing* from a list of compatible components. Sometimes the clues are more subtle. We noticed, for example, that to purchase a software developer's certificate from VeriSign or Thawte we needed to first identify the object signing technology with which the certificate was to be used. It was possible that

[1] Originally, *signtool*, a Netscape product, was called "*zigbert.*"
[2] *javakey* is from Sun Microsystems and comes with Sun's JDK.

these companies were collecting this information for planning purposes but it was more likely that this information was necessary to correctly configure the certificate—suggesting that a single certificate did not work with a different signing technology. This turned out to be the case.

We already knew from the direct IIOP model solution at the end of Chapter 13 that *signtool* could be used with Netscape certificates to sign Java applets. However, we quickly discovered from reading the Netscape FAQ that Java applets signed using *javakey* would not be accepted by Netscape Navigator. This is because the signature (.rsa) file that *signtool* constructs is different than the one that *javakey* constructs. A large part of the difference is that *javakey* includes the entire signature (.sf) file in the .rsa file. As a result of this discovery, we were required to eliminate javakey as a component option, and the HotJava browser with it.

We next needed to determine if *signtool* could be used to sign applets using Java or Authenticode certificates. Recall from our earlier discussion that to digitally sign an object you need the object (naturally) and the developer's certificate and private key. Both Navigator and *signtool* know where to look for the certificate and private key in two files, cert7.db and key3.db. Examining the usage information for *signtool,*[3] we discovered two critical pieces of information. First, we discovered the –d option, which instructs *signtool* in which directory to look for these two files (that is, cert7.db and key3.db). Second, we discovered the –L option that lists all the certificates in these database files, marking certificates that are available for object signing with an asterisk.

Figure 15-3 shows the output of running the *signtool* command with the –L flag option on a Netscape certificate database. It can be seen from this listing that "Scott A. Hissam's Personal DIRS ID" and "myEntrustTestCert" certificates can be used for object signing. These certificates must have some property that distinguishes them from other certificates in the list that cannot be used for object signing. It was necessary to learn more about the content of these certificates.

Through earlier serendipitous discoveries we had learned about two utilities, *SSLeay* and *pfx*. The contents of a certificate can be viewed using the *SSLeay* utility. Unfortunately, *SSLeay* had no knowledge of the Netscape certificate database format. A bit of persistence was needed to get things into the right format. The first step was to export the object signing certificate of interest from the Netscape certificate database. Netscape Navigator can be used to export a certificate in PFX format through the security dialog window by selecting the certificate to export and pressing the export button.[4] PFX, invented by Microsoft, is a predecessor to

---

[3] Usage information for *signtool* is displayed when the command is run without parameters, or with incorrect parameters.

[4] Confusing things further, Netscape uses the extension .p12 and describes these files as being in "PKCS#12" format when they are actually in PFX format.

```
% signtool -L -d ~/.netscape
using certificate directory: ~/.netscape
- ------------
   GlobalSign Primary Class 3 CA
   VeriSign Class 1 Primary CA
   Verisign/RSA Commercial CA
   Deutsche Telekom AG Root CA
   Digital Signature Trust Co. Global CA 2
   Intranet Certificate Authority - Thawte Consulting
 * Scott A. Hissam's Personal DIRS ID
   VeriSign Class 3 Primary CA
   Verisign Class 1 Public Primary Certification Aut
   Thawte Premium Server CA
 * myEntrustTestCert
   GTE CyberTrust Global Root
```

Figure 15-3   Output from *signtool*.

PKCS#12. PFX specifies a format for storing or transporting a user's private keys, certificates, and miscellaneous secrets. Not surprisingly, the *SSLeay* tool has no knowledge of the PFX format either, so we needed to use the *pfx* utility to extract the certificate from the .p12 formatted file and save it as a PEM-encoded X.509v3 certificate:

```
% pfx -print_certs -in testcert.p12
```

This command generates a list of certificates and private key information contained in the .p12 in PEM format. We were only interested in the portion of the output representing Scott Hissam's certificate, shown in Figure 15-4.

```
subject=/C=US/O=DIRS/OU=Pittsburgh/UNKNOWN=shissam
        /CN=Scott Hissam/Email=shissam@sei.cmu.edu
issuer=/C=US/O=DIRS/OU=Pittsburgh/CN=Pittsburgh CA
-----BEGIN CERTIFICATE-----
MIICOjCCAaOgAwIBAgIBBjANBgkqhkiG9w0BAQQFADBQMQswCQYDVQQGEwJVUzEQ
MA4GA1UEChMHSkVETUlDUzETMBEGA1UECxMKSHVudHN2aWxsZTEaMBgGA1UEAxMR
SHVudHN2aWxsZSBTdWlgQ0EwHhcNOTgwMjEwMTgzMzEzWhcNOTgwODA5MTgzMzEz
+EIBAQQEAwIA8DAfBgNVHSMEGDAWgBR8pXRpZSjdpMGFqyDZPncn6PcNsjANBgkq
hkiG9w0BAQQFAAOBgQCJGjDKxCW+SAou7XioXekMLRw1qBw66TLAKlaqtnNBE9O+
LIn7VdhUYZqRaqFFux1LmWD3c4ywpMrnEWf38spkOHvDfLySMd4IP/5b2dH+ubqG
ScikBuoyxkgDcjEeVmbPFLOlQch5IIy/q/er18LUjqqYjG6FlC1lixCCg7eHPw==
-----END CERTIFICATE-----
```

Figure 15-4   Scott A. Hissam's Personal DIRS Certificate.

The portion of this output between "BEGIN CERTIFICATE" and "END CERTIFICATE" was saved to a file. Finally, we had a format that *SSLeay* understood, and we used it to display the contents of the certificate, as shown in Figure 15-5. The fragment of this output that was of interest is shown in boldface. This all sounds much more straightforward now than it seemed at the time. If nothing else, this illustration vividly demonstrates the kind of low-level, detailed analysis needed to analyze component dependencies.

After examining the decoded certificate, we noticed that the "Netscape Cert Type" X.509v3 extension was missing from both the Java and Authenticode certificates. Performing a search on "Netscape Cert Type" on the Netscape site we discovered the following information:

> Object Signing Certificates must have the **netscape-cert-type** extension. Object Signing CA certs must have the *Object Signing* CA bit set. Object Signing certs must have the *Object Signing* bit set.

```
% ssleay x509 -in testcert.pem -inform PEM -text
Certificate:
    Data:
        Version: 3 (0x2)
        Serial Number: 6 (0x6)
        Signature Algorithm: md5WithRSAEncryption
        Issuer: C=US, O=DIRS, OU=Pittsburgh, CN=Pittsburgh CA
        Validity
            Not Before: Feb 10 18:33:13 1998 GMT
            Not After : Aug  9 18:33:13 1998 GMT
        Subject: C=US, O=DIRS, OU=Pittsburgh/UNKNOWN=shissam,
                 CN=Scott Hissam/Email=shissam@sei.cmu.edu
        Subject Public Key Info:
            Public Key Algorithm: rsaEncryption
            RSA Public Key: (512 bit)
                Modulus (512 bit):
                    29:5e:30:b7:99:f7:50:e3:d0:f6:4a:78:64:1c:67:
                    60:4c:9a:7c:11:7d:8f:cb:c8:5a:96:0c:8a:61:22:
                    20:b6:16:d0:9c:17:c7:eb:6c:94:02:2d:90:f5:f4:
                Exponent: 65537 (0x10001)
        X509v3 extensions:
            Netscape Cert Type:
                ....
            X509v3 Authority Key Identifier:
                0...|.tie(..... .>w'..
    Signature Algorithm: md5WithRSAEncryption
...
```

Figure 15-5   Netscape certificate contents.

We had thus discovered that *signtool* is unable to use Java or Authenticode certificates to sign objects because these certificates lack the Netscape certificate extension identifying them (to *signtool*) as valid developer certificates.[5] This further explained why other Netscape certificates listed by *signtool* in Figure 15-3 were not marked as object signing certificates: they did not have the *Object Signing* bit set as also required by *signtool*. Microsoft Authenticode's object signing tool, *signcode*, does not require any special certificate extensions to be present to sign an object. Authenticode needs only to have a valid certificate, certificate authority, and private key to sign an object. However, *signcode* can sign 32-bit `.exe`, `.cab`, `.ocx`, and `.class` files but not the `.jar` or `.zip` files required by Netscape Navigator. This effectively eliminates *signcode* from consideration. But eliminating *signcode* has a further unpleasant ramification. Applets signed with *signtool* will work with Navigator but not with Microsoft IE because they are packaged as a `.jar` or `.zip` file and not in the `.cab` format required by IE. We had discovered yet another reason why the applet ensemble would not work with IE and Navigator. Things were going from bad to worse.

The binding box that is the product of these investigations is shown in Figure 15-6. These experiments confirmed our suspicions that object signing and certificate technologies from JavaSoft, Netscape, and Microsoft were largely incompatible.

	Javasoft	Microsoft	Netscape
Web browser	~~HotJava~~	~~Internet Explorer~~	Navigator
Web server	~~Java Web server~~	~~Internet Information Server (IIS)~~	Enterprise server
X.509 signing	~~Java certificate~~	~~Authenticode certificate~~	Netscape certificate
Signing tool	~~Javakey~~	~~Signcode~~	Signtool
Certificate manager	~~Javakey~~	~~CertMgr~~	Certificate management server

Figure 15-6   Component binding box.

[5] The skeptics might be thinking that we could have saved a great deal of time and effort if we had simply read the documentation. While this may be true, it is also true that the information in this case was stored on an obscure Web page on the Netscape site that we were unlikely to discover and read if we did not know what information we were looking for. Also, learning how to use these tools to discover this information often goes further in increasing your understanding of the underlying technology than just reading about it in the product documentation. Knowledge of these tools will most likely prove invaluable in the development and debugging of the system down the road.

SECURE SESSIONS

The principles of secure session were discussed in "PKI in Secure Sessions" in Chapter 14. Secure sessions are required in DIRS to ensure that data is kept confidential and that only authorized users obtain access to data. The ability to establish secure HTTP sessions is implied by the Web authentication ensemble which, as we have determined, works out of the box with Internet Explorer and Navigator. However, it still remained to be seen how IIOP sessions will be secured. Figure 15-7 extends the direct IIOP ensemble to show the three forms of interaction involving IIOP:

- Interactions between the applet and DIRS services, for example, the calls to the getImage box and getImage methods.

- Interactions among servers within the DIRS system, that is, within its *trusted computer base* (TCB); for example, the call to the audit method.

- Interactions among DIRS servers that span TCBs; for example, the call to the check remote index method.

Of these, the first and third need to be secured (as suggested by the IIOPS stereotype, mimicking the HTTPS convention used to distinguish between secured and unsecured HTTP transactions), while the second, being restricted to a single TCB, is already, by definition, secured. As is clearly depicted in the blackboard, the ORB plays a key role in securing these interactions. As with object signing, we needed to understand if there were product commitments implied by the use of certificate technology for single sign-on and applet signing.

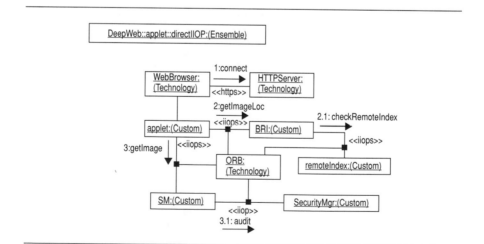

Figure 15-7   Secure interactions in direct IIOP ensemble.

Not surprisingly, there were. And, also not surprisingly, we had made the wrong initial choice of ORB.

The ORBs used to implement the direct HTTP and direct IIOP model solutions were IONA's Orbix and OrbixWeb. At this time, IONA's Orbix security solution was based on the OpenGroup's distributed computing environment (DCE) and not on secure socket layer (SSL), the industry quasi-standard defined by Netscape. SSL uses certificates to negotiate the details of an SSL session; the DCE approach did not use certificates. Continuing to use IONA's products implied the need to use—and administer—two different security infrastructures, one for HTTP-based interactions, one for IIOP. This was clearly unacceptable. If we wished to adopt PKI, we were forced to switch from IONA's ORB to an alternative ORB.

We previously had performed a risk/misfit evaluation of two popular ORBs: IONA's Orbix and Visigenics'[6] VisiBroker so we had a good understanding of the capabilities of both products. We knew that Visigenics provided an add-on product called the VisiBroker SSL Pack that could be used to secure communications between a VisiBroker client and server using SSL. Moreover, at just about the same time the DIRS redesign effort was initiated, Visigenics and Netscape had announced a strategic partnership which, among other things, bundled a VisiBroker ORB with Navigator to enable just the sort of ensemble we were investigating.[7] For these reasons we decided to reimplement the direct IIOP and direct HTTP model solutions with the VisiBroker 3.0 and VisiBroker SSL Pack 3.0.

Things proceeded smoothly until we attempted to use Netscape certificates to configure an SSL connection using the SSL Pack services. A little bit of investigation revealed the problem: while SSL Pack worked with Consensus certificates, it did *not* work with either Netscape or Java certificates. This was a rather serious problem that prevented us from supporting secure sessions between a Java application and a CORBA server or between CORBA servers using Netscape certificates which, to this point, were the only certificates we were able to use in code signing. We contacted Visigenics to report the problem, and they assured us that they were fixing the problem, and that we would soon receive a version of SSL that supported Netscape certificates.

But there was no disguising the fact that, once again, we had been thwarted. At this point, for the first time, we were beginning to question the feasibility of the entire family of applet ensembles. The rather disappointing result of the ORB switchover is shown on the blackboard depicted in Figure 15-8, which highlights the interactions needed to create secure (that is, SSL-based) IIOP connections between an applet and DIRS servers.

---

[6] Visigenics has since been purchased by Borland, who then changed its name to Inprise.

[7] It turned out that Netscape had bundled an already obsolete version of VisiBroker, which made this particular vendor partnership moot for our purpose.

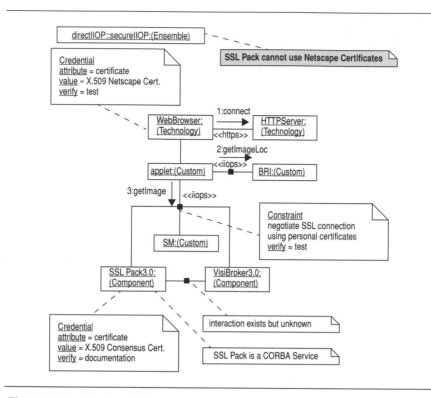

Figure 15-8   Another failure.

15.3   Sustaining the Public Key Infrastructure

An important consideration in the design of any large-scale information system is the policy and technical infrastructure needed to administer and sustain the deployed system. This is especially true where commercial components are used—there are analogous design problems introduced by the sustainment infrastructure to those already encountered for the deployed system.

CERTIFICATE MANAGEMENT POLICIES

Certificate management concerns such things as how certificates are requested, how the identity of the requestor is established, how certificates are issued and published, and, ultimately, how certificates are revoked. One option is to use the services of a certificate authority (CA) such as Verisign and Thawte. Once you have trust in an organization's policies for assigning certificates, you can trust that certificates generated by this organization are authentic. A second option is to create an enterprise-wide certificate authority (ECA). Both options were worth investigating, and each has its own advantages and disadvantages. Interestingly, the decision to use a CA or to establish an ECA involves deciding between a commercial service and a commercial component.

When we initially discovered in Chapter 13 that we needed a certificate for code signing, we thought that our only option was to obtain a certificate from VeriSign or another certificate authority. We also did not yet understand how the various types of certificates differed. We decided to obtain developer certificates from VeriSign, since these were the least expensive. To obtain a developer certificate from VeriSign, personal information must be submitted to VeriSign for verification of identity. VeriSign compares this information, such as social security number, home address, and credit card number, with information held by credit bureaus, in this case Equifax. Since two of the authors had recently relocated, Equifax did not have their correct home addresses. This led to time-consuming delays as we had to obtain copies of our credit record, update the information in the credit record, and resubmit a request to VeriSign. Even if your identity is correctly verified on the first pass, it can take three to four weeks of processing time to obtain a certificate.

While we were awaiting our certificates from VeriSign, we discovered that we could use the Netscape Certificate Manager Server to generate our own certificates, and in fact, we used these certificates in Chapter 13 to complete the implementation of our direct IIOP transfer model problem solution. We now had to decide which approach (commercial certificate services versus "roll-your-own" certificates) would be most appropriate for the DIRS program.

To help the DIRS program make this decision we developed a list of questions:

- How many, and what type of, certificates are needed? How often do these certificates expire? Will certificates need to be revoked?
- What are the initial and continuing costs of using a CA? Alternatively, what are the costs of setting up and maintaining an enterprise capability for managing certificates?
- What software exists for managing certificates? Does this software satisfy all the certificate management requirements? How much does it cost to buy and maintain this software?
- What type of processes are implemented by the CA? Does the CA have access to the criteria to decide which individuals/organizations should be granted certificates? Does the CA have adequate policies in place to ensure that only these individuals are granted certificates? Are these processes acceptable to the organization using the certificate authority?
- Can the CA ensure that legitimate certificate requests are handled in a timely fashion while still maintaining processes of sufficient rigor to warrant trust in the certificates they issue?

Incidentally, most of the issues underlying these questions were brought to the surface during our development of the model solutions in Chapter 13. It is highly unlikely that we would have obtained the requisite competence to ask these and similar questions on the basis of reading documentation alone.

Based on the earlier model problem, it was clear that DIRS would need *personal, server,* and *developer* certificates. One developer certificate would be sufficient for code signing purposes. Several server certificates would be needed to secure communications between the users and HTTP servers, users and CORBA servers, and between CORBA servers. At this point the exact number of servers in the final system was not known, but it was thought that the number would most likely be a single digit. However, personal certificates would need to be issued for each user. Since this is a large system installed at numerous locations with numerous users at each location, the number of personal certificates required would be quite large, possibly in the thousands.

Given the type and number of certificates required, we could estimate the initial and continuing costs of using a commercial CA. In 1997, individual certificates from VeriSign cost approximately $50 each.[8] Assuming 100 users at each of the 36 DIRS locations, user certificates alone would cost $180,000 for the first year—not an insignificant figure. Costs for other types of certificates are generally higher, as these are considered more "specialized."

As a result of this analysis, DIRS decided to adopt an enterprise-managed certificate process for two principal reasons:

- DIRS needed to establish custom processes for certificate management that would ensure that certificates were created for legitimate users in a *timely* fashion.[9]

- DIRS required a large number of certificates. The cost of setting up and maintaining an enterprise capability for managing certificates was considerably lower than using a commercial CA.

Before a final determination was made, however, it was necessary to ensure that software tools were available to manage certificates, and that these certificates would support the range of third-party systems that, in the long run, were intended to interoperate with DIRS.

CERTIFICATE MANAGEMENT SOFTWARE

The selection of certificate management software essentially depends on your ability to map the features and functions of the product to your organization's security policy and procedures. The specific choice of certificate management

---

[8] At the time of writing, in the waning days of the millennium, 50 certificates could be obtained from VeriSign for $747.50 USD.

[9] Current Enterprise offerings from VeriSign allow an organization to establish their own policies for issuing certificates although the cost of the service is still relatively high.

software is heavily dependent on the type of certificates needed, as we have seen, and the applications that are to use the certificates.

As we had decided, at least for the short term, to focus more narrowly on Netscape, we looked first at the Netscape solution. The Netscape Certificate Management Server (CMS) and Netscape Directory Server (DS) already have been mentioned in conjunction with applet signing. DS acts as a global repository for a wide range of application data, including user and group information, application preferences, CORBA object locations, and public-key certificates. The DS supports the open Internet standard lightweight directory access protocol (LDAP) and could communicate using LDAP over SSL. DS is used to store the certificates for users who are authorized to use the DIRS system. This implies that the DIRS website server requires authorized users to have a valid entry within DS.

Figure 15-9 illustrates the process that occurs to assign a personal certificate to an end-user using Netscape products—it is a blackboard in the form of a sequence chart. This process follows the general PKI process described in Chapter 14 which entails:

1. Requesting a personal certificate from a CA.

2. Reviewing the request and issuing the certificate by the CA.

3. Retrieving the issued certificate by end-user making the request.

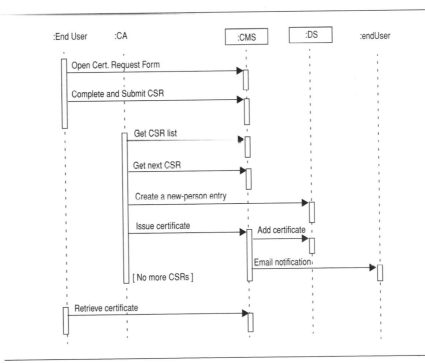

Figure 15-9 Generating a personal certificate.

Using Netscape products, the certificate issuing process is initiated by the end-user, who uses Netscape Navigator to access the public menu of the Netscape CMS. The user enters the required information, including the values that are included in the distinguished name field of the certificate and the user's contact information. When the form is submitted, Navigator generates a private and public key and retains the private key. The public key and required information is submitted for certification in the form of a certificate signing request (CSR).

The individual acting under the authority of the CA also uses Netscape Navigator to access the privileged menu within the CMS. This menu allows the CA to list pending CSR, revoke certificates, and update the directory server, among other functions. In this case, the CA retrieves the list of CSRs and processes each one. The information submitted by the requester is scrutinized and if the request is determined to be legitimate, the CA creates a new-person entry in the DS and issues the certificate. CMS, if configured correctly, automatically adds the certificate to the DS and e-mails notification to the end-user with instructions on how to retrieve the certificate. The newly issued certificate is considered "published" once it is stored in the DS.

We did not spend much time evaluating interoperability issues with respect to certificate management software, since by now we were well within Netscape's gravity field. As expected, personal certificates created by Netscape CMS version 1.01 were fully compatible with Netscape Navigator.

Netscape also provided patches to CMS that permitted Microsoft's Internet Explorer versions 3.02 and later to obtain personal certificates from CMS. This patch worked by first sensing if the incoming request was from Netscape Navigator. If the browser was Navigator, it would be redirected to the original site having access to all CMS functions. Otherwise, the browser would be directed to an alternate site providing only the function-supporting requests for a personal certificate. The patch did not allow non-Netscape browsers to perform other CMS functions such as requesting server certificates, listing other certificates generated by that site, and reviewing certificate revocation lists.

Here, too, it seems that the vendors have forced us into a proprietary solution, in this case the requirement for using Navigator to access CMS functions. However, this was not considered a failure with respect to the multi-browser criterion, since it was not thought that this criterion applied to system administrators.

15.4   Evaluation

As a result of the investigations described in this chapter, the applet ensemble appears, if anything, less feasible than when the chapter began. The direct HTTP ensemble had appeared at first to be feasible, at least in a limited sense. However, the lack of secure IIOP now called even that minimal feasibility into question. Moreover, the entire ensemble was now contingent on two events: the Java Protection

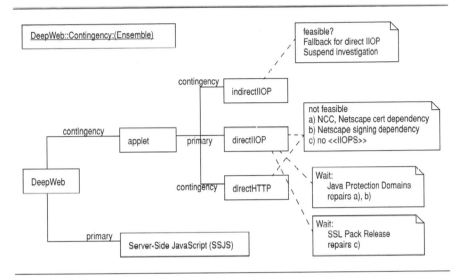

Figure 15-10   Revised DeepWeb Contingency.

Domains, which promised a nonproprietary alternative to Netscape capability classes, and the Visigenics patch that would enable their SSL Pack product to work with Netscape certificates. This state of affairs is depicted in the contingency blackboard in Figure 15-10.

Meanwhile, the server-side ensemble team continued to make progress. Consequently, the cost of switching from the server-side ensemble to the applet ensemble was increasing with each passing day.

15.5 Summary

Certificates play a key role in the DIRS system, supporting object signing, fine-grain access control, identification and authorization, and secure sessions. Due to incompatibilities in certificate formats and elsewhere, certificates from Sun, Microsoft, and Java proved to be largely incompatible. We were able to use certificates from a single vendor, in this case Netscape, to perform most of the security functions listed above. However, we were not able to use Netscape certificates to secure sessions because of incompatibilities with the VisiBroker SSL Pack. Another serious problem was the inability of a Java applet running in the Netscape browser to retrieve the private key for its corresponding certificate from the Netscape key store. Without this ability, the applet cannot establish secure sessions with CORBA servers, and the applet ensemble must be abandoned. As you will see, this problem is not resolved until the end of our narrative.

15.6 Discussion Questions

1. In this chapter we attempted to identify valid ensembles of security components. Although significant effort was spent in this endeavor, we did not consider every possible combination. For example, we discarded IONA's Orbix out of hand because its security model was based on DCE and not on SSL, without taking the time to compare DCE with SSL. Was this the correct decision?

2. The decision to support a Netscape product (Navigator) quickly snowballed into a decision to use the entire suite of Netscape products largely because of incompatibilities. How important is it to require products from multiple vendors to work together?

16

Applet Ensemble: The Middlegame

> *I have yet to see any problem, however complicated, which, when you looked at it in the right way, did not become still more complicated.*
> —Poul Anderson

In this chapter we end the R^3 cycle begun in Chapter 13, and begin a new R^3 iteration to address the design risks and misfits that had been exposed in the applet ensemble. We define three new model problems. One model problem takes the applet ensemble into the realm of security authorization. The second explores performance issues relating to large image transfer. The third explores a repair strategy that enables secure IIOP sessions.

16.1   Where Are We?

At the start of Chapter 13, we initiated an R^3 cycle to explore the technical ramifications of a design contingency, the applet ensemble. A model problem was specified for the applet ensemble, and two model solutions were created, one for the direct IIOP ensemble, and one for the direct HTTP ensemble. The direct IIOP ensemble had the merit of architectural simplicity, but only worked with Netscape certificate and object-signing technology. The direct HTTP ensemble was unwieldy, using IIOP to initiate service requests and HTTP to deliver image data.

Chapter 13 evaluated the model solutions with respect to component dependencies introduced by object signing and other uses of certificate technology. As a result of this evaluation, the applet ensemble was at risk of being infeasible because of these dependencies, and because of difficulties securing (specifically with respect to confidentiality) IIOP interactions.

Figure 16-1 shows the case study narrative in light of the overall design process. One set of model solutions had been developed and evaluated. Now it was

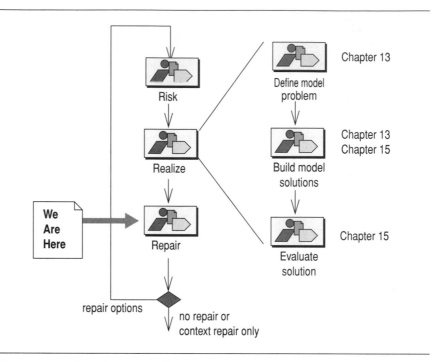

Figure 16-1   Completing an R^3 iteration.

time to consider if repairs were required for these model solutions and, if so, what were they?

16.2   Repair Analysis

While it might have been acceptable to become locked into Netscape products on the server side of DIRS, the user community would never accept a solution that restricted their freedom to choose their own browser. As a result, some repair was needed to remove the client-side dependency on Navigator. The two sources of this dependency were:

- Use of Netscape Capability Classes to extend the applet sandbox to allow ImageEdit to be launched.
- Use of Netscape Certificates for signing applets, a requirement imposed by Netscape Capability Classes.

Of course, applet signing might have been a good idea in any event, but the problem still remained that Netscape signing technology would not work with

Internet Explorer, and this was unacceptable. Yet there were hopeful signs that the market would produce an answer in the form of Java Protection Domains and the Java 2 plug-in. Java protection domains were a new feature built into the Java 1.2 JVM that provided an open alternative to Netscape's proprietary NCC API. The Java 2 plug-in would allow the applet to be bundled with the Java 1.2 JVM for its runtime environment. This simultaneously would provide a standard way of extending the applet sandbox and remove the dependency on Netscape object signing technology, which failed because Internet Explorer's embedded JVM only recognized cabinet files (files with a `.cab` extension) and not Java archive files (files with a `.jar` extension). Thus, it made sense to wait on a market event for this, the more so since there were other pressing issues that we could address while in the wait state.

In addition to these rather serious dependencies on Navigator, there was the still unresolved problem of how to secure IIOP interactions. The Visigenics SSL Pack *should* have worked with any X.509v3 certificates, but of course it did not. We were still waiting on a repair from Visigenics that would at least permit us to use Netscape Certificates to operate IIOP over SSL connections, even if the solution was restricted to work only with Netscape Certificates. Since Visigenics assured us that the repair was imminent, we began to prepare to build a model solution to demonstrate secure IIOP interactions. Unfortunately, there was another unpleasant surprise: Navigator did not have an API for obtaining the private keys stored in its proprietary database, yet SSL Pack required the private key to create an SSL connection. Even if the Visigenics repair arrived, it would be of no use at this point. The applet could not obtain the private key it needed from Navigator to open an SSL connection! There were three possible strategies to repair these problems with securing IIOP connections:

1. Develop our own API to the closed Navigator certificate and key databases

2. Use an alternative, possibly a custom certificate and key database

3. Use an alternative, possibly custom implementation of SSL or its equivalent

It was uncertain if the first of these options could be achieved. Netscape had been reluctant to publish the details of its certificate database format, arguing that to do so might have been interpreted as a violation of export control laws pertaining to key management technology. The certificate databases in question, after all, were the way Navigator managed its keys, and that certainly *sounded* like key management. But we thought that by applying appropriate black-box visibility techniques, we could discover the format of these key databases and develop our own public API wrapper to access the Navigator key database, not for export purposes, but for the purpose of component integration. Our adventures exploring this repair strategy are recounted in Chapter 21.

We were confident that the second option could be achieved, but were uncertain about the viability of this approach. Nevertheless, as a temporary fallback, it might be necessary to have an alternative handy. We were certain that the third option could be achieved, although it was not clear if it would be cost effective.

As with the custom database, however, it might prove useful to have a temporary alternative to SSL Pack while we awaited the market event—the next release of SSL Pack—that promised to repair the deficiency. The investigation of this repair is described in Chapter 19.

Around this time it became obvious that the root cause of most of these difficulties was the *browser itself*. The DIRS program commitment to a browser-based client had become something of a sacred cow, and belief in this as a fundamental tenet of the DIRS redesign had become, in the minds of some, a matter of intense religious belief. Notwithstanding this, one repair strategy became self-evident: get rid of the browser altogether. Instead, deploy the client as a stand-alone Java program. In a flash, most of the difficult integration problems we had encountered would simply disappear:

- The stand-alone Java client could open IIOP, HTTP, and SSL connections to backend servers, using nonproprietary interfaces.

- The Java client could still be user-deployed; users could connect to DIRS using a browser of choice and download the self-installing client, digitally signed with technology recognized by that browser.

- There would be no issue of security sandbox, and therefore no need to use proprietary browser interfaces to launch components such as a third-party image viewer.

Although this was a sensitive topic, the architect decided it was worth considering. What tipped the scales in favor of applying precious resources to exploring this radical repair option was that it could be combined with the investigation of a custom or alternative (to Netscape) certificate and key database. These combined investigations are described in Chapter 17.

The DIRS design space resulting from this repair analysis is depicted in Figure 16-2. Note that customDB is simultaneously a repair for the applet ensemble and a part of the application ensemble. Having identified a range of repair strategies, it was time for us to embark on another exploration—and to initiate another R^3 discovery cycle.

16.3   Risk Analysis

The first step of R^3 is risk analysis. It is important to take stock of the overall design situation to accommodate circumstances that may have changed in light of other developments. This is precisely what occurred in our case study. The main design option was able to retrieve images. However, system performance was not all that had been hoped, partly, it was thought, due to the overhead incurred in encrypting and decrypting images before and after transmission.

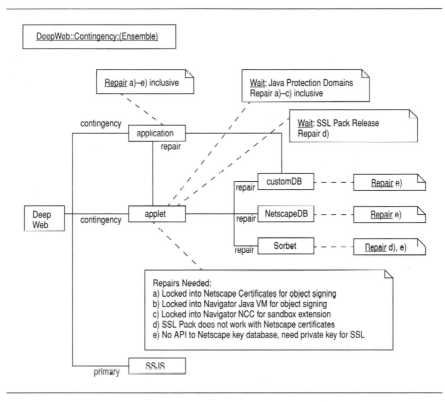

Figure 16-2   DeepWeb contingencies.

This tended to put questions of performance in sharp relief. Accordingly, we posed additional design questions:

Design Question #1: Could the direct IIOP and direct HTTP ensembles be distinguished with respect to performance measures pertaining to the transfer of very large images? In what way are these ensembles tunable for better performance?

Rather than burden the investigation of the above to repair options with additional questions, we decided to tackle performance in its own model problem workflow. Performance analysis of the direct HTTP and direct IIOP ensembles is discussed in Chapter 18.

While performance concerns may have been instigated by others on the design team, we had our own questions about the applet ensemble. With all of the effort expended worrying about browser dependencies and secure sessions, we had not lost sight of the question of authorization. Once users have been identified and authenticated, they will have permission to do different sorts of things. A quality assurance specialist might be allowed to insert images into the image store, while maintenance engineers might only be allowed to retrieve images. There were a variety of ways to implement user authorization with straightforward extensions of the applet ensemble. But given the propensity for the ensemble to surprise us (usually in unpleasant ways), we assumed the worst. We decided it would be prudent to demonstrate an authorization scheme in the applet ensemble, and so posed the following question:

> Design Question #2: Could the applet ensemble be extended to include user-level authorization in a way that piggybacks transparently (to the user) on the out-of-the-box identification and authentication mechanism supported by Web browsers and servers?

The need to obtain answers quickly required that we work on these questions concurrently. This called for additional staff effort, but every day without an answer meant an increase in overall design risk, since it was becoming more and more difficult to back out of earlier commitments. Figure 16-3 depicts the process

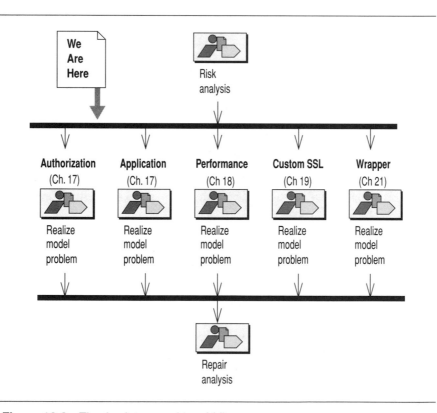

Figure 16-3   The Applet ensemble middlegame.

structure for these parallel investigations.[1] Each investigation was assigned its own workflow for specifying model problems and developing model solutions. Each workflow is also cross-referenced to the appropriate chapter. We leave the substance of Chapter 20 to be as much of a surprise to you as it was to us.

16.4   Summary

In this chapter there was a pause in the action as we studied the results of the model problem. We identified two repair strategies for the known deficiencies in the applet ensemble. One repair strategy proposed replacing browser-based Java applet clients with stand-alone Java application clients. The other proposed developing an API to allow an applet programmatic access to the Navigator certificate key databases. Meanwhile, new concerns surfaced involving system performance and user authorization. The need to address these concerns quickly required parallel investigation.

16.5   Discussion Questions

1. In what ways does the R^3 process just illustrated differ from Boehm's spiral model, in which each iteration is preceded by a risk analysis? In what ways is R^3 similar to the spiral model?

2. Of the five concurrent tasks depicted in Figure 16-3, are all equally important? How might you allocate resources to these activities? What sorts of questions would you ask?

3. Are there any dependencies among the tasks depicted in Figure 16-3 that suggest an ordering that is not apparent in their representation as concurrent activities?

[1] "Authorization" for extensions of applet ensemble for user authorization; "Application" for the Java client *sans* Web browser; "Performance" for performance analysis of different ensembles; and "Wrapper" for the custom API to the proprietary Netscape key databases.

17

Secure Applet Ensemble

For every problem, there is one solution which is simple, neat and wrong.
—Henry Louis Mencken (1880–1956)

In this chapter we construct two model solutions. The first demonstrates the feasibility of extending the applet ensemble to user authorization, while the second demonstrates the feasibility of a stand-alone Java application in place of the Web browser-based applet. Although the model solutions address different design risks, their structural similarity makes it convenient to consider them within the same model problem.

17.1 Where Are We?

At this point we divided work into several concurrent tasks, each addressing its own design risks. One of these tasks was to investigate the feasibility of extending the applet ensemble with user-level authorization. We started with the signed applet ensemble developed in Chapter 13. The intent of this task was twofold: first, to anticipate the imminent release of a Visigenics patch that would permit signed applets to open SSL connections to remote CORBA services; and second, to allay suspicions that some other unpleasant surprise awaited us when we extended the ensemble to authorization. At the same time, we investigated the consequences of replacing Java applets with Java applications for the client. The intent of this task was simplicity itself: bypass the Web browser and all of the integration difficulties attendant to Web browser-based clients.

Although these seem, on the surface, to involve different design questions, their solutions are structurally quite similar. The blackboards depicted in Figure

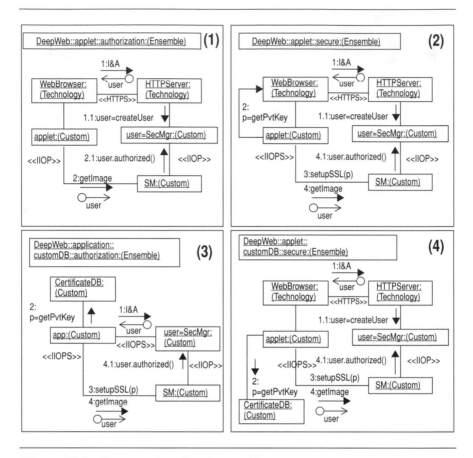

Figure 17-1 Four security-related ensembles.

17-1 show just how similar these are.[1] Although these blackboards are discussed in detail later, the following may be observed here.

The applet authorization ensemble (1) introduces a straightforward extension to the authentication blackboard described in Chapter 15. After authenticating, the HTTP server constructs a user object that is then passed back to the applet. The user object is included in all subsequent service requests made by that applet for interrogation by the service provider. Assuming this ensemble can be made to work (that is, we can bind components to this blackboard), a fully secure applet is not far away. In ensemble (2), the applet only has to obtain the private key associated with a user certificate to fully secure its interactions with DIRS. Of course, it is precisely this detail that has eluded us to this point. For this reason

---

[1] The ORB has been omitted for simplicity.

we need to investigate the browserless alternative (3). This ensemble is obtained by replacing the browser in (2) with a custom-built key database and removing the now superfluous HTTP server. The result would be as secure as (2), but without any browser or object-signing dependencies. Java applications easily can be converted to applets, and, in fact, it is relatively easy to create a Java program that can run as either an applet or an application. Simply reintroducing the Web browser and HTTP server to the secure Java application ensemble in (3) should be straightforward. The resulting ensemble (4) will again satisfy our security requirements. Of course, the applet in (4) must be signed for it to access a browser-side certificate database. This reintroduces the dependency on Navigator.

Thus, ensemble (4) can be considered a fallback position in case ensemble (2) does not work out, and ensemble (3) may well constitute an alternative to both (2) and (4). Clearly, all of these ensembles are closely related. The work described in Chapter 21 tackles the difficult task of discovering the format of Netscape's proprietary certificate database so that the browser-side API to this database could be developed. However, ensembles (1) and (3) appeared to be relatively straightforward. We expected these to work and were more concerned about encountering unexpected obstacles. And, if (3) could be developed, and we were confident of this, then (4) would involve only a small matter of programming. Since (1) and (3) were in our grasp, and were so closely related, we decided to deal with both in the same model problem.

17.2   Model Problem

To define a model problem, we need a hypothesis, evaluation criteria, and design constraints. (See "From Toy to Model Problem" in Chapter 6.) The hypothesis and criteria are easily dispatched given the preceding discussion. A discussion of design constraints is more involved, as you will soon see.

> Hypothesis #1: An applet ensemble can be constructed that transparently (to the user) uses off-the-shelf Web Browser to HTTP Server I&A as a basis for fine-grained, operation-level access control based on user- or role-specified permissions.

> Hypothesis #2: A Java application ensemble (no Web Browser) can be constructed that supports I&A and fine-grained, operation-level access control based on user- or role-specified permissions, and the Java application can be converted easily to run as an applet.

It may appear as if we are cheating since the model problem has more than one hypothesis, and not very similar hypotheses at that. However, the evaluation criteria are almost identical:

> Criterion #1: The ensemble must identify and authenticate users requesting access to the system.

Criterion #2: Authenticated users are authorized to access privileged resources but prevented from accessing restricted resources.

Criterion #3 (Java application only): Communication between the applet running in the browser and back-end servers is confidential.

Criterion #4: The overhead required to implement operation-level access control should be acceptable with respect to responsiveness.

Criterion #5: The resulting system must be easy to operationally manage and maintain.

Most of these criteria are straightforward, though the last two are somewhat ambiguous. Notwithstanding the ambiguity, the criteria can be evaluated, and bear sufficiently well upon the hypotheses. The third criterion only applies to the Java application, as the inability of applets to satisfy this criterion was what motivated us to remove the browser in the first place. What remains are the design constraints that model solutions must satisfy.

In the previous model problem (Section 13.3), the constraints involved binding components to technologies and products. However, design constraints often reflect business processes and business rules (or policies). Such is the case with the current model problem, and criteria #1 and #2 imply as much. In particular, both criteria tacitly refer to some underlying security policy. Referring to criterion #2, for example, how are authorizations granted and revoked? Will user authorization refer to specific services, or specific data images? Are permissions allocated to *individuals*, or to *roles* that may be played by individuals? To make sense of these and many analogous questions, it is necessary to define the security context in which the model solutions operate. This means defining security policies and creating the infrastructure to install and administer these policies. These constitute the constraints imposed by the model problem.

SECURITY POLICY

The security policy defines, among other things, how users and servers identify themselves. The security policy defines user roles, their associated privileges, and the scope of these privileges. In defining the security policy, we want to keep things as simple as possible, but no simpler. This means that some of the functionality in the end-solution is omitted from model solutions.

Users supply personal certificates to the system for purposes of identification and authentication. DIRS servers likewise supply server certificates to identify and authenticate users. Since role-based access control was not required by the evaluation criteria (and involved more work), we defined only a single class of user. These users can access the DIRS installation which issued their certificate—but no others. To access more than one DIRS installation, the user must be issued a certificate from each installation, as shown in Figure 17-2. This is an important simplifying assumption, but it does have an effect on how the certificate authority structure is defined.

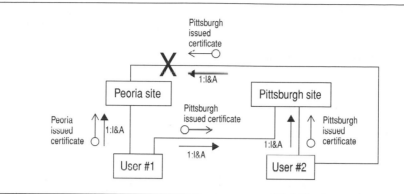

Figure 17-2 Certificate issuing and acceptance policy.

Instead of setting up a single CA at one location, responsibility for issuing certificates was delegated to subordinate CAs. This was a logical approach given the decision to require users to obtain certificates from each DIRS site. The X.509 standard supports setting up a hierarchy of CAs. In this model, the root CA is at the top of the hierarchy and has a self-signed certificate. The root CA can delegate the authority to issue certificates to a subordinate CA. These subordinate CAs can also delegate issuing authority to other CAs.

We established a simple CA hierarchy for DIRS, shown in Figure 17-3. This consists of a root CA at the DIRS program office and subordinate CAs at the Pittsburgh and Peoria DIRS installations. The ou, o, and c fields correspond respectively to the *organizational unit, organization,* and *country* fields in the distinguished name. The client or server will accept certificates signed by all of the subordinate CAs without user-intervention dialog boxes on the client. If a new subordinate CA is added, the server will automatically accept certificates

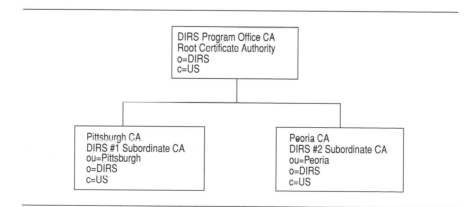

Figure 17-3 Certificate authority hierarchy.

signed by the new subordinate CA. If, as in the model problem security policy, a server in Pittsburgh (for example) wishes only to accept certificates issued by the Pittsburgh CA, it can load the Pittsburgh CA certificate into its local database, and mark that CA as trusted, while marking the root CA as untrusted.

CERTIFICATE MANAGEMENT INFRASTRUCTURE

To develop model solutions that implement the CA just defined, we needed a certificate management server (CMS) for each CA in the hierarchy. A CMS was installed as the root authority at the DIRS program office and as subordinate authorities at the Pittsburgh and Peoria locations. In addition, we needed to establish operational environments in both Pittsburgh and Peoria. It required installing a Netscape Enterprise Server and Netscape Directory Server (DS) at each of these locations.

We simulated geographic distribution in our lab by installing the servers on different workstations. This eliminated the possibility that servers installed on the same machine were interacting indirectly with each other or communicating via shared memory or other mechanisms. Figure 17-4 shows the certificate management infrastructure. At the same time, it shows the component binding decisions that govern the model solutions. Once again, we have opted to use Netscape components to implement the required infrastructure. Note that it was not necessary that the DIRS program office be at a separate location, so we located the root authority CMS at the Pittsburgh location.

Once installed, we configured the servers to support the security policy outlined earlier. Root CAs were chained to each subordinate CA using CMS menus. This enforced the CA hierarchy defined in Figure 17-3. We then installed root CA certificate and marked it as an *untrusted* CA in each subordinate CMS. Each site's server was enabled for SSL using the corresponding subordinate CA as the

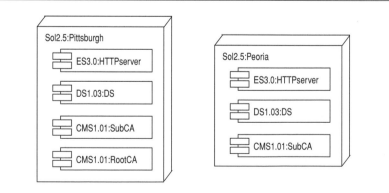

Figure 17-4   Deployment view of certificate infrastructure.

issuing authority. For example, the subordinate CA at Pittsburgh issues the SSL site certificate for the Pittsburgh server. Similarly, the subordinate CA at Peoria issues the SSL site certificate for the Peoria server. The corresponding subordinate CA was installed and marked as trusted in the server's certificate database (using the management software menus provided with the enterprise server). Each directory service was added to the corresponding enterprise server and CMS. Each DS could then be updated with the user, server, and CA certificates for the site.

17.3 Model Solutions

With hypothesis, criteria, and design constraints all defined, it was time to construct the model solutions. The first model solution implements the applet authorization ensemble (1) from Figure 17-1, the second implements the Java application ensemble (3), also from Figure 17-1.

JAVA APPLET AUTHORIZATION

This model solution, which implements ensemble (1) in Figure 17-1, automatically handles authentication between the browser and the HTTP server. The HTTP server interrogates the browser for the client certificate, validates the client certificate, and matches the supplied certificate with the one in the directory server. Figure 17-5 shows the sequence diagram for the model solution. The steps above the dashed line refer to the identification and authorization performed by the Web browser and HTTP server. The steps below refer to the user authorization.

Once the enterprise server authenticates the client certificate, some additional steps are required before the HTML page containing the applet can be downloaded to the browser. In particular, some form of session identifier is needed that can be passed as a parameter on calls from the applet to back-end servers to prove that the client already has been authenticated. This is important as it is too costly (in terms of performance) to reauthenticate the client on each request. In this model solution, a *user object* is created to act as a session identifier. The user object is implemented as a CORBA distributed object, encapsulating information about the user—including information derived from the user's certificate. A reference to the user object is passed as a parameter in all method calls from the applet to the back-end servers. Back-end servers can invoke the user object to verify user authorization or to audit an event.

Creating the user object relies on two features of the Netscape enterprise server: *Server-side JavaScript* (SSJS) and *LiveConnect*. JavaScript is Netscape's scripting language for adding dynamic behavior to an HTML page. JavaScript comes in two different varieties: client-side JavaScript runs within the browser process and allows an application, for example, to place elements on an HTML form and respond to user events such as mouse clicks, form input, and page navigation.

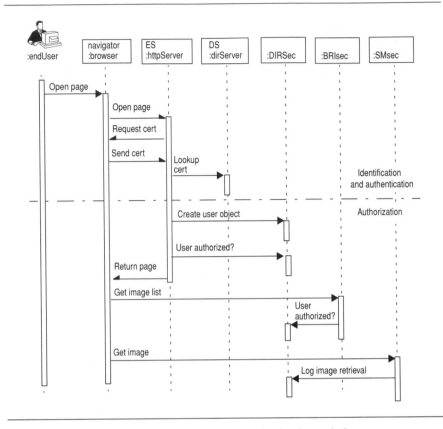

Figure 17-5 Sequence diagram for applet authorization solution.

Server-side JavaScript runs on the server platform. It allows applications, for example, to communicate with a relational database, provide continuity of information from one invocation to another, and to perform file manipulations on a server. LiveConnect connects server-side JavaScript applications to Java components or classes on the server. It is then possible, through Java, to connect to CORBA-compliant servers using VisiBroker for Java.

To create the user object, we must first initialize the ORB and then connect to the *user factory*. The user factory is an implementation of the factory creation design pattern [Gamma+ 94]. Since the creation of the user factory and the initialization of the ORB only need to be performed once, both these operations are implemented on the SSJS `start.html` page, shown in Figure 17-6.

The `start.html` page runs when the enterprise server is started. SSJS uses LiveConnect during the execution of the `start.html` page to invoke Visi-Broker methods in Java. These methods initialize the ORB and establish a connection with the user factory object. Both the ORB reference and user factory

```
<server>
// initialize the orb
project.orb = Packages.org.omg.CORBA.ORB.init();

// establish connection to the "UserFactory" service
project.DIRsecUserFactory =
   Packages.DIRsec.UserFactoryHelper.bind(
      project.orb,
      "UserFactory"
   );
</server>
```

Figure 17-6   start.html.

references are stored as properties of the *project* object. The project object is one of four session management objects predefined by SSJS for storing and retrieving information between HTTP connections. The project object is used to share data among multiple clients accessing the same application.

The user factory and user objects interface are defined in the DIRS security (DIRsec) module. The DIRS security module is a CORBA server, added to the basic Web ensemble to support security functionality. Figure 17-7 shows the IDL for the security server. The user object contains methods for checking to see if a user is authorized to use the DIRS system and for logging image retrievals. It will be observed that the security server is quite trivial. That is, of course, intentional. A successful model solution is one that focuses on the essentials of the model problem. It would, of course, be possible to implement a more realistic security service, but such effort would not be justified.

```
// DIRsec.idl
module DIRsec {
interface User {
    boolean authorized();
    void logImageRetrieval(in string image);
  };
interface UserFactory {
typedef sequence<octet> DERcert;
User createUser(
      in string uid, in string cert, in string ip);
User createDERUser(
      in string uid, in DERcert cert, in string ip);
  };
};
```

Figure 17-7   IDL for security service DIRsec.

Initializing the ORB and creating the user factory occur just once—when the enterprise server is started. We also need to execute SSJS logic to create a new user object upon the start of each new client session. To implement this functionality, we created the `index.html` SSJS page shown in Figure 17-8. This SSJS code is to used to retrieve the client's certificate from the enterprise server and uses the certificate to create a user object. Netscape servers assign values to a set of environment variables, called CGI variables, when setting up the context for running a CGI script. The CGI variable `CLIENT_CERT` contains the client certificate. This CGI variable can be accessed from JavaScript applications using the `ssjs_getCGIVariable()` method as shown on line 2 of the SSJS code in Figure 17-8. The certificate is used, in conjunction with other information retrieved from the *request* object, to create the user object. The request object is another of the four predefined SSJS objects and contains data about the current

```
1.  <server>
2.  cert = ssjs_getCGIVariable("CLIENT_CERT");
3.  __userObj = project.DIRSsecUserFactory.createUser(
4.      request.auth_user, cert, request.ip);
5.  __strUserObj=project.orb.object_to_string(__userObj);
6.  __authorizedUser = __userObj.authorized();
7.  if ( __authorizedUser) {
8.    write("<P>Enter the search criteria:");
9.    write("</td></tr></table>");
10.   write("<center>\n");
11.   write("<applet\n");
12.   write("code=DIRSapplet.class\n");
13.   write("codebase=\"DIRSappletDemo\"\n");
14.   write("archive=\"dirsec.zip\"\n");
15.   write("width=600 height=250>\n");
16.   write("<param name=USE_ORB_LOCATOR value=>\n");
17.   write("<param name=org.omg.CORBA.ORBClass
18.         value=com.visigenic.vbroker.orb.ORB>\n");
19.   write("<param name=strUserObject value=");
20.   write(__strUserObj);
21.   write(">\n");
22.    write("<h2>Error running applet");
23.    write("</applet>\n");
24.    write("</center>\n");
25. }
26. else {
27.   write("Unauthorized client access\n");
28.   write("</td></tr></table>");
29. }
30. </server>
```

Figure 17-8 ORB and applet initialization in Index.html.

What You Don't Know Can Hurt You

During the design of the model solution, we decided to store the user object in the SSJS *client* object. The client object is one of the four predefined SSJS objects. As there is one user object per client object, this appeared to be the logical location to store this information.

When implementing the model solution, we discovered a peculiarity about SSJS; namely, that the client object cannot be used on the application's initial page. In our case, this meant that the user object had to be assigned to either a local attribute or to an attribute of the project object. This is representative of the type of information that can only effectively be gained by implementing model problems. This problem was mainly an annoyance, but similar problems can invalidate a design. Defining model problems and implementing model solutions can reduce these risks.

—rCs

client request. In this case, we extract the name of the authorized user and the originating IP address of the request and store this information in the user object.

After the user is authenticated, the HTML page is constructed using the SSJS `write()` function. The generated HTML includes an `applet` tag (lines 11–23 in Figure 17-8) that downloads the DIRS applet to the browser. The DIRS applet accepts several parameters including a "stringified" reference to the user object, as shown in lines 19 and 20. Once downloaded and launched, the applet reconstitutes the user object from the stringified reference and presents it as a session ID on calls to back-end servers to prove that the client has been authenticated. As this object reference is also passed as a parameter on each remote method invocation, these servers can invoke this remote object to validate that the client is authorized to access a particular resource or to make a record of an auditable event.

JAVA APPLICATION

Recall that we proposed the Java application ensemble as a repair strategy for the dependency on Netscape Navigator. Although this certainly seemed to be an effective way to deal with that dependency, we knew it was a rather draconian measure. We also knew that Java applications, in theory, can be developed to make them run as stand-alone clients and, with minor modification, as Web browser applets. We were, in effect, letting this model solution do double duty. First, to demonstrate the viability of a non-browser solution for DIRS. Second, to allow us to implement the needed client-side infrastructure if we chose to stay with the applet ensemble but still required a client-side certificate database. (One thing our experience has taught us is to never do anything for just one reason.)

Since we tackled the application ensemble first, we implemented the I&A interactions formerly performed by the (now missing) Web browser and server. To save effort, we piggybacked on the applet model solution described earlier in this chapter and extended the DIRS security server so that it could authenticate a personal certificate presented by the Java application. As we have seen already, Netscape Navigator retrieves a certificate from its own internal certificate database and presents it to the HTTP server for authentication. Since this certificate is not available, we must extract a certificate from a custom certificate database instead. Unfortunately, this means that in an applet solution two certificates need to be presented, and each certificate must be authenticated. However, this was always implied by repairs that bypassed the Navigator certificate database.

Figure 17-9 shows the sequence diagram for the Java application model solution. When the end-user logs in, `DIRSclient` (the Java application) reads the certificate from the custom certificate database. The custom certificate database is simply a directory containing DER-encoded certificates in the format *uid*.der, where *uid* is the user's ID. The DIRS client creates a user object by passing the certificate, user ID, and local IP address to the `createDERUser()` method in the user factory. The code that runs on the client platform for reading in the certificate and creating the user object is shown in Figure 17-10.

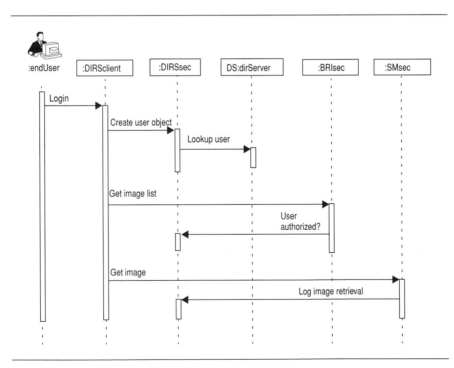

Figure 17-9   Java application (custom certificate DB) model solution.

```
FileInputStream f = null;
byte[] myCert = null;
String UserID = "hd";

factoryRef = DirSec.UserFactoryHelper.bind(
   orb, "UserFactory"
);
f = new FileInputStream (UserID + ".der");
myCert = new byte[f.available()];
f.read (myCert);

userRef = factoryRef.createDERUser(
   UserID, myCert,
   java.net.InetAddress.getLocalHost().getHostAddress()
);

if (userRef.authorized()) {
    System.out.println ("Welcome");
} else {
   System.out.println ("Unauthorized Access!");
   System.exit(0);
}
```

Figure 17-10   A simple Java application.

The user factory in the security server uses the certificate and the other data as parameters to the `createDERUser()` method to determine if the user is authorized to use the system. The user object uses the Netscape LDAP Java SDK v. 1.0 to retrieve the user's certificate from the directory server and compares the certificate presented by the user to this retrieved certificate. If the user is authenticated, a user object is created. The remaining interactions between the client and DIRS services follow the model solution outlined for the applet authentication model solution, except an application, not an applet, makes the requests. For the user to be authenticated, the following conditions must be true:

- The certificate presented must be issued from the site.
- The X.509 distinguished name fields, `cn=`, `uid=`, `email=`, `ou=`, `o=`, and `c=`, must be found in the LDAP server.
- The certificate presented must match the certificate found in the LDAP server.
- The certificate must not have expired or been revoked.

The security server used the `java.security.cert` package in the (then) newly released JDK 1.2 release for parsing and managing certificates. Although we used the JDK 1.2 certificate API for certificate management in the model solution, we did not use Java certificates because they were incompatible with both Netscape Navigator and the Netscape Enterprise Server. To use Netscape certificates in our custom database solution, we had to first convert them into DER-encoded certificates following the process described in "Object Signing" in Chapter 15.

EVALUATION

The applet authorization model solution worked without a hitch, and satisfied each criterion of the model problem, except for the one concerning confidential communication, but that did not apply. For once, we had good news to report, however modest an accomplishment the model solution seemed. Still, one significant outcome of the applet authorization work (besides a few moments of cheer) was an elaboration of alternative certificate management policies, and rationale for selecting the one chosen to constrain the model solutions just described.

The results of the Java application model solution were decidedly mixed. Certificate management is a major weakness of this ensemble. Netscape certificates are managed using the Netscape certificate management server, directory server, and browser. Installing these certificates in the custom certificate database meant manually extracting them from Navigator and installing them in the custom database. This makes certificate management awkward for the end user. It also makes it impossible to use a single database of certificates for authentication by the browser and by a Java applet or application running on the client platform. Moreover, the flexibility to define DIRS-specific I&A policies was more than outweighed by the cost of developing and maintaining a custom I&A solution.

In short, we had learned enough to sustain embers of hope for the applet ensemble. However, we were forced to admit that the Java application ensemble looked better on paper than in implementation. Still, we did not rule out a custom certificate database, although everyone agreed that due to the increased complexity of administering multiple certificates, this design option could only be exercised under extreme duress, and even then only as a very short-term contingency.

17.4   For Further Reading

A paper by Seacord and Hissam, "Browsers for Distributed Systems: Universal Paradigm or Siren's Song?," provides an in-depth discussion of the pros and cons of browser and browserless approaches [Seacord+ 98]. The paper (the title says much about the point of view expressed in the paper) was a healthy sanative to much of the hype that surrounded the use of the Web as a panacea for enterprise integration.

17.5   Summary

In this chapter, we defined a model problem to explore two design alternatives. One alternative remained rooted in the applet ensemble. It was contingent on a repair that would enable IIOP interactions to take place over SSL. The second alternative was identified during repair analysis. It sought to eliminate the browser from the design, and with it the source of a great many integration difficulties. However, a closer look at these two alternatives revealed commonalities. In particular, both combined the custom certificate database from the Java application ensemble with the Web browser from the applet ensemble. This meant that we could design one model problem to explore both ensembles, and could use the model solutions to give our design effort flexibility in the form of a fallback position (applet ensemble with custom database) and a fallback for that fallback (the Java application ensemble).

17.6   Discussion Questions

1. It is clear that the Java application ensemble posed no serious technical challenges. Should additional work have been performed to test the assertion that the Java application could be turned into an applet? Why or why not?

2. Propose two alternative approaches for adding authorization to the applet ensemble, and produce blackboards for these alternatives. What criteria can be defined to compare and, ultimately, to choose one from among these alternatives?

18

Instrumented Model Problem

with Daniel Plakosh[1]

> *One never notices what has been done.*
> *One can only see what remains to be done.*
> —Marie Curie

This chapter describes a model problem that analyzed the performance characteristics of different approaches to moving large image data in DIRS, varying in size
from approximately 25MB to 2GB.

18.1   Where Are We?

Chapter 14 identified repair options and additional risks that needed to be understood before the applet ensemble could be considered feasible. One area of risk
was system performance. We were less than satisfied with early performance testing on the main server-side design option, and we assumed that the applet ensemble would only exacerbate performance problems. What was unclear, however,
was the extent of this degradation, or if performance overhead might be outweighed by ease of system maintenance or other quality attributes. In addition,
there are different ways to implement file transfer using CORBA. Before deciding if the performance of the applet ensemble was adequate, we first had to determine the method of transferring files that provided the best performance. For
these reasons, the design team decided to analyze the applet ensemble in terms of
latency of large-image transfer. While we could have studied many other aspects
of performance, image transfer latency presented substantial risk.

---

[1] Daniel Plakosh is a senior member of the technical staff at the Software Engineering
Institute, Carnegie Mellon University.

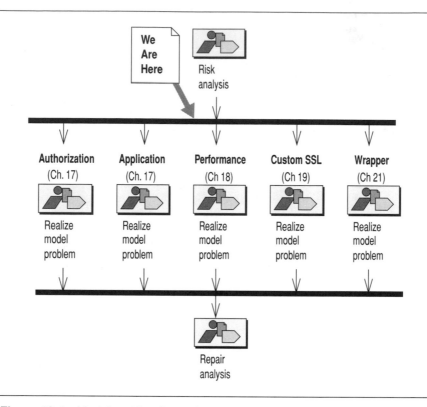

Figure 18-1   Model problem for performance analysis.

Figure 18-1 shows process context of this investigation. The analysis that follows was not intended to be conclusive or exclusive; rather, the evidence generated was to be just one factor in determining the feasibility of the applet ensemble.

18.2   Model Problem

The File Transfer Protocol, commonly referred to as FTP, is one of the fastest ways to transfer large files between two computers in a distributed environment because it is a very thin layer implemented on top of sockets. FTP represents a gold standard for performance analysis. Benchmarking with FTP would give us a lower bound for further comparisons.

CORBA provides a mechanism for distributed objects analogous to remote procedure call (RPC), and was not designed to transfer large amounts of data. For example, CORBA does not transfer sequences of octets (8-bit data) without a complete memory-to-memory transfer of the entire octet sequence. That is,

CORBA performs the transfer by first allocating the required amount of memory in both the client and server. This can easily result in a transfer failure and/or unpredictable performance problems due to memory swapping or a memory allocation failure when the sequence size approaches or surpasses a machine's physical or virtual memory capacity. Thus, to reliably transfer a large data set using CORBA, the data set must broken down into smaller, manageable pieces and transferred in fragments. This introduces application complexity and run-time overhead.

HTTP has its own problems, chief among which is the run-time expense of the required MIME-encoding of 8-bit image data into a form suitable for transmission as 7-bit ASCII data. This encoding would be, of course, in addition to any prior encoding; for example, encrypting of image data.

The performance discussion of FTP, IIOP (by way of CORBA), and HTTP was expressed as the following hypothesis and evaluation criterion:

> Hypothesis: An applet ensemble can be implemented that provides adequate performance with respect to the latency required to transfer images ranging in size from 25MB to 2.5GB of 8-bit data.

> Evaluation Criterion: Image transfer latency in the applet ensemble should be perceived by users as commensurable with data transfer latency using Web browsers and servers.

The evaluation criterion involves user perception. For the evaluation phase, we substituted our own judgments for actual users. Of course, this can be a dangerous decision. But at this point in the design effort, we could evaluate as well as actual users reasonable latency for Web-based access to large data. Besides, getting actual user input at this point could be risky. We did not want to go to the time and expense of developing user-friendly graphical interfaces or finding appropriate users from the various DIRS installations.

We imposed two constraints on the model solutions. First, the model solutions were constrained to use VisiBroker 3.0 and VisiBroker for Java 3.0. Second, the model solutions needed to guarantee reliable data delivery. It would not be acceptable to sacrifice reliability on the altar of performance.

18.3   Model Solutions

We were, of course, constrained to use the applet ensemble in its two varieties: the direct IIOP ensemble, and the direct HTTP ensemble. There still remained considerable flexibility in these ensembles, especially in terms of how CORBA would be used. This flexibility resulted in a number of ensemble refinements, which became the basis for model solutions. These model solutions were then instrumented. The following sections describe these ensemble refinements and their instrumentation.

ENSEMBLE REFINEMENTS

CORBA provides four basic ways to transfer data:

- Synchronous method invocation
- Asynchronous "one-way" method invocation
- Deferred synchronous method invocation
- Event channels

Each of these can implement different patterns of interaction than those already encountered in the applet ensemble. Thus, each of these can be thought of as refinements of the applet ensemble.

Synchronous Method Invocation. Synchronous method invocation is the equivalent of classic RPC. Its advantages include simplicity and reliability. The synchronous method is similar to simple method invocation. The programmer can be shielded, to some extent, from the complexities of distribution. Since an application can always determine if the remote call was successful, it is reliable. On the other hand, synchronous invocation requires the caller to be in lock step with the remote server, possibly limiting application performance.

Asynchronous "One-way" Method Invocation. A CORBA one-way method invocation allows the application to continue executing immediately after the invocation. This can improve application performance. However, since no return values can be provided, including exceptions, this method must be considered as unreliable. The application has no way of determining if the operation was successful.

Deferred Synchronous Method Invocation. The CORBA dynamic invocation interface (DII) allows a client to asynchronously invoke a method and later synchronously retrieve the status of the operation along with any return values. This method allows applications to continue with other processing after the invocation. This improves performance without sacrificing reliability. Its disadvantage is client-side programming complexity. Moreover, it is still necessary to synchronize with the server to check the status of an operation. Since a constraint of this model problem is reliable delivery of data, we must perform a synchronous rendezvous with the image server for each image fragment delivered. Thus, it was unclear that DII held any benefits for DIRS, at least in the context of this model problem.

Figure 18-2 shows the four ensembles that correspond to the most natural ways of using synchronous and one-way communication in CORBA. The applet client pull (1) is the most straightforward. It involves a series of synchronous calls to the storage manager (SM) by the client applet to receive an image. The applet server push ensemble requires the applet to provide a client-side helper object. It, in turn, provides an interoperable object reference (IOR) to receive data pushed to it by SM. The remaining two ensembles recapitulate the direct HTTP ensemble (4) and its equivalent by substituting FTP for HTTP (3). We did not consider using DII. In our judgment, DII did not provide sufficient advantage to

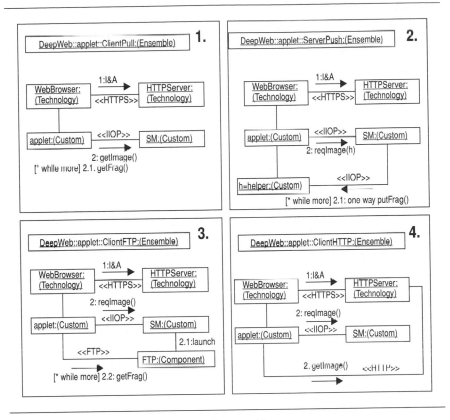

Figure 18-2   Four non-event channel ensembles.

outweigh added client-side complexity. These four ensembles were implemented as instrumented model solutions. We also investigated a variety of ensembles using event channels.

CORBA Event Channels.   Event channels support one-to-one, one-to-many, and many-to-many interactions. Producers and consumers register with event channels. Each may choose to implement a *push* or *pull* interface. A *push producer* invokes the event channel to push data onto the channel. A *pull producer* has its interfaces invoked by the event channel whenever there is demand for data. Conversely, a *push consumer* has its interface invoked when there is data available on the channel. A *pull consumer* invokes the event channel when it wishes to receive data from the channel. An event channel can have any number of push and pull producers and consumers. This distribution method returns control immediately to the application. It also allows multiple consumers and producers, and permits the consumers to individually select the push or pull model to receive data. However, this model has two severe disadvantages. The reliability of

CORBA event channels is implementation-defined. Also, at that time, vendors only transferred data of type "CORBA:Any" over an event channel. "CORBA:Any" objects allow any type data to be inserted into them and to be retrieved. However, experience has shown that the use of the "CORBA:Any" object incurs a significant performance penalty.

Figure 18-3 depicts three additional ensembles that we instrumented. In ensembles (5) and (6), SM provides the IOR for its dedicated event channel. In ensemble (7), the client must provide the IOR for its helper, which is then installed as a push consumer of the SM event channel. Ensemble (8) is pathological in the present circumstance. There is never any stimulus that provokes an event channel to pull data from a producer.

In all cases but (4), the image is transmitted to the client in fragments. Of these, all but (3) required the client and SM to agree on the fragment size before initiating the transfer. In (3), fragments were purely a client-side decision about the number of bytes pulled from the FTP connection. The fragment size used in (4) was not under our control.

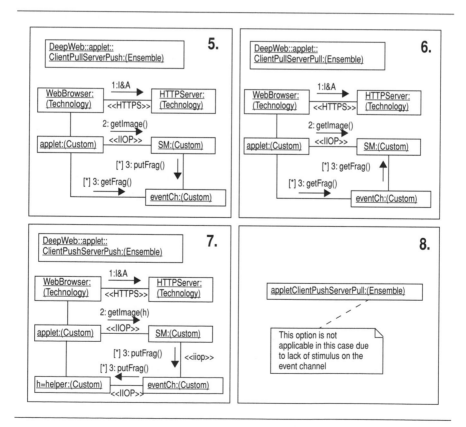

Figure 18-3 Three event channel ensembles.

INSTRUMENTING WITH THE TEST HARNESS

We developed a test harness to measure the image transfer latency of our model solutions. The test harness had two parts, the client side and server side. We could "hot switch" from one ensemble to another without restarting the client or server applications. In addition, we designed the server software to support all of the selected data transfer models. The server software included a file search feature that was implemented using CORBA and Java. The client software could be executed as either a Java applet or Java application. In this way, we could determine if a browser had any effect on transfer performance.

All software was written in the Java programming language. The FTP server was the standard software included with all Unix operating systems. Note that the FTP software in the client was written in Java to limit the effects of language difference with respect to performance. However, the FTP software on the server remained in a compiled programming language.

Using the test harness, we could search for a particular file name, select the transfer method and fragment size, and download a file from the server. During the file transfers the following statistics were captured:

- Image size
- Transfer time
- Transfer rate
- Fragment size
- Number of fragments

Once a file download was complete, the statistics of the transfer were appended to a comma-delimited log file for import into Microsoft Excel, and presented on screen to the user as shown in Figure 18-4. The test harness and server

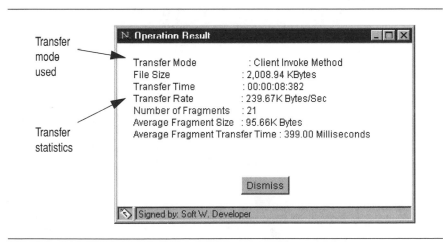

Figure 18-4   Results interface.

software were designed to be "throw-away software." We developed this software and gathered data in approximately three person-weeks of effort.

18.4 Evaluation

As with most experiments, some of the results were expected, while other results were quite surprising. The results are summarized in Table 18-1.

Our first discovery concerned CORBA one-way method invocations in the applet server push ensemble (2). We expected that one-way invocations would always be reliable notwithstanding the lack of return values for error codes or exceptions. However, we encountered approximately one failure in fifteen thousand invocations on the remote server—the "helper" IOR in ensemble (2). That is, 1 in 15,000 invocations were never executed on the remote server. This caused us to change the one-way calls in applet server push ensemble (2) to synchronous method invocation.

We also did not expect the poor performance of the modified (to remove the one-way calls) applet server push ensemble (2). In theory, it should have performed similarly to the applet client pull ensemble (1). Further testing (by comparing runs of applets and applications) determined that the performance discrepancy was caused by the CORBA server within the browser. If the browser was not in the way, and one-way worked as expected, this ensemble could possibly rival FTP. But established fact suggested otherwise.

Table 18-1   Summary Test Results

Method (ensemble #)	Fragment Size (K)	XFER Time (hh:mm:ss)	XFER Rate (KB/Sec)	#Fragments	Avg. Fragment Size (K)	Fragment XFer Time (ms)
Client Pull (1)	0.50	0:06:42	55	44,304	0.50	9.0
	1.00	0:03:36	103	22,152	1.00	9.0
	10.00	0:01:25	261	2,216	10.00	38.0
	100.00	**0:00:55**	**401**	**222**	**100.00**	**248.0**
Server Push (2)	0.50	1:02:02	6	44,304	0.50	84.0
	1.00	0:31:13	12	22,152	1.00	84.0
	10.00	0:03:59	93	2,216	10.00	107.0
	100.00	0:01:26	258	222	100.00	387.0
Client FTP (3)	0.50	0:00:32	686	49,508	0.44	0.7
	1.00	0:00:32	689	25,195	0.87	1.2
	10.00	**0:00:31**	**701**	**5,764**	**3.84**	**5.0**
	100.00	0:00:36	614	5,644	3.92	6.0
Client HTTP (4)	N/A	0:00:54	408	N/A	N/A	N/A
Event Channel Push-Push (7)	0.5					
	1.00					
	10.00					
	100.00	0:12:40	29	222	100.00	3,421.0

The poor performance of CORBA event channels also took us by surprise. In fact, the performance was so poor that testing was suspended. The culprit was the "CORBA:Any" objects combined with the Java programming language. Running the same tests using C++ in place of Java improved performance by a factor of four, but still did not provide acceptable results. Naturally, we eliminated event channels from our list of viable options.

We were not surprised to observe that an excessive number of fragments reduces the transfer rates. There is on-the-wire overhead associated with each message on the network. As a consequence, the overhead becomes proportionately larger as the size of the messages becomes progressively smaller. Additionally, each method invocation also increases processing (CPU) time to both the client and the server. In our tests, 100K fragments performed best.

Also, as expected, FTP provided the best overall performance, approaching the line speed of 10 Mbps ethernet at 75% utilization. The fragment sizes for FTP in these experiments are the size of buffer for the read operation in the FTP client software. As discussed earlier, this is because FTP does not support a fragment transmission size. For the CORBA-based solutions, the best performance was achieved using the applet Client Pull ensemble (1), which provided about one-half the performance of FTP.

The ensembles that performed best, highlighted in Table 18-1 in boldface, are the applet Client Pull and applet Client FTP ensembles. The worst, applet Client Push Server Push, is underlined. Having identified the best, we then ran tests to simulate user-perceived performance for images of sizes varying from 2.5MB to 2.5GB. This analysis is presented in Table 18-2. It shows that using CORBA to transfer files, from the user perspective, can significantly increase the amount of time to transfer a file. In the worst case, the user would have to wait an additional 37 minutes! To fully appreciate this impact, it would be necessary to determine the distribution of image sizes over the DIRS image population, usage patterns against this image population, and other factors.

Still, it was difficult to escape the conclusion that these results were going to reduce the feasibility of a pure-IIOP solution. Despite added complexity when compared with a pure-IIOP solution, using FTP or developing a (probably quite simple) custom image transfer protocol directly on top of TCP now appeared to

Table 18-2   The FTP/IIOP Difference

Ensemble	File Size	Transfer Time (HH:MM:SS)	IIOP Difference (HH:MM:SS)
appletClientFTP	25MB	00:00:37	+00:00:27
appletClientPull		00:01:04	
appletClientFTP	2048MB	00:49:52	+00:37:18
appletClientPull		01:27:10	

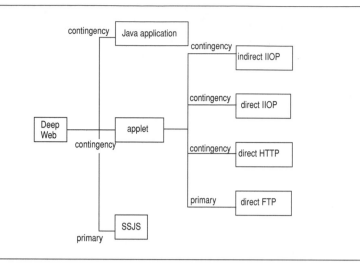

Figure 18-5 DeepWeb contingencies.

be the leading candidate, as is reflected in the revised DeepWeb contingency structure shown in Figure 18-5 (annotations have been eliminated for clarity).

18.5 Summary

The problem of moving large images was central to DIRS, so it was critical that images be transferred in an efficient manner. Ensuring that the core system functionality can be achieved is a precept of software engineering—akin to the idea in law enforcement of "following the money." In the case of DIRS, if these large images could not be transferred efficiently, the design was a non-starter.

Analyzing performance through benchmarking and simulation is no more than good engineering practice. However, using both ensembles and model problems provides an effective way of structuring performance analysis. Ensembles (and their blackboards) express detailed contextual assumptions relating to performance measures. They also organize the results of benchmarking efforts in a way that is easily grasped by design decision makers. Model problems are a management tool for allocating and tracking resource expenditures for technical explorations.

18.6   Discussion Question

1. From the test results in Table 18-1, the server invoked push and CORBA event file transfer methods show dramatically poor performance relative to the other methods discussed in this chapter. Explain under what circumstances it would be acceptable to use these slower modes of file transfer.

19

Sorbet: A Custom Ensemble

with Fred Long[1]

> *It has been related that dogs drink at the river Nile running along, that they may not be seized by the crocodiles.*
> —Phædrus, 8 AD

Sometimes it is necessary to develop custom components even when commercial alternatives exist. This may be true even if the commercial alternatives are more capable than the custom alternative. For example, a commercial component might be deficient in some way, but it is expected that a future release will remove the deficiency. In this scenario, the custom component can be a stopgap repair measure. A custom component can also be a fallback position in case an anticipated component release is late or never arrives.

19.1   Where Are We?

The Visigenics SSL Pack provided a robust implementation of SSL, but Visigenics had not yet delivered a version that worked with Netscape certificates. In Chapter 16 we thought of developing a custom alternative to SSL Pack to repair the applet ensemble. At first this appeared to be a drastic remedy. However, it became apparent that a custom alternative to SSL Pack could be developed with a modest level of effort. Moreover, the approach we had in mind was highly complementary with the authentication and custom key database ensembles that were concurrently being investigated (see Figure 17-1). In fact, we were able to share code with these ongoing investigations to improve the efficiency of the prototyping effort.

---

[1] Fred Long is a senior lecturer in the Department of Computer Science at the University of Wales, Aberystwyth, in the UK.

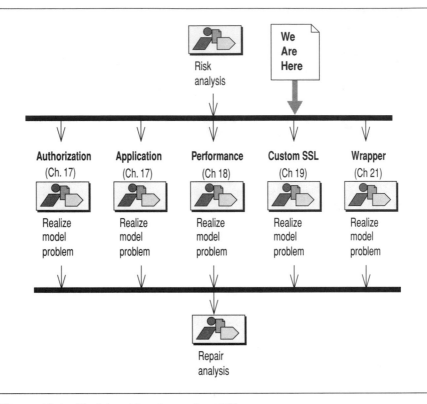

Figure 19-1   Model problem for custom SSL.

In this chapter we define a model problem to assess the feasibility of developing a custom alternative to SSL Pack. If this proves feasible, the custom alternative might replace SSL Pack. More likely, though, it could provide a temporary remedy until a version of SSL Pack that worked with Netscape certificates was available. Figure 19-1 shows the context of this investigation.

19.2   Model Problem

The question we posed was whether we could construct a custom alternative to SSL in time and within a limited budget. Moreover, this custom alternative could not sacrifice robustness. It had to support all of the security-related quality attributes that we hoped to obtain by using IIOP over SSL in general, and Visigenics SSL Pack in particular, including:

- bidirectional identification and authentication (I&A)

- confidentiality
- integrity

Each of these security attributes was discussed in Chapter 14. We have already seen unilateral I&A in the model solutions of Chapter 15 and Chapter 17. Bilateral I&A is just that: it involves a mutual process of determining who resides at the other end of an interaction. Confidentiality is typically achieved by encryption, and, where PKI is used, data integrity is achieved by digital signature.

In addition to security quality attributes, there was a growing concern about performance. While the final results of Chapter 18 were not yet available, there was a widely shared concern that the performance of the applet ensemble might not scale well, especially when handling large images (200MB and more). For this reason we felt that we had to demonstrate a solution that scaled well to large image transfer. This led to the following hypothesis for the model problem:

> Hypothesis: A custom alternative to SSL can be created within 30 days that supports bidirectional I&A and confidentiality, can be implemented with little effort, performs well when handling large images, and is as robust as its commercial (SSL) counterparts.

This was a tall order, but, as in many aspects of life, what was more important than the statement of objective was a statement of how success would be measured. After some discussion, we developed evaluation criteria that balanced the architect's desire for visible, tangible proofs of feasibility (that is, running code) against the reality of compressed schedules and limited resources. There were, after all, several other contingencies being investigated concurrently, and in some cases by the same design team members.

Evaluation Criterion #1: Unidirectional I&A is demonstrated.

Evaluation Criterion #2: Conceptual demonstration of how confidentiality and integrity would be achieved.

Evaluation Criterion #3: The solution should be easy to build and to maintain.

Evaluation Criterion #4: Measured performance is comparable with SSL Pack.

Parsing these criteria shows what had been achieved in negotiating with the architect. First, we only needed to demonstrate unidirectional I&A. It was understood that if I&A worked in one direction, it could be made to work in both directions. We also convinced the architect that a good, clear specification of how we intended to achieve confidentiality and integrity in the custom ensemble would be sufficient to prove its feasibility. As it turned out, we did better than that by providing a prototype demonstration. We thought that the limited time available to produce a model solution would adequately demonstrate ease of development and maintenance. In fact, we already had in mind a model solution, and suspected that it involved only a small amount of code. However, the architect insisted (and rightly so) on a proof of performance, and this remained an essential measure of success.

As for constraints, we were required to use the Visigenics ORB, and to use Netscape certificates. This reflected a continuing desire to implement a "single sign on" approach through the Web browser, which meant certificate-based I&A. However, we were enjoined to develop the model solution as an application and *not* as an applet. Since the model solution must implement certificate-based I&A, the client-side is required access to a certificate database. This was a known problem with applets and a principal cause for concern. We would develop other model solutions to deal with the certificate database—either implementing a custom API "wrapper" of Navigator or a custom certificate database. This model problem was to focus on SSL-like functionality.

19.3 Model Solution

The model solution implemented the Sorbet (Secure ORB Enterprise Transactions) ensemble, which is described by its blackboard in Figure 19-2. We used a feature of the Visigenics ORB, called interceptors, to make Sorbet (mostly) transparent to developers of DIRS clients and servers. At that time, interceptors were optional features of CORBA ORBs. Interceptors are placed between the sender and receiver of a request. We used interceptors to inject session information into IIOP messages on the requestor side, and to strip off this information on the provider side. The details of how interceptors are used are described later.

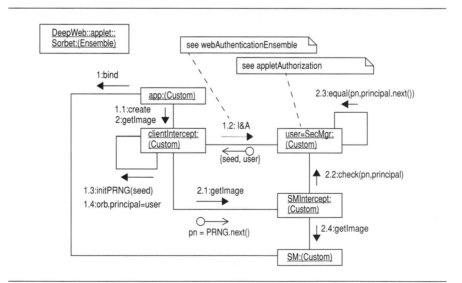

Figure 19-2 Blackboard for Sorbet ensemble.

The blackboard does not show the details of certificate-based identification and authentication, which have already been described elsewhere (see Figure 15-2). An annotation on the I&A interaction references the pertinent blackboard. Similarly, the Sorbet ensemble reuses the pattern of interaction centered on the security manager (SecMgr) component in the applet authorization ensemble (see Figure 17-1). An annotation links Sorbet to the pertinent blackboard. Note also that the I&A operation is unidirectional in Sorbet. The interpretation of the blackboard is that the client is authenticating to the server.

At start-up, the client and server each register interceptor factories with the ORB. The client then calls an application server such as the SM. This call causes the client interceptor factory to create a client interceptor. The client interceptor initiates a series of steps to authenticate to the SecMgr and receive a valid session object.

The details of I&A and session object creation are shown in Figure 19-3. To initiate I&A, the client interceptor loads its credentials from a keystore[2] located on the client platform and presents these to SecMgr. SecMgr creates a challenge consisting of a random stream of bytes and returns it to the client interceptor. The client interceptor formulates a response to the challenge by signing the challenge with the user's private key and returns the response to SecMgr. SecMgr uses the

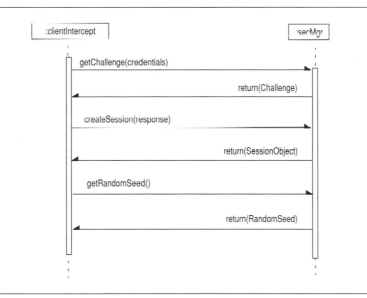

Figure 19-3   Client authentication.

[2] A database of private keys and their associated X.509 certificate chains. This is the same implementation used to develop the custom certificate database model solution discussed in Chapter 17.

client's public key to verify that the response received was in fact the random data signed using the client's private key. If the response is verified, SecMgr creates a session object and returns it to the client along with a seed that is encrypted using the client's public key. The client and session object use this seed to initialize a cryptographically secure pseudo random number generator (PRNG). On the client side, the session object is set as the default *principal* for all further messages emanating from that client. A principal is a CORBA-defined element that may be inserted optionally into IIOP messages, and is intended to identify the initiator of a request (although it can be used for other purposes).

Assuming client authentication is successful, both the session object and the client now use the same seed to start tandem pseudo random number generators (PRNGs) to provide a synchronous step operation. At this point, the client can begin making calls to the application service. The first call causes the server interceptor to be created.

The server interceptor, client interceptor, and session object work together to provide a secure session. For each method call made by the client, the client interceptor steps the client's PRNG and injects the generated random number into the message. The server interceptor strips the random number from the message and invokes the session object, which it identifies from the principal, to verify the random number. When the session object receives this request, it steps its own PRNG and compares this with the random number extracted from the message. The session object returns a result of true if the random numbers are the same, and false otherwise. If true, the server passes the request through to the application server. If false, the server interceptor throws an exception that is caught by the client interceptor. Further action can be taken on the application server side to log the attempt or break the connection as required by the security policy.

So far, Sorbet has handled I&A. The synchronized session object even provided an additional measure of security in that now it will be exceedingly difficult for eavesdroppers to interpose themselves and "hijack" a session, even though the session may be operating in the clear. That is, an eavesdropper may discover the random number sent as part of a client request (since neither it nor the message has yet been encrypted), but this discovery cannot be used to predict what the *next* random number will be. Even the discovery of the session object is of no value. For example, the eavesdropper may attempt a denial of service attack by invoking the session object's verify method. If executed, this would cause the session object to become "out of synch" with the client, causing a service disruption. However, this is easily remedied in one of two ways. First, we can assume that server-to-secMgr interactions take place within a trusted computing base, in which case the identity of all servers is known a priori by the SecMgr and can be checked prior to invoking the verify method (or, rather, the random number step function that is part of that method). Second, we can apply the Sorbet idea uniformly, thus requiring all servers (except SecMgr, of course) to have their own session objects. This second approach is rather stringent, however, and the first was considered sufficient for DIRS.

It still remains, however, to ensure confidentiality. It would be possible to use asymmetric key encryption, but that would guarantee that Sorbet would fail to satisfy its performance criterion. To meet performance objectives, we need to use symmetric key cryptography. But how could client and server establish a shared, secret key? The answer lies in the Diffie-Hellman algorithm, defined by RSA and put in the public domain [Diffie+ 76]. Diffie-Hellman allows two parties to establish a shared secret key by exchanging information in the clear. The algorithm begins with two parties, P1 and P2, publicly agreeing on a prime number p and base number g. Each party then selects a secret number, s, and computes a temporary number t:

$$P1_t = g^{P1_s} \bmod p$$

and

$$P2_t = g^{P2_s} \bmod p$$

P1 and P2 then exchange their temporary numbers $P1_t$ and $P2_t$, and use the information just received to generate a seed k:

$$P1_k = P2_t^{P1_s} \bmod p$$

and

$$P2_k = P1_t^{P2_s} \bmod p$$

At this point $P1_k = P2_k$ and these values can now be used to generate a shared secret key.

The strength of Diffie-Hellman depends on the size of the prime modulus p. At the time the Sorbet ensemble was being tested, it took over seven hours to compute a 1,024-bit prime modulus on (then) high-end Pentium desktops. Of course, it would be possible for DIRS to pre-compute a large set of prime numbers and to periodically refresh this set. Alternatively, clients could choose to generate p on demand, opting to accept a smaller modulus and some start-up penalty in exchange for guaranteed uniqueness of the shared secret. It was not clear how this tradeoff would influence Sorbet's ability to meet its performance criterion.

Using the VisiBroker for Java ORB, we developed prototype CORBA objects for P1 and P2 that implemented the Diffie-Hellman key exchange, and from this, demonstrated Triple-DES encryption of data passed between P1 and P2. Since it would be only a small matter of programming to incorporate this demonstration into the client and server interceptor code that already implemented I&A and session object instantiation, we had, in effect, satisfied the criterion for confidentiality. Further, since we were still free to digitally sign all encrypted messages, Sorbet guaranteed data integrity. If Sorbet demonstrated comparable performance to SSL Pack, it would be proven feasible with respect to its evaluation criteria.

Since the selection of encryption mechanism was in some respects orthogo-nal to Sorbet, and in any event could be negotiated at runtime, we decided to benchmark Sorbet and VisiBroker SSL Pack performance without data encryp-tion; SSL Pack used without encryption is referred to as *SSL null*. SSL null elim-inates encryption (and therefore confidentiality) but retains I&A. For testing purposes we used 2MB files, transmitted in 0.5KB, 1KB, 10KB, and 100KB fragments. (We naturally borrowed code from the performance analysis model problem discussed in Chapter 18.) We discovered that even though the overall shape of their performance curves was comparable, Sorbet was noticeably slower than SSL Pack. The results are summarized in Figure 19-4. A (very) little analy-sis showed why this is so: in Sorbet, every client-side IIOP request is translated into two server-side IIOP requests, one to check the session object, and, if that turns out to be valid, one to satisfy the client request.

Throughout the development of the Sorbet model solution, we had been, in effect, mixing the tasks of producing a model solution and evaluating our results, beginning first with establishing interceptor-based I&A with session objects, then moving on to confidentiality and integrity, and, finally, to performance analysis. It was only during performance analysis that we discovered the need to at least consider repairs to improve Sorbet performance. Clearly, we needed to eliminate the extra server-side IIOP call. The most obvious repair was to move the code that stepped the PRNG into the server interceptor. This option is labeled *opti-mized Sorbet* in Figure 19-4. Unfortunately, this optimization assumes that clients communicate with just one server, which would invalidate much of the justifica-tion for applets in the first place. Recall that the originating idea for applets was that the client could open channels to multiple DIRS services. Pressed for time, we were not able to repair Sorbet.

We did, however, investigate other ways to improve Sorbet performance. Sorbet used the Sun Java Cryptologic Extension (JCE) technology for signing and verifying signatures. Signing and verification in Sorbet takes place during

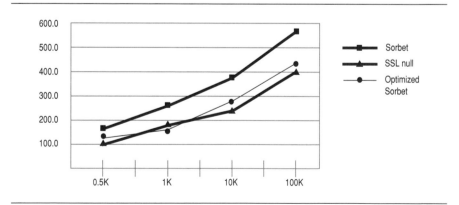

Figure 19-4   Performance comparison: Sorbet versus SSL Pack.

Table 19-1   Signing Performance

	Solaris 2.5.1 (first)	Solaris 2.6 (first)	WinNT (first)	Solaris 2.5.1 (average)	Solaris 2.6 (average)	WinNT (average)
Crypto-J	2.4	2.1	2.1	7.7	4.9	0.08
SunJCE	16.1	9.9	5.5	1.3	0.9	0.08

Table 19-2   Verification Performance

	Solaris 2.5.1 (first)	Solaris 2.6 (first)	WinNT (first)	Solaris 2.5.1 (average)	Solaris 2.6 (average)	WinNT (average)
RSA	3.2	2.5	2.0	1.5	0.9	0.1
Sun	0.3	0.2	0.2	0.2	0.1	0.1

initialization of a connection; for example, in a CORBA-based application, this initialization occurs during the `bind()` operation. The time it takes to sign and verify can vary significantly (see Table 19-1 and Table 19-2) based on the product used to perform the cryptologic functions and the platform.

Both signing and verification measures were taken on three platforms (Solaris 2.5.1, Solaris 2.6, and WinNT). Data was collected for the first time the function was invoked and an average of the subsequent four invocations. This was important in that, for some operations, there was greater than an order of magnitude difference in performance between the first and subsequent calls.

The Crypto-J package had much better times than SunJCE for signing, but verification times were better in SunJCE. If we replaced the use of SunJCE with Crypto-J in Sorbet, we would expect to see an overall decrease in the time spent in initialization, which could improve throughput in systems with many connections.

19.4   Evaluation

Sorbet had clearly satisfied several of its success criteria. The model solution clearly demonstrated unilateral I&A. With a little effort, it easily could be extended to bilateral I&A. Confidentiality was demonstrated in two ways. First, through the public-domain Diffie-Hellman key exchange algorithm. Second, in a prototype demonstration of the use of Diffie-Hellman to generate secret keys and the subsequent use of these keys for data encryption. Integrity was demonstrated by using certificates for I&A. These same certificates could "sign" encrypted data images, thus ensuring data integrity. The implementation of Sorbet was also quite compact, and built on an existing security management infrastructure (that is, the session object factory) that already had been developed for other model solutions.

Whether Sorbet had satisfied its performance criterion was not so certain. In absolute terms, Sorbet was noticeably slower than SSL Pack. On the other hand, there is a difference between "noticeably slower" and "unacceptably slower" performance. The shape of the overall performance curves indicates that the difference in performance between Sorbet and SSL null diminish as the size of images increases. Moreover, switching to alternative signing and verification components would likely diminish the performance gap. At least with respect to latency, the performance analysis had been inconclusive. (In all of this, the feasibility of the optimized Sorbet had to be discounted.) One remaining wild card was the performance impact of generating the prime modulus for the Diffie-Hellman algorithm. However, since it was, in principle, possible to generate prime numbers off-line, this particular performance issue was not a dominant concern.

Overall, Sorbet had satisfied all but the performance criterion. Even with respect to this criterion, the results were ambiguous. Thus, Sorbet might remain a viable repair option, especially if it were used only as an interim repair.

19.5   Summary

It is sometimes necessary to consider developing custom components as alternatives to commercial components. A custom component might be required to implement special functionality, or it might serve as an interim repair. It is important to avoid a dogmatic approach to component-based development, and, in particular, to avoid being trapped by a "commercial at any cost" mindset.

19.6   Discussion Questions

1. Assuming that Sorbet was used as an interim repair, could you justify a later switchover to a commercial alternative such as SSL Pack? How might this justification be expressed in a quantifiable way?

2. Was the decision to benchmark Sorbet without encryption justifiable, or should data encryption have been included? Explain the pros and cons of each position.

20

Hardware Components

It is a capital mistake to theorize before one has data. Insensibly, one begins to twist facts to suit theories, instead of theories to suit facts.
—Sir Arthur Conan Doyle

One often hears analogies drawn between hardware and software components. For example, the "plug and play" cliché is used to describe the ideal state of component-based software development. Whether or not the software component industry ever compares to the PC hardware component industry remains to be seen. One thing is certain: the boundaries between software and hardware are blurring. What was formerly the exclusive domain of hardware components can now be found in software components, and vice versa. This phenomenon should not be surprising given how we defined software component—essentially as an implementation of functionality with an interface. If software components are truly "black boxes," then, in principle, we should not know, or care, whether the implementation is compiled from Java or C++, is interpreted byte code, or, for that matter, is printed in hardware circuitry.

Of course, there is a often a big difference between principle and practice. The component-based systems integrator will surely recognize the distinction between software and hardware components. Yet, as this chapter illustrates, the same techniques that we have been illustrating—blackboards, model problems, black-box visibility, repair analysis—apply equally to either software or hardware. Indeed, some techniques, such as black-box visibility, are absolutely essential to both.

One aspect of component-based development runs through the following chapter: the ever-present possibility that the technology market will spring a surprise, pleasant or otherwise, that disrupts the development process. This is what happened to the DIRS design team.

20.1 Where Are We?

The design team was in the midst of exploring repair options for the applet ensemble. The difficulties centered on integrating the security features of different components. The applet ensemble was limited to a single browser, Netscape Navigator. Also, we had not yet demonstrated how data confidentiality and integrity were to be achieved over IIOP-based sessions.

About this time a sales representative from NICNAK.com walked in.[1] NICNAK.com provided a hardware-based, network-level security solution. At first glance, it appeared to resolve a number of integration difficulties. Most computers are connected to a network via a network interface card (NIC). Such cards are available from 3Com, SMC, Intel, and many other vendors. This is a logical place to insert an encryption device, as most confidentiality concerns center on network communication. Replacing the existing NIC with one that performs encryption and decryption, such as the one sold by NICNAK.com, ensures that that all network traffic leaving the computer is encrypted and all network traffic arriving is decrypted. Even legacy applications can now, *without* modification, send and receive confidential communication over the network.

This obviously appealed to DIRS program management. If all data were automatically, and transparently, encrypted, wouldn't the need for Visigenics SSL Pack be obviated? In fact, wouldn't the same encryption apply equally well to HTTP, IIOP, FTP, or any other application-level protocol? Further, wouldn't hardware encryption be much faster than software encryption? Shouldn't that be important to consider given the concerns expressed about DIRS performance? The NICNAK.com representatives, of course, answered each of these in the affirmative. Then they went further by promising hardware-level support for data labeling, which could be used to implement fine-grained access control policies. This topic was already of some concern. In fact, we had developed an authorization ensemble back in Chapter 17.

Project management posed the question: should the design team suspend its investigation into the security aspects of the applet ensemble and focus instead on acquiring and integrating the NICNAK.com security solution? It is fair to say that to some, NICNAK.com offered an easy way out of the complexities facing DIRS. (Alas, component-based development is never easy!) Fortunately for DIRS, cool heads prevailed, and we determined to treat the NICNAK.com solution just like any other commercial component—as something that required a dedicated R^3 discovery effort. If NICNAK.com was the answer, it would have to prove itself in the lab!

---

[1] This is the only instance in this case study where we have obscured the name of a component vendor.

20.2   Risk Analysis

Before we could proceed sensibly, we needed to learn something about NIC-NAK.com's product, called (oddly enough) the NICNAK NIC, or NN. Engineers from NICNAK.com and DIRS discussed how to apply NN to DIRS. We focused on the interface between software applications and NN and the behavior of the hardware based on those interfaces.

WHAT IS NICNAK?

NICNAK is a network subsystem comprised of a network interface card (NN), a user-assigned smart card, and smart card reader, and a central management work-station called NNCentral. NN replaces the typical NIC found in most workstations and servers. NN software drivers supported the platforms used by DIRS, includ-ing the Microsoft Operating Systems, Sun Microsystem's Solaris, and Silicon Graphic's IRIX. NN differed from traditional NICs, however, in that it could sup-port a range of security features:

- **Encryption:** NN could be programmed to support DES, Triple-DES, and military grade cryptography.
- **Security data labeling:** NN could be programmed to insert data labels into the network stream to enforce separation of network packets from difference security enclaves.
- **Network firewall:** NN could be programmed to enforce constraints on host and port connectivity.

NN is configured to operate with a *profile* during system start-up. The profile controls which network filtering, encryption protocols, and security labels are used during system operation. Network traffic that originates from the NIC is encrypted and labeled according to its configuration. Conversely, network traffic is received by NN and decrypted if, and only if, the label on the packet matches a label found in NN's configuration. Any attempt to generate or receive network traffic that does not match NN's configuration is rejected and an audit record is sent to NNCentral.

NN Configuration.   Users can configure NN at any point after the host com-puter is turned on. The user inserts an assigned smart card (something he or she has) into the NN smart card reader, and enters a personal identification number (something he or she knows).[2] The user then selects a profile via a toggle switch on the card reader. NN then sends station identification, user data, and profile information to NNCentral. NNCentral performs the necessary table lookups and responds to NN with the appropriate configuration. It then programs NN to the desired security label(s) (Figure 20-1).

NN Operation.   When writing, NN encrypts the data and places the assigned security label on every network packet transmitted. This security label is placed in the Internet Protocol's (IP) options field defined in RFC791 (the original protocol specification for IP) as a subtype for security, otherwise known as the Internet Protocol Security Option (IPSO) defined in RFC1108. This security option is simply appended to the normal IP header shown in Figure 20-2.

When reading, NN queries the IP options field, looking for both the set security option and the contents of that security label. If the label does not match one found in the configuration of the receiving NN, the receiving NN ignores the IP packet (except to audit the rejection). Otherwise, the payload of the packet is decrypted and processed normally.

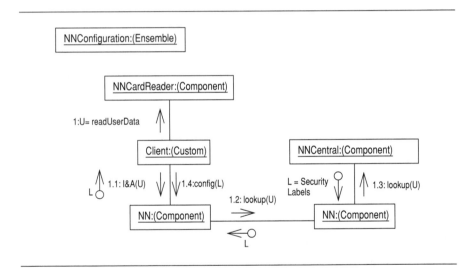

Figure 20-1   NICNAK configuration ensemble.

[2] The combination of "something he has, something he knows" is considered more secure than either element by itself. Something a user has could be lost or stolen and something a user knows might be discovered. The archetypical example of "something he has, something he knows" are Automated Teller Machines (ATMs) that require a bank card and a personal identification number (PIN).

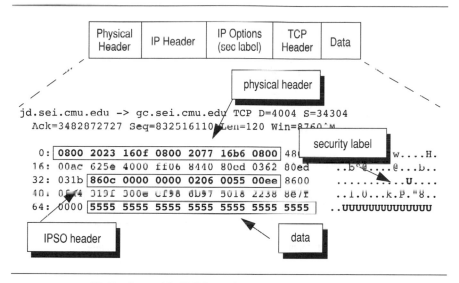

Figure 20-2 IP Packet with IPSO option.

Since the option field used for the security data label is actually part of the IP header, NN is capable of labeling TCP and UDP network traffic, as well as any other IP based protocol.

NN Modes of Operation. NN can operate in either *autonomous* or *application* mode. These modes are only significant to data labeling for network write operations, not read operations or encryption.

In autonomous mode, NN labels outgoing IP network traffic with the security label assigned and configured by NNCentral. The NN software device driver reads the assigned security label from the memory on NN. The device driver formats this information to conform to the IPSO specification, building a properly formed IP header with options. On a write, the IP header, options, and data are passed to NN for transmission (see Figure 20-3a). NN can only generate a single label in autonomous mode.

In application mode, the data label placed on outgoing data comes from the user application and not NN memory. This label is set by the application through the POSIX set socket options function as shown in Figure 20-3b. In application mode, NN can transmit different network packets with different labels—although those labels must still match those allowed by NN.

RISK ANALYSIS

We now had a basic understanding of NN. However, we still needed to know how to integrate NN with DIRS and how this integration would affect users. In spite

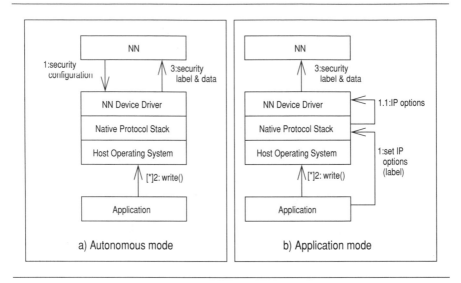

Figure 20-3   NN modes of operation.

of vendor enthusiasm, the design team did not understand many issues, and we suspected that nasty risks lurked in these recesses. Our first area of concern was NN setup and administration. With so many DIRS sites and client machines, this could be a source of severe difficulty. The second area of concern went right to the heart of NN itself: some vendor claims seemed to be at odds with our understanding of the TCP/IP standards. To expose these risks and, if possible, their remedies, we defined two model problems.

The first model problem ostensibly was to validate vendor claims about hardware level encryption. We say "ostensibly" because we were confident that NN could handle the encryption, and we were sure NICNAK.com would help us set up our NN testbed to show off this product feature. Our real objectives for this first model problem were twofold: first, to learn more about NN administration; second, to establish a test environment for the second model problem.

The second model problem focused on NN support for data labeling. There was a great deal of uncertainty about how NN could be configured to support the multi-user/multi-role fine-grained access control desired by DIRS. We also suspected mismatches between the operational concept for data labeling as described by the vendor engineers, and the TCP/IP protocol. If our suspicions were proven, the entire NN scheme would be exposed as a house of cards. Table 20-1 summarizes the design questions and their allocation to the two model problems.

Armed with these four (not so innocent as they appear) design questions, we set out to find the answers.

Table 20-1   Design Questions Surfaced from Risk Analysis of NICNAK NIC

Design Question	Model Problem
Design Question #1: Could NN be used in the applet ensemble to provide data confidentiality through encryption without impact on any DIRS client or server software? Design Question #2: Were administrative aspects of NN acceptable?	Confidentiality
Will NN work in application mode on all DIRS platforms? Does NN guarantee that all packets are properly labeled?	Authorization

20.3   Realize Confidentiality Model Problem

DEFINE MODEL PROBLEM

We kept the confidentiality model problem intentionally simple. Our intent was to gain experience administering NN. The only constraints imposed on the model solution were that it needed to be demonstrated on the major DIRS platforms, specifically: Microsoft Windows NT 4.0 using the Intel-based PCI-bus architecture, Sun Solaris 2.6 using the SBus, and SGI IRIX 5.3, also using the SBus. Table 20-2 summarizes the hypotheses and evaluation criteria for the first model problem. Hypothesis and criterion #1 addresses Design Question #1, while Hypothesis and criterion #2 addresses Design Question #2.

BUILD MODEL SOLUTION

Installing the NN hardware suite was straightforward. We put NNCentral—the heart of NN configuration support and control, on a dedicated machine. We could have installed it on the existing Windows NT machine, but selected a separate, dedicated workstation to match the expected deployment environment. We did,

Table 20-2   Hypothesis and Criteria for Authentication Model Problem

Hypothesis	Evaluation Criteria
Hypothesis #1: NN supports data confidentiality and integrity through hardware encryption on all major DIRS platforms, and this encryption is completely transparent to DIRS applications (clients and servers).	Criterion #1: Direct evidence must be provided that conclusively shows that data is encrypted "on the wire" for NN configured on Windows NT 4.0, Solaris 2.6, and IRIX 5.3 platforms.
Hypothesis #2: NN can be configured and administered with a reasonable level of effort.	Criterion #2: Configuration and administration are not deemed to be excessive in comparison with other DIRS hardware and software components.

however, discover numerous configuration options and settings that were never discussed by the vendor. So, while installation was straightforward, it certainly was not trivial. All told, the complexity was within acceptable limits.

Once NNCentral was installed and configured, we assigned each NN device a primary, secondary, and tertiary NNCentral controller (the reverse of the service configuration step in NNCentral). Reciprocating tables were needed both in NN itself as well as NNCentral. Finally, to complete the setup we issued one smart card for each NN device. Each NN came with two blank, nonreusable smart cards. Someone had to insert the blank, unused smart card into the card reader (which was also a writer on NNCentral) and issue the menu command and passwords to "burn" the card. More smart cards could be ordered from the vendor.

Next, we set up the experiment apparatus. We added another Sun Workstation to the testbed LAN. It was configured with a normal (non-NN) NIC. An FTP session between two NN machines verified that the network connection was working. Then, using the snooping technique described in Chapter 11, we ran the snoop utility on the Sun Workstation with the normal NIC and examined data transferred via FTP between the NN hosts. What was sent as clear, readable text appeared as binary data on the network. This indicated that the transferred data was, in fact, encrypted. Additionally, the transferred file compared equally with its original source file, indicating that the data decryption was also successful. Further analysis of the captured network packets confirmed that IP security was being used as claimed by the vendor.

We next installed a variety of applet ensembles onto the NN platforms. They worked without modification, and all data appearing on the network was properly encrypted, as promised.

EVALUATE MODEL SOLUTION

The results of our experiment looked promising: NN had provided confidentiality (through hardware-based encryption) for network clients and servers. The first evaluation criterion was satisfied. Administration was tedious but acceptable. Naturally, physically administering all of the client machines was going to be expensive, but that burden was implied in a NIC-level approach to security.

As is often the case with model problems, though, it is not the a priori evaluation criteria that dominate the analysis, but rather the a posteriori criteria—those that are discovered as a result of building the model solution. In this respect, we found that NN was deficient in several ways:

- **Human in the loop**. To configure NN, a human operator must physically place a smart card in an attached card reader, select a profile, and press a "set" button. But DIRS servers operate 24x7x365 and they reboot automatically in the event of a catastrophic power failure or system crash. In the event of an unattended restart, NN would not configure until the "set" button was pressed. This means that the unattended servers would reboot, but network services would be unavailable to them.

- **Users with multiple profiles**. To change profiles under NN, a user must power-cycle the NN by power-cycling its host machine. This was absurd because many DIRS users routinely played different roles at different times. In some cases, users needed to interleave activities that spanned roles.

- **Closed system**. There was no way for an application running on an NN machine to determine whose smart card was in the attached card reader, or to determine anything else about the card, for that matter. As a result, the smart card only could be used to authorize the user for the NN. DIRS users would need additional authentication mechanisms to obtain authorization to use other resources. This violated the DIRS objective of a single sign-on security solution.

- **Communication breakdown**. Machines configured with NN worked as advertised. However, we discovered that computers configured with NN could not communicate directly with computers not configured with NN. The NICNAK.com solution was to use a router to send packets from an NN machine onto a network with a machine configured with both a normal NIC and NN. This repair would obviously complicate network administration.

These were all deficiencies that would need to be addressed by NIC-NAK.com, and we received assurances that they would do so. Without such repairs, however, NN began to look more questionable. As it turned out, the results of the second model problem made these repairs moot.

20.4   Realize Authorization Model Problem

DEFINE MODEL PROBLEM

Design Question #3 asked whether NN would work in application mode on all DIRS platforms. Our particular concern was with Windows NT. In fact, we were not sure NN would work consistently across *any* set of DIRS platforms. Design Question #4 asked whether NN would work in application mode on TCP/IP connections *at all*. Table 20-3 summarizes the hypotheses and evaluation criteria corresponding to these design questions. Hypothesis #3 corresponds to Design Question #3, while Hypothesis #4 corresponds to Design Question #4.

BUILD MODEL SOLUTION

We developed three distinct model solutions, or experiments, to test the above hypotheses:

1. Experiment one evaluated platform support for the POSIX set socket options function. It was critical that each of the operating systems hosting DIRS servers provided the interfaces required by NN to set data labels.

Table 20-3   Hypothesis and Criteria for Authorization Model Problem

Hypothesis	Evaluation Criteria
Hypothesis #3: NN will work in application mode on all major DIRS platforms.	Criterion #3: Direct evidence must be provided that applications can set IPSO data labels on Windows NT 4.0, Solaris 2.6, and IRIX 5.3 platforms.
Hypothesis #4: NN guarantees that packets are always correctly labeled.	Criterion #4: Tests must demonstrate that no incorrectly labeled packets are generated when applications change data labels during the course of one or more sessions.

2. Experiment two evaluated how network packets were affected by insertion of IPSO labels. NICNAK.com had made ambiguous statements about the behavior of the NN in multi-level secure networks. This experiment was designed to remove these ambiguities.

3. Experiment three considered the effect of labeled packets on a network in which different hosts had access to different labels.

Experiment 1: Setting Socket Options.   To use NN, it was necessary for DIRS servers to programmatically set IPSO labels on outgoing images. This capability had to be supported by all three operating systems used in DIRS: Microsoft Windows NT, Sun Solaris, and Silicon Graphics IRIX. To perform this experiment, we modified a test program we received from NICNAK.com for setting IPSO labels. Using the vendor-supplied test program saved effort and also eliminated some doubt as to the validity of the test. Our approach to this experiment was simple. The test program would be compiled and executed on each of the three operating system platforms, after which we would evaluate the results.

Microsoft Windows NT 4.0 – Microsoft's operating systems have struggled with the IP for years, including TCP and UDP. This is still true today. At the time of this experiment, Microsoft's TCP/IP stack was WinSock version 2.0. It was supported under Windows 95, Windows 98, and Windows NT 4.0. WinSock 2.0 only provided limited support for configuring, or parameterizing, the IP, TCP, and UDP protocols. It did not support Internet Protocol Options (IP_OPTIONS)—a feature needed to support IPSO data labeling.

We modified NICNAK.com's test program to compile and execute under the Microsoft Windows operating systems, and to conform to the WinSock API. Using the snoop program under Solaris, we determined that the Microsoft OS did not support setting various IP parameters, including the Internet Protocol Options and Internet Protocol Time To Live (IP_TTL). These findings were corroborated by Quinn [Quinn 98].

Figure 20-4 shows the output from the test (WinNT_clt) program. On line 5, the test program reports the current value for the IP parameter time-to-live (TTL) is 0x20 (decimal 32). On line numbers 6–9, the test program instructs

```
 1:Winnt_clt -n gc.sei.cmu.edu -e 4004
 2:IpsoLabel size is '12'                     ┌─────────────────┐
 3:Client connecting to: gc.sei.cmu.edu       │ Silent Failures │
 4:performing getsockopt(): can we get IP_TTL?└─────────────────┘
 5:  getsockopt() returned: retval 0, ttl 0x20, error 0
 6:performing setsockopt() on IP_TTL
 7:  setsockopt() returned: retval 0, error 0
 8:performing getsockopt(): can we get IP_TTL?
 9:  getsockopt() returned: retval 0, ttl 0x40, error 0
10:performing getsockopt(): can we get IP_OPTIONS?
11:  getsockopt() returned: retval 0, lenop 0x0, error 0
12:performing setsockopt()
13:  setsockopt() returned: retval 0, error 0
14:performing getsockopt(): can we get IP_OPTIONS?
15:  getsockopt() returned: retval 0, lenop 0xc, error 0
16:Sent Data [This is a small test message [number 0]]
```

Figure 20-4 Sample execution of WinNT_clt.

WinSock to set the TTL to 0x40 (decimal 64). It also retrieves the TTL parameter from WinSock to confirm that TTL was set correctly. All operations are performed without any indication of error. As we were to discover, however, WinSock was failing, but failing silently. Lines 10–15 use the same WIN32 calls to set the IP options field to the IPSO header, and again all operations are performed without error.

Analysis of the network traffic generated by the test program (shown in Figure 20-5) demonstrates that the calls to update the TTL and the IP options to include the IPSO header had failed. Worse, these calls failed silently as the getsockopt(), setsockopt(), and WSAGetLastError() operations all returned 0 indicating successful execution. In particular, three failures must be noted:

1. The TTL field of the IP packet is actually 0x80 (decimal 128). This field was incorrectly reported as 0x20 on line 5 or 9 in Figure 20-4 and was not set to 0x40 (decimal 64) as expected.

```
pcbj.sei.cmu.edu -> gc.sei.cmu.edu TCP D=4004 S=2701
  Ack=4100106949 Seq=254254011 Len=128 Win-8760

 0: 08 |TTL| 16af 0060 97 |IHL| 0800 4500  .. #...`.a....E.
16: 00       4000 8006 9a        057b 80ed  ..U)@........{..
32: 031b 0a8d 0fa4 0f27 9bbb f462 aac5 5018  .......'...b..P.
48: 2238 f552 0000 5468 6973 2069 7320 6120  "8.R..This is a
64: 736d 616c 6c20 7465 7374 206d 6573 7361  small test messa
80: 6765 205b 6e75 6d62 6572 2030 5d00 c00c  ge [number 0]...
                   :
176: fa77 1400 0000                          úw....
```

Figure 20-5 A captured WinSock 2.0 network packet.

2. Lines 13 and 15 of Figure 20-4 report success in setting and getting the IP options field for the IPSO header. However, the actual network packet does not include the IP options set by the test program.

3. The actual Internet header length (IHL) of 0x05 (decimal 5) confirms that the length of the Internet header did not increase as expected if the IP options field had been set. The length of the IPSO header is 12 bytes (three 4-byte words). An IHL of 5 words plus an IPSO header of 3 words should have resulted in a total IHL of 0x08.

Solaris and IRIX – We used the original, unmodified, test program from NIC-NAK.com to exercise Sun's Solaris and SGI's IRIX. These operating systems behaved correctly and set the IP options via the set socket options function. However, retrieving the socket options using the get socket options function, `getsockopt()`, behaved differently for each operating system. This was unexpected and troubling.

Both Solaris and IRIX returned an additional 4 bytes not associated with the IPSO label. This appeared to be a bug stemming from the set socket options function call. When setting IP options, special processing is performed to handle source routing. An additional 4 bytes is added to the beginning of the IP options data to account for the first hop when using source routing. This processing appears to occur even when the IP options data does not contain source routing information. The first 4 bytes are not actually included in the IP options data that go out on the wire. However, this bug results in an additional 4 bytes being returned for all get socket options function calls requesting the current IP options.

Under Sun Solaris, the get socket options function returns the 4 bytes and the data contained in the IPSO label (`IpsoLabel`) structure shown in Figure 20-6. If the buffer used to retrieve the socket options did not account for these additional bytes, Solaris would inadvertently overwrite memory not allocated to the IPSO label structure. Under SGI's IRIX, get socket options also returned the 4 bytes not associated with the IPSO label structure, but would not overwrite memory as on Solaris. As with Solaris, the data returned in the IPSO label structure was not correct and was offset by 4 bytes.

Results from Experiment 1.

1. WinSock version 2.0 did not support IPSO data labeling. Therefore, we could not use Microsoft Windows NT as a host for any DIRS servers without modifying the WinSock networking stack or finding an (unidentified) alternative to WinSock.

2. Given the POSIX specification and the behavior of the set socket options and get socket options functions for Solaris and IRIX, it would be impossible for a DIRS client to read the actual security label applied to network packets for a document retrieved from a DIRS server.

3. The set socket options function under Solaris and IRIX did perform as expected, as IPSO data labels could be programmatically set.

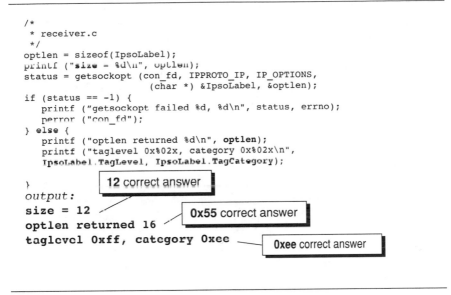

```
/*
 * receiver.c
 */
optlen = sizeof(IpsoLabel);
printf ("size = %d\n", optlen);
status = getsockopt (con_fd, IPPROTO_IP, IP_OPTIONS,
                     (char *) &IpsoLabel, &optlen);

if (status == -1) {
   printf ("getsockopt failed %d, %d\n", status, errno);
   perror ("con_fd");
} else {
   printf ("optlen returned %d\n", optlen);
   printf ("taglevel 0x%02x, category 0x%02x\n",
   IpsoLabel.TagLevel, IpsoLabel.TagCategory);
}
output:
size = 12
optlen returned 16
taglevel 0xff, category 0xee
```

12 correct answer

0x55 correct answer

0xee correct answer

Figure 20-6   The get socket options function under Solaris.

Experiment 2: IPSO Labels.   The second experiment assessed how network packets were affected by inserting IPSO labels. In other words, were the IPSO data labels set in the previous experiment being communicated across the network? In this experiment, we only examined applications running under Sun Solaris and Silicon Graphics IRIX, since the Microsoft platforms were now out of contention. We built a test harness to complete this experiment. Figure 20-7 depicts the test harness which is comprised of a Sender, Receiver, and Sentinel.

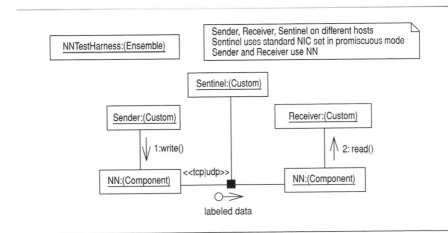

Figure 20-7   Authorization test harness.

Sender endlessly transmits data at different security levels, U for unclassified, S for secret, and T for top secret. The content of unclassified data is a sequence of ASCII U characters, and analogously for S and T data. Sender uses the set socket options function to set the data label to match the security level of the data being transmitted. Sender also accepts a number of command line options, listed in Table 20-4, that change the characteristics of the experiment and permit fine-grained control over program execution and behavior.

Receiver waits for data to appear on an inbound socket. As data is read from the socket, its classification is reported (from the contents of the message, as described above). Receiver also reports if it encountered data with different classification levels in a single read buffer.

Sentinel watches network traffic between Sender and Receiver. We did this by programming the network interface of Sentinel's host to read the network in promiscuous mode. Promiscuous mode allows an NIC to receive all packets on the network, regardless of the machine for which they are addressed. This is the same mechanism used by Solaris' snoop utility. We could have used snoop to isolate network traffic, but manually decoding the network traffic proved to be labor-intensive. We needed Sentinel to programmatically sense IPSO data labels and to enhance processing and analysis.

Sentinel was programmed to look for IP packets with security violations. A security violation was defined (by us) as an IP packet containing an IPSO label that did not match the data in the packet. This definition, though limited, covered our interests. The violations included:

- Packet mislabeling: TCP or UDP data is mislabeled in the IP packet header. That is, data appears in the network packet with an incorrect data label (for example, top-secret data labeled as unclassified).

Table 20-4   Sender Command Line Options

Option	Meaning	Function
-i	TCP NO DELAY	Data is sent immediately. Does not permit the operating system to buffer any data before sending.
-n	NON-BLOCKING WRITES	Operating system is instructed to copy user data into the kernel and not wait for resources—not all data may be sent due to available kernel resources.
-o	RUN ONCE	Program is only to send one message and stop.
-p [port]	PORT NUMBER	Sets the port number at which to contact the receiver.
-s [size]	BUFFER SIZE	Sets the size of the message to be sent to receiver (1 byte or greater).
-u	UDP DATAGRAM	Use UDP datagrams (TCP is the default).

- Data mixing: TCP or UDP data requiring different labels appearing in the same IP packet (for example, both top-secret and unclassified data appear in the same packet).

The test harness quickly demonstrated a number of critical problems with NN.

Results of Experiment 2.

1. Packets were mislabeled, leading to a security violation. The cause of this mislabeling made a repair unlikely. In UNIX there are two paths to the network interface device, the `write()` system call and the `setsockopt()` library call (which uses the `ioctl()` system call), as shown in Figure 20-8. In the first path (labeled data stream in Figure 20-8), blocks of data are moved from the user (application) space to the kernel space. Data are queued in kernel buffers to be processed by the network stack, presented to the network driver, and finally sent though NN onto the network. The second path is a direct command path to any functional layer through the kernel, to the network driver (see Figure 20-8). Such I/O control commands are not queued through the kernel stack along with the data stream. Because of these two paths to the NN, an inherent race condition exists that is difficult to predict or control, and is, at best, problematic. This race condition is illustrated by the following example. While a data stream is making its way through the kernel buffers and protocol stack(s), an I/O control is issued to one of the kernel routines or the device driver before, during, or after the data stream reaches that same logical place in the kernel. Our test harness demonstrated this by writing a sequence of Ts to a network socket and later calling the set socket options function to label subsequent packets with the label U. In many instances, latency in the kernel writes resulted in data streams of Ts to be labeled by NN as U data. This represented a mislabeled network packet (that is, T data labeled as U) and therefore a security violation. This was detected using the native Solaris snoop utility and Sentinel, as

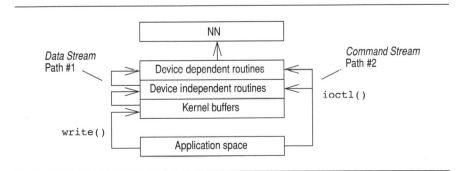

Figure 20-8   Race condition in Unix network device driver architecture.

```
jd.sei.cmu.edu -> gc.sei.cmu.edu TCP D=4004 S=34302
  Ack=1740419550 Seq=3395512586 Len=1000 Win=8760
```

```
 0   data    2023 160f  IPSO Header  6 0800 4800  label   #.... w....H.
16:  ....  625e 4000 ff06 8440 80ed 0362 80ed  ..^`@....@...b..
32:  031b 860c 0000 0000 0206 0055 00ee 8600  ...........U....
48:  0 a4 319f 300e cf98 6b97 5018 2238 8e7f  ..1.0...k.P."8..
64: 0000 5454 5454 5454 5454 5454 5454 5454  ..TTTTTTTTTTTTTT
```

```
IP_OPTION number   = 0x86 (CIPSO)
IP_OPTION length   = 0x0c (12)
IPSO taglevel      = U    (unclassified)
Security Violation
   from '128.237.3.98': found 'T' when expecting 'U' at 0 of 1000
```

Figure 20-9 A captured mislabeled network packet.

shown in Figure 20-9. This race condition existed for the Sun Solaris 2.5.1, Sun Solaris 2.4, and Silicon Graphics IRIX 5.3 platforms.

2. Data at different classification levels were not segregated, but rather became mixed, leading to a security violation. In this case, however, it is not the operating system at fault, but the design of TCP itself [Postel 81]. TCP is a byte-stream protocol and does not insert record markers between application writes. An application receiving 100 bytes of data, for example, cannot tell if the sender wrote 50 bytes followed by another 50 bytes or 30 bytes, followed by 35 bytes, followed by an additional 35 bytes. The TCP specification also allows the network to combine data from individual writes into a single TCP packet or to fragment a single write into multiple packets. As a result, there is no way to guarantee how data is packaged. Figure 20-10

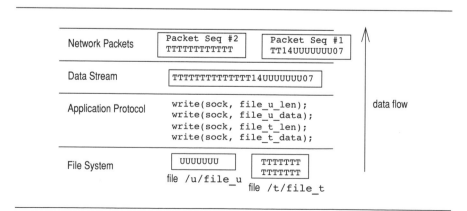

Figure 20-10 Arbitrary file boundaries ignored by TCP.

illustrates this point. Two files containing unclassified and top-secret data are written to a TCP socket. For performance reasons, the kernel attempts to package data into the maximum size packets allowed on the network. Since `file_u` in this example contained less data than the maximum packet size, the kernel padded the packet with data from subsequent writes. By monitoring the network traffic, we can see that the first packet has data from both `file_u` (unclassified) and `file_t` (top-secret), while the second packet has the remaining data from `file_t`. Correctly labeling the first packet is now impossible as the same packet contains both unclassified and top-secret data. This problem was also detected using snoop and Sentinel during the lab experiments discussed earlier. Both unclassified and top-secret data appeared in a single packet, causing a security violation to be reported.

Experiment 3: Labels and TCP/IP. Our last experiment was a "thought experiment." Given what we had learned so far, we deduced cases where IPSO labels in an NN-hardened network could cause problems with TCP connections. In particular, we could predict problems with respect to TCP acknowledgments (ACKs) and TCP error processing.

TCP Acknowledgments – The TCP protocol allows acknowledgments (ACKs) to be sent along with data—a process referred to as piggybacking. Piggybacking usually occurs when one of the communicating processes needs to simultaneously send data and acknowledge received data. When this occurs, the ACK is sent in the same packet as the data. This means, of course, that a single IPSO header is used for both the acknowledgment and the data. Unfortunately, the label can be set based on the classification of either the new data or the acknowledgment. Since, in a secure environment, one would expect the IPSO header in an acknowledgment to be required to match the classification of the data received, this would lead to a security violation. Figure 20-11 illustrates this risk.

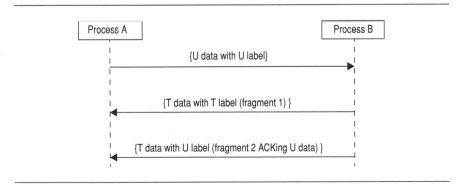

Figure 20-11 TCP acknowledgment failure.

Two processes are communicating via TCP. Process A sends process B unclassified data, while process B sends process A top-secret data. The TCP drivers on each platform must ACK receipt of data. When process B's OS prepares the top-secret data for transmission to process A, the OS is free to piggyback the TCP ACK for the unclassified data received from process A. As a result, the label assigned to this packet cannot be determined. It may be labeled top-secret based on the data or it may be labeled unclassified based on the acknowledgment. Neither assignment decision can be considered correct.

TCP Error Processing – When an incoming or outgoing packet violates a security constraint, NN silently discards the packet without notifying the application or operating system. This feature will cause problems for TCP if a packet is discarded by NN once a connection has been established. Since TCP is a reliable protocol, it resends the unacknowledged packets, which the receiving card drops for the same reason it did so before. Eventually, the TCP connection will be broken due to retransmission failures. The sending application has no way of determining the cause of the failure (for example, was it a TCP circuit failure or a security violation?). We concluded that this behavior was not only acceptable, but it was the only correct behavior possible because it removed a covert channel (for example, transmitting information in the form of system response to error conditions), which would itself present a potential security hazard.

20.5   Repair Analysis

At the outset of the R^3 discovery process, NICNAK.com claimed that their product, NN, would provide full data confidentiality and integrity transparently to DIRS clients and servers. Moreover, NICNAK.com claimed that their product would, through data labeling, support DIRS authorization services. After subjecting NN to the type of testbed analysis that typifies the R^3 process, however, the NICNAK.com claims lost much of their luster.

First, on the positive side, NN did indeed provide network-level data confidentiality and integrity. If NN could be used, it would avoid the need for the repairs to the applet ensemble centered on data confidentiality. With NN in place, applets simply could create IIOP sessions and expect all data to remain confidential without having to resort to SSL. This would greatly simplify the DIRS design effort, and would significantly boost the feasibility of the applet ensemble, which up to this point was questionable, at least in part because of problems encountered establishing IIOP sessions over SSL.

On the negative side, however, NN suffered various deficiencies, none of which DIRS could repair. One set of deficiencies, exposed in the confidentiality model problem, would need to be repaired by NICNAK.com. These included the requirement for human intervention in the case of a server shut-down and the provision of APIs to allow DIRS software to interrogate the NN card reader to obtain user data. Until these repairs were made, NN could not be considered feasible as a DIRS solution for confidentiality and integrity. We had not discounted using NN, however. We merely noted it as being "provisionally feasible," depending on a market event—receipt of vendor repairs.

Much more serious deficiencies were encountered by the authorization model problem. Some of these deficiencies were an outgrowth of the Unix network device driver architecture. Others arose from mismatches between using NN in application mode for data labeling and the TCP/IP standard itself. The only way to repair these problems would be to guarantee that each TCP session operated at only a single security level, with a single data label. However, DIRS was a repository containing data from hundreds of sources; users would construct work plans using image data drawn from a variety of sources. To require the user to establish different sessions for each data label was wholly unacceptable.

The DIRS architect, with the concurrence of program management, conceded that NN did not, after all, solve our component integration problems. On the other hand, it was apparent that a modest investment in a single R^3 iteration had saved the DIRS architect and DIRS program from making a costly mistake.

20.6 Summary

The commercial marketplace has a penchant for springing surprises. A component-based design effort must be agile enough to respond to these surprises, whether they are welcome or not. While the DIRS project had encountered numerous unpleasant surprises along the way, the NICNAK.com surprise appeared to be very good news.

Before committing to it, however, the design team rightly instantiated a dedicated R^3 workflow to investigate the claims made by NICNAK.com. The R^3 process provided the structure and focus needed to investigate the product in the most efficient manner possible. The major findings were obtained in less than two weeks, a modest investment when compared to the potential cost of installing NN cards on each DIRS server and workstation.

One other point about the NICNAK.com experience bears noting. Investigating NN required a significant level of systems expertise by the design team. The need for such expertise and skills to diagnose and effect repairs in component-based systems is quite common. In this chapter the expertise pertains to networking issues, but the skills might just as well have involved transactions, security, performance, or a variety of other subdisciplines of computer science. In many cases, these skills can and must be brought to bear in component-based systems through model problems, experimentation, black-box visibility, repair analysis, and the other techniques described in this book.

20.7   Discussion Questions

1. Would you suggest using NN as a repair to the confidentiality aspects of the applet ensemble? What are the arguments for and against this?

2. Devise application protocol repairs to allow DIRS to use multiple labels per session while avoiding security violations. Is another round of R^3 needed?

21

Into the Black Box

with Daniel Plakosh[1]

> *The winds and waves are always on the side of the ablest navigators.*
> —Edward Gibbon, 1737–1794

Component vendors often supply only user-level documentation. In most cases, this level of documentation is adequate. In some cases, however, the developer may need to learn about the internal operation of a component; for example, the algorithms used and perhaps internal data formats. Component vendors are often reluctant to release such information because of its proprietary value. As a result, it is sometimes necessary for the developer to extract the required information from the component itself. In such cases, black-box visibility is required, often requiring ingenuity and persistence on the part of the investigator. Nevertheless, as a last resort, a facility with these sorts of probing capabilities can mean success or failure for a component-based development effort.

21.1 Where Are We?

If the applet ensemble was to succeed, we had to prove that component interactions using IIOP would meet the confidentiality and integrity standards required by DIRS. Coupled with the architect's preference to deliver a "single sign-on" solution to customers, this requirement led to the conclusion that IIOP interactions must be conveyed over SSL sessions. The only ORB then available that supported SSL was Visigenics with their SSL Pack. Unfortunately, SSL Pack required a user's private key to initiate an SSL session. Netscape did not provide an API that would retrieve private keys from its key databases.

---

[1] Daniel Plakosh is a senior member of the technical staff at the Software Engineering Institute, Carnegie Mellon University.

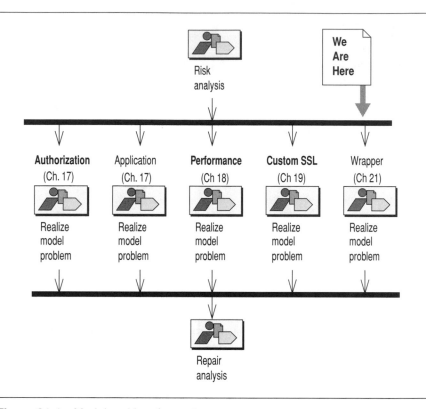

Figure 21-1   Model problem for custom wrapper.

As it stood, the applet ensemble needed several major repairs before it was feasible. One repair strategy was to develop a custom API "wrapper" for the non-published, proprietary Netscape key database. To demonstrate the feasibility of this repair option, we created a model problem workflow, as depicted in Figure 21-1.

21.2   Define Model Problem

Operationally, we needed to extract private keys and certificates from version 4.5 of Netscape Communicator's internal databases. The Netscape certificate database (`cert7.db`) and key database (`key3.db`) contain certificates and private keys that ultimately are used to provide authentication and secure communication. Netscape did not, however, make the format of their key and certificate databases publicly available because they were afraid of violating the International Traffic in Arms Regulations (ITAR) for key management in cryptographic systems. The feasibility of a custom API hinged on whether we could discover the structure and interpretation of these databases. Logically, then, this discovery would lead us to develop an API. As a result, we focused on the database format rather than on the API itself (which, as you will see, is more involved than might at first be suspected).

There were no significant constraints placed on model solutions, other than the tacit prohibition of code-level reverse engineering. We limited ourselves to documentation and other resources provided by Netscape and to resources that we could obtain from the Web. We also ensured that the results of our work could not be used to subvert or crack the standard encryption algorithms used by Netscape Corporation to protect certificate and key material stored in Communicator's databases.

The hypothesis and evaluation criteria were straightforward:

Hypothesis: It is possible to construct an API to the Netscape Navigator certificate and key databases to retrieve a private key that corresponds to a user's certificate.

Evaluation Criterion: A demonstration is required of programmatic extraction of certificate and private key information from the Navigator database, and demonstrated understanding of how an API could be constructed that retrieves the private key that corresponds to a user certificate.

As the evaluation criteria makes clear, we had to demonstrate that *some* API can be constructed, but not necessarily *the* API that would be used by Java applets. The model solution must demonstrate a certain understanding of the database formats, and provide a proof by existence that an API could be constructed.

21.3 Model Solution

The most obvious choice for a model solution was to develop a database dump utility. It would both demonstrate access to the Navigator databases as well as help us discover the structure and interpretation of the data within the `key3.db` and `cert7.db` databases. This effort required four steps:

1. Discover the basic database mechanisms used by these databases.
2. Discover the structure of `cert7.db` so that certificates could be retrieved.
3. Discover the structure of `key3.db` so that private keys could be retrieved.
4. Discover the connection between `cert7.db` and `key3.db` so that private keys could be looked up for particular personal certificates.

DATABASE MECHANISM

The first step was to determine the type of database system that Netscape used to store information. If Netscape used a proprietary database, this step was going to be difficult. We recalled that Netscape released some initial source code of their Mozilla browser. Although the released source code did not contain support for security, we suspected that Netscape used the same database to store more than just security-related items. If this suspicion held true, we could use this detail to gain programmatic access to the Netscape databases.

We downloaded the Mozilla source, unzipped it, and discovered a dbm directory. After a closer investigation, we discovered that the files in the directory were the source code files for the Berkeley DB 1.85 database. We obtained the source for the Berkeley DB 1.85 and used it to build a library. We wrote a simple test program called DBDump to open a database, dump all the records, and access the keys in binary form.

The Berkeley DB 1.85 database supports three different types of database files:

- DB_HASH: allows arbitrary key/data pairs to be stored in data files.

- DB_BTREE: allows arbitrary key/data pairs to be stored in a sorted, balanced binary tree.

- DB_RECNO: allows both fixed-length and variable-length flat text files to be manipulated using the same key/value pair interface as in DB_HASH and DB_BTREE. For DB_RECNO, the key consists of a record (line) number.

The test program executed successfully on both the key and certificate databases. Thus, we verified our suspicion that the Berkeley DB 1.85 was the database system Netscape used to create, access, and modify the databases. Figure 21-2 shows the output from DBDump when given a key3.db file as input. We determined

```
Record 1
Key Data: (7 bytes)
00000000 56 65 72 73 69 6f 6e                               Version
Record Data: (1 bytes)
00000000 03 .
<stuff deleted>
Key Data: (65 bytes)
00000000 00 b1 e0 ad 39 e7 09 41 b9 d3 21 90 9b 0f 95 78    ....9..A..!....x
00000010 e6 fd ef d3 62 34 51 4d 79 02 83 17 9f 4f 09 68    ....b4QMy....O.h
00000020 5c 81 a2 e6 2d b1 f7 bb e6 69 ba 39 a5 f4 17 0b    \...-....i.9....
00000030 a9 a9 ea b0 4c 7f ff 55 a5 46 a7 67 10 3a 1f e1    ....L..U.F.g.:..
00000040 7b {
Record Data: (436 bytes)
00000000 03 08 23 47 eb a8 ce fc 4b c0 6b 53 63 6f 74 74    ..#G....K.kScott
00000010 20 41 20 48 69 73 73 61 6d 27 73 20 56 65 72 69     A Hissam's Veri
00000020 53 69 67 6e 2c 20 49 6e 63 2e 20 49 44 00 30 82    Sign, Inc. ID.0.
<stuff deleted>
00000190 d2 9d e3 00 63 72 4f 79 d4 e9 ad 1d 1e cd 79 3f    ....crOy......y?
000001a0 89 9a 66 e4 f6 a2 1d ec a0 3e 61 35 81 cc b8 83    ..f......>a5....
000001b0 5c df 87 24                                         \..$
```

Figure 21-2   Output of DBDump (key3.db file as input).

that both the certificate and key databases are in the DB_HASH format by attempting to open these files using the different database formats until we were successful.

Things were proceeding exactly as planned.

CERTIFICATE DATABASE

Next, we determined the format of the data and access keys for each database record. Decoding the certificate database was much easier than expected. We searched the Web and news groups for information describing Netscape's certificate database for terms such as *cert7.db, decode, ASN.1, DER, certificate-database, format, specification, certificate, security*, and *Netscape*.

We found that useful information describing the content and format of the Netscape certificate database was readily available on the Internet. All records in the certificate database have a common header that describes the type of record. This information was described in some detail at various Web sites.[2] We observed that at least one of these sites was overseas. This called into question whether export control laws are material insofar as Netscape's products are concerned. This provided little comfort, however, since it was unlikely that Netscape would reverse their policy about revealing the information we needed.

The information at these Web sites did not describe every field of the header or every field of each record. We obtained a copy of the Netscape Security Services (NSS) library from Netscape. Netscape documented, to a certain extent, the exact format of the common header as well as the format for each possible type of record in the database. The common header shown in Figure 21-3 has the following fields:

1. A Version field that indicates the database version (currently 7)

2. A Type field that indicates the *type* of record

3. A Flags field (always zero).

Using some of the NSS header files, we determined the list of possible record types—the Type field in Figure 21-4. Some, but not all, of this information was also available on the Internet. To construct a database structure that we

```
typedef struct {
  unsigned char Version;
  unsigned char Type;
  unsigned char Flags;
} DBHeader;
```

Figure 21-3   Certificate database record type header.

[2] See: *http://www.drh-consultancy.demon.co.uk/cert7.html, http://www.columbia.edu/~ariel/good-certs/, http://www.netscape.com/eng/security/downloadcert.html*

```
// Record Types
#define CERT7VERSION          0
#define CERT7CERTIFICATE      1
#define CERT7NICKNAME         2
#define CERT7SUBJECT          3
#define CERT7REVOCATION       4
#define CERT7KEYREVOCATION    5
#define CERT7SMIMEPROFILE     6
#define CERT7CONTENTVERSION   7
```

Figure 21-4   Certificate database record types.

could test with the DBDump utility, we patched together information assembled from different sources.

We then focused on determining the format of each record. This task was simple thanks to the NSS header files. Figure 21-5 and Figure 21-6 show the C structures that define the format of each record type in the database. We had to derive these structures from information such as the byte offsets of fields within a record and hexadecimal dumps from the DBDump tool described earlier. We discovered that records in the certificate database were in big endian format, so all fields that are of the type "unsigned short" had to be byte swapped. Most of the important information is DER encoded.

By analyzing the contents of several databases we determined that the CERT7VERSION record (shown in Figure 21-7) and the CERT7CONTENTVERSION record (shown in Figure 21-8) are always present and can identify a certificate database. These records have the access keys "\0Version\0" and "\7ContentVersion\0" respectively. Access keys are determined by sequencing through the hash table and retrieving each record. The database iterator function returns both the access key and the record data.

Once we had determined the record formats for the certificate database, we built a tool to browse the database. This tool (shown in Figure 21-9) lists each record in the database. The user can select a particular record and the tool displays the key index for the record as well as its contents. Record fields that are DER encoded can be displayed in abstract syntax notation one (ASN.1) or Hex/ASCII format. Additionally, the tool can save a certificate to a file in DER format.

The database key information shown in Figure 21-9 at the beginning of the record content is used to retrieve a record quickly. A record is typically retrieved using the key information as shown below:

```
DBT key, data;
key.data=(void *)"Version";
key.size=strlen("Version")+1;
if ((db->get)(db,&key,&data,0)==RET_SUCCESS) {
  DisplayRecord(&data);
}
```

```
#define NICKNAMEHEADERFIXEDSIZE 2
typedef struct {
  unsigned short NickNameDERLength;
  unsigned char *NicknameDER;
} NickNameHeader;

#define SUBJECTHEADERFIXEDSIZE 6
typedef struct {
  unsigned short NumberOfCertificates;
  unsigned short NicknameLength;
  unsigned short EmailAddressLength;
  char * NickName;
  char * EMailAddress;
  unsigned short * CertificateKeyLength;
  unsigned short * KeyIDLength;
  unsigned char  * CertificateKeys;
  unsigned char  * KeyIDs;
} SubjectHeader;
#define MIMEHEADERFIXEDSIZE 6
typedef struct {
  unsigned short  DERSubjectNameLength;
  unsigned short  MimeOptionsLength;
  unsigned short  OptionsDateLen;
  unsigned char * DERSubjectName;
  unsigned char * MimeOptions;
  unsigned char * OptionsDate;
} MimeHeader;

#define REVOCATIONHEADERFIXEDSIZE 4
typedef struct {
  unsigned short DERCertificateLength;
  unsigned short URLLength;
  unsigned char *DERCertificate;
  char *URL;
} RevocationHeader;

#define CERTVERSIONHEADERFIXEDSIZE 0
typedef struct {
  // Contains just the common header
} CertVersionHeader;

#define CERTCONTENTVERSIONHEADERFIXEDSIZE 1
typedef struct {
  unsigned char ContentVersion;
} CertContentVersionHeader;
```

Figure 21-5 Certificate database record formats.

In the above code fragment, the key and data variable are the type DBT (data base thang [sic]) as described in the Berkley 1.85 documentation.

We had come a long way, but we still didn't know how Netscape selected keys for each record type. In some cases, the database key appeared to contain DER-encoded information. In other cases, the key appeared to be just a string. We had more to discover, and things were about to become much more difficult.

```
#define CERTIFICATEHEADERFIXEDSIZE 10

// Flags for Object Signing, E-mail and SSL
#define CERT7DB_VALID_PEER          (1<<0)
#define CERT7DB_TRUSTED             (1<<1)
#define CERT7DB_SEND_WARN           (1<<2)
#define CERT7DB_VALID_CA            (1<<3)
#define CERT7DB_TRUSTED_CA          (1<<4)
#define CERT7DB_NS_TRUSTED_CA       (1<<5)
#define CERT7DB_USER                (1<<6)
#define CERT7DB_TRUSTED_CLIENT_CA   (1<<7)
#define CERT7DB_INVISIBLE_CA        (1<<8)
#define CERT7DB_GOVT_APPROVED_CA    (1<<9)
#define CERT7DB_PROTECTED_OS_CA     (1<<10)

typedef struct {
  unsigned short SSLFlags;
  unsigned short EMailFlags;
  unsigned short ObjectSigningFlags;
  unsigned short DERCertificateLength;
  unsigned short NickNameLength;
  unsigned char *DERCertificate;
  char *Nickname;
} CertificateHeader;
```

Figure 21-6 Certificate data format.

```
Key Data:
  Size is :9 bytes
  0    0056 6572 7369 6F6E 00        .Version.

Record:
  Size:    3 bytes
  Version: 7
  Type:    Version
  Flags:   0x00
```

Figure 21-7 Certificate version record.

```
Key Data:
  Size is :16 bytes
  0    0743 6F6E 7465 6E74 5665 7273 696F 6E00    .ContentVersion.

Record:
      Size:      4 bytes
      Version: 7
      Type:      Content Version
      Flags:     0x00
Content Version: 0x12
```

Figure 21-8 Certificate content version record.

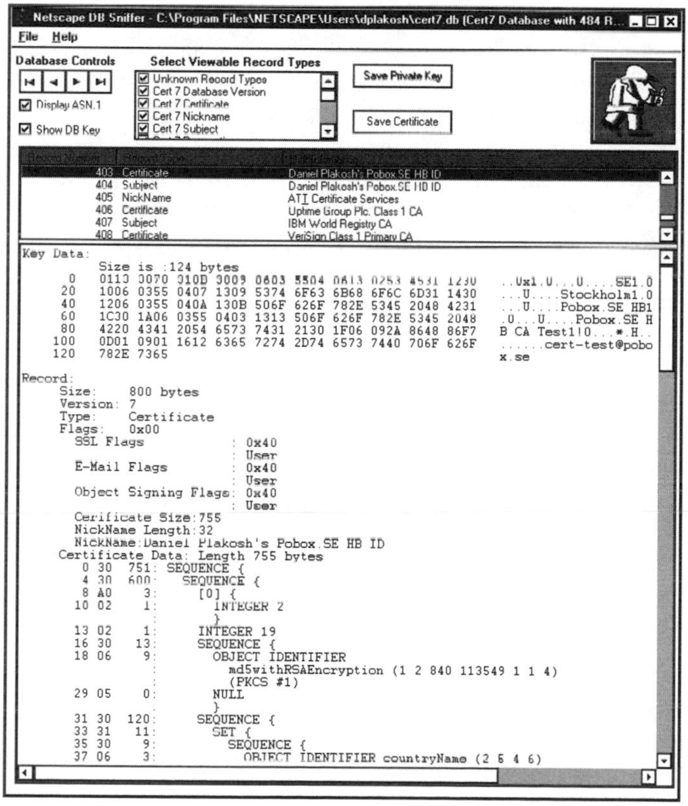

Figure 21-9 Database browsing tool.

KEY DATABASE

Decoding the key database was significantly more difficult than decoding the certificate database. This difficulty was mainly due to the lack of available documentation, and the fact that the private key record in the data is encrypted with a password. Unlike the certificate database, the NSS does not provide *any* information describing the format of this database or the encryption used. In trying to decode this database, we first dumped all of the records in the database. This led to the discovery that there are only four different types of records in the key database. Only two of these records contain the common header depicted in Figure 21-3. The types of records that use the common header are shown in Figure 21-10.

The other two records (that do not contain the common header) are the `Version` record and the `Global Salt`[3] record. These records can be identified easily by their access keys, `"Version"` and `"global-salt"` respectively. The key database can be confirmed by the existence of the version record independent of the file name. Additionally, if the key database contains any private key records, it must also contain a password check record that can be accessed using "`password-check`" as the database access key.

As in the certificate database, records in the key database are in big endian format. The key database record formats shown in Figure 21-11 were fairly easy to determine by dumping out several records from different databases with different values and looking for patterns in data. However, determining how to use these key database record formats to decrypt a private key was a different story. Determining the role of each record in the decryption of a private key was going to be a challenge.

We started by dumping a private key record header and data (ASN.1 encoded) as shown in Figure 21-12. The software used to decode the ASN.1 encoded information, dumpasn1, was written by Peter Gutmann.[4] The dumpasn1 utility revealed an object identifier (OID)[5] of "06 0B 2A 86 48 86 F7 0D 01 0C 05 01 03." The dumpasn1 utility makes use of a configuration file to map common OIDs to description strings. The description string for this OID is:

    pkcs-12-PBEWithSha1AndTripleDESCBC

```
//Record Types
#define PRIVATEKEY 8
#define PASSWORDCHECK 16
```

Figure 21-10   Key record types.

---

[3] A string of random bits concatenated with a key or password to foil precomputation attacks.

[4] See *http://www.cs.auckland.ac.nz/~pgut001/*

[5] A concept defined by the ASN.1 specification.

```
typedef struct {
  unsigned char GlobalSalt[16];
}GlobalSaltHeader;

typedef struct {
  // Contains just the common header
} KeyVersionHeader;

#define KEYPASSCHKFIXEDSIZE 18
typedef struct {
  unsigned char Salt[16];
  unsigned short CryptAlgLength;
  unsigned char *AlgInfo;
  unsigned char *EncryptedAccessKey; // "password-check"
                                     // Encrypted 16 bytes
} PasswordCheckHeader;

#define KEYHEADERFIXEDSIZE 8
typedef struct {
  unsigned char Salt[8];
  char * NickName;
  unsigned char * KeyInfoDER;
}KeyHeader;
```

Figure 21-11   Private key database record formats.

This string describes the specific encryption technique used to encrypt the private key. If you guessed that this OID description specifies password-based encryption (PBE) with secure hash version one (SHA1) and the Triple-DES in cipher block chaining mode (CBC), you have a bright future in component-based development. The octet string and the integer contained in the sequence following the OID are the salt and iterator value for the PBE scheme. Finally, the last octet string is the encrypted private key.

We needed a document that described the PBEWithSha1AndTripleDESCBC password-based encryption technique. An initial search of the Web did not reveal any additional information about the OID. However, we located documentation that described the password-based encryption technique for a similar OID called PBEWithSha1And3-KeyTripleDESCBC in the RSA laboratories PKCS#12 Personal Information Exchange Standard [RSA 99]. We thought that both object identifiers used the same password-based encryption technique.

We now needed an encryption package that supported the hashing function SHA1 and Triple DES CBC encryption. In Chapter 13 we discussed the use of SSLeay, an encryption package that contains cryptographic libraries and certificate support software. Additionally, we located a software package that enhanced the certificate support software in SSLeay by adding support for the PKCS12

```
Record:
  Size:     436 bytes
  Version: 3
  Type:     Private Key
  Flags: 0x23
  Initial Vector:   47 EB A8 CE FC 4B C0 6B
  Key Name:Scott A Hissam's VeriSign, Inc. ID
  Name Length:34
  Encrypted ASN.1 Private Key
    0 30   386: SEQUENCE {
    4 30    28: SEQUENCE {
    6 06    11: OBJECT IDENTIFIER
      :   pkcs-12-PBEWithSha1AndTripleDESCBC (1 2 840 113549 1 12 5 1 3)
      :  (PKCS #12 OID PBEID (1 2 840 113549 1 12 5 1).  Deprecated, use
         the incompatible but similar (1 2 840 113549 1 12 1 3) or
         (1 2 840 113549 1 12 1 4) instead)
   19 30    13: SEQUENCE {
   21 04     8: OCTET STRING
      :    47 EB A8 CE FC 4B C0 6B
   31 02     1: INTEGER 1
      :         }
      :       }
   34 04   352: OCTET STRING
      :       BF 3E 52 71 3E 07 94 73 25 F2 28 8D 06 D6
      :       B3 EC FA 59 17 06 EC F9 8F 92 19 FE 4C FF C3 81
<<stuff deleted>>
      :     }
```

Figure 21-12   Private key record header and key.

standard. This was fantastic—we had found on the Web all of the software we needed to decrypt a Netscape private key record!

We examined the source code from the downloaded software and incorporated into DBDump the portions that were needed to decrypt a private key. However, our attempt to decrypt a private key using the code extracted from the implementation of the PKCS12 [RSA 98] standard ended in failure—the cipher was not able to complete successfully.

Humbled, but not dismayed, we decided to take a closer look at the NSS software. Upon examination, we noticed the SECKEY_ChangeKeyDBPasswordAlg function call. This API call appeared to change the encryption algorithm used to encrypt the database. This was a guess because the NSS documentation only describes the higher level API calls necessary for using SSL and the Netscape Portable Runtime (NSPR). It does not include any documentation (other than undocumented C header files) describing the lower level APIs. Examining the header files yielded two password-based encryption algorithm identifiers of interest:

1. SEC_OID_PKCS12_PBE_WITH_SHA1_AND_TRIPLE_DES_CBC
2. SEC_OID_PKCS12_V2_PBE_WITH_SHA1_AND_3KEY_TRIPLE_DES_CBC

The first algorithm appeared to be the OID for which we were unable to find information. The second algorithm appeared to be the OID for which we had obtained some documentation and an implementation. It appeared that our earlier assumption that both OIDs were compatible was incorrect.

We wrote a program to change the database encryption algorithm to SEC_OID_PKCS12_V2_PBE_WITH_SHA1_AND_3KEY_TRIPLE_DES_CBC. After trying to figure out the semantics of Netscape's undocumented interface, we successfully produced the code shown in Figure 21-13. This exercise turned out to be informative. We learned that the global salt record was used with the password

```
#include <stdio.h>
#include <string.h>
#include <secitem.h>
#include <key.h>
int main (int argc, char **argv)
{
 SECKEYKeyDBHandle *Handle;
 SECItem            *st;
 char                passwd[512];
 if (argc!=2) {
  printf("usage: changedb <database file>\n");
  return -1;
 }
 if ((Handle=SECKEY_OpenKeyDBFilename(argv[1],0))==NULL) {
  printf("database open error\n");
  return -1;
 }
 printf("Enter Password:");
 fgets(passwd,sizeof(passwd),stdin);
 if (strlen(passwd)) passwd[strlen(passwd)-1]='\0';
 st=SECKEY_HashPassword(passwd,Handle->global_salt );
 if (SECKEY_CheckKeyDBPassword(Handle,st)!=SECSuccess) {
   printf("Incorrect Password\n");
   SECKEY_CloseKeyDB(Handle);
   return -1;
 }
 // Original Database format was
 // SEC_OID_PKCS12_PBE_WITH_SHA1_AND_TRIPLE_DES_CBC
 if (SECKEY_ChangeKeyDBPasswordAlg(Handle,st, st,
     SEC_OID_PKCS12_V2_PBE_WITH_SHA1_AND_3KEY_TRIPLE_DES_CBC)==
     SECSuccess)
     printf("Database Format Change Success\n");
 else printf("Database Format Change Falied\n");

 SECKEY_CloseKeyDB(Handle);
 return 0;
}
```

Figure 21-13   Code to change the DB encryption algorithm.

```
Unsigned char HashPassword[20];
void __fastcall TForm1::SetHashPassword(char *Password)
{
  SHA_CTX c;
  SHA1_Init(&c);
  if (HaveGlobalSalt) SHA1_Update(&c,GlobalSalt, 16);
  SHA1_Update(&c, (unsigned char *)Password,strlen(Password));
  SHA1_Final(HashPasswd,&c);
}
```

Figure 21-14   Password and global salt hash function.

(exact details were not known at this time) and that, contrary to what we had thought, the two OIDs were *not* compatible.

Next, we tried to decrypt a private key record in the converted database. Initially we were unsuccessful, but after some trial and error with different password formats (unicode or non-unicode), we decrypted a private key. The output from the NSS API call `SECKEY_HashPassword` needed to be the input password to the PBE PKCS12 decryption software that we obtained from the Web. After further trial and error, we determined that the `SECKEY_HashPassword` actually performs the hashing function shown in Figure 21-14. Our trial and error attempts were motivated by an observation that all passwords were 20 bytes long, indicating that the user input password and salt were most likely being used as input to SHA1, since SHA1 is a hashing function that always returns a 20-byte digest.

On our first attempt, we used the `SHA1_Update` call in the hash function shown in Figure 21-14 to concatenate salt onto the password; however, this failed. Next we changed the order (salt then password); this worked.[6] Almost incidentally, we determined that key databases do not always contain a "Global Salt" record, which is the reason for the `HaveGlobalSalt` flag in the password hashing function, and which explains the "if" statement in the hash function. The hashed password, however, is *always* 20 bytes in length.

At this point, our tool could decrypt all of the records in the private key database that had been converted to use the `SEC_OID_PKCS12_V2_PBE_WITH_SHA1_AND_3KEY_TRIPLE_DES_CBC` encryption algorithm. However, requiring a database conversion was unsatisfactory. We were too close to stop here! We needed to determine the details of the `PBEWithSha1AndTripleDESCBC` encryption algorithm. An exhaustive search of the Web was performed until we discovered information about this *uncommon* OID (note again the overseas addresses in one of the sources):

---

[6] This contingency is best explained by the Gibbon quotation in the epigraph to this chapter.

- Personal Information Exchange Syntax and Protocol Standard Version 0.020 27, January1997 Microsoft Corporation
- a PFX software program (`pfx-012.tar.gz`) written by Dr. Stephen Henson (shenson@drh-consultancy.demon.co.uk)
- PKCS #1 RSA Cryptography Specifications Version 2.0
- RFC 2104 HMAC: Keyed-Hashing for Message Authentication the TLS Protocol Version 1.0

Using the above resources and *still more* trial and error to decipher the documentation, we decrypted the private key information in the database without using NSS to change the database password encryption algorithms. The private keys were decrypted as shown in Figure 21-7.

1. The user input password and global salt (if present) are used to generate a hash password using the `SetHashPassword()` method shown in Figure 21-14.

2. The "Key" and the "Initial Value" for Triple DES Cipher are generated by calling the `BEPGetKeyIV()` method shown in Figure 21-15 using the `HashPassword` for the password value, salt and iterator from the ASN.1 object. A 24-byte key and 16-byte *initial value* are returned.

3. The decrypt function shown in Figure 21-16 is called using the *initial value* and key generated in step 2 and the encrypted data portion of ASN.1 object. If decryption is successful, a pointer to decrypted data as well as its length is returned.

We incorporated this software into our browsing tool. This tool could now examine and decrypt all the records in Netscape's certificate and key databases. Next, we investigated Netscape's password check record. After some trial and error, we determined that this record contained a 16-byte salt, an encryption algorithm OID, and 16 bytes of encrypted data. When the encrypted data is decrypted correctly, the plain text turns out to be the string "`password-check.`" This is how Netscape determines if a password is correct without decrypting a private key record.

Now our database-browsing tool was robust enough to examine the Netscape databases. We investigated how Netscape uses database keys to link certificates in the certificate database to the private key database. After studying a certificate and private key record that was known to match, we noticed that Netscape included an octet string in the certificate record. This octet string is the access key used to retrieve the private key from the private key database. Q.E.D.

```
void __fastcall TForm1::PBEGetKeyIV(
  unsigned char *Password, unsigned char *Salt,
  int SaltLength, int Iterator,
  unsigned char *Key, unsigned char *IV)
{
  unsigned char Digest[20], SecondDigest[20], DK[40];
  SHA_CTX c;
  HMAC_SHA1_CTX   hmac_ctx;
  memset(SecondDigest, 0, 20);
  memcpy(SecondDigest, Salt, SaltLength);
  SHA1_Init(&c);
  SHA1_Update(&c, Password,20);
  SHA1_Update(&c, Salt,SaltLength);
  SHA1_Final(Digest,&c);
  for (int i = 1; i < Iterator; i++) {
    SHA1_Init(&c);
    SHA1_Update(&c,Digest, 20);
    SHA1_Final(Digest,&c);
  }

  for (int i = 0; i < 2; i++) {
    HMAC_SHA1_Init(&hmac_ctx, Digest,20);
    HMAC_SHA1_Update(&hmac_ctx, SecondDigest, 20);
    HMAC_SHA1_Update(&hmac_ctx, Salt, SaltLength);
    HMAC_SHA1_Final(&hmac_ctx, &DK[i*20], NULL);
    HMAC_SHA1_Init(&hmac_ctx, Digest,20);
    HMAC_SHA1_Update(&hmac_ctx, SecondDigest, 20);
    HMAC_SHA1_Final(&hmac_ctx, SecondDigest, NULL);
  }
  memcpy (Key, DK,24);
  memcpy (IV, DK + 32, 8);
}
```

Figure 21-15   Key and IV generation.

```
unsigned char * __fastcall TForm1::TrippleDESDecrypt(
  unsigned char *CryptData, int CryptDataLen,
  unsigned char *Key, unsigned char *IV, int  *DecryptDataLen)
{
  DES_EDE3_CBC_Type cipher_ctx;
  unsigned char *DecryptData;
  int tmp;
  if ((DecryptData = (unsigned char *)malloc(CryptDataLen + 8))
      ==NULL) {
    *DecryptDataLen=0;
    return(NULL);
  }
  DES_EDE_3_CBC_Init(&cipher_ctx, Key, IV,DECRYPT);
  DES_EDE_3_CBC_Update(
    &cipher_ctx,DecryptData,Decrypt  DataLen,CryptData,
    CryptDataLen);
  if (!DES_EDE_3_CBC_Final(&cipher_ctx, DecryptData+*Decrypt
      DataLen,&tmp)) {
    free(DecryptData);
    *DecryptDataLen=0;
    return(NULL);
  }
  (*DecryptDataLen)+=tmp;

  return(DecryptData);
}
```

Figure 21-16   Triple DES decrypt function.

21.4   Evaluation

Needless to say, the model solution satisfied its evaluation criterion, and the hypothesis of the model problem was sustained. It was clear that our efforts had resulted in a clear understanding of the Netscape key databases,[7] and a convincing demonstration that an API to this database could be constructed.

---

[7] See *http://www.mozilla.org/projects/security/pki/nss/db_formats.html* and *http://www.mozilla.org/crypto-faq.html#1-6* for Netscape's oblique acknowledgment of this work.

21.5   Summary

The most obvious conclusions to draw from this part of the case study is that remarkable perseverance and considerable ingenuity are required to discover hidden component properties. But there are other lessons:

1. If you need to look inside a product (a black box), you must know what you are looking for. In this case study, deep and detailed knowledge of computer security was necessary. Without this knowledge, it is doubtful that progress could have been made.

2. For good and sufficient reasons, vendors such as Netscape use standards in building their products (for example, ASN.1). Knowledge of these standards is crucial for developers who want to peer inside a product. From a security perspective, this shows that standards can be a two-edged sword.

3. A significant degree of systems expertise is needed to look inside a product. Programs must be written, raw data dumps must be interpreted, networks "sniffed," and other techniques used to crack the puzzle. Moreover, strong problem solving skills and perseverance are needed, since there is rarely just one puzzle to be cracked.

All of this supports the observation that building systems from commercial components often requires more, rather than less, technical sophistication on the part of software developers.

21.6   Discussion Questions

1. Can DIRS rely on the information discovered about Netscape databases? What are the arguments for and against the conclusion that this information will remain stable over new component releases?

2. Is it possible to train someone to perform the sort of investigation described in this chapter?

22

Applet Ensemble:
The Endgame

As the design process unfolds, it demands more knowledge of components and their interactions. This is especially so whenever we consider changing direction. As the DIRS design activity progressed, each passing day imposed a greater burden of proof on the applet ensemble, both with respect to its feasibility and to its benefits. A contingency plan (such as the applet ensemble) is, in essence, a hedge against, or an investment to preserve, a particular design option. At some point, the cost of switching to the contingency will outweigh its benefits. The challenge is to locate this point in time and cease nonproductive exploration before reaching this point of diminishing return.

22.1   Where Are We?

The applet ensemble had satisfied the critical performance and security-related requirements of DIRS. However, meeting these requirements meant "locking into" Netscape components on both the server and client side. This was unacceptable. Until we resolved browser dependency, the applet ensemble was infeasible. But removing browser dependency was no easy matter. It required several different, and in some cases competing, repair options. In Chapter 16 we proposed a number of repair strategies that would result in a browser-independent and secure ensemble. Having completed their assigned tasks, each of the model problem workflows synchronized on the third R of the initiating R^3, repair analysis (Figure 22-1).

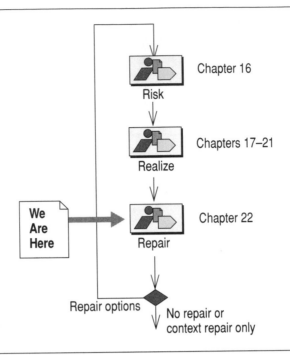

Figure 22-1   Time to reflect and repair.

22.2   Repair Analysis

We evaluated a number of active repair strategies (besides waiting for market events). We had proved the feasibility of

- The stand-alone application. But no amount of persuasion would prevail against deeply ingrained user preconceptions.
- Extending the applet ensemble to address user authorization; for example, fine-grained access control.
- Performing IIOP transfers on par with traditional RPC. This provided performance that was more than sufficient for small images. Larger images could be handled by the direct FTP ensemble, an alternative to the more cumbersome direct HTTP ensemble.
- Developing an API to the Navigator certificate and key databases. This eliminated the need for a custom key database. This was good news, as the custom database solution was mismatched with the DIRS requirement for a single sign-on security solution.

More good news was in store from the component marketplace. Visigenics released a version of SSL Pack that, at long last, worked with Netscape certificates. This eliminated the need for Sorbet, and brought the design effort within striking distance of secure IIOP interactions. Naturally, we tested the new release of SSL Pack with Consensus and Netscape certificates, and were pleased to find that the product worked as advertised.

Best of all was news of the release of the Java 2 plug-in from Javasoft. The Java 1.2 release implemented Java Protection Domains directly in the JVM, providing a portable, "open" alternative to Netscape's NCC API. The plug-in allows developers to bundle a JVM along with an applet. This allowed the applet ensemble to control the execution environment of applets, and removed the dependency between signing technology and browser (recall that the JVM in Microsoft's Internet Explorer only accepted signed .cab files, not signed .jar files as required by non-Microsoft signing technologies, as we discovered in Chapter 15).

The design team was confronted with several questions. Had the applet ensemble been proven feasible? Were there any repairs of the applet ensemble that were speculative? Would other ensembles or DIRS requirements need to be repaired to make room for the applet ensemble? Opinions on these fundamental questions varied. Until we reached consensus on these questions there would be little point in posing the next question: should we switch from the current main design option to the applet ensemble?

The question of ensemble feasibility invariably arises in component-based design. Operationally, the question amounts to a decision to commit to full-scale implementation based on an ensemble. The criteria for answering this question vary from project to project. Ultimately, all criteria depend on intangible factors such as:

- the level of uncertainty a designer will tolerate
- the ingenuity and talent of the development team
- the importance of the project
- schedule and funding pressures

If the design activity has been conducted efficiently, the answer to the question of feasibility balances on the knife's edge. A judgment based on insufficient evidence is, in effect, a gamble. On the other hand, if the evidence of feasibility is overwhelming, then perhaps resources have been squandered, proving the obvious. One challenge of component-based design is to recognize when the necessary criteria for proving ensemble feasibility have been satisfied. After that point, everything else is excess.

Returning to our case study, what judgment would be reasonable at this point in the narrative? We find that:

- Prototypes of key elements of the applet ensemble had been demonstrated— secure IIOP, I&A, authorization, and large-image transfer, and retrieval of keys from the Netscape certificate and key databases.

- The arrival of the Java 2 plug-in, in principle, was the last element required to pull all of the pieces together. All that remained was to develop an API to the Netscape key database, and use the new features of the Java 1.2 release, what is sometimes called "a small matter of programming."

In the case study, the designer decided that we had not established the feasibility of the applet ensemble to the desired level of certainty. The experience of the design team had suggested that it was, perhaps, not yet time to uncork the Champagne. While there were no repairs remaining, the designer wanted more evidence before anointing the applet ensemble as the preferred design alternative.

22.3 Risk Analysis

We were tantalizingly close to testing the fruits of our labor, but one more last great effort was needed. The areas of uncertainty boiled down to:

- Would all of the different facets of the applet ensemble work together?
- Did the Java 2 plug-in and JVM 1.2 protection domains remove the browser dependency?
- Did the applet ensemble achieve interoperability of certificate and signing technology?

We used these questions to initiate the final model problem of the case study. Only then would the designer be prepared to make a decision about switching from the main design option to the applet ensemble.

22.4 Summary

The results of active repair work, combined with anticipated market events, had improved the prospects of the applet ensemble. But feasibility is not usually a question of black or white, but one of subtle shades of grey. A designer with more courage may have ruled decisively at this point in the narrative. But our particular designer was more conservative. However, given the role of model problems as decision aids, and the subjective aspects of judgment in design decision making, it is easy to understand that opinions on feasibility can vary greatly.

22.5 Discussion Questions

1. Based on the evidence presented so far, would you have ruled in favor of, or in opposition to, the applet ensemble? Or would you, like the case study designer, ask for further evidence? Explain your answer.

2. Refine the model problem and R^3 processes to ensure that only necessary feasibility criteria are proven. What kinds of assumptions are necessary for these refinements to be effective?

23

Secure Applet Ensemble Redux

> *Once more, unto the breech, dear friends, once more.*
> —Henry V, in William Shakespeare's *Henry V*

The design process was converging on the fate of the applet ensemble. Evidence indicated that the ensemble was feasible, but experience tempered that judgment. One last model problem was needed to prove the applet ensemble would support the requisite quality attributes (primarily security and performance), and would support alternative Web browser, certificate, and signing technologies.

23.1   Model Problem

The design questions in the previous chapter pointed to a model solution that united the design threads from earlier model problems: browser and certificate-based I&A, user authorization for fine-grained access control, secure IIOP connections, and reading the Navigator certificate and key databases to initiate SSL sessions using SSL Pack. We still had to convert the DBDump program developed in Chapter 21 into an API callable by an applet, but this was considered to be a small matter of programming.

Accommodating the Java 2 Plug-in and its security infrastructure required more substantive effort. While we were engrossed in the study of the Netscape certificate database and performed the other activities described in this book, Sun Microsystems enhanced both its Java Cryptography Architecture[1] (JCA) and Java Cryptography Extensions (JCE). The JCA was originally introduced with the JDK 1.1 release. It provided the framework for accessing and developing cryptographic functionality for the Java platform. The JCA encompasses the parts of the

---

[1] Also referred to as the Java Cryptographic Architecture.

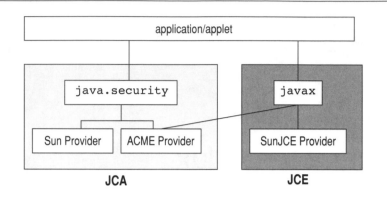

Figure 23-1   Java security infrastructure (JCA/JCE).

JDK 1.1 Java Security API related to cryptography along with other interfaces and conventions.[2] The JCA also introduced the *provider* architecture to support multiple and interoperable cryptography implementations.

The JCE extends the JCA API to include encryption, key generation and key agreement, and message authentication code (MAC) algorithms.[3] Sun historically provided the JCE in a separate release because it could not be exported outside the United States.[4] JCA and JCE were important elements to our model solution because they removed the applet ensemble dependency on any one vendor's security components.

> Hypothesis: An ensemble can be constructed that implements I&A, supports fine-grained authorization, ensures data confidentiality and integrity for all client/server interactions over HTTP and IIOP, provides a certificate-based, single sign-on security infrastructure, is "open" to different security service providers, and works with Netscape and Microsoft Web browsers.

The DIRS architect was satisfied that this hypothesis, if sustained, would indeed prove the feasibility of the applet ensemble. Since the most critical elements of the hypothesis were support for Netscape and Microsoft browsers and openness to alternative security providers, we called these out in evaluation criteria and constraints:

[2] *http://java.sun.com/products/jdk/1.2/docs/guide/security/CryptoSpec.html*

[3] *http://java.sun.com/products/jce/index.html*

[4] This restriction no longer applies as of the JCE 1.2.1 release, which is exportable outside the U.S. and Canada due to mechanisms it implements to ensure that only qualified providers can be plugged into the framework.

Evaluation Criterion #1: Demonstrate an end-to-end use case involving user sign-on, I&A, authorization, and image retrieval.

Evaluation Criterion #2: Demonstrate Microsoft and Netscape Web browsers using the use case defined for Criterion #1.

Evaluation Criterion #3: Demonstrate alternative security service providers using the use case defined for Criterion #1.

Evaluation Criterion #4: Demonstrate that interactions over HTTP and IIOP are secured (that is, <<HTTPS>> and <<IIOPS>> are used).

These criteria all required actual demonstration. To further clarify the problem, we defined the following implementation constraint:

Constraint #1: The model solution must use Crypto-J and Entrust as cryptographic security provider components.

An analogous implementation constraint for key store services was not required. It was implied by Evaluation Criterion #2.

23.2 Model Solution

The first step was to construct a blackboard for the model solution. Having developed several model solutions, this was not too difficult. Figure 23-2 shows the resulting blackboard. It appears daunting at first glance, but most of the details should seem familiar by now. For example, the interactions among the Web server HTTPServer, security manager SecMgr, the applet, and the storage manager *SM* were worked out in the authorization model problem (see Figure 17-1). The details of certificate-based I&A using Web browser WebBrowser and HTTPServer were evaluated in the initiating model problem (see Figure 15-2). The interactions among applet, SSL Pack, and VisiBroker first appeared in the security-related model problem (see Figure 15-7).[5]

Only the grey region in Figure 23-2 was uncharted. Operationally, this region is less complicated than it looks (though perhaps that is hindsight). The applet is downloaded with version 1.2 of the JVM. This JVM is launched, which in turn executes the applet. At this point, the applet connects to the security manager and requests the certificate presented by the user for the purpose of I&A; there is sufficient information in the user (session) object to allow the security manager to locate the proper certificate. The applet then uses the certificate to retrieve the alias of that certificate from the keystore, and uses this alias to locate the private key associated with that certificate. Once it holds the private key, the

---

[5] Note that we have not shown the three-way interaction between the applet, the storage manager, and the ORB, as was shown in earlier blackboards. Such details may always be omitted if they are not material to what is being proven.

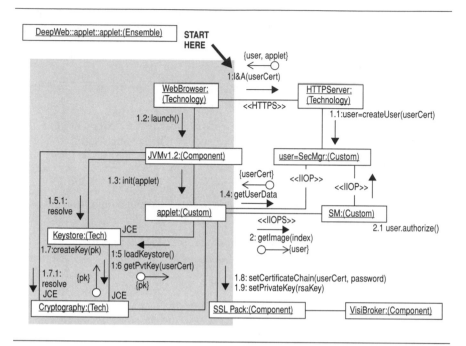

Figure 23-2   The ultimate secure applet ensemble.

applet configures an SSL connection with SSL Pack, which secures all further interactions over IIOP.

CERTIFICATE INTEROPERABILITY TOY

By now we understood the high-level details of the secure applet ensemble. However, that is not the same thing as saying its implementation was easily realized. For example, the Keystore and Cryptography *technologies* in Figure 23-2 are classifiers that must be bound to components; the constraints on the model solution stipulated that Keystore was to be bound to the Navigator databases and to some other keystore component. We had not yet developed the API to the Navigator databases—we had only demonstrated that such an API *could* be constructed (Chapter 21). Before developing an API, it made sense to use an off-the-shelf keystore. After all, if for some reason the ensemble proved infeasible, developing an API to the Navigator databases would have been wasted effort. We selected JKS, the free Java KeyStore component, as our keystore service provider.

This presented an interesting question: how did we know that JKS would work with Netscape certificates? Just because JKS implemented the service provider interfaces (SPI) for keystore providers did not mean it would work with all forms of certificate. Before setting up the Java 2 Plug-in and developing the

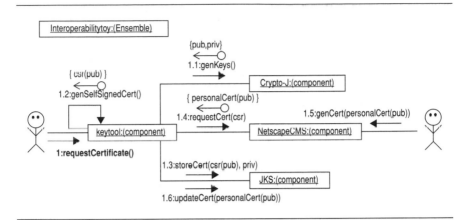

Figure 23-3   Certificate interoperability toy.

applet code, we decided to test certificate interoperability between JKS and Netscape certificates. For similar reasons, we also decided to introduce a cryptography service provider from a third vendor by using RSA's Crypto-J. If we could prove interoperability of JKS and Crypto-J with respect to Netscape certificates, we would be well on our way to proving the secure applet ensemble.

What we needed was a toy—something we could quickly integrate without introducing the overhead of browser, server, and security manager. The toy ensemble is shown in Figure 23-3. Another free utility distributed by Sun for generating keys, requesting certificates, signing objects, and managing a keystore is KeyTool. The interactions in our toy are logical rather than actual. In reality, all interactions except for 1.4:requestCert and 1.5:genCert are command-line invocations of the keytool itself. When the keytool is installed, it is configured with a cryptographic service provider (in this case, Crypto-J rather than the default Sun-JCE) and keystore service provider (in this case, JKS). The 1.4:requestCert interaction required manual manipulation of the self-signed certificate csr generated by keytool. Despite these slight departures from the actual interactions, the blackboard is useful.

Being optimistic by nature but pessimistic by experience, we were not sure whether the interoperability ensemble would work. As usual, experience got the better of nature. Things worked fine only up to 1.6:updateCert. This was distressing. We had succeeded in using Crypto-J to generate RSA public and private keys which were recognized by both keytool and Netscape CMS. What follows is a good, practical illustration of black-box visibility. The error we had encountered was puzzling:

```
test> keytool -v -debug -import \
              -alias Hissam -file hissam.cer \
              -keypass mypassword \
              -keystore newStore -storepass mypassword
```

```
keytool error: Public keys in reply and keystore don't match
java.lang.Exception: Public keys in reply and keystore don't match
    at sun.security.tools.KeyTool.establishCertChain(Compiled Code)
    at sun.security.tools.KeyTool.installReply(Compiled Code)
    at sun.security.tools.KeyTool.doCommands(Compiled Code)
    at sun.security.tools.KeyTool.run(Compiled Code)
    at sun.security.tools.KeyTool.main(Compiled Code)
```

This command instructs keytool to import a new certificate (personalCert in the interoperability ensemble), where it is known by the alias Hissam and can be found in the file hissam.cer. It is imported into keystore newStore, managed by JKS. What puzzled us was that Netscape CMS is only supposed to chain the Netscape CA certificate to the one submitted in the signing request (csr in the interoperability ensemble), and then digitally sign the new certificate using its CA private key. This operation should not have corrupted the public key in csr. Could it be that the Netscape certificate returned by CMS (personalCert) was corrupt? To test this theory, we imported personalCert into Netscape Navigator to determine if the certificate itself was valid. This test was successful. So the problem could not be with personalCert.

Perhaps there was something about the public key that keytool or JKS did not like. To examine this possibility, we examined the keytool program itself. The keytool program, on Microsoft Windows platforms, is a small 20K application. Since this is quite small for an application that does certificate and public/private key generation and manipulation, we suspected additional libraries or classes were being invoked. Using hexedit, we discovered the string "sun.security.tools.KeyTool" within the keytool executable. KeyTool is a Java class within the package sun.security.tools package.

It seemed that the *keytool* program was a thin wrapper around the KeyTool class. To verify this hypothesis we invoked the KeyTool class directly as shown in Figure 23-4. The KeyTool class appeared to contain most, if not all, of the functionality of the keytool program. By examining this class, we would understand the inner workings of the keytool program. A quick inspection of rt.jar file (the JDK runtime) using

```
jar tvf rt.jar | find "sun/security/tools/KeyTool"
```

confirmed the location of the class. After extracting the class file (again using the jar command), and disassembling the byte codes using javap, we confirmed that the KeyTool class was responsible for displaying the error message. Using jad to decompile this class, we found further evidence of this problem. Output from jad is shown in Figure 23-5, with the applicable code shown in boldface.

As a result of the conditional test on the equality of the two public keys, the error message is printed, and accompanying exception thrown. Since we believe these keys are the same, it seemed that this error was incorrect. To explore this possibility, we modified our decompiled version of keytool class by commenting out the Java statement that throws the questionable exception. We then recompiled this modified version and reran the failed certificate import command. This time,

```
% java sun.security.tools.KeyTool \
      -list -keypass mypassword \
      -keystore newStore  storepass mypassword

Keystore type: jks
Keystore provider: SUN

Your keystore contains 2 entries:

Hissam, Thu Sep 21 12:57:37 EDT 2000, keyEntry,
Certificate fingerprint (MD5):
8D:E7:CA:B0:20:BF:14:AD:33:31:E9:FF:E1:BA:F7:F0
seiroot, Fri Sep 22 12:08:01 EDT 2000, trustedCertEntry,
Certificate fingerprint (MD5):
9C:38:EC:9E:CE:78:81:CE:27:D3:09:F3:F6:C5:B5:41
```

Figure 23-4   Directly invoking the KeyTool class.

```
% jad KeyTool.class
Parsing KeyTool.class... Generating KeyTool.jad

% more KeyTool.jad
....
if (certificate != null) {
  java.security.PublicKey publickey =
                            certificate.getPublicKey();
  java.security.PublicKey publickey1 =
                            certificate1.getPublicKey();
  if (!publickey.equals(publickey1)) {
    String s = "Public keys in reply and keystore don't match";
    throw new Exception(s);
  }
}
....
```

Figure 23-5   javap and jad: the game is afoot.

after displaying the error message, keytool continued to import the reply certificate. Now we needed to verify that the certificate and its public key were valid, and that we had not simply short-circuited a properly functioning error-handling mechanism. For this we built two additional toys, as depicted in Figure 23-6. The first toy, signThis, used Crypto-J to read the private key assigned to the keystore alias "Hissam" and digitally signed a message using that key. The second program, verifyThis, obtained the certificate assigned to the keystore alias "Hissam" and verified that it was a valid certificate using the trusted CA certificate keystore

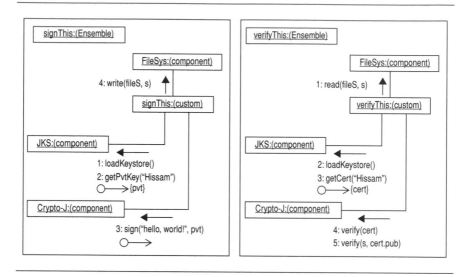

Figure 23-6   The `signThis` and `verifyThis` toys.

alias "seiroot" (as "seiroot" issued the "Hissam" certificate). If the "Hissam" certificate was authentic, signThis used the public key from that certificate to verify the signature of the message.

We applied these two toys and discovered that we could indeed sign and verify an object. This was clear evidence that the exception thrown in keytool was in error and that the two public keys were identical. The expression in the `KeyTool` class, `publickey.equals(publickey1)`, was almost certainly returning an incorrect result. Since the keys involved in this example are RSA keys, the `equals()` method returning the incorrect result was actually supplied by the cryptographic service provider, RSA's Crypto-J.

We submitted our toys, the decompiled `KeyTool` class, and a bug description to the support team for Crypto-J at RSA. They sent word back that the RSA Crypto-J development team had not implemented the `equals()` method of either the `PublicKey` or `PrivateKey` classes and that `KeyTool`'s use of `equals()` was inherited from the default Java `Object` class. Since this class has no semantic knowledge of either the `PublicKey` or `PrivateKey` classes, it simply compares the object references to determine if they are referring to the same object. Within five days, RSA emailed us an updated `JSAFE.jar` that included an implementation of the `equals()` method. We subsequently imported the reply certificate without any problems.

NETSCAPE DATABASE (NDBS) TOY

The first toy demonstrated certificate interoperability. This indicated that a future model solution would satisfy the evaluation criterion concerning alternative security service providers. The next logical step was to take the plunge and develop a C library API and Java bindings to the Netscape cert7.db and key3.db databases.

To begin, we examined the specification of the Sun JCA key store SPI. This interface is an abstract class consisting of 16 methods. Of these 16 methods, 11 were "read-only" and the remaining 5 were "read/write." This was an important distinction because the DBDump toy only read information from cert7.db and key3.db. Figuring out how to read the database was difficult enough—learning how to insert new records would be another matter entirely. In addition, the JCA-defined engineGetCreationDate() method returns the creation date stamp for when a key store entry was created. This information was not available in the Netscape databases. So, if we accepted that our service provider interface for Netscape certificate and key databases would only open the databases in "read-only" mode, and that we would be unable to learn the creation data of a certificate or private key entry, then we had a match to Sun's JCA for key store providers.

Developing the C-library that implemented the 11 read-only keystore methods, and the JNI binding to this library, was uneventful. (Some things really are just a small matter of programming.) We installed NDBS as a trusted keystore service provider by following an installation process similar to the one followed to install JKS as the keystore service provider. Since NDBS was in place, we re-applied the signThis and verifyThis toys. The results were a success.

We had gone as far as we could go with toys. It was time to graduate to the model solution.

MODEL SOLUTION

Up to this point only toys had been built. However, we had built them with the objective of paving the way for the model solution. Comparing the lower left quadrant of Figure 23-2 with the two toys depicted in Figure 23-6 indicates that both exhibit the same pattern of interaction with the keystore and cryptographic service providers. Thus, developing the applet was going to be straightforward. Beyond the applet itself, we still needed to incorporate the Java 2 Plug-in.

Java 2 Plug-In. Unlike Java applets, which are identified by the <APPLET> tag, plug-ins are embedded into an HTML stream using browser-dependent HTML tags. Netscape Communicator uses <EMBED> to identify a plug-in, whereas Internet Explorer uses <OBJECT>. This appears problematic, but it is not. It is possible to place both tags in the same HTML stream and have both Netscape Communicator and Internet Explorer work correctly. Thus, it was a trivial matter to modify the DIRS server-side logic running in the Netscape Enterprise Server (ES) to use the Java 2 Plug-in.

Next, we addressed how the applet would check and request permissions from the Java 2 Plug-in JVM to access different hosts on the network and to access local machine resources. Access to machine resources was necessary to invoke the JNI interfaces to the keystore, and to launch ImageEdit (a third-party image viewer). The most direct approach was to instruct the Java 2 Plug-in JVM that any applet coming from the DIRS secure Web server could be trusted with the keys to the kingdom. To do this, we needed only to add the following stanza to the `java.security` file that is part of the trusted directory structure of the Java 2 Plug-in JVM (usually found in the `lib/security` directory):

```
grant codeBase "https://gc.sei.cmu.edu/dirs/-" {
    permission java.security.AllPermission;
};
```

This little stanza does wonders. It grants all permissions to the applets that are loaded from the identified codebase. This is not an optimal configuration for any operationally secure web ensemble. However, the purpose of our model solution was to demonstrate the feasibility of the ensemble. At this point a more fine-grained approach to extending the applet sandbox was not essential.

With the plug-in installed on the server-side, and with calls to the proprietary Netscape NCC removed, our applet was ready for the last modifications.

Applet Modifications.   To complete the model solution, we started with the applet previously developed for the authorization model problem. It already implemented the necessary interactions with the security manager. All that remained was to modify the applet to:

- request the certificate used by the browser to identify and authenticate the user from the security manager;
- use this certificate to retrieve its associated private key data from the key-store service provider (NDBS); and
- use this private key and certificate to configure SSL Pack to initiate SSL sessions for all future IIOP connections between applet and DIRS servers.

The first interaction was already substantially tested and in place. The rest were similar to interactions already tested in the toys just built.

All that remained was to decide where to locate the `cert7.db` and `key3.db` databases, and how to convey this location to applets. We assigned the location of the keystore to the JVM system property `user.home`. Further, we changed the applet to display a dialog box to prompt for a password to open `key3.db` database. If the private key could be located successfully using the X.509 certificate retrieved from the user (session) object, and if the user presented the correct password, the applet would proceed. Otherwise it would throw an appropriate exception and stop. This code is shown in Figure 23-7.

Armed with a private key and its corresponding certificate, the applet would initialize the Visigenics ORB and SSL Pack (which is known by its service name as `SSLCertificateManager`). This code is shown in Figure 23-8.

```
KeyStore myKeyStore = KeyStore.getInstance ("NDBS");
FileInputStream myKeyStoreFile =
   new FileInputStream (System.getProperty("user.home") +
                        File.separator + "testdb");
String ksPassword = this.promptAndGetPassword();
myKeyStore.load (myKeyStoreFile, ksPassword.toCharArray());

// userRef is this users security token created by SSJS
X509Certificate myCert = userRef.getLoginCert();
String myCertID = myKeyStore.getCertificateAlias (myCert);
PrivateKey myPrivateKey = (PrivateKey) myKeyStore.getKey
                          (myCertID, ksPassword.toCharArray());
```

<stuff omitted>

Figure 23-7   Secure applet and NDBS.

<stuff omitted>

```
CertificateManager manager = CertificateManagerHelper.narrow(
      orb.resolve_initial_references("SSLCertificateManager"));
byte[][] certificates = {
      myCert.getEncoded()
};
manager.setCertificateChain(certificates);
manager.setClearPrivateKey(myPrivateKey.getEncoded());
smRef = SMsecHelper.bind(orb, "SMsec"); // Locate the SM server
Current current = CurrentHelper.narrow
      (orb.resolve_initial_references("SSLCurrent"));
// Check the cipher
System.out.println("Negotiated Cipher:  " +
   CipherSuite.toString(current.getNegotiatedCipher(smRef)));
System.out.println("Protocol Version:   " +
   current.getProtocolVersion(smRef));
System.out.println("The SMsec Server's certificate: " +
   current.getPeerCertificateChain(smRef));
```

<stuff omitted>

Figure 23-8   Secure applet and SSL.

With the applet modified, we now configured the Java 2 Plug-in to find the classes supporting NDBS, Crypto-J, and SSL Pack. This was set using the non-standard −Xbootclasspath flag.[6] It defines the search path for the Java 2 Plug-in to bootstrap classes and resources. Since both Sun and Visigenics defined the class org.omg.CORBA.ORB, Visigenics must appear before the Java libraries:

```
-Xbootclasspath:c:\dirs\vbjorb.jar;
               c:\dirs\vbjapp.jar;
               c:\dirs\vbj30ssl.jar;
               c:\dirs\NDBS.jar;
               c:\dirs\jsafeJCE.jar;
               c:\dirs\jsafe.jar;
               C:\PROGRA~1\JavaSoft\JRE\1.3\lib\jaws.jar;
               C:\PROGRA~1\JavaSoft\JRE\1.3\lib\rt.jar
```

As you can see from the −Xbootclasspath option, all the classes needed for NDBS, Crypto-J, and SSL Pack are included in the path. The last two jar files, jaws.jar and rt.jar, are needed as well; jaws.jar contains the java classes needed by the Java 2 Plug-in, while rt.jar contains all of the other Sun Java classes.

With the Java 2 Plug-in set up and configured and all the changes made to the secure Web ensemble, we were now ready to exercise our complete model solution of the secure web ensemble.

NETSCAPE NAVIGATOR TEST

Our first test of the secure applet was a dramatic affair. We instrumented the applet code so that we could monitor the internal progress of the scenario. The first demonstration used the Netscape browser. To our complete astonishment, the model solution worked without a hitch!

The Web browser was launched, and the user entered the URL to the secure DIRS server. At contact, the DIRS (Netscape Enterprise Server) HTTP server requested client authentication from the incoming browser. Navigator presented a dialog box asking the end user to select a personal certificate identification and authentication. Once the certificate was selected, the DIRS HTTP server identified and authenticated the user. The HTML then returned to Navigator to include the <OBJECT> and <EMBED> tags discussed earlier. Upon receipt, Navigator loaded the Java 2 Plug-in.

At this point, the Java 2 Plug-in processed the command line parameters, including the "stringified" user object holding the user certificate just used for I&A, and loads the applet for the secure Web ensemble. The applet initializes the ORB and reconstitutes the stringified CORBA-based user object passed in as a

---

[6] javahelp reports that the −X options are nonstandard and subject to change without notice.

parameter. Once initialized, the applet binds to the user object and requests the X.509 certificate it contains. We'll point out that the certificate that is returned to the applet running within the Java 2 Plug-in is actually passed in the clear. This was fine, as you'll recall, since certificates contain only public information—including a public key.

Once the certificate was retrieved, the applet used the NDBS keystore via the JCA SPI, to load the user's certificate and private key. The NDBS was asked to return the Netscape alias of the certificate retrieved from the reconstituted user Object. The alias is then used to retrieve the corresponding private key (to that certificate alias). Once the applet had the corresponding private key to the certificate, it could initialize Visigenics SSL Pack. This was done before any CORBA bindings occur to the storage manager. When the applet binds to the storage manager, an SSL connection was established, and from this point forward all IIOP messages had guaranteed confidentiality and integrity. Our "instrumentation" interrogated the connection to the storage manager and confirmed that, indeed, a cipher had been negotiated, and that the applet had communicated with the authentic image server.

With all the connections to the back-end CORBA servers established (some using SSL and others not), the applet now presented its interface to the user. In this simplistic model solution, the user entered a simple free text search parameter against the available list of drawing (using a simple algorithm). The applet then presented the search results in a list box. The user double-clicked in the text box on the image's name, and the applet would request the image (via IIOP over SSL) from the storage manager. Once the image had been retrieved, the applet opened a file on the local hard disk and wrote the image data. Once the image server had completed sending the image data, the applet closed the file on the local hard disk and launched the image editor on the newly created file. A sample of that execution is shown in Figure 23-9.[7]

Needless to say, the design team was ecstatic. Finally, we had obtained an end-to-end demonstration of all of the functional and nonfunctional requirements imposed on the applet ensemble. All but one, that is.

INTERNET EXPLORER TEST

One last difficulty remained. We had developed a keystore service provider for Navigator's `key3.db` and `cert7.db` databases, but we had not developed a comparable service provider for the Microsoft platform. When a user connects to the DIRS Web server using Explorer, the certificate Explorer presents for I&A is retrieved from the registry. This same certificate must also be present in NDBS, as otherwise there is no way to retrieve the private key from NDBS.

---

[7] Note that the screenshot shows Microsoft Photo Editor rather than ImageEdit because we were using JPG rather than the proprietary image format used by DIRS.

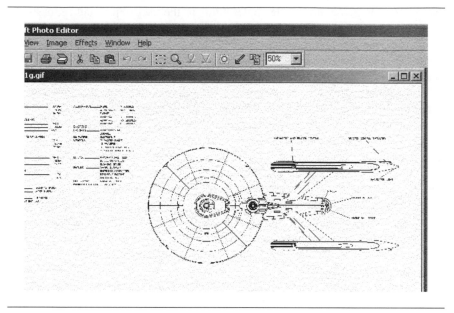

Figure 23-9   Launching the legacy editor.

We had several options. We could look for a commercial keystore service provider for the Microsoft platform, but there was little time to do that. We could figure out how Microsoft managed its keys in the registry, and then develop an analog to NDBS. But if we had no time to look for commercial providers, we certainly had no time to embark on another black-box visibility journey comparable to that described in Chapter 21.

The remaining option was circuitous, but workable, and that was to ensure that certificates stored in the registry were also stored in NDBS. We used a Netscape browser to export certificates manually from NDBS, and then we translated these certificates into a form recognized by Microsoft's certificate manager. This ensured that duplicate certificates and keys were available, one set for I&A in the registry, the other for SSL and IIOP in NDBS. This solution was ugly but it did the trick—the Explorer test was successful.

23.3   Evaluation

Had the model solution satisfied its evaluation criteria? The use case demonstrated an end-to-end scenario involving I&A, authorization, and image retrieval (Criterion #1). True, the NDBS provider did not implement all of the JCA methods for keystore providers, but applets did not have to insert data into the keystore.

We successfully demonstrated multiple security service providers (Criterion #3). By inspecting the debug output from the applet we confirmed that SSL sessions had been established for IIOP interactions (Criterion #4). But what about Criterion #2, browser independence?

We could hardly argue that the model solution *in itself* demonstrated browser independence. To demonstrate the end-to-end scenario, we had coerced Explorer into using a keystore service provider based on the Netscape certificate and key databases. It was a delicious irony, but a limitation of the model solution nonetheless. Furthermore, we had to use the Netscape browser to export the key material for later import into the Microsoft keystore (its registry). Therefore, we had not actually removed the Netscape browser at all. It was still required in the end-to-end scenario even if its "off-line" use was not directly visible.

But as we discussed in Chapter 22, the question of feasibility, and hence criteria satisfaction, rests on judgment. Model problems are *not* designed to develop production code, but to reduce design risk. The question of whether the secure applet satisfied its multi-browser criterion did not hinge on whether the model solution directly satisfied the criterion. Instead, it is only necessary for the model solution to demonstrate the *feasibility* of satisfying this (or any other) criterion in a production system. It is difficult to overestimate the importance of this distinction, since without it, the utility of model problems as an efficient way of reducing design risk vanishes.

Returning to the multi-browser criterion, satisfaction depends on whether we could acquire or develop a JCA-compliant keystore provider for Microsoft platforms. At this point, no such keystore provider had been found. If Microsoft did not publish an API for using certificates to retrieve private keys from its registry-based keystore, then we would require a feat of discovery analogous to what transpired in Chapter 21. If this was the case, then clearly the secure applet ensemble would be infeasible.

Fortunately, Microsoft did publish its crypto-API (CAPI, pronounced "cap-ee"). Two methods in particular were relevant: `CryptGetUserKey`, and `CryptAcquireCertificatePrivateKey`. Although we had no direct experience using CAPI, the documentation and sample programs associated with these methods, and discussions on newsgroups, suggested that these would be a suitable basis for developing a Microsoft analogue to NDBS.

At this point the design team had a decision to make: whether to prove the feasibility of using CAPI to develop a JCA-compliant keystore, or to argue the feasibility of the ensemble on the basis of what was already known. As noted elsewhere, each passing day increased the cost of abandoning the pure server-side SSJS design in favor of the secure applet design. Working with the DIRS designer, we decided that time was dear. The benefit of increasing our confidence in the applet ensemble would be outweighed by the cost of achieving this increased confidence. It was time to decide.

23.4   Summary

Even at this late stage, the applet ensemble had proven capable of springing surprises. Without last-minute black-box visibility techniques, the secure applet ensemble would have failed to satisfy its evaluation criteria. And, despite all of the earlier prototyping, we could not honestly state that the proof of feasibility was airtight. It depended on a judgment call with respect to browser independence. Nevertheless, absolute certainty is not, and usually should not be, the test of feasibility. After all, little is certain in the development of complex systems until they are completed. And while this is generally true for all system development efforts, it is nearly a law for component-based efforts.

23.5   Discussion Questions

1. How could you extend the design representations and processes described in this book to include probability as a measure of confidence of criterion satisfaction and ensemble feasibility?

2. Are the lines between design and implementation more or less sharply defined in component-based development than in custom development? Explain your answer.

3. Is waiting for a market event for Microsoft to release a JCA-compliant keystore a reasonable repair strategy? Explain your answer.

24

Conclusion & Retrospective

I hear and I forget. I see and I remember. I do and I understand.
—Confucius

Explorers may be motivated by the desire for adventure, but financiers usually have more pragmatic ends in mind. We began the DIRS case study with a simple design objective that unexpectedly triggered a series of design explorations. Now we had to take stock of what we had discovered and act on that knowledge. Figure 24-1 shows the design space, as we now understood it, with feasible ensembles appearing in gray. Our case study focused on the applet contingency. Within the applet contingency were four separate design contingencies, the main one being the use of FTP to transfer images. Indirect IIOP transfer was considered feasible but overshadowed by direct IIOP transfer, which shared all the advantages of the indirect approach but eliminated some of the problems. Of the three contingency plans for implementing direct IIOP, only event-based image transfer had been eliminated because of its severe performance problems.

Of the remaining ensembles, the Java application was deemed infeasible due to the difficulty of obtaining user buy-in. Moreover, it became unnecessary to pique the users once we had proven the applet ensemble to be feasible. The SSJS ensemble had been considered feasible from the start, and in fact, significant progress had been made in the design and implementation of an SSJS-based solution.

At this point, the designer faced a set of possible ensembles. Each ensemble was feasible, each ensemble had its own strengths and weaknesses, and each was independent. As discussed in Chapter 9, these are necessary conditions for using multi-attribute utility technology (MAUT). Now that we had proven the feasibility of the alternatives through prototyping, we applied this analytical and judgment-based decision aid.

345

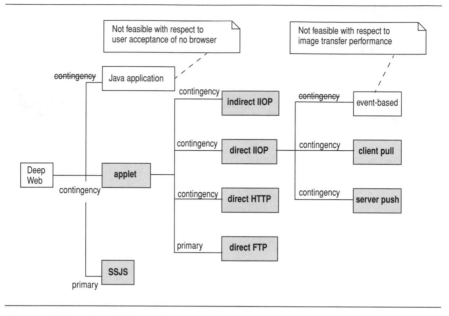

Figure 24-1 DeepWeb contingencies.

24.1 Multi-Attribute Evaluation

To evaluate the strengths and weaknesses of each ensemble, we had to define a preference structure. The preference structure does not make a decision process objective. Rather, it formalizes the process of applying judgment, so that the constituents of a judgment are explicit. In essence, a preference structure simultaneously provides a tool for making judgments and for explaining how any particular judgment was reached.

Figure 24-2 illustrates the preference structure for the DIRS ensemble selection. Note that there are no criteria for data integrity, data confidentiality, or I&A. These critical attributes are missing precisely because they are critical attributes. No ensemble would be considered feasible unless it supported the requisite quality attributes.

We weighted the preference structure to show a strong bias of sustainability (.75) over functionality (.25). The explanation for this is that certain functional requirements, such as the ability to search and retrieve images, are feasibility criteria for any ensemble. As such, they do not need to appear in a MAUT preference structure. Bass, Clements, and Kazman observed that the design task's primary concern is ensuring that a system satisfies quality attributes [Bass+ 98].[1]

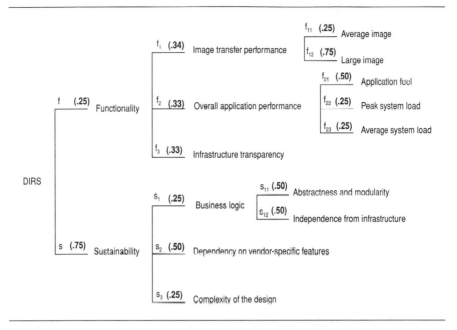

Figure 24-2   DIRS preference structure.

Thus, sustainability, the cost of keeping a deployed system up and running over time, surpasses functionality in the DIRS preference structure.

The definition of measures and utility scales for the frontier of the preference structure is also of interest. Ensemble performance attributes have objective, repeatable measurement scales. Attributes such as *design complexity* and *infrastructure transparency* may have measures, but devising them would most likely be a waste of time. In this case, we decided that nonrepeatable judgments were acceptable.

We eliminated indirect IIOP from consideration because it was dominated by the direct IIOP option. Table 24-1 shows the architect's judgment as to how well each contingency in the design space met each preference in the DIRS preference structure. Each preference is assigned a total value of 1, which is proportioned among the contingencies.[2]

We observe that the SSJS option is the least preferred, although all the contingencies are generally close. Some preference for client pull and direct FTP contingencies is shown, although the winner is "too close to call."

---

[1] It might be argued that performance should not be classified under functionality, since performance, like security and modifiability, are often defined, categorically, as nonfunctional attributes. Fortunately, such distinctions do not matter when constructing decision aids, so long as the resulting aid reflects the judgment of the decision maker and other stakeholders.

[2] Some columns do not exactly total one because values have been rounded to the hundredths.

Table 24-1 Contingency Evaluation

Option	f11	f12	f21	f22	f23	f3	s11	s12	s2	s3	Pref.
Client pull	.2	.15	.22	.2	.2	.24	.25	.23	.23	.25	.24
Server push	.1	.05	.22	.1	.1	.24	.25	.23	.23	.25	.23
Direct HTTP	.2	.15	.22	.2	.2	.24	.15	.23	.23	.15	.21
Direct FTP	.3	.5	.24	.3	.3	.24	.18	.23	.23	.1	.24
SSJS	.2	.15	.1	.2	.2	.04	.18	.08	.08	.25	.14

Now that we have come this far in the analysis, it is easy (and fun!) to play with the values. By altering the weightings in the preference structure, we can perform a sensitivity analysis. This will let us know how sensitive our decision is to differences in preference. Table 24-2 illustrates what happens if we inverse the weightings for functionality and sustainability and calculate new preference values.

In this analysis, we can see some reordering in preferences between the contingencies. The direct HTTP solution moves ahead of the server push option, and, more importantly, the direct FTP option moves out in front over the client pull option. However, a relatively large shift in preference between functionality and sustainability was required to change the rankings, so the decision model is fairly stable with respect to this preference.

The last point that requires attention is cost justification. In the DIRS case study, the applet ensemble was a "blue sky" design contingency. The design team felt that the applet ensemble would perform better and would be more sustainable than its low-risk SSJS competitor. However, work had already commenced on the low-risk alternative. So, in addition to establishing the technical superiority of applets over pure SSJS, the design team also had to weigh its efficacy against switchover cost.

At the next design team meeting, the results of the study were reviewed by the architect, designers, and management. At this meeting, it was decided that the advantages of the applet approach did not outweigh the cost of switching over, so the main SSJS design was carried on through completion.

Table 24-2 Sensitivity Analysis

Option	f(.25), s(.75)	f(.75), s(.25)
Client pull	.24	.26
Server push	.23	.22
Direct HTTP	.21	.24
Direct FTP	.24	.33
SSJS	.14	.15

24.2   Conclusion

Although the direct FTP applet was the most desirable ensemble, we were not able to implement this approach due to cost and schedule constraints. While work proceeded on proving the feasibility of the applet ensemble, significant progress had been made on the SSJS approach and there was simply no time left to discard this work and begin implementing the user interface in a completely different language, with completely different constraints and capabilities. Although the applet ensemble we had spent so much time and effort evaluating was not used in DIRS, this was a perfectly acceptable result of the R^3 process and contingency management approach.

Increasingly, cycle time and time to market are critical factors in a software development effort. This was true of DIRS, as it is of many systems. The fact that the development group had little competence with Web technology at the beginning of the effort was a huge hurdle for the team. Through judicious use of R^3, the team was able to anticipate risks and devise solutions for problems that would have been discovered much later using traditional development methods.

The fact that the applet ensemble was not selected is immaterial to the demonstration of our approach. DIRS was a close run race, and the final outcome easily could have been different. Perhaps more importantly, our success in proving the feasibility of the applet ensemble would have consequences on the next project, and the one after that.

24.3   Retrospective

Having reached the terminus of the active design effort, it is time to reflect on and enlarge the themes of the book.

THE ENSEMBLE'S THE THING

It is noteworthy that at no place in this case study did we discuss the topic of formal component evaluation. A reference to evaluation, appearing in a sidebar in Chapter 13, emphasizes the futility of premature multi-criteria component evaluation. Instead, we have emphasized the importance of understanding design dependencies, repairs, and contingencies as a basis for making component selection decisions.

The proper focus of evaluation in component-based development is the *ensemble*. While the components that form an ensemble ultimately determine its feasibility, the components are only the means to that end. The ensemble defines the context for components and is adapted to accommodate the strengths and weaknesses of its constituent components. The ensemble is one of the few remaining elements of the component-based architecture still under the designer's control.

Consider, for example, the conditions that led us to component selections in the case study. In Chapter 15, "A Certificate Odyssey," we eliminated a number of products and technologies based on previous component selections, even though these decisions were tentative. These prior selections bound components to an abstract role within an ensemble. Change these decisions and components that were previously eliminated may once again be viable. Again, consider the selection of an ORB in the case study. The original selection was Orbix. However, we later eliminated Orbix and introduced VisiBroker, because Orbix did not support a required pattern of interaction in an ensemble.

IMPLEMENTATION SUPPORTS ANALYSIS

It is absurd to think that one can discover the integration constraints that govern ensemble feasibility and, ultimately, component selection using purely analytical decision aids. No purely analytical approach, whether multi-criteria evaluation or object and component modeling techniques, can expose the deep and subtle integration dependencies that arise within and across ensembles.

To uncover component dependencies and to prove ensemble feasibility, it is essential to use sharply focused prototypes such as *model solutions*. The reliability of analytical approaches to system design decreases as the number of commercial components in a system increases. Commercial components are opaque by intent, and usually exhibit complex behavior. The most reliable way to determine if a component is feasible is to evaluate it in the context of an ensemble. This is the purpose of prototyping.

NONLINEAR DESIGN

Following a linear design process from problem statement, through use cases, component specifications, and ultimately software architecture, is reasonable when the designer has control over components and their interfaces. This process is anachronistic, however, when commercial components dominate. In this case, it is essential to explore multiple design paths early in the process, especially when innovative and evolving components are used.

Instead of a linear process, component-based design is best represented by a hierarchy (or lattice) of nested contingencies. Design commitments are made in the face of uncertainty about component or ensemble feasibility. These decisions rely on a speculation that nothing will be discovered that will contradict these commitments. But, as we have seen, this sort of discovery is commonplace. In the face of such uncertainty, contingency plans must be put in place by the conscientious designer.

On a more positive note, the component market can be expected to respond to customer demand. Component vendors usually bridge integration gaps in future product releases. It would make sense to leave a design option open in anticipation of these market events, but we must recognize that a commitment to the design option must occur within a defined time interval. Again, the possibility that an event might not occur should be mitigated with contingency plans. We saw just such an example with the Sorbet contingency described in Chapter 19. In this case, the contingency was not exercised, but that is beside the point. The investment in Sorbet kept a design option open, and reduced risk.

LOW-LEVEL SYSTEMS SKILLS ARE MORE, NOT LESS, CRITICAL

There is perhaps nothing quite so irritating as when people who are confronted with component integration challenges exclaim, "Oh, that's just plumbing. That's being solved by <insert vendor name here>!" The plumbing analogy conveys the idea that the problem is amenable to routine skill. It also conveys the idea that focusing on infrastructure is at odds with the goal of a design effort: adding value to an enterprise. If we follow this logic, we must conclude that building applications adds value to an enterprise, while building infrastructure is an expense.

Unfortunately, this implication does not withstand even gentle scrutiny. As the case study abundantly demonstrates, there is nothing routine about infrastructure construction. So long as commercial component vendors lock customers into proprietary infrastructure mechanisms, infrastructure development remains a complex and daunting challenge.

It is also clear that business logic and infrastructure technology cannot be easily separated. (Herzum and Sims base their approach to business component development on the feasibility of this separation, but do not describe how to fully achieve it [Herzum+ 00].) Whether business rules are embedded as stored procedures in a relational database, encoded as Java servlets running in a Web-server hosted JVM, or encoded in enterprise beans running in an Enterprise JavaBean container, the dependency between infrastructure and business logic is unmistakable. Given this dependency, it is neither feasible nor sensible to divorce infrastructure development from application development; at least not yet.

Finally we want to emphasize that, at a low level of abstraction, all integration efforts appear quite similar: data and control are passed by means of some intercomponent communication mechanism. The components of interest change far more rapidly than these low-level integration mechanisms. As we often have seen, expertise in low-level integration and systems interfaces can achieve better results than high-level, component-specific expertise. Thus, if forced to choose, we would select software engineers with system rather than component or application skills.

24.4   Summary

This chapter brings the DIRS case study to a conclusion. Having identified a design option that was perhaps optimal for future systems, we nonetheless selected a nonoptimal path to accommodate cost and schedule constraints. Although this decision may leave a bad taste in the mouth of purists and technologists, from a software engineering perspective it was the correct decision.

We also summarized the key themes that, we believe, run throughout the case study. Those themes include the central role of *ensemble* in component-based design and component selection, the crucial role of prototyping in support of design analysis, the fundamental role of contingency planning, and the premium placed on low-level systems skills. We believe the case study, drawn from our own real-life experience, effectively illustrates these themes.

24.5   Discussion Questions

1.   Complete the multi-criteria decision aid started in Figure 24-2 using, if possible, a commercially supported tool. Break into teams and see how you might reconcile competing preferences.

2.   Describe what you would need to do to completely separate business logic from infrastructure. Use Herzum and Sims' model of distributed object components and business components as a foundation.

3.   Assuming that you decide to not develop a way to insulate business logic from infrastructure, what sort of organizational and technical processes are needed to manage the deployed systems and new projects, given a steady stream of new releases of infrastructure components?

PART III: ONWARD

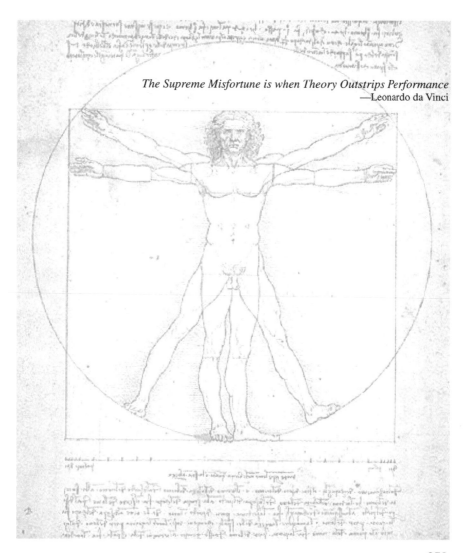

The Supreme Misfortune is when Theory Outstrips Performance
—Leonardo da Vinci

25

Getting Started

The Road goes ever on and on
Down from the door where it began.
Now far ahead the Road has gone,
And I must follow, if I can,
Pursuing it with eager feet,
Until it joins some larger way
where many paths and errands meet.
And whither then? I cannot say.
—Bilbo Baggins' *Walking Song*, by J.R.R. Tolkien

Commercial software components are not new to software engineering. However, many organizations do not realize that they have, by adopting commercial components, changed the way they develop systems. A different circumstance arises when a project decides to adopt, for example, an object-oriented approach to software development. In that circumstance, there is a clear port of departure: the old procedure-oriented development style. There is also a clear destination: a well-understood software development method based in object-oriented abstractions. Last, there are well-charted routes: there is considerable industrial experience in adopting object-oriented methods. The situation pertaining to software components could hardly be more different.

In place of a clear point of departure, there is a blurry frontier. Many organizations find themselves dependent on software components without having made an overt decision to adopt component-based development. Where adopting object technology involves a self-conscious decision, component technology is imposed by necessity. Choice (and therefore, decision) is banished where necessity rules. The modern enterprise is only free to decide which commercial software components to use, and how to use them. It is not, in most cases, free to decide whether to use components.

The port of destination is no clearer than the port of departure. What makes a development method component based rather than object based? Can a method be both component based and object based? We are inclined to answer "yes" to this last question, although the title of Szyperski's influential book, *Component-Software:*

355

Beyond Object-Oriented Programming, suggests that others may disagree [Szyperski 98]. In our view, the most significant challenges of software components are those posed by the market regime; that is, by the use of preexisting commercial off-the-shelf software components. These challenges are quite distinct from, and independent of, those addressed by object-oriented concepts.

It is too early to say whether standard component infrastructures, and the component-based methods founded on the simplifying assumptions they make possible [Cheesman+ 00], will come to dominate the software development landscape. What is known, however, is that commercial software components—including, but not limited to, component infrastructures—will become more, not less, important. This book makes (at least some of) the constituents of a development method for commercial components explicit. We are not reluctant to say, however, that more work is needed.

The conclusion that we can draw from this discussion is that there is widespread experience with *using* commercial software components. There are, however, few (if any) well-defined *commercial* component-based development methods. There is still less documented experience in making the transition to commercial components. Given this, you may be wondering how you or your organization might begin to master the challenges of commercial components. In this chapter, we outline four ways to get started.

25.1   Build a Competence Center

As the case study demonstrates, success in component-based development depends, to a considerable degree, on the designers and developers possessing expertise in the components being integrated. The gap between available and required component expertise is a source of project risk. To reduce this risk, expertise must be developed during the project at the expense of time, money, or both. Alternatively, expertise can be obtained independently of particular projects, with the cost of obtaining it amortized across projects. In short, component expertise is an asset that can (and should) be managed like any other enterprise asset.

One way to do this is to develop a *competence center*, a testbed of computer hardware and software components. A competence center can be used to develop proofs-of-feasibility using components, conduct training, support personal growth, or other such activities. Three conditions must hold, however, if a competence center is to be effective.

1. The center must be independent of particular development projects. This is important for administrative and psychological reasons. Administratively, the cost of sustaining a competence center should be tracked separately from project costs. Psychologically, the users of the center should be focused on obtaining competence, not delivering products.

2. The center must have an *agenda*. Competence building should be independent of particular projects, but should be guided by an enterprise's strategic technology objectives. If an enterprise has made a commitment to e-commerce, the competence center should have e-commerce components installed. Model problems should be used to guide exploration of new technologies, and to train engineers in how to develop model solutions.

3. The center must be linked to individual performance expectations. One point is critical: a competence center should not become a separate research and development unit. Instead, it should be a resource for all developers. Personal performance evaluations should require a specific amount of time to be spent in the competence center.

All of this implies that, while not a separate research and development unit, the competence center nevertheless must be managed separately. Its objectives must be defined, and its environment sustained. There are many ways of doing this. For example, an enterprise architect might be responsible for defining a competence agenda, and line managers might be required to staff the center on a rotating basis. The important point is to find an effective way to promote, and manage, the development of appropriate, component-specific expertise.

25.2 Define Your Infrastructure

Infrastructure means different things to different people: it is best defined as whatever a person needs to do his or her job. This point is reflected quite nicely in Herzum and Sims' *Business Component Factory* [Herzum+ 00]. They make clear that the developer of an infrastructure and the user of that infrastructure are liable to be different people, possessing different skills. The user of an infrastructure should not be required to understand how the infrastructure works, or how it has been integrated. Moreover, infrastructure can be layered so that developers at each tier can have specialized skills and well-specified, recurring tasks, much like an assembly-line worker. The success of this approach depends on making the infrastructure a well-defined, managed set of software services.

However, there is another aspect of infrastructure that is often overlooked. An enterprise uses an infrastructure as a foundation on which to provide its customers with business value. From this perspective, an organization defines as infrastructure that which does not provide business value, but rather enables it. For example, the DIRS project assumed workstations, network services, Web technology, terabyte disk farms, and database management as infrastructure. The business value provided by DIRS consisted of services such as disaster recovery, service availability, and secure data enclaves. Why is it important to distinguish that which enables business value from the value itself? Because an organization should seek to maximize investment in business value and minimize investment in infrastructure.

This is more than idle business philosophy: it has direct consequence on the design of component-based systems, and on identifying required competence. It made sense for DIRS to "own" the security aspects of its design. This did not mean that DIRS had to develop its own encryption algorithms. It did mean, however, that DIRS had to use commercially available technologies in a distinctive way so that it could provide its customers with business value not available elsewhere. The result was a secure applet ensemble that was, at that time, innovative and risky, both in the components used and in the way they were integrated. The risk was justified by the potential business value, and therefore the investment in design contingencies was commensurate with risk and value. Had innovative security services not been considered a core business value for DIRS, a purely off-the-shelf security ensemble would have sufficed.

The important point is that a substantial amount of the risk associated with commercial components comes from technologies that are on "the bleeding edge." Sometimes it pays to be on the edge. In these situations, it is especially important to be prepared with contingencies, black-box visibility, R^3, and other techniques described in this book. Conversely, it is useful to know when being on the edge is unnecessary.

Building a competence center and defining your infrastructure are good things to do, but it may be difficult to turn these ideas into concrete accomplishments unless you have something specific in mind. The next two ideas serve this purpose.

25.3   Build an Enterprise Design Handbook

In Chapter 8, we described how you could structure a design handbook centered on component ensembles. A handbook project would be an effective way to inaugurate a competence center, and to provide clarity on what is core business value, and what is infrastructure.

You might begin by documenting the component-based aspects of one or more exemplar applications. It should not be difficult to find an exemplar—any application that made good use of commercial software components would serve. Existing design documents may provide enough information to construct reference and supplier ensembles. More likely, though, you will need to interview project members to discover which design alternatives were considered, and why they were abandoned. You might also begin with a clean slate rather than from exemplars. Which you choose depends on how many component-based applications your organization has developed; the extent to which these make use of components are representative of future projects.

You might also develop a handbook to specify design standards. Some organizations have units that are responsible for setting enterprise technology standards. Often, there is a considerable gap between these units and those that develop end applications. In these situations, another gap also arises: between the level of abstraction used to describe enterprise standards, and the information needed to apply these standards. This abstraction gap arises because the enterprise standards have to apply to a large class of applications. A handbook that describes, in concrete terms, how enterprise standards are to be used in applications would effectively reduce both gaps.

Whether you begin with exemplars or a clean slate, an ensemble handbook is a concrete artifact that can be measured, distributed, and used. Its utility can be improved with experience. And, it can be used to structure development activities in the competence center. For example, development staff might be asked to develop "starter kits" along the lines described in Chapter 8.

25.4   Certify Designers and Lead Engineers

This idea will no doubt cause more than a few raised eyebrows. How could we advocate certifying designers and developers in the discipline of component-based development, when, earlier in this same chapter, we argued that the discipline is still nascent? We could put the matter differently, however. We could ask whether there are things that every designer and lead engineer should know before embarking on a component-based development effort. If there is, and we think there is, then certifying that they have this knowledge is not just reasonable, but prudent. This is true even if component-based development methods are still immature.

There are three classes of expertise that pertain to component-based development:

1. Expertise pertaining to commercial software components in general. In this book, we have described and illustrated a number of necessary skills. These could form the basis for training or other forms of professional development. There are other necessary skills that we have not discussed, such as license management, configuration management, and reference modeling.

2. Expertise pertaining to specific component technologies. It should be clear from the case study that the design process is decisively influenced by components. Senior designers, developers, and even program managers should have substantive knowledge about critical components. It is the lack of this knowledge that poses the most substantive risks in component-based development.

3. Expertise pertaining to enterprise design standards. Design standards are required to ensure that large-scale enterprise concerns are addressed even by small- and mid-scale applications. For example, achieving application sustainability and interoperability requires that certain design decisions be made in a consistent way. An ensemble handbook is one way of conveying these standards.

Of course, these are skills that are above and beyond other necessary software engineering skills.

25.5   Summary

The best way to get started is to recognize the distinctive nature of component-based development:

- Application requirements and components are mutually constraining.
- Component competence is a fundamental design asset.
- Competence is a wasting asset.
- Competence can be packaged and sustained as an enterprise asset.
- No amount of competence will insulate you from technology surprises.
- Contingencies and competence generation are therefore essential.

Most of all, recognize that using commercial software components is an adventure.

26

The Prophecies

What does it matter now if men believe or no?
What is to come will come.
And soon you too will stand aside,
To murmur in pity that my words were true.
—Cassandra, in *Agamemnon* by Aeschylus

Prophesying the future (especially in print) is risky business. Some famous examples of cloudy crystal balls include:

- "... computers in the future may have only 1000 vacuum tubes and perhaps weigh only 1 [and] 1/2 tons"
  —*Popular Mechanics,* 1949 [Hamilton 49]

- "I think that there is a world market for maybe five computers."
  —Thomas Watson, chairman of IBM, 1943[1]

- "640K ought to be enough for anybody."
  —Bill Gates, 1981[2]

However, in the service of advancing the state of software engineering, we accept the risk of being wrong.

26.1 Programmers Won't Get Any Smarter

The Bureau of Labor Statistics predicts 70% growth in computer and data processing jobs by the year 2005. At the same time, the U.S. Department of Education

---

[1] IBM believes that this quote is a misunderstanding of remarks made by Thomas Watson at IBM's annual stockholders meeting on April 28, 1953 (not 1943 as commonly attributed). See *http://www-1.ibm.com/ibm/history/reference/faq_0000000047.html* for more information on this theory.

[2] In an article written by Bill Gates in 1996 and distributed by the *New York Times* Syndicate; Bill Gates denied ever having said this.

shows that the number of graduates in computer science has dropped 43% since 1986. This trend will continue. In response, programming will be "outsourced" to developing countries. Programming will be vastly simplified, even at the expense of flexibility. Programmers will be increasingly specialized "blue collar" workers, and many will work on component assembly lines. Software engineers will fare better, and they will be trained to build the factory infrastructures in which software development will occur.

26.2   Technology Changes Faster Than Programmers

Lawrence Sanders' novel *The Tomorrow File* describes an anti-utopian future where technology change is so rapid that people become obsolete, or "obso," within months of beginning their professional careers [Saunders 75]. Those that became obso were quickly marginalized by society. We see a similar phenomenon at work in the software technology marketplace. However, the vast and still growing demand for software is a safeguard against the marginalization of programmers. Nonetheless, in the near future, the majority of programmers will be obsolete but still employed.

26.3   Component Standards Emerge

The situation today, with vendors having free reign over the design of their components, will give way to more restrictive component standards. In the future, component developers will be required to comply with one or more component standards. A component standard imposes interface and other conventions on vendors so that deployment of components, and integration of component-based systems, becomes routine. Component models such as Sun Microsystems' Enterprise JavaBeans and Microsoft's COM+ are prominent exemplars of this emerging trend.

26.4   Component Standards Expand and Merge

Microsoft, Sun, Object Management Group (OMG), and others will expand their component standards in the enterprise computing domain. Two or three major enterprise component standards will become well established by 2003. Each standard will include comparable functionality, but will do so inconsistently, ensuring that components cannot be developed, deployed, or integrated across standards.

26.5   Niche-Specific Frameworks Emerge

In a complementary trend to the emergence of enterprise component standards, niche-specific component standards will arise within selected vertical business areas. Education, manufacture, health care, emergency response, telephony, and other major economic sectors will each converge on their own component standards, and markets of software components will emerge for each such standard.

26.6   Component Product Lines, Not Commodities, Emerge

Markets in commodity components will not materialize in the near term. Instead, vendors will produce product lines of components. These will comprise components that have been designed to work together. Mass customization will be the dominant form of software commerce. Variability will be provided through configuration and parameterization tools. Consumers will buy applications from product line vendors by specifying their unique parameters, and custom solutions will be delivered in a matter of minutes or days. Many product lines will emerge, but an industry shake-out will leave only a few major players. Only at this point will commodity component markets emerge, and these will support particular product-line-specific supply chains of components.

26.7   Liability Will Lead to Component Certification

Component license agreements that disclaim responsibility for loss of property or life will prove unenforceable. The increasingly vital role of software in post-industrial economies will lead to well-publicized failures and, ultimately, to successful legal action against software developers and component vendors. The software industry will respond by insuring themselves against liability. This, in turn, will lead insurers to make use of independent testers and certifiers, such as Underwriters Laboratories, to limit their liability exposure.

26.8   Systems Are Predictably Assembled

With certified components and component standards will come predictable assembly. Beginning in selected application domains, component standards and the infrastructures that implement them will be explicitly designed to support compositional reasoning. For example, performance, availability, safety, or security properties of an assembly of components will be predicted from certified component properties. The component standard and infrastructure will guarantee, by construction, that the assumptions underlying the compositional reasoning scheme have been honored by an implementation.

26.9   Reasoning Systems Automate System Assembly

Component specification standards will be defined. Components will document the properties that are needed for component integration. These specifications will be certified and, together with the component and certificate, will be made tamper resistant. Component integration rules will define which component properties are compatible, and which are incompatible. Component integrators will provide an ensemble specification to an automated assistant. The specification will include functional and nonfunctional requirements. Nonfunctional requirements will be specified using a "quality equalizer" like the one shown in Figure 26-1. Based on the ensemble specification, component specifications, and integration rules, the automated assistant will identify and rank ensembles. The system integration task will, to a large extent, consist of finding the correct settings on the equalizer for the system being developed.

26.10   Federated Virtual Component Repositories Emerge

Components will be found using search technologies that have been adapted for component search. Vendors will make their components available through these search engines. In addition, component boutiques and component warehouses

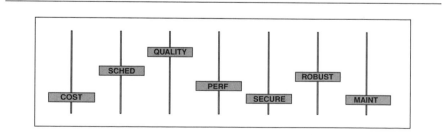

Figure 26-1   Quality equalizer.

will also emerge. Supplier agreements will link brand-name software components to particular distribution channels. Enterprises will store their components in local repositories. If needed components are not available in a local repository, the search will be extended to organizational, domain, and finally global repositories. Different companys' component repositories will be interconnected, with users able to search the entire repository network. Both proprietary and commercial components will share the same virtual repository, taking advantage of advanced security services to control access.

26.11 Component Standard-Independent Components Emerge

One area in which components have been successful is in the area of graphical user interface (GUI) controls. Libraries of GUI components emerged as early as 1966. Later, competing platform-independent GUI standards emerged, such as Graphical Kernel System in 1985 and Programmer's Hierarchical Interactive Graphics System in 1989. Eventually, these were replaced by platform-dependent GUI components, such as Motif Widgets and Windows controls. Platform-specific GUI controls made it difficult to develop cross-platform applications, spawning an industry of virtual GUI toolkits and user interface management systems. These are now giving way to platform-independent GUI components, such as Java Swing controls. Swing GUI controls are based on the JavaBeans component standard, and are composable by GUI builder tools, even when these tools have no preexisting knowledge of the controls. Many third-party companies have developed additional GUI controls to extend the core set of controls provided by Sun. This history will repeat itself, this time with server-side components rather than GUI components. The next step will be the development of framework-independent components. These will implement business logic that easily can be adapted to a variety of standards and infrastructures.

26.12 Software Systems Are Assembled Without Coding

In selected domains, applications will be developed without coding. Instead, they will be visually assembled from existing components in a way similar to how drawing tools allow complex drawings to be composed from primitive drawing objects such as circles, lines, and polygons. Zero code assembly will first take hold in domains that require *transient* applications. These are applications that are built quickly, for a well-defined and functionally constrained purpose, and are then discarded. Such composition environments already exist for data instrumentation and mathematics. Many more such application areas will emerge as programming becomes more of an end-user activity.

26.13 The Distant Future

The above prophecies span the next ten years. But what about the more distant future? The first prediction concerns the future of information security, which has some relevance considering the prominence of information security in the case study. The second concerns a long-term solution to the shortage of talented programmers.

INFORMATION CRIME SYNDICATES ARISE

The value of personal and corporate information will surge, and information security will become ever more important to society. Crime syndicates will engage in all varieties of information crime, including: extortion, corporate espionage, identity theft, and e-commerce fraud. In response, the biometric security market will explode. Retinal scans, voice print, and handprint identification will become commonplace. Information syndicates will become increasingly unscrupulous. There will be a 700% increase in emergency room admissions of people missing fingers and eyes.

PROGRAMMERS ARE GROWN ON FARMS

Programming will not fundamentally change. Instead, programmers will be genetically engineered and grown on farms. Unnecessary organs will be eliminated to make programmers more efficient. For example, it will be discovered that it is cheaper to genetically modify programmers to have 5 rows of 8 fingers on each hand than it is to replace QWERTY keyboards. Programmers will be psychologically conditioned to see problems as challenges, and really big problems as opportunities.

Bibliography

[Allen+ 97] Robert Allen and David Garlan, "A Formal Basis for Architectural Connection," ACM Transactions on Software Engineering and Methodology, July, 1997.

[ANSI 85] Accredited Standards Committee on Financial Services, X9, American National Standard, Financial Institution Key Management (Wholesale), American Bankers Association, Section 7.2. ANSI X9.17-1995. New York: American National Standards Institute, 1985.

[Bachmann+ 00] Felix Bachman, Len Bass, C. Buhman, F. Long, Santiago Cornella Dorda, John Robert, Robert Seacord, Kurt Wallnau, Technical Concepts of Component-Based Software Engineering, Technical Report CMU/SEI-2000-TR-008, Software Engineering Institute, Carnegie Mellon University, Pittsburgh. *http://www.sei.cmu.edu/ publications/documents/00.reports/00tr008/00tr008title.html.*

[Bass+ 98] Len Bass, Paul Clements, and R. Kazman, *Software Architecture in Practice.* Reading, Mass: Addison-Wesley, 1998.

[Bauer 97] F. L. Bauer, *Decrypted Secrets: Methods and Maxims of Cryptology.* Berlin: Springer-Verlag, 1997.

[Beker+ 82] H. Beker, and F. Piper, *Cipher Systems.* London: Northwood Books, 1982.

[Belton 86] Valerie Belton, "A Comparison of the Analytic Hierarchy Process and a Simple Multi-Attribute Value Function," *European Journal of Operational Research*, 26, no.1: 7–21, July 1986.

[Boehm 88a] Barry Boehm, "A Spiral Model of Software Development and Enhancement," *Computer*, May 1988: pp. 61–72.

[Boehm 88b] Barry Boehm, "COCOMO II Model Definition," Center for Software Engineering, Los Angeles: University of Sourthern Califoria. 1998.

[Boehm+ 00] Barry Boehm and Fred Hansen, eds., Spiral Development: Experience, Principles, and Refinements, Special Report CMU/SEI-2000-SR-008, Software Engineering Institute, Carnegie Mellon University, Pittsburgh. *http://www.sei.cmu.edu/ cbs/spiral2000/february2000/SR08html/SR08.html.*

[Boehm+ 78] B. Boehm, J. Brown, J. Kaspar, M. Lipow, G. McCleod, M. Merit, *Characteristics of Software Quality.* Los Angeles: University of Sourthern California— Center for Software Engineering. 1978.

[Booch+ 99] Grady Booch, James Rumbaugh, and Ivar Jacobson, *The Unified Modeling Language User Guide.* Reading, Mass.: Addison Wesley, 1999.

[Breshahan 96] J. Breshahan, "Mission Possible," *CIO Magazine*, October 15, (1996): 54–64.

[Brown 84] Dave Brown, "My Accordian's Stuffed Full of Paper or Why We Did So Badly in the Design Phase," Software Engineering Notes, July 1984: pg. 58–60.

[Cheesman+ 00] John Cheesman and John Daniels, *UML Components: A Simple Process for Specifying Component-Based Software*. Boston: Addison-Wesley, 2001.

[Cifuentes 94] Cristina Cifuentes, "Reverse Compilation Techniques," Ph.D. diss. University of Queensland, Brisbane, Australia, 1994.

[Cifuentes+ 95] C. Cifuentes and K. J. Gough, "Decompilation of Binary Programs," *Software - Practice & Experience*. 25, no. 7, (1995): 811–829.

[Cox 95] B. Cox, "No Silver Bullet" Reconsidered, *American Programmer Magazine*, Ed Yourdan (ed.) Arlington MA: Cutter Information Corp., 8, no. 11 (November 1995).

[Cusumano+ 95] Michael A. Cusumano and Richard W. Selby, *Microsoft Secrets*. New York: The Free Press, 1995.

[Denning 83] D. E. R. Denning, *Cryptography and Data Security*. Reading, Mass: Addison-Wesley, 1983.

[Diffie+ 76] W. Diffie and M. E. Hellman, "New Directions in Cryptography," *IEEE Transactions on Information Theory, IT-22*, 6, (1976): 644–654.

[D'Ipollito+ 92] Richard D'Ippolito, Ken Lee, Chuck Plinta, Jeff Stewart, Paul Bailor, "Putting the Engineering in Software Engineering," Paper presented at the Conference on Software Engineering Education, Software Engineering Institute, San Diego, CA. 1992.

[Drucker 99] Peter Drucker, "Beyond the Information Revolution," *Atlantic Monthly* 284, no. 4, (October 1999): 47–57.

[D'Souza+ 99] Desmond F. D'Souza and Alan Cameron Wills, *Objects, Components, and Frameworks with UML: The Catalysis Approach*, Reading, Mass: Addison-Wesley, 1999.

[ECMA 91] European Computer Manufacturers Association (ECMA), *Reference Model for Frameworks of Software Engineering Environments*, Technical Report ECMA TR/55, 2nd ed. Geneva, Switzerland: ECMA, 1991.

[Edwards+ 82] Ward Edwards and J. Robert Newman, *Multiattribute Evaluation: Series on Quantitative Applications in the Social Sciences*. Beverly Hills, CA: Sage Publications, 1982.

[El Gamal 85] T. El Gamal, "A Public Key Cryptosystem and Signature Scheme Based on Discrete Logarithms," *IEEE Transactions on Information Theory* IT-31, (1985): 469–473.

[Ellis 87] J. H. Ellis, "The Story of Non-Secret Encryption." Cheltenham, UK: Communications Electronics Security Group, 1987. *www.cesg.gov.uk/about/nsecret/ellis.htm*.

[Fenton 93] Norman Fenton, *Software Metrics: A Rigorous Approach*. London: Chapman & Hall, 1993.

[Ford+ 97] Warwick Ford and Michael Baum, *Secure, Electronic Commerce: Building the Infrastructure for Digital Signatures and Encryption*. Upper Saddle River, NJ: Prentice-Hall, 1997.

[Gamma+ 94] Erich Gamma, Richard Helm, Ralph Johnson, John Vlissides, *Design Patterns: Elements of Reusable Object-Oriented Software*. Reading, Mass: Addison-Wesley, 1995.

[Garfinkel+ 97] Simson Garfinkel and Gene Spafford, *Web Security & Commerce*, Sebastapol, Calif.: O'Reilly & Associates, 1997.

[Garlan+ 95] David Garlan, R. Allen, and J. Ockerbloom, "Architectural Mismatch: or Why It's Hard to Build Systems Out of Existing Parts," in *Proceedings of the International Conference on Software Engineering* (ICSE-95, Seattle, Wash.) New York: ACM, 1995, pp 179–185.

[Gerck 97] E. Gerck, Overview of Certification Systems: X.509, CA, PGP, and SKIP. *http://www.mcg.org.br/cert.htm.*

[Gibbs 94] W. Wayt Gibbs, "Software's Chronic Crisis," *Scientific American*, 271, no. 3 (September 1994), pp. 86–95.

[Greenspan 99] Alan Greenspan, Testimony Before the Joint Economic Committee, U.S. Congress, June 14, 1999. *http://www.federalreserve.gov/boarddocs/testimony/1999/19990614.htm.*

[Gries+ 93] David Gries and Fred B. Schneider, A Logical Approach to Discrete Math, New York: Springer-Verlag, 1993.

[Harold 97] Rusty Harold, Java Network Programming, Sebastapol, Calif: O'Reilly & Associates, 1997.

[Harrison+ 96] Michael Harrison and Pamela Zave, "Introduction," in *Proceedings of the Second IEEE International Symposium on Requirements Engineering.* Los Alamitos, California: IEEE Computer Society Press, 1996.

[Hazelrigg 99] G. A. Hazelrigg, "A Framework for Decision-Based Engineering Design," *Journal of Mechanical Design*, 1999.

[Herzum+ 00] Peter Herzum and Oliver Sims, *Business Component Factory: A Comprehensive Overview of Component-Based Development for the Enterprise.* New York: John Wiley (OMG Press): 2000.

[Hickman 95] K.E.B. Hickman, *The SSL Protocol*, December 1995. *http://home.netscape.com/eng/security/SSL_2.html.*

[Hissam+ 99] Scott A. Hissam and David Carney, "Isolating Faults in Complex COTS-based Systems," *Journal of Software Maintenance: Research and Practice*, 11, no. 4 (May–June 1999): 183–199.

[Hong+ 81] S. Hong and R. Nigam, "Analytic Hierarchy Process Applied to Evaluation of Financial Modeling Software," in *Proceedings of the First International Conference on Decision Support Systems*, Austin, TX: Execucom Syst. Corp., 1981.

[IEEE 89] IEEE Computer Society, "Standards for a Software Quality Measurement Methodology," P-1061/D20, 1989.

[IEEE 90] IEEE Computer Society, et al., IEEE Standard Glossary of Software Engineering Terminology, IEEE Std610.12-1990, New York: IEEE Publishing, 1990.

[IETF 99] Internet Engineering Task Force, "The TLS Protocol Version 1.0," Request for Comments: 2246, January 1999. *http://www.rfc-editor.org/rfc/rfc2246.txt.*

[ISO 97] International Telecommunications Union, *Information technology—Open Systems Interconnection—The Directory: Overview of concepts, models, and services.* Geneva, Switzerland: ITU, 1999.

[ISO9000-3 94] International Organization for Standardization (ISO), *Guidelines for the Application of ISO 9001 to the Development, Supply and Maintenance of Software*, Geneva, Switzerland: ISO-9001, June 1994.

[ITU-T 97] International Telecommunications Union, *Information Technology—Open Systems Interconnection—The Directory, Authentication Framework: Data Systems and Open System Communication, Directory.* Geneva, Switzerland: ITU, 1996.

[Jacobson+ 99] Ivar Jacobson, Grady Booch, and James Rumbaugh. *The Unified Software Development Process.* Reading, Mass.: Addison Wesley, 1999.

[Jordon+ 91] K. A. Jordon and A. M. Davis, "Requirements engineering metamodel: An integrated view of requirements," in *Proceedings of the Fifteenth Annual International Computer Software and Applications Conference*, Los Alamitos, CA: IEEE Computer Society Press, 1991, 472–478.

[Kontio 95] Jyrki Kontio, "OTSO: A Systematic Process for Reusable Software Component Selection," Technical Report CS-TR-3378, UMIACS-TR-96-63, University of Maryland College Park, December 1995.

[Kontio 96] Jyrki Kontio, "A Case Study in Applying a Systematic Method for COTS Selection," in *Proceedings of the 18th International Conference on Software Engineering*, Los Alamitos, CA: IEEE Computer Society Press, 1996: 201–209.

[Kuhn 62] Thomas Kuhn, *The Structure of Scientific Revolutions*, 3rd ed. Chicago: University of Chicago Press, 1996.

[Lai 92] X. Lai, "ETH Series on Information Processing, in *On the Design and Security of Block Ciphers,* Vol 1, ed. J. L. Massey. Konstanz, Switzerland: Hartung-Gorre Verlag, 1992.

[Marca+ 87] D. Marca and C. McGowan, *Structured Analysis and Design Technique.* New York: McGraw-Hill, 1987.

[McGowan 94] Clement L. McGowan, "Requirements Engineering—A Different Analogy" in *Proceedings of the First International Conference on Requirements Engineering.* Los Alamitos, Calif.: IEEE Computer Society Press, 1994, p. 147.

[Meyer 00] Bertrand Meyer, *Design by Contract*, Prentice Hall, 2000.

[Min 92] Hokey Min, "Selection of Software: The Analytic Hierarchy Process," in *International Journal of Physical Distribution and Logistics Management*, 22, no. 1, (1992): 42–52.

[Morisio+ 97] M. Morisio and A. Tsoukiàs, "IusWare: A methodology for the evaluation and selection of software products," in *IEE Proceedings of Software Engineering*, 144, no. 3 (June 1997).

[Naur+ 69] P. Naur and B. Randall, eds. *Software Engineering: A Report on a Conference Sponsored by the NATO Science Committee*, Brussels: The Scientific Affairs Committee, NATO, 1969.

[NIST 93] National Institute of Standards and Technology, Data Encryption Standard (DES) (FIPS PUB 46-2). Gaithersburg, Md., January, 1993. *http://www.nist.gov/itl/div897/pubs/fip46-2.htm.*

[NIST 95] Secure Hash Standard (FIPS 180-1). Gaithersburg, Md.: National Institute of Standards and Technology, April 1995. *http://www.nist.gov/itl/div897/pubs/fip180-1.htm.*

[NYTIMES 99] Matt Richtel, "Need for Computer Experts is Making Recruiters Frantic," *New York Times*, Thursday, 18 November, 1999, Section A, p. 1.

[Offutt+ 95] A. J. Offutt, Z. Jin and J. Pan, "The Dynamic Domain Reduction Approach to Test Data Generation." (1995). pp. 1–19. *http://www.isse.gmu.edu/faculty/ofut/rsrch/papers/dd-gen.ps.*

[Parnas 71] David Parnas, "Information Distribution Aspects of Design Methodology," in *Proceedings 1971 IFIP Congress*, Amsterdam: North Holland Publishing, 1971, pp. 339–344.

[Polya 45] G. Polya, *How to Solve It*, Princeton, NJ: Princeton University Press, 1945.

[Postel 81] J. Postel, "Transmission Control Protocol, DARPA Internet Program Protocol Specification" (RFC-791). Information Sciences Institute, September 1981. *http://info.internet.isi.edu:80/in-notes/rfc/files/rfc793.txt*.

[Quinn 98] B. Quinn, "WinSock Version 2.0: Overview, Status and Pointers," March 1998. *http://sockets.com/ws2_stat.htm*.

[Rivest 91] R. Rivest, *The MD5 Message Digest Algorithm*. Cambridge, Mass.: MIT Laboratory for Computer Science, 1991.

[Roy 91] Bernard Roy, "The Outranking Approach and the Foundations of the ELECTRE Methods," in *Theory and Decision*, Vol. 31. Dordrecht, Netherlands: Kluwer Academic Publishers, 1991, 49–73,

[Royce 70] W. W. Royce, "Managing the Development of Large Software Systems: Concepts and Techniques" in *Proceedings*, Los Angeles: WESCON. August, 1970, p. 8.

[RSA 91] PKCS #1: RSA Encryption Standard, Version 1.4. San Mateo, Calif.: RSA Data Security, 1991.

[RSA 98] RSA Laboratories, "PKCS #1: RSA Cryptography Specifications," Version 2.0, Bedford, MA.: September 1999.

[RSA 99] RSA Laboratories, "PKCS 12 v1.0 Personal Information Exchange Syntax," Version 1.0, Bedford, MA.: RSA, June 1999.

[Saaty 90] T. L. Saaty, *The Analytic Hierarchy Process*, New York: McGraw-Hill, 1990.

[Salomaa 96] A. Salomaa, *Public-Key Cryptography*, 2nd ed. Berlin: Springer-Verlag, 1996.

[Saunders 75] Saunders, L., *The Tomorrow File*, New York, NY: Berkley Books, 1975.

[Schneier 96] Bruce Schneier, *Applied Cryptography: Protocols, Algorithms, and Source Code in C*, 2nd ed. New York: John Wiley & Sons, 1996.

[Seacord+ 98] Robert Seacord and Scott Hissam, "Browsers for Distributed Systems: Universal Paradigm or Siren's Song?" *World Wide Web Journal,* Vol. 1, no. 4, (1998). 181–191.

[Seacord+ 99] Robert C. Seacord, Kurt C. Wallnau, John E. Robert, Santiago Comella Dorda, Scott A. Hissam, "Custom vs. Off-The-Shelf Architecture," in *IEEE Proceedings of Enterprise Distributed Object Computing*, Mannheim, Germany, Piscataway, NJ: IEEE, 1999, pp. 270–278.

[SEI 87a] *Characterizing the Software Process: A Maturity Framework*, Technical Report CMU/SEI-87-TR-11, Software Engineering Institute, Carnegie Mellon University, Pittsburgh.

[SEI 87b] W. Humphrey and W. Sweet, *Method for Assessing the Software Engineering Capability of Contractors*, Technical Report CMU/SEI-87-TR-23, Software Engineering Institute, Carnegie Mellon University, Pittsburgh.

[SEI 94] Frank J. Sisti and Sujoe Joseph, Software Risk Evaluation Method Version 1.0, CMU/SEI-94-TR-19, December 1994.

[SEI 96] Ronald P. Higuera and Yacov Y. Haimes, *Software Risk Management*, Technical Report CMU/SEI-96-TR-012, Pittsburgh: Software Engineering Institute, Carnegie Mellon University. June 1996.

[Shaw 96] Mary Shaw, "Truth vs. Knowledge: The Difference Between What a Component Does and What We Know it Does," in *Proceedings of the Eighth International Workshop on Software Specification and Design*, March, 1996. Los Alamitos CA: IEEE, 1996.

[SPC 94] Software Productivity Consortium, Appendixes for Software Reuse Business Model, SPC-94062-C, Herdon, VA: Software Productivity Consortium, November 1994.

[Szyperski 98] Clemens Szyperski, *Component Software: Beyond Object-Oriented Programming*. Reading, Mass.: Addison-Wesley, 1998.

[Thomas+ 92] I. Thomas and B. Nejmeh, "Definitions of tool integration for environments," *IEEE Software* 9, no. 3, (March 1992): 29–35.

[Toulmin 87] S. E. Toulmin, "Philosophy of Science," in *Encyclopedia Britannica*, Vol. 25, Chicago: Encyclopedia Britannica (1987): 661–678.

[Trammell 95] C. Trammell, "Quantifying the Reliability of Software: Statistical Testing Based on a Usage Model," Proceedings of the Second IEEE International Symposium on Software Engineering Standards. Montreal, Quebec, Canada, August 21–25, 1995. Los Alamitos, CA.: IEEE Computer Society Press, 1995, 208–218.

[Weiss 99] David Weiss, C. Tau, and R. Lai, *Software Product Line Engineering*, Reading, Mass: Addison-Wesley, 1999.

Acronyms

ACL	Access Control List
ACM	Association of Computing Machinery
AHP	Analytic Hierarchy Process
ANSI	American National Standards Institute
API	Application Programming Interface
ASCII	American Standard Code for Information Interchange
ASN	Abstract Syntax Notation
ATM	Automated Teller Machine
BRI	Business Rule Interpreter
CA	Certificate Authority
CAPI	Cryptography Application Programming Interface
CBC	Cipher Block Chaining
CERT	Computer Emergency Response Team
CGI	Common Gateway Interface
CIO	Chief Information Officer
CIPSO	Commercial Internet Protocol Security Option
CMM	Capability Maturity Model
CMS	Certificate Management Server
CMU	Carnegie Mellon University
CN	Common Name
COBOL	Common Business Oriented Language
COCOMO	Constructive Cost Model
COM	Component Object Model
CORBA	Common Object Request Broker Architecture
COTS	Commercial Off-the-Shelf
CPU	Central Processing Unit
CSR	Certificate Signing Request
CTO	Chief Technology Officer
DARPA	Defense Advanced Research Projects Agency
DB	Database
DBMS	Database Management System

DBT	Database Thang
DCE	Distribute Computing Environment
DDE	Dynamic Data Exchange
DER	Distinguished Encoding Rules
DES	Data Encryption Standard
DII	Dynamic Invocation Interface
DIRS	Distributed Information Retrieval System
DLL	Dynamic Link Library
DOS	Disk Operating System
DS	Directory Server
DSTO	Defense Science and Technology Organization
ECA	Enterprise-wide Certificate Authority
ECMA	European Computer Manufacturers Association
EDE	Encrypt-Decrypt-Encrypt
EJB	Enterprise JavaBeans
ES	Enterprise Server
FAQ	Frequently Asked Questions
FDDI	Fiber Distributed Data Interface
FIPS	Federal Information Processing Standard
FTP	File Transfer Protocol
GB	Gigabyte
GCHQ	Government Communications Headquarters
GDW	Graphics Display Workstation
GEE	Generic Enterprise Ensemble
GMT	Greenwich Mean Time
GUI	Graphical User Interface
HMAC	Hashing for Message Authentication Codes
HTML	Hypertext Markup Language
HTTP	Hypertext Transfer Protocol
HTTPS	Hypertext Transfer Protocol Secure
I&A	Identification and Authentication
IBM	International Business Machines
ICSE	International Conference on Software Engineering
IDE	Integrated Development Environment
IDEA	International Data Encryption Algorithm
IDL	Interface Definition Language
IE	Internet Explorer
IEE	Institution of Electrical Engineers

IEEE	Institute of Electrical and Electronics Engineers
IETF	Internet Engineering Task Force
IFIP	International Federation for Information Processing
IHL	Internet Header Length
IIOP	Internet Interoperable Object Protocol
IIOPS	Internet Interoperable Object Protocol Secure
IIS	Internet Information System
IO	Input/Output
IOR	Interoperable Object Reference
IP	Internet Protocol
IPSO	Internet Protocol Security Option
ISO	International Standards Organization
IT	Information Technology
ITAR	International Traffic in Arms Regulations
ITU	International Telecommunication Union
IV	Initial Value
J2EE	Java 2 Enterprise Edition
JCA	Java Cryptography Architecture
JCE	Java Cryptography Extension
JDBC	Java Database Connectivity
JDK	Java Development Kit
JPEG	Joint Photographic Experts Group
JKS	Java KeyStore
JNI	Java Native Interface
JRE	Java Runtime Environment
JVM	Java Virtual Machine
KAI	Kuck & Associates, Inc.
KB	Kilobyte
KISS	Keep it Simple, Stupid!
KM	Kilometer
LAN	Local Area Network
LDAP	Lightweight Directory Access Protocol
MAC	Message Authentication Code
MAUT	Multi-Attribute Utility Theory
MB	Megabyte
MIME	Multipurpose Internet Mail Extensions
MS	Microsoft
MTS	Member of the Technical Staff

NATO	North American Treaty Organization
NCC	Netscape Capability Classes
NDBS	Netscape Database Keystore
NIC	Network Interface Card
NN	NIC Nak
NNC	NIC Nak Central
NS	Netscape
NSPR	Netscape Portable Runtime
NSS	Netscape Security Services
NT	New Technology
OCL	Object Constraint Language
OID	Object ID
OLE	Object Linking and Embedding
OMG	Object Management Group
OOA	Object-Oriented Analysis
OOD	Object-Oriented Design
ORB	Object Request Broker
OS	Operating System
OTSO	Off-the-Shelf Option
OU	Organizational Unit
PBE	Password Based Encryption
PC	Personal Computer
PCI	Peripheral Component Interconnect
PEM	Privacy Enhanced Mail
PFX	Personal Information Exchange
PGP	Pretty Good Privacy
PID	Process ID
PIN	Personal Identification Number
PKCS	Public-Key Cryptography System
PKI	Public Key Infrastructure
POSIX	Portable Operating System Interface for UNIX
PPID	Parent Process ID
PRNG	Pseudo Random Number Generator
RAD	Rapid Application Development
RDBMS	Relational Database Management System
RFC	Request for Comment
ROI	Return on Investment
RPC	Remote Procedure Call

RPG	Report Program Generator
RSA	Rivest, Shamir, and Adelman
RUP	Rational Unified Process
SASD	Structured Analysis and Structured Design
SATAN	Security Administrator Tool for Analyzing Networks
SDK	Software Development Kit
SEI	Software Engineering Institute
SGI	Silicon Graphics, Inc.
SHA	Secure Hash Algorithm
SKIP	Simple Key-management for Internet Protocols
SM	Storage Manager
SPI	Service Provider Interface
SQL	Structure Query Language
SSJS	Server-Side JavaScript
SSL	Secure Sockets Layer
STL	Standard Template Library
TCB	Trusted Computing Base
TCO	Total Cost of Ownership
TCP	Transmission Control Protocol
TLS	Transport Security Layer
TTL	Time to Live
TTY	Teletype
UDP	User Datagram Protocol
UI	User Interface
UID	User ID
UML	Unified Modeling Language
URL	Uniform Resource Locator
USD	United States Dollars
VM	Virtual Machine
WAN	Wide Area Network
WWW	World-Wide Web

Index

The SEI Series in Software Engineering

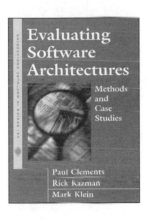

Evaluating Software Architectures
Methods and Case Studies
Paul Clements, Rick Kazman, and Mark Klein

This book is a comprehensive, step-by-step guide to software architecture evaluation, describing specific methods that can quickly and inexpensively mitigate enormous risk in software projects. The methods are illustrated both by case studies and by sample artifacts put into play during an evaluation: view-graphs, scenarios, final reports—everything you need to evaluate an architecture in your own organization.

0-201-70482-X • Hardcover • 304 Pages • ©2002

Software Product Lines
Practices and Patterns
Paul Clements and Linda Northrop

Building product lines from common assets can yield remark-able improvements in productivity, time to market, product quality, and customer satisfaction. This book provides a frame-work of specific practices, with detailed case studies, to guide the implementation of product lines in your own organization.

0-201-70332-7 • Hardcover • 576 Pages • ©2002

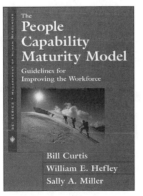

The People Capability Maturity Model
Guidelines for Improving the Workforce
Bill Curtis, William E. Hefley, and Sally A. Miller

Employing the process maturity framework of the Software CMM, the People Capability Maturity Model (People CMM) describes best practices for managing and developing an organization's workforce. This book describes the People CMM and the key practices that comprise each of its maturity levels, and shows how to apply the model in guiding organizational improvements. Includes case studies.

0-201-60445-0 • Hardback • 448 Pages • ©2002

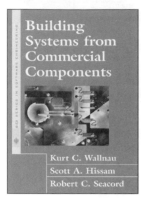

Building Systems from Commercial Components
Kurt C. Wallnau, Scott A. Hissam, and Robert C. Seacord

Commercial components are increasingly seen as an effective means to save time and money in building large software systems. However, integrating pre-existing components, with pre-existing specifications, is a delicate and difficult task. This book describes specific engineering practices needed to accomplish that task successfully, illustrating the techniques described with case studies and examples.

0-201-70064-6 • Hardcover • 416 pages • ©2002

CMMI Distilled
A Practical Introduction to Integrated Process Improvement
Dennis M. Ahern, Aaron Clouse, and Richard Turner

The Capability Maturity Model Integration (CMMI) is the latest version of the popular CMM framework, designed specifically to integrate an organization's process improvement activities across disciplines. This book provides a concise introduction to the CMMI, highlighting the benefits of integrated process improvement, explaining key features of the new framework, and suggesting how to choose appropriate models and representations for your organization.

0-201-73500-8 • Paperback • 240 pages • ©2001

The CERT Guide to System and Network Security Practices
By Julia H. Allen

The CERT Coordination Center helps systems administrators secure systems connected to public networks, develops key security practices, and provides timely security implementations. This book makes CERT practices and implementations available in book form, and offers step-by-step guidance for protecting your systems and networks against malicious and inadvertent compromise.

0-201-73723-X • Paperback • 480 pages • ©2001

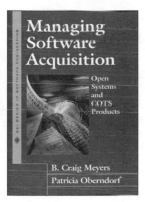

Managing Software Acquisition

Open Systems and COTS Products
B. Craig Meyers and Patricia Oberndorf

The acquisition of open systems and commercial off-the-shelf (COTS) products is an increasingly vital part of large-scale software development, offering significant savings in time and money. This book presents fundamental principles and best practices for successful acquisition and utilization of open systems and COTS products.

0-201 70454-4 • Hardcover • 288 pages • ©2001

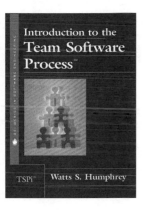

Introduction to the Team Software Process

Watts S. Humphrey

The Team Software Process (TSP) provides software engineers with a framework designed to build and maintain more effective teams. This book, particularly useful for engineers and students trained in the Personal Software Process (PSP), introduces TSP and the concrete steps needed to improve software teamwork.

0-201-47719-X • Hardcover • 496 pages • ©2000

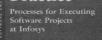

CMM in Practice

Processes for Executing Software Projects at Infosys
Pankaj Jalote

This book describes the implementation of CMM at Infosys Technologies, and illustrates in detail how software projects are executed at this highly mature software development organization. The book examines the various stages in the life cycle of an actual Infosys project as a running example throughout the book, describing the technical and management processes used to initiate, plan, and execute it.

0-201-61626-2 • Hardcover • 400 pages • ©2000

Measuring the Software Process
Statistical Process Control for Software Process Improvement
William A. Florac and Anita D. Carleton

This book shows how to use measurements to manage and improve software processes within your organization. It explains specifically how quality characteristics of software products and processes can be quantified, plotted, and analyzed, so that the performance of software development activities can be predicted, controlled, and guided to achieve both business and technical goals.

0-201-60444-2 • Hardcover • 272 pages • ©1999

Cleanroom Software Engineering
Technology and Process
Stacy Prowell, Carmen J. Trammell, Richard C. Linger, and Jesse H. Poore

This book provides an introduction and in-depth description of the Cleanroom approach to high-quality software development. Following an explanation of basic Cleanroom theory and practice, the authors draw on their extensive experience in industry to elaborate the Cleanroom development and certification process and show how this process is compatible with the Capability Maturity Model (CMM).

0-201-85480-5 • Hardcover • 400 pages • ©1999

Software Architecture in Practice
Len Bass, Paul Clements, and Rick Kazman

This book introduces the concepts and practice of software architecture, not only covering essential technical topics for specifying and validating a system, but also emphasizing the importance of the business context in which large systems are designed. Enhancing both technical and organizational discussions, key points are illuminated by substantial case studies.

0-201-19930-0 • Hardcover • 480 pages • ©1998

Managing Risk

Methods for Software Systems Development
By Elaine M. Hall

Written for busy professionals charged with delivering high-quality products on time and within budget, this comprehensive guide describes a success formula for managing software risk. The book follows a five-part risk management road map designed to take you from crisis to control of your software project.

0-201-25592-8 • Hardcover • 400 pages • ©1998

Software Process Improvement

Practical Guidelines for Business Success
By Sami Zahran

This book will help you manage and control the quality of your organization's software products by showing you how to develop a preventive culture of disciplined and continuous process improvement.

0-201-17782-X • Hardcover • 480 pages • ©1998

Introduction to the Personal Software Process

By Watts S. Humphrey

This workbook provides a hands-on introduction to the basic discipline of software engineering, as expressed in the author's well-known Personal Software Process (PSP). By applying the forms and methods of PSP described in the book, you can learn to manage your time effectively and to monitor the quality of your work, with enormous benefits in both regards.

0-201-54809 7 • Paperback • 304 pages • ©1997

Managing Technical People
Innovation, Teamwork, and the Software Process
By Watts S. Humphrey

Drawing on the author's extensive experience as a senior manager of software development at IBM, this book describes proven techniques for managing technical professionals. The author shows specifically how to identify, motivate, and organize innovative people, while tying leadership practices to improvements in the software process.

0-201-54597-7 • Paperback • 352 pages • ©1997

The Capability Maturity Model
Guidelines for Improving the Software Process
By Carnegie Mellon University/Software Engineering Institute

This book provides the authoritative description and technical overview of the Capability Maturity Model (CMM), with guidelines for improving software process management. The CMM provides software professionals in government and industry with the ability to identify, adopt, and use sound management and technical practices for delivering quality software on time and within budget.

0-201-54664-7 • Hardcover • 464 pages • ©1995

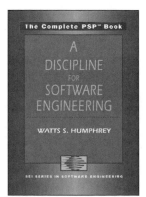

A Discipline for Software Engineering
The Complete PSP Book
By Watts S. Humphrey

This book scales down to a personal level the successful methods developed by the author to help managers and organizations evaluate and improve their software capabilities—methods comprising the Personal Software Process (PSP). The author's aim with PSP is to help individual software practitioners develop the skills and habits needed to plan, track, and analyze large and complex projects, and to develop high-quality products.

0-201-54610-8 • Hardcover • 816 pages • ©1995

Software Design Methods for Concurrent and Real-Time Systems
By Hassan Gomaa

This book provides a basic understanding of concepts and issues in concurrent system design, while surveying and comparing a range of applicable object-oriented design methods. The book describes a practical approach for applying real-time scheduling theory to analyze the performance of real-time designs.

0-201-52577-1 • Hardcover • 464 pages • ©1993

Managing the Software Process
By Watts S. Humphrey

This landmark book introduces the author's methods, now commonly practiced in industry, for improving software development and maintenance processes. Emphasizing the basic principles and priorities of the software process, the book's sections are organized in a natural way to guide organizations through needed improvement activities.

0-201-18095-2 • Hardcover • 512 pages • ©1989

Other titles of interest from Addison-Wesley

Practical Software Measurement
A Foundation for Objective Project Management
By John McGarry, David Card, Cheryl Jones, Beth Layman, Elizabeth Clark, Joseph Dean, and Fred Hall

A critical task in developing and maintaining software-intensive systems is to meet project cost, schedule, and technical objectives. This official guide to Practical Software Measurement (PSM) shows how to accomplish that task through sound measurement techniques and the development of a software measurement process. It provides a comprehensive description of PSM's techniques and practical guidance based on PSM's actual application in large-scale software projects.

0-201-71516-3 • Hardcover • 512 pages • ©2002

Making the Software Business Case
Improvement by the Numbers
By Donald J. Reifer

This book shows software engineers and managers how to prepare the *business* case for change and improvement. It presents the tricks of the trade developed by this well-known author over many years, tricks that have repeatedly helped his clients win the battle of the budget. The first part of the book addresses the fundamentals associated with creating a business case; the second part uses case studies to illustrate cases made for different types of software improvement initiatives.
0-201-72887-7 • Paperback • 224 pages • ©2002

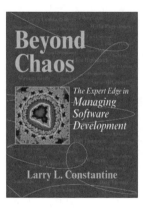

Beyond Chaos
The Expert Edge in Managing Software Development
Larry L. Constantine

The essays in this book, drawn from among the best contributions to Software Development magazine's Management Forum, reveal best practices in managing software projects and organizations. Written by many top names in the field— including Larry Constantine, Karl Wiegers, Capers Jones, Ed Yourdon, Dave Thomas, Meilir Page-Jones, Jim Highsmith, and Steve McConnell—each piece has been selected and edited to provide ideas and suggestions that can be translated into immediate practice.

0-201-71960-6 • Paperback • 400 pages • ©2001

Component-Based Software Engineering
Putting the Pieces Together
By George T. Heineman and William T. Councill

This book provides a comprehensive overview of, and current perspectives on, component-based software engineering (CBSE). With contributions from well-known luminaries in the field, it defines what CBSE really is, details CBSE's benefits and pitfalls, describes CBSE experiences from around the world, and ultimately reveals CBSE's considerable potential for engineering reliable and cost-effective software.

0-201-70485-4 • Hardcover • 880 pages • ©2001

Software Fundamentals
Collected Papers by David L. Parnas
By Daniel M. Hoffman and David M. Weiss

David Parnas's groundbreaking writings capture the essence of the innovations, controversies, challenges, and solutions of the software industry. This book is a collection of his most influential papers in various areas of software engineering, with historical context provided by leading thinkers in the field.

0-201-70369-6 • Hardcover • 688 pages • ©2001

Software for Use
A Practical Guide to the Models and Methods of Usage-Centered Design
by Larry L. Constantine and Lucy A. D. Lockwood

This book describes models and methods that help you deliver more usable software-software that allows users to accomplish tasks with greater ease and efficiency. Aided by concrete techniques, experience-tested examples, and practical tools, it guides you through a systematic software development process called usage-centered design, a process that weaves together two major threads in software development: use cases and essential modeling.

0-201-92478-1 • Hardcover • 608 pages • ©1999

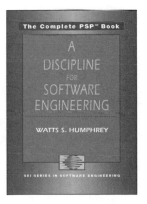

CMM Implementation Guide
Choreographing Software Process Improvement
by Kim Caputo

This book provides detailed instruction on how to put the Capability Maturity Model (CMM) into practice and, thereby, on how to raise an organization to the next higher level of maturity. Drawing on her first hand experience leading software process improvement groups in a large corporation, the author provides invaluable advice and information for anyone charged specifically with implementing the CMM.

0-201-37938-4 • Hardcover • 336 pages • ©1998

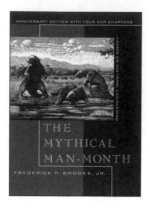

The Mythical Man-Month, Anniversary Edition
Essays on Software Engineering
By Frederick P. Brooks, Jr.

Fred Brooks blends software engineering facts with thought-provoking opinions to offer insight for anyone managing complex projects. Twenty years after the publication of this influential and timeless classic, the author revisited his original ideas and added new thoughts and advice, both for readers already familiar with his work and for those discovering it for the first time.

0-201-83595-9 • Paperback • 336 pages • ©1995